The Economics of Green Growth

T0300352

The Economics of Green Growth investigates the possibility of creating an integrated indicator covering three pillars of sustainable development: economy, society and the environment. The excessive pursuit of economic efficiency has resulted in severe environmental problems, such as climate change and biodiversity loss, and societal human issues, such as inequality and disparity.

This book aims to change the direction of economic growth towards one which is more sustainable. It explores beyond the conventional indicator – the GDP – that measures economic growth and human well-being. It also introduces new indicators relevant to sustainable development and a green economy and discusses the key issues for these indicators.

Shunsuke Managi is Professor of Technology and Policy, School of Engineering, at Kyushu University, Japan, while also holding positions as IGES fellow at the Institute for Global Environmental Strategies and an Adjunct Professor at the University of Tokyo. He is an editor of *Environmental Economic and Policy Studies*, a lead author for the Intergovernmental Panel on Climate Change, and is the author of *Technology, Natural Resources and Economic Growth: Improving the Environment for a Greener Future* and editor of *The Routledge Handbook of Environmental Economics in Asia*.

Routledge Studies in Ecological Economics

The Economics of Green Growth

New indicators for sustainable societies

Edited by Shunsuke Managi

Routledge
Taylor & Francis Group

LONDON AND NEW YORK

First published 2015
by Routledge
2 Park Square, Milton Park, Abingdon, Oxfordshire OX14 4RN

Simultaneously published in the USA and Canada
by Routledge
711 Third Avenue, New York, NY 10017

First issued in paperback 2017

*Routledge is an imprint of the Taylor & Francis Group,
an informa business*

British Library Cataloguing in Publication Data
A catalogue record for this book is available from the British
Library

Library of Congress Cataloging-in-Publication Data
The economics of green growth : new indicators for sustainable
   societies / edited by Shunsuke Managi.
(Routledge studies in ecological economics ; 40)
   Includes index.
  1. Sustainable development. 2. Economic development—
Environmental aspects.   3. Environmental economics.
I. Managi, Shunsuke.
   HC79.E5E28155 2015
   338.9'27—dc23
   2014047660

ISBN 13: 978-1-138-06730-1 (pbk)
ISBN 13: 978-1-138-81715-9 (hbk)

Typeset in Galliard
by Apex CoVantage, LLC

Contents

Figures

Tables

Notes on contributors

Aoki-Suzuki, Chika is a researcher at Sustainable Consumption and Production Area, Institute for Global Environmental Strategies.

Bhattacharya, Tania Ray is the founder and chief executive officer at The Celestial Earth Consultants.

Fujii, Hidemichi is Associate Professor at the Graduate School of Fisheries Science and Environmental Studies, Nagasaki University.

Huijuan, Cao is a PhD student at the Graduate School of Environmental Studies, Tohoku University.

Ito, Yutaka is Assistant Professor at the Graduate School for International Development and Cooperation, Hiroshima University.

Kabaya, Kei is a researcher at Green Economy Area, Institute for Global Environmental Strategies.

Kawahara, Hiromitsu is Director General at Japan Network for Climate Change Actions.

Kojima, Satoshi is a principal researcher at the Institute for Global Environmental Strategies.

Managi, Shunsuke is Professor at the School of Engineering, Kyushu University, and IGES Fellow, Institute for Global Environmental Strategies.

Mizobuchi, Hideyuki is Assistant Professor at the Faculty of Economics, Ryukoku University.

Okayasu, Sana is a researcher at the Natural Resource and Ecosystem Service Area, Institute for Global Environmental Strategies.

Sato, Masahiro is a Research Officer at the Economic and Social Research Institute, Cabinet Office, Government of Japan.

Sato, Masayuki is Associate Professor at the Graduate School of Human Development and Environment, Kobe University.

Tanaka, Kenta is Assistant Professor at the Faculty of Economics, Musashi University.

Tsurumi, Tetsuya is Lecturer at the Faculty of Policy Studies, Nanzan University.

Preface

Overviewing the current trends of internationally developed indicators, this book investigates the possibility to create an integrated indicator covering three pillars of sustainable development, namely economy, society and environment. Our fundamental objective is to contribute to changing the direction of economic growth towards a more sustainable way. It is expected that we could show a better indicator to measure economic growth and human well-being beyond the conventional GDP.

An indicator enables us to evaluate the current situation and to set up future targets in general. For the last several decades we have heavily focused on the maximization of one indicator, namely GDP. Excessive pursuit of economic efficiency has resulted in severe environmental problems, such as climate change and biodiversity loss, and societal human issues, including inequality and disparity.

So as to shift the paradigm from a GDP orientation to a sustainable and happy society orientation, some global initiatives (e.g. Beyond GDP and Inclusive Wealth Index) have been initiated since the latter half of the 2000s. At Rio+20 in 2012, the need for broader measures of progress to complement GDP was discussed and set forth in the outcome document. To sum up, a new integrated indicator is highly demanded in the global society.

This book is suitable for the undergraduate level as a text to widen and deepen knowledge on the domains mentioned previously. The potential university courses which this book could contribute to include economics, international political economics, environmental/ecological/resource economics, environmental policies, econometrics and statistics.

This book also targets policy makers, government officials, business leaders and global citizens as general audiences who have skepticism in current economic growth and intelligential interests in human well-being, happiness and sustainable development.

This book is a compilation of both new materials and revised manuscripts from existing papers. I would thus like to thank all the contributing authors for their involvement in our research and also for their permission to include materials from their previous work in this book. I also wish to acknowledge the following journals for their permission to reproduce some of their previously published papers: *Environmental Economics and Policy Studies, Journal of Cleaner Production* and *International Journal of Biodiversity Science, Ecosystem Services & Management*. This research was partially funded by Specially Promoted Research of a Grant-in-Aid for Scientific Research from the Japanese Ministry of Education, Culture, Sports, Science and Technology (MEXT) and Ministry of Environment. Of course, all errors that may remain are my responsibility alone.

Shunsuke Managi

Introduction

Shunsuke Managi and Kei Kabaya

What is sustainable development? This concept was first officially presented in the report entitled "Our Common Future," prepared by the World Commission on Environment and Development in 1987, when a wide range of environmental problems arose driven by over-consumption and poverty. It has since been defined as "development that meets the needs of the present without compromising the ability of future generations to meet their own needs" (WCED, 1987). Today the world poverty rate has decreased to 21 percent of people in the developing world from 43 percent in 1990 (World Bank, 2014), and deforestation rates have slowed to 5.2 million hectares per year in the 2000s in comparison to 8.3 million in the 1990s (FAO, 2011). We can thus observe some progress towards sustainable development. However, the question remains on where the ultimate goal of sustainable development should be set. How much have we achieved for this goal so far? Even today, there still exist huge income gaps within and between nations, and we have yet to solve global environmental issues such as climate change and biodiversity loss.

Faced with these challenges, we need to set goals and identify indicators to measure our progress so as to promote actions for sustainable development. At the United Nations Conference for Sustainable Development in 2012 (i.e. Rio+20), the launch of discussions on the Sustainable Development Goals (SDGs) was agreed upon in order to prepare for the post Millennium Development Goals (MDGs), which will be terminated in 2015. The proposed SDGs total 17 goals as of now, encompassing a wide range of global issues, including poverty, education, gender, food, water, energy, cities, climate, oceans and forests (UN-DESA, 2014). Another major theme discussed at Rio+20 was green economy, which can be defined as "one that results in improved human well-being and social equity, while significantly reducing environmental risks and ecological scarcities" (UNEP, 2011). In the discussion of green economy some countries underlined the necessity of measuring the progress of green economy with timelines and indicators, resulting in the development of green growth indicators by the Organisation for Economic Cooperation and Development (OECD) (OECD, 2011).

The attempts to develop indicators to measure sustainable development or wealth "beyond GDP" are not necessarily new. For instance, the World Bank proposed the Adjusted Net Savings (ANS) in 1998, which takes into account investment in education, health and environment to calculate the "genuine" savings in an economy. With a stronger focus on the environment and the economy, the United Nations has developed the System of Environmental-Economic Accounts (SEEA) since 1993, which widens the scope of the conventional System of National Accounts (SNA) to include environmental inputs and impacts of an economy, such as natural resources and wastes. Meanwhile, the United Nations Development Programme (UNDP) has publicized the Human Development Index (HDI) since 1990, which focuses more on human needs (i.e. income, education and health). However, there still is room to improve such indicators in terms of their scope and methodologies. The United Nations University (UNU) and the United Nations Environment Programme (UNEP) developed the Inclusive Wealth Index (IWI) in 2012 and 2014, with a similar approach to the ANS but with broader measurement categories (see UNU-IHDP and UNEP [2014] and Muñoz et al. [2014] for detailed computation). In addition, integrated databases have been developed to understand sustainability (World Resource Table [WRT] by Managi, [2015], Miyama and Managi [2014], and Yang et al. [2015]). The SEEA will be extended to incorporate natural capital and ecosystem services in the accounting framework.[1] Human well-being is measured with broader aspects in the Better Life Index (BLI) proposed by the OECD in 2011, which consists of 11 indicators including income, education, health, safety and life satisfaction.

Again, the capacity for enhancing these upgraded indicators in terms of their scope and methodologies still exists. Such recognition was the starting point of this book. We split the book into three parts. Part I introduces the roles of relevant indicators in addressing global issues such as green economy, emission reduction, natural capital investment, sustainable consumption and international trade and so forth. Part II discusses how to improve existing sustainability and well-being indicators, mainly focusing on the Inclusive Wealth Index and the OECD Better Life Index. Part III investigates the mutual relationships between the economy and the environment and seeks opportunities to promote private actions towards green growth. A brief introduction of each chapter is given as follows:

Chapter 1 introduces and compares the new concepts of green economy and green growth established by five international organizations, and investigates similarities and dissimilarities among them. The composite indicators developed by the UNEP Green Economy Initiative and the OECD Green Growth Strategy are also introduced in detail, with the lists of respective indicators.

Chapter 2 raises the issue of over-consumption in developed countries and under-consumption in developing countries. Following the discussion on sustainable development indicators from the perspective of planetary boundaries, this chapter analyzes the indicator for sustainable resource management and stresses the importance of equity of resource use.

Chapter 3 analyzes the impact of economic growth on environmental quality from the perspectives of economic scales, technical improvement and change in industrial structures. With the empirical datasets and the semi-parametric method, the relationships between economic (e.g. GDP) and environmental indicators (e.g. SO_2 and CO_2) are investigated.

Chapter 4 discusses the concept, roles, and estimation methods of embodied environmental impact indicators, which can contribute to sustainable development by bridging national-level indicators and global sustainability. Focusing on the actual water use embodied in the world trade network, the estimation results will be presented.

Chapter 5 focuses on the SEEA and Experimental Ecosystem Accounting (EEA). Followed by the brief history of these accounting schemes, current progress towards development of ecosystem accounting in some countries is introduced. Several challenges faced in developing such accounts are also discussed.

Part II begins with Chapter 6, which considers the economic theory and framework for sustainability indicators (e.g. IWI) and points out the technical challenges in the measurement of various capitals in monetary terms.

Chapter 7 discusses the ways to estimate the temporal movement of inclusive wealth paths. Presenting the methodology to estimate the inclusive wealth-based total factor productivity (TFP), taking into account both technological progress and efficiency change, the contribution of TFP to sustainable development will be evaluated.

Chapter 8 shifts the focus to the Better Life Index (BLI). Recognizing the problem that weighting each index is in the hands of users, this chapter proposes methods to construct a composite indicator which aggregates the 11 elements of the BLI so as to understand the overview of well-being in each country and to compare them with the uniform approach.

Chapter 9 explores the monetary values of various aspects of life in reference to the BLI. Customizing some indices to the Japanese lifestyles and applying the Life Satisfaction Approach, the results of questionnaire survey and subsequent statistical analysis are demonstrated.

As the first chapter of Part III, Chapter 10 explores the impacts of natural disasters on the stock market. Based on the understanding of economic damages caused by the disasters, this chapter analyzes the effects of two recent gigantic earthquakes in Japan on the stock price behavior in an empirical manner.

Chapter 11 examines the environmental impacts of an international mega event. Taking the example of the 2008 Summer Olympic Games in Beijing, which aimed for a "Green Olympics," the short-to-midterm effects on air quality are revealed in comparison with that in other regions in China.

Chapter 12 investigates the relations between environmental regulations and private actions. The latter is represented by the improvement in the TFP of an enterprise which includes environmental performance. By measuring and comparing its temporal changes, the contribution of environmental regulations is considered.

Chapter 13 focuses on private activities for the conservation of global biodiversity and scrutinizes the factors influential to companies' environmental decision-making. This chapter also proposes a framework for biodiversity loss mitigation action.

Chapter 14 examines the cost effectiveness of tax reductions and subsidies with regard to the purchases of hybrids and eco-cars. Classifying the several subsidy and tax reduction schemes, the respective cost effectiveness will be evaluated comparatively, and more favorable policies will be considered.

Note

1 Ecosystem accounting is separated from the SEEA Central Framework at this stage (see more detail in Chapter 5).

Bibliography

Food and Agricultural Organization (FAO) (2011). *Deforestation and Net Forest Area Change.* http://www.fao.org/forestry/30515/en/ (Last access: 1 Aug. 2014).

Managi, S. (Ed.) (2015). *The Routledge Handbook of Environmental Economics in Asia.* New York: Routledge.

Miyama, E., and Managi, S. (2014). "Global Environmental Emissions Estimate: Application of Multiple Imputation," *Environmental Economics and Policy Studies* 16 (2): 115–135.

Muñoz, Pablo, Petters, Kira, Managi, Shunsuke, and Darkey, Elorm. (2014). Chapter 1: Accounting for the Inclusive Wealth of Nations: Key Findings of the IWR 2014, in UNU-IHDP and UNEP (2014). *Inclusive Wealth Report 2014. Measuring Progress Toward Sustainability.* Cambridge: Cambridge University Press.

Organisation for Economic Cooperation and Development (OECD) (2011). *Towards Green Growth: Monitoring Progress.* Paris: OECD Publishing.

United Nations Department of Economic and Social Affairs (UN-DESA) (2014). *Introduction to the Proposal of The Open Working Group for Sustainable Development Goals.* http://sustainabledevelopment.un.org/focussdgs.html (Last access: 1 Aug. 2014).

United Nations Environment Programme (UNEP) (2011). *Towards a Green Economy: Pathways to Sustainable Development and Poverty Eradication.* http://www.unep. org/GreenEconomy/InformationMaterials/Publications/Publication/ tabid/4613/language/en-US/Default.aspx?ID=4188

UNU-IHDP and UNEP (2014). *Inclusive Wealth Report 2014. Measuring Progress Toward Sustainability.* Cambridge: Cambridge University Press.

World Bank (2014). *Poverty Overview.* http://www.worldbank.org/en/topic/poverty/overview (Last access: 1 Aug. 2014).

World Commission on Environment and Development (WCED) (1987). *Our Common Future.* Oxford: Oxford University Press, p. 43.

Yang, J., Managi, S., and Sato, M. (2015). "The Effect of Institutional Quality on National Wealth: An Examination Using Multiple Imputation Method," *Environmental Economics and Policy Studies.* DOI 10.1007/s10018-014-0084-z

Part 1
Global issues and indicators

1 Green Economy and Green Growth in international trends of sustainability indicators

Chika Aoki-Suzuki

The necessity for an indicator which complements GDP (Gross Domestic Product) has been widely discussed by the international community. This matter has arisen due to the limits of GDP as a measurement of social and economic development, as well as to the change to the recognition of happiness. With this background, the development of an indicator system which covers a comprehensive area including sustainability and well-being has been widely discussed internationally.

International organisations that have recently expanded their activities to develop a practical and structured indicator system for sustainability and well-being include OECD (Organisations for Economic Cooperation and Development) Green Growth indicators, UNEP (United Nations Environment Programme), Inclusive Wealth Index (IWI) and WAVES (Wealth Accounting and the Valuation of Ecosystem Services) by the World Bank. As a prerequisite of these activities, some countries have already accumulated experience of relevant indicator systems and their policy utilisation, such as natural capital accounting and material flow accounting, including the resource productivity indicator. In addition, a central framework for the System of Environmental-Economic Accounting (SEEA) was agreed upon by the United Nations (United Nations, 2014). And at Rio+20, the United Nations Conference on Sustainable Development (UNCSD) in 2012, discussions on Sustainable Development Goals (SDGs) began in the context of the post-2015 Development Agenda/Millennium Development Goals.

Green Economy/Growth is not only recognised as indicator development but is also widely recognised as an important item on the international policy agenda towards sustainability, especially after Rio+20, which highlighted a green economy in the context of sustainable development and poverty eradication. Various organisations have been working on the policy concept as well as indicators of Green Economy/Growth.

This chapter focuses on growing international activities on Green Economy/ Growth, and mainly discusses the definitions and purposes by analysing terms used in the definitions. This is followed by an examination of the system of UNEP Green Economy/OECD Green Growth indicators which are major examples of Green Economy/Growth indicators.

1.1 International discussion of Green Economy/Growth

Major international organisations and international initiatives have been working on this issue, with UNCSD, UNEP Green Economy Initiative and European Environment Agency (EEA) looking at Green Economy, and OECD and United Nations Economic and Social Commission for the Asia and the Pacific (UNES-CAP) focusing on Green Growth. However, such international recognition and proactive actions by international organisations do not equate to the existence of an internationally shared definition.

This section starts by examining the concept of Green Economy and Green Growth developed by various international organisations, followed by a comparative analysis of definitions of Green Economy/Green Growth, considering the difference between sustainability and sustainable development.

1.1.1 Concepts and definitions of Green Economy and Green Growth

There are many common items among the concepts and definitions of Green Economy and Green Growth developed by UNEP, OECD and EEA as described later and in Table 1.1. Examples of common items are (1) resource efficiency, low-carbon, ecosystem service and natural capital as components of Green Economy/Growth; (2) employment, economic development, social inclusiveness, poverty alleviation and happiness as objectives/goals of Green Economy/Growth.

a) UNEP

A report on Green Economy published by UNEP entitled "Towards a Green Economy: Pathways to Sustainable Development and Poverty Eradication" (UNEP, 2011a) comprises three parts: "Investing in natural capital"; "Investing in energy and resource efficiency" and "Supporting the transition to a global green economy". The part on "Investing in natural capital" gives approaches for improving the quality and quantity of natural capital, mainly focusing on industries which are directly linked with natural capital, such as agriculture, fisheries and forestry. On the other hand, "Investing in energy and resource efficiency" focuses on efficient use of inputs from natural capital in economic systems (human-made capital), and mainly discusses industries such as renewable energy, manufacturing, waste, infrastructure, transportation, tourism and cities.

b) OECD

The main components of OECD Green Growth are the environmental and resource productivity of the economy, the natural asset base, the environmental dimension of quality of life and economic opportunities and policy responses

Table 1.1 Example of definitions of Green Economy/Growth

Green Economy	UNEP (2011a)	Green economy as one that results in "improved human well-being and social equity, while significantly reducing environmental risks and ecological scarcities". In its simplest expression, a green economy is low-carbon, resource efficient, and socially inclusive. In a green economy, growth in income and employment are driven by public and private investments that reduce carbon emissions and pollution, enhance energy and resource efficiency, and prevent the loss of biodiversity and ecosystem services.
	EEA (EEA website)	Green economy is one that generates increasing prosperity while maintaining the natural systems that sustain us. (. . .) The objectives of a green economy are to meet our needs – for food, transport, energy and so on – in a sustainable and equitable way. (. . .) In balancing environmental, economic and social elements, the green economy concept evidently has much in common with the notion of sustainable development – albeit with a focus primarily on the environmental and economic aspects.
	UNCSD (2012)	Para 56. (. . .) In this regard, we consider green economy in the context of sustainable development and poverty eradication as one of the important tools available for achieving sustainable development and that it could provide options for policymaking but should not be a rigid set of rules. We emphasize that it should contribute to eradicating poverty as well as sustained economic growth, enhancing social inclusion, improving human welfare and creating opportunities for employment and decent work for all, while maintaining the healthy functioning of the Earth's ecosystems.

Para 60. We acknowledge that green economy in the context of sustainable development and poverty eradication will enhance our ability to manage natural resources sustainably and with lower negative environmental impacts, increase resource efficiency and reduce waste.

Para 61. We recognize that urgent action on unsustainable patterns of production and consumption where they occur remains fundamental in addressing environmental sustainability and promoting conservation and sustainable use of biodiversity and ecosystems, regeneration of natural resources and the promotion of sustained, inclusive and equitable global growth. |

(*Continued*)

Table 1.1 (Continued)

Green Growth	OECD (2011a)	*Green growth is about fostering economic growth and development while ensuring that the natural assets continue to provide the resources and environmental services on which our well-being relies. To do this it must catalyse investment and innovation which will underpin sustained growth and give rise to new economic opportunities.*
	UNESCAP (2012)	*Green growth is, in general terms, economic progress that fosters environmentally sustainable, low-carbon and socially inclusive development. By "recalibrating" the economy to synergise economic growth and environmental protection, green growth" strategies work to bring economic growth trajectories in better alignment with sustainable development objectives. Such strategies can help build a "green economy," characterized by substantially increased investments in economic activities that build on and enhance the earth's natural capital, while reducing ecological scarcities and environmental risks – activities such as renewable energy, low-carbon transport, energy- and water-efficient buildings, sustainable agriculture and forest management and sustainable fisheries.*

Source: Table compiled by author based on various sources

(Figure 1.1). More details are shown in section 1.2.2 "OECD Green Growth indicator".

c)   EEA

Green Economy of EEA consists of maintaining ecological resilience in the ecosystem (natural capital) and improving resource efficiency in the economy (manufactured and financial capital), as well as comprising a part of human well-being (social and human capital) (Figure 1.2).

1.1.2   Relationship between "Green Economy/Growth" and "sustainability/sustainable development"

Regardless of the commonness, the context of Green Economy/Growth slightly varies among the international organisations. To examine the definitions more deeply, the author aims to take the major terms used in concepts and definitions of Green Economy/Growth and to classify them into components, objectives and direction, as well as goals of Green Economy/Growth (Table 1.2).

This typology also can show that Green Economy/Growth contain the context of the three pillars of sustainable development, which are Environment, Economy and Society. Environment is reflected in the necessary components of Green

Measurement framework

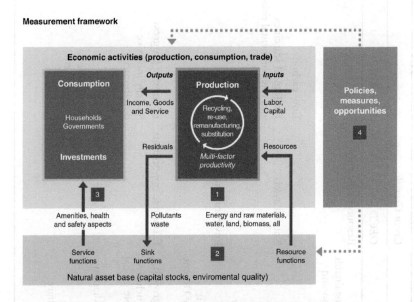

Figure 1.1 Framework of OECD Green Growth indicators

Source: OECD Website; http://www.oecd.org/greengrowth/greengrowthindicators.htm

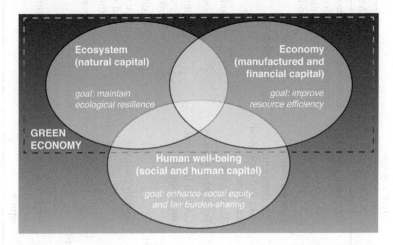

Figure 1.2 Conceptual diagram of EEA Green Economy

Source: EEA Website; http://www.eea.europa.eu/themes/economy/intro

Economy/Growth, such as resource efficiency, low-carbon, natural capital and ecosystem. Economy and Society are reflected in objectives such as economic opportunity/progress/growth, employment, decent work and social inclusion. Green "Economy" puts relatively more attention on the Environment–Society nexus, whereas Green "Growth" focuses on the Environment–Economy nexus. Sustainable development and human welfare are reflected as goals of Green

Table 1.2 Typology of terms in the concepts and definitions of Green Economy/Growth

		Green Economy			Green Growth	
		UNEP	EEA	UNCSD	OECD	UNESCAP
Components	Resource efficiency	Resource efficiency	Resource efficiency	Resource efficiency Sustainable consumption and production	Resource efficiency	
	Low-carbon	Low-carbon				Low-carbon
	Natural capital	Environmental risks and ecological scarcities	Natural system		Natural assets	Ecological scarcities and environmental risks
	Biodiversity	Biodiversity		Biodiversity		
	Ecosystem services	Ecosystem services		Ecosystem	Environmental services	
	Employment	Growth in income and employment		Employment opportunity Decent work		
Objectives, direction	Economic development			Economic growth	Economic opportunity	Economic progress
	Social inclusiveness	Socially inclusive		Sustained, inclusive and equitable global growth		Socially inclusive development
	Poverty alleviation			Poverty eradiation		
	Sustainable development		Sustainable development			Sustainable development
Goals	Happiness	Improved human well-being and social equity	Prosperity	Human welfare		

Source: Table compiled by author based on various sources

Economy/Growth. This could mean that Green Economy/Growth is not the same as sustainable development.

Relationships between Green Economy/Growth and sustainable development are clearly mentioned in the output documents of Rio+20 "The Future We Want" (UNCSD, 2012), which defines the Green Economy as one of the important tools through which sustainable development could be achieved.

> *Para 56. (. . .) In this regard, we consider green economy in the context of sustainable development and poverty eradication as one of the important tools available for achieving sustainable development and that it could provide options for policymaking but should not be a rigid set of rules. (. . .)*
>
> (UNCSD, 2012)

The UNEP (2011a) report on Green Economy also clearly states that sustainable development is not equal to Green Economy. This can be seen in the statement:

> *The concept of a green economy does not replace sustainable development; but there is a growing recognition that achieving sustainability rests almost entirely on getting the economy right. Decades of creating new wealth through a "brown economy" model based on fossil fuels have not substantially addressed social marginalisation, environmental degradation and resource depletion.*
>
> (UNEP, 2011a)

Furthermore, UNEP (2011a) expresses sustainable development from the perspective of capital stock and states that:

> *Society must decide how best to use its total capital stock today to increase current economic activities and welfare. Society must also decide how much it needs to save or accumulate for tomorrow, and ultimately, for the well-being of future generations.*[1]
>
> (UNEP, 2011a)

To summarise and provide a perceptible image of the previous discussion, the author illustrates the relationship between sustainable development and Green Economy/Growth in Figure 1.3.

Looking at these differences between sustainable development and Green Economy/Growth, the discussion of sustainable development is based on capital stock, whereas the discussion of Green Economy/Growth is based on flow of capital. This can be reflected in different ways to develop indicators for sustainable development and Green Economy/Growth. Examples of integrated indicators for sustainable development are Genuine Savings and Inclusive Wealth Index (UNEP and UNU-IHDP, 2012). These are integrated indicators for sustainability based on an economic capital approach through evaluation of the change

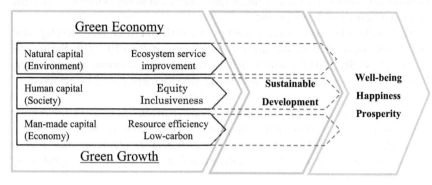

Figure 1.3 Relationship between sustainable development and Green Economy/
        Growth

Source: Author

of wealth (capital stock) produced by the input of human, human-made and natural capitals. More details of these sustainability integrated indicators will be discussed in other chapters.

The next section will focus more on indicators of Green Economy/Growth. This section gives details of the UNEP Green Economy indicator as well as details of the OECD Green Growth indicator, both of which are the most internationally recognised indicators on Green Economy/Growth.

1.2   Indicator development on Green Economy/Growth

1.2.1   *UNEP Green Economy indicator*[2]

a)   *Background*

Based on international discussions regarding the necessity of developing Green economy, the Statistical Office of the United Nations and UNEP need a new approach to assess Green Economy. In paragraph 63 of the outcome documents of Rio+20, "The Future We Want", it states that organisations which address Green Economy should be involved in the establishment of assessment methodology for Green Economy (UNCSD 2012).

In line with this document, the Green Economy initiative was established in 2008 under UNEP-DTIE and initiates discussions on developing indicators for Green Economy. UNEP published a report which introduces a basic framework for Green Economy indicators, namely "Measuring Progress Towards an Inclusive Green Economy" (UNEP 2012). In the report, UNEP expects that Green Economy indicators will be used as evaluation tools for policies on Green Economy in various countries, and that they also should be customised to fit each country's situation.

The framework of the UNEP Green Economy indicator suggests that indicators evaluate human well-being, social equity, reduction of environmental risk and ecological scarcity, which are components included in the definition of Green Economy. The framework also recommends assessing not only the current status of Green Economy, but also the policy process to achieve Green Economy, due to the fact that Green Economy is a tool for sustainable development and poverty eradication.

b)   Structure, groups and topics of the indicator

The UNEP Green Economy indicator is made up of three stages: first setting an agenda, followed by policy development and finally policy evaluation (Figure 1.4). These three stages apply indicators which fit the context of each stage. The agenda-setting stage applies indicators for environmental issues and targets. Policy development applies indicators for policy intervention, and policy evaluation applies indicators for policy impacts on well-being and equity. Tables 1.3 to 1.5 show the details of indicators at each stage, introduced as example indicators by UNEP. UNEP claims that indicators are basically determined by each county to fit the context of that country.

INDICATORS FOR ENVIRONMENTAL ISSUES AND TARGETS

UNEP perceives environment as an area which UNEP should address first, as well as the starting point of Green Economy indicators. This is based on the recognition of UNEP that Green Economy will not be achieved without solving environmental issues. This indicator area is the stage of agenda setting. Thus, indicators of this area are to be used for identifying issues, prioritising and monitoring the issues as well as understanding cause and effects.

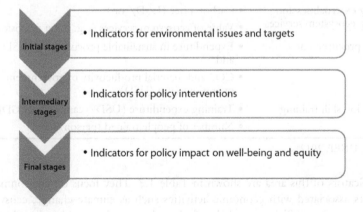

Figure 1.4 Three stages of the Green Economy indicator
Source: UNEP, 2012

Table 1.3 Illustrative environmental issues and related indicators

Issues	Indicators
Climate change	• Carbon emissions (ton/year) • Renewable energy (share of power supply) (%) • Energy consumption per capita (Btu/person)
Ecosystem management	• Forestland (ha) • Water stress (%) • Land and marine conservation area (ha)
Resource efficiency	• Energy productivity (Btu/USD) • Material productivity (ton/USD) • Water productivity (m3/USD) • CO2 productivity (ton/USD)
Chemicals and waste management	• Waste collection (%) • Waste recycling and reuse (%) • Waste generation (ton/year) or landfill area (ha)

Source: UNEP, 2012

Table 1.4 Illustrative green economy policy interventions and related indicators

Issues	Indicators
Green investment	• R&D investment (% of GDP) • EGSS investment (USD/year)
Green fiscal reform	• Fossil fuel, water and fishery subsidies (USD or %) • Fossil fuel taxation (USD or %) • Renewable energy incentive (USD or %)
Pricing externalities and valuing ecosystem services	• Carbon price (USD/ton) • Value of ecosystem services (e.g. water provision)
Green procurement	• Expenditure in sustainable procurement (USD/year and %) • CO2 and material productivity of government operations (ton/USD)
Green job skill training	• Training expenditure (USD/year and % of GDP) • Number of people trained (person/year)

Source: UNEP, 2012

Indicators of this area are shown in Table 1.3. They focus on environmental impacts associated with economic activities such as climate change, ecosystem services, resource efficiency and chemicals and waste. Areas which directly relate to pollution and daily life, such as water/air pollution, are not included here, but are included in the indicators for well-being and equity.

Table 1.5 Examples of well-being and equity indicators

Issues	Indicators
Employment	• Construction (person, %) • Operation and management (person, %) • Income generated (USD/year) • Gini coefficient
EGSS performance	• Value added (USD/year) • Employment (jobs) • CO2 and material productivity (e.g. USD/ton)
Total wealth	• Value of natural resource stocks (USD) • Net annual value addition/removal (USD/year) • Literacy rate (%)
Access to resources	• Access to modern energy (%) • Access to water (%) • Access to sanitation (%) • Access to health care (%)
Health	• Level of harmful chemicals in drinking water (g/litre) • Number of people hospitalised due to air pollution (person) • Road traffic fatalities per 100 000 inhabitants (transport related)

Source: UNEP, 2012

INDICATORS FOR POLICY INTERVENTION

The UNEP guidebook on Green Economy indicators introduces example indicators such as green investment, green fiscal reform, pricing externalities and valuing ecosystem services, green procurement and green job skill training, as shown in Table 1.4 (UNEP, 2012).

UNEP's Green Economy approach is to identify the area which produces the most co-benefits among environment, society and economy, and to invest in those areas (UNEP, 2012). UNEP observes that policy intervention under a Green Economy approach should focus ways to change investment flow to address issues and achieve targets, and states that policy options for addressing issues and achieving targets are capital investment incentive and regulations (UNEP, 2012). UNEP also states that policy intervention indicators to evaluate policy options aim to support the estimation of cost and benefits of each option, as well as to help evaluate whether polices are adequate to achieve targets (UNEP, 2012).

WELL-BEING AND EQUITY INDICATORS

These indicators evaluate policy impacts in well-being and equity. Indicators of this area show additional policy outcomes to targets set for environmental issues at the policy development stage, expressed as indirect (health etc.) and direct effects by Green Economy policies. For example, policy intervention with targets to reduce per capita CO_2 emissions is investing 1 % of GDP in technology for renewable energy. In this case, policy impacts on income and employment are expected in addition to CO_2 reductions (UNEP, 2012).

Well-being indicator   Under the Green Economy approach, economic indicators can significantly describe aspects of human well-being. Thus, a well-being indicator focuses on the environmental goods and service sector (EGSS) and green jobs. UNEP claims that employment in these sectors should be decent work (UNEP, 2012).

Equity indicators   Equity indicators evaluate human and social development like poverty alleviation, equity, social inclusiveness and inclusive wealth, which are affected by the direct impacts (resource access, nutrients, employment) and indirect impacts (health, education/skills) of Green Economy (UNEP, 2012).

Example indicators based on the previous ideas are shown in Table 1.5.

1.2.2   OECD Green Growth indicator

A Green Economy/Growth indicator expresses the "flow" of capital, including natural capital.

a)   Background

The development of a Green Growth indicator is part of the activities of the Green Growth Strategy initiated in 2009 by OECD member countries. The OECD first published a provisional indicator set (OECD, 2011b) in combination with its comprehensive strategy "Towards Green Growth" in May 2011 (OECD, 2011a). The OECD has continued to develop headline indicators as well as individual indicators and a re-proposed indicator set in 2014 (OECD, 2014). The purpose of a Green Growth indicator is to identify determinants of Green Growth and to provide information on policy analysis and progress evaluation towards the achievement of Green Growth.

b)   Structure, groups and topics of the indicator

OECD Green Growth indicators consists of five indicator groups (OECD, 2011b; OECD, 2014): (1) The socio-economic context and characteristics of growth which express the economy of a country, (2) Environmental and resource productivity, (3) Natural asset base, (4) Environmental quality of life which describes interlinkages between economic activity and the natural asset base and (5) Economic opportunities and policy responses. A conceptual measurement framework for the OECD Green Growth Indicator shown in

Measurement framework

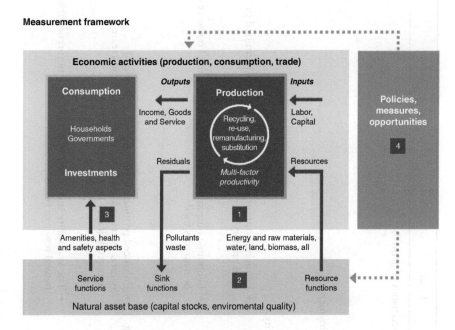

Figure 1.5 Framework of OECD Green Growth indicators (re-shown)

Source: OECD Website; http://www.oecd.org/greengrowth/greengrowthindicators.htm

Figure 1.5 describes the relationship between the five indicator groups. This indicates that Green Growth as a whole is improved through increased performance in each group. Table 1.6 shows the Green Growth indicator set proposed by OECD. However, OECD noted that the structure should be flexible to fit the context of a country and should continue to be elaborated on as long as there is data availability, concept development and feedback of policy application.

(1) THE SOCIO-ECONOMIC CONTEXT AND CHARACTERISTICS OF GROWTH

Indicators in this group show the effects of Green Growth policies, linking them to social goals such as poverty reduction, social equity and inclusion. These are considered the basis for Green Growth.

(2) INDICATORS MONITORING THE ENVIRONMENTAL AND RESOURCE PRODUCTIVITY OF THE ECONOMY

Indicators belonging to this group aim to look at the efficiency of production and consumption in economic activity, using energy, material resources and other natural resources, as well as environmental services from natural capital, to describe the transition to a low-carbon, resource-efficient economy.

Table 1.6 Overview of OECD Green Growth Indicators

Main indicator groups	Topics covered	Focus
	The socio-economic context and characteristics of growth	
Economic growth, productivity and competitiveness	Economic growth and structure Productivity and trade Inflation and commodity prices	
Labour markets, education and income	Labour markets (employment/unemployment) Socio-demographic patterns Income and education	
	Environmental and resource productivity	
Carbon and energy productivity	1. CO_2 productivity (demand-based, production-based) 2. Energy productivity	• Economic output generated per unit of CO_2 emitted or total primary energy supplied
Resource productivity	3. Material productivity (demand-based, production-based), non-energy materials, waste materials, nutrients 4. Water productivity	• Economic output generated per unit of natural resources or materials used
Multi-factor productivity	5. Multi-factor productivity reflecting environmental services	• Enhanced productivity through efficient use of natural assets and environmental services can create opportunities for new markets and jobs
	Natural asset base	
Renewable stocks	6. Freshwater resources 7. Forest resources 8. Fish resources	• The availability and quality of renewable or non-renewable natural resource stocks
Non-renewable stocks	9. Mineral resources	

Biodiversity and ecosystems	10. Land resources 11. Soil resources 12. Wildlife resources	• Biological diversity and ecosystems, including wildlife as well as the productivity of land and soil
	Environmental quality of life	
Environmental health and risks	13. Environmentally induced health problems and related costs 14. Exposure to natural or industrial risks and related economic losses	• Human exposure to pollution and environmental risks (natural disasters, technological and chemical risks), the associated effects on human health and on quality of life and the related health costs and impact on human capital and on labour productivity
Environmental services and amenities	15. Access to sewage treatment and drinking water	• Public access to environmental services and amenities, characterising the level and type of access that different groups of people have to environmental services such as clean water, sanitation, green space or public transport
	Economic opportunities and policy responses	
Technology and innovation	16. R&D of importance to GG 17. Patents of importance to GG 18. Environment-related innovation	• Technology and innovation that are important drivers of growth and productivity in general, and of Green Growth in particular • Production of environmental goods and services that reflect an important, albeit partial, aspect of the economic opportunities which arise in a greener economy

Source: OECD (2011b), OECD (2014) and OECD Website; http://www.oecd.org/greengrowth/greengrowthindicators.htm

For energy productivity and resource productivity, both production- and demand-based indicators are used. A production-based indicator covers energy or resources used or generated by domestic production and subsequent final consumption. A demand-based indicator, or consumption-based indicator, covers energy and resources that are embodied in imports and extracts those that are embodied in exports.

(3)   INDICATOR DESCRIBING NATURAL ASSET BASE

To help identify risks to future growth due to the degradation of the natural asset base, indicators in this group monitor whether the natural asset base is being maintained within sustainable thresholds in terms of quantity, quality or value.

(4)   INDICATORS MONITORING THE ENVIRONMENTAL DIMENSION
      OF QUALITY OF LIFE

Indicators in this group monitor environmental conditions, environmental risks and amenities which affect quality of life and well-being. These indicators also observe how income growth influences well-being as well as environmental quality.

(5)   INDICATORS DESCRIBING POLICY RESPONSES AND ECONOMIC
      OPPORTUNITIES

OECD states that indicators in this group monitor trends of policy instruments to promote the transition to (and to tackle obstacles to) Green Growth, such as environmentally related taxes and subsidies. These indicators also evaluate the economic opportunities associated with Green Growth, such as growth of the environmental goods and services sector and "green jobs". Although the current proposed indicators in this group focus mainly on technology and innovation, OECD states that this group covers prices and taxes so as to internalise externalities, education, training and skills, as well as investment and financing for uptake and dissemination.

c)   Headline indicators

OECD made improvements to the indicator set and re-published it in 2014 with headline indicators that proposed to facilitate communication with policy makers, media and citizens, as shown in Table 1.7 (OECD, 2014). OECD considered proposing a single-composite indicator, but in the end a small-balanced indicator set was chosen due to the difficulties of aggregating and weighting data for a single-composite indicator.

Table 1.7 Overview of proposed headline indicators

Environmental and resource productivity	
Carbon productivity	1. CO_2 productivity
Resource productivity	2. Non-energy material productivity
Multi-factor productivity	3. Multi-factor productivity (including environmental services)
The natural asset base	
Renewable and non-renewable stocks	4. Natural resource index
Biodiversity and ecosystems	5. Changes in land use and cover
Environmental quality of life	
Environmental health and risks	6. Air pollution (population exposure to PM 2.5)
Economic opportunities and policy responses	
Technology and innovation, environmental goods and services, prices and transfers, etc.	Placeholder – no indicator specified

Source: OECD (2014)

1.3   Conclusion

This chapter analysed interlinkages and common aspects among Green Economy, Green Growth and sustainable development by examining the concepts and definitions of Green Economy/Growth of several international organisations such as UNEP, OECD, EEA, UNESCAP and UNCSD. Green Economy and Green Growth have high commonality, especially with regard to their components and goals. However, some differences were found in the objectives and processes towards these goals. Green Economy emphasises social and well-being aspects like the improvement of income and employment, which are achieved through rehabilitation of natural capital and ecosystems as well as through improvements in resource efficiency and low-carbon, which are components of Green Economy. Green Growth focuses more on creating economic opportunity and economic development through the improvement of the components. So in the end, the goals of Green Economy and Green Growth converge on happiness or prosperity. Regardless of any differences, the trend by international organisations to develop and promote Green Economy/Growth seems to show a willingness on the part of a global society to take action to achieve prosperity and sustainable development.

This chapter also summarised the system of indicators in the form of the UNEP Green Economy indicator and OECD Green Growth indicator. These indicators are important to monitor and evaluate the progress of Green Economy/Growth, as well as critical to guiding countries in the appropriate direction on this matter. To develop and facilitate the indicators, both UNEP and OECD state that international communities must address the issue of data development, especially the harmonisation of statistical bases and analytical methodologies (UNEP, 2012, and OECD 2011b, 2014). In addition, UNEP indicates that capacity development for data collection and analysis is crucial in developing countries (UNEP, 2012). UNEP also states that many international common databases on the environment should be utilised, including those of the International Energy Agency (IEA), the Food and Agriculture Organisation (FAO) and the United Nations Framework Convention on Climate Change (UNFCCC). Both UNEP and OECD claim that is vital to make use of the SEEA as an international integrated database (UNEP, 2012, and OECD 2011b, 2014). To move forward on Green Economy/Growth leading to sustainable development, the international community is expected to strengthen its evaluation system by utilising international integrated and common databases. There also needs to be some improvement in the definition of Green Economy/Growth and sustainability.

Appendix

Resource productivity: an indicator for resource efficiency – one key component of Green Economy/Growth and sustainable development

Resource efficiency, as explained in this chapter, is a critical component of Green Economy/Growth and sustainable development. Resource productivity is an indicator for resource efficiency, which has recently attracted attention as an environmental policy tool in industrialised countries.

Resource productivity is derived from the methodologies of Material Flow Analysis/Accounting (MFA). MFA methodologies have been developed by industrial ecology experts (e.g. Adriaanse et al., 1997; Fischer-Kowalski, 1998; Fischer-Kowalski and Hüttler, 1998; Matthew et al., 2000; Eurostat, 2001; Weisz, 2007; Moriguchi, 2007; OECD 2008; Bringezu et al., 2008; Bringezu et al., 2009; Fischer-Kowalski et al. 2011). This development on methodologies was used in international collaborative research work under OECD and Eurostat. Details of MFA methodologies and the definition of each indicator can be referred to in their publications (Eurostat, 2001, 2013; Weisz, 2007; OECD 2008)

MFA at the national level, so-called economy-wide MFA (EW-MFA), is the most widely used analytical tool to monitor national resource efficiency. In EW-MFA, existing national and international statistical data on production, consumption, trade and environment are used to show not only material inputs and outputs (in tonnes) of the economy, environment and trade in a country, but also material flow relating to efficient use of resources and environmental impact (OECD, 2008).

Resource productivity usually evaluates both energy and material resources, whereas resource productivity indicators for energy and material resources are distinguished by the UNEP Green Economy indicator and OECD Green Growth indicator. The author, here in this appendix, focuses on resource productivity, which covers both energy and material resources in accordance to the methodologies found in OECD or Eurostat publications.

Resource productivity is calculated as GDP/Direct Material Input (DMI) or Domestic Material Consumption (DMC). DMI comprises all materials with economic values directly used in an economy for both production and consumption (DMI = Domestic extraction used (DEU) + import). DMC is the total quantity of materials consumed within an economy (DMC = DMI – Exports). Discussion of the raw material equivalent of DMC and DMI has recently arisen in the European Commission and Japan, calling for more appropriate evaluation as they cover the embodied resources of import products. Parallel with resource productivity and DCM/DMI, Total Material Requirement (TMR) is often calculated to check

Annex

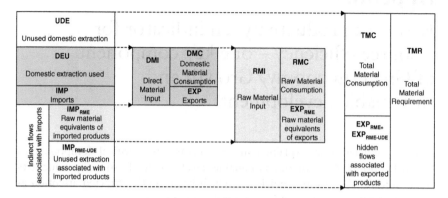

Figure A1.1 Correlation chart of Material Flow indicators
Source: EC 2012

indirect flows associated with imports (known as hidden flows or an "ecological rucksack", such as mining overburden, harvest losses, pollution and waste generated upstream in the production process, etc.) from an environmental point of view. Overview of these MFA derived indicators is shown in Figure UN1.

With increasing international recognition of resource efficiency, recently there has been an expansion in the development of resource efficiency policies using assessment by resource productivity and other MFA indicators. In 2011, the European Union (EU) announced "A Resource-Efficient Europe – Flagship Initiative of the Europe 2020 Strategy", (EC, 2011a; EC, 2011b). The following year the German Resource Efficiency Programme (ProgRess) was created, a policy for improving resource productivity in Germany (BMU, 2012). There was also the Resource Efficiency Action Plan (REAP) announced by Austria in January 2012 (BMLFUW, 2012). In Asia, Japan has developed resource efficiency policies in the context of the three Rs (reduce, reuse and recycle) and has conducted policy assessments based on MFA (MOEJ, 2003; 2013). China has also set resource productivity indicators for a circular economy in the Twelfth Five-Year Plan for National Economic and Social Development of the People's Republic of China (PRC) (Chapter 23: Vigorously Develop Circular Economy) and in its national circular economy development plan (Chinese Government, 2011). The definition of resource productivity is slightly different depending on the context of each country. In addition, the calculation of the raw material equivalent of DMC and DMI has been discussed for more appropriate evaluation of the environmental impact of material flow.

In addition to national initiatives, the International Resource Panel (IRP), established in 2007 with the support of UNEP, has published several evaluation reports on resource efficiency, aiming to decouple economic growth from resource consumption and associated environmental degradation. The panel also draws up policy cases using resource productivity (UNEP, 2011b) that highlight its significance and recommend it into the process of Sustainable Development Goals (UNEP, 2014a). In OECD, the policy development on resource productivity, as well as development MFA methodologies, has been discussed and still ongoing.

Resource productivity is a well-accepted indicator for understanding the overall situation of resource efficiency, especially from the perspective of material resources. It is also crucial to improve resource efficiency policies whilst recognizing the limitations of MFA and resource productivity (data reliability, difficulties of aggregation and the limitations of showing real environmental impact due to the unit being in tonnes). Looking at growing resource consumption on a global level, resource productivity will most likely gain more international attention from the perspective of sustainability.

Notes

1 According to the UNEP Green Economy report (2011a), this is based on general consensus at the World Commission on Environment and Development (WCED) in 1987: "sustainable development as development that meets the needs of the present without compromising the ability of future generations to meet their own needs" (WCED 1987), which can be translated economically as "an increase in well-being today should not result in reducing well-being tomorrow. That is, future generations should be entitled to at least the same level of economic opportunities – and thus at least the same level of economic welfare – as is available to current generations".

2 UNEP continued discussion on the development guidance manual on Green Economy indicators after the publication of the report "Measuring Progress Towards an Inclusive Green Economy" (UNEP, 2012), which is one of main bases of this chapter. Based on the discussion, UNEP newly published (after the author finished writing this chapter) a guidance manual for Green Economy indicators entitled "Using Indicators for Green Economy Policymaking" (UNEP, 2014b). The guidance manual provides a framework of Green Economy indicators for the implementation Green Economy policies at the national level, not intending to propose the examples of Green Economy indicators (UNEP, 2014b). The manual suggests three stages: (1) issue identification and agenda setting, (2) policy formulation and assessment and (3) monitoring and evaluation, and sub-steps to identify and utilize Green Economy indicators in the cycle of integrated policy-making (UNEP, 2014b).

Bibliography

Adriaanse, A., S. Bringezu, A. Hammond, Y. Moriguchi, E. Rodenburg, D. Rogich and H. Schütz. (1997) *Resource Flows: The Material Basis of Industrial Economies.* Washington, DC: World Resources Institute.

Austrian Federal Ministry of Agriculture, Forestry, Environment and Water Management (BMLFUW). (2012) *Ressourceneffizienz Aktionsplan (REAP)* [Resource Efficiency Action Plan: REAP]. www.lebensministerium.at/publikationen/umwelt/umweltpolitik_nachhaltigkeit/REAP.html

28   *Chika Aoki-Suzuki*

BMLFUW (Austrian Federal Ministry of Agriculture, Forestry, Environment and Water Management) (2012) *Ressourceneffizienz Aktionsplan* (REAP) [Resource Efficiency Action Plan]. Available at: www.lebensministerium.at/publikationen/umwelt/umweltpolitik_nachhaltigkeit/REAP.html

BMU (Federal Ministry for the Environment, Nature Conservation and Nuclear Safety) (2012) German Resource Efficiency Programme (ProgRess) Programme for the Sustainable Use and Conservation of Natural Resources. Available at: www.bmub.bund.de/en/topics/economy-products-resources/resource-efficiency/german-resource-efficiency-programme-progress/

Bringezu, S., H. Schütz and S. Moll. (2008) 'Rationale for and Interpretation of Economy-Wide Materials Flow Analysis and Derived Indicators', *Journal of Industrial Ecology*, 7(2): 43–64.

Bringezu, S., I.V.D. Sand, H. Schütz, R. Bleischwitz and S. Moll. (2009) Analysing Global Resource Used of National and Regional Economies Across Various Levels. In S. Bringezu and R. Bleischwitz (Eds.), *Sustainable Resource Management. Trends, Visions and Policies for Europe and the World*. Sheffield, UK: Greenleaf Publisher.

Chinese Government. (2011) *Twelfth Five-Year Plan of National Economic and Social Development, China*. www.gov.cn/2011lh/content_1825838_7.htm

European Commission (EC). (2011a) *A Resource-Efficient Europe – Flagship Initiative Under the Europe 2020 Strategy*, COM (2011) 21, Brussels. eur-lex.europa.eu/LexUriServ/LexUriServ.do?uri=COM:2011:0021:FIN:EN:PDF

EC. (2011b) *A Roadmap to a Resource-Efficient Europe*, COM (2011) 571 final, Brussels, 20 Sep., 2011.eurlex.europa.eu/LexUriServ/LexUriServ.do?uri=COM:2011:0571:FIN:EN:PDF

EC. (2012) *Options for Resource Efficiency Indicators*. Consultation paper. ec.europa.eu/environment/consultations/pdf/consultation_resource.pdf

Eurostat. (2001) *Economy-Wide Material Flow Accounts and Derived Indicators: A Methodological Guide*, Luxembourg. ec.europa.eu/eurostat/en/web/products-manuals-and-guidelines/-/KS-34-00-536

Eurostat. (2013) *Economy-wide Material Flow Accounts (EW-MFA) Compilation Guide 2013*. ec.europa.eu/eurostat/documents/1798247/6191533/2013-EW-MFA-Guide-10Sep2013.pdf/54087dfb-1fb0-40f2-b1e4-64ed22ae3f4c

Federal Ministry for the Environment, Nature Conservation and Nuclear Safety (BMU). (2012) *German Resource Efficiency Programme (ProgRess) Programme for the Sustainable Use and Conservation of Natural Resources*. www.bmub.bund.de/en/topics/economy-products-resources/resource-efficiency/german-resource-efficiency-programme-progress/

Fischer-Kowalski, M. (1998) 'Society's Metabolism, The Intellectual History of Materials Flow Analysis, Part I, 1860–1970', *Journal of Industrial Ecology*, 2(1): 61–78.

Fischer-Kowalski, M., and W. Hüttler. (1998) 'Society's Metabolism, The Intellectual History of Materials Flow Analysis, Part II, 1970–1998', *Journal of Industrial Ecology*, 2(4): 107–136.

Fischer-Kowalski, M., F. Krausmann, S. Giljum, S. Lutter, A. Mayer, S. Bringezu, Y. Moriguchi, H. Schütz, H. Schandl and H. Weisz. (2011) 'Methodology and Indicators of Economy-Wide Material Flow Accounting, State of the Art and Reliability Across Sources', *Journal of Industrial Ecology*, 15(6): 855–876.

Matthews, E., C. Amann, S. Bringezu, M. Fischer-Kowalski, R. Kleijn, C. Ottke, E. Rodenburg, D. Rogich, H. Schütz, H. Schandl and E.V.D. Voet. (2000) *The*

Weight of Nations: Material Outflows from Industrial Economies. Washington, DC: World Resources Institute.

Ministry of the Environment, Japan. (2003) *Dai 1 ji jyunkan gata syakai keisei suisin kihon keikaku* [The First Fundamental Plan for Establishing Sound Material-Cycle Society], Tokyo, Japan. www.env.go.jp/en/recycle/smcs/f_plan2.pdf

Ministry of the Environment, Japan. (2013) *Dai 3 ji jyunkan gata syakai keisei suisin kihon keikaku* [The Third Fundamental Plan for Establishing Sound Material-Cycle Society], Tokyo, Japan. www.env.go.jp/en/recycle/smcs/3rd-f_plan.pdf

Moroguchi, Y. (2007) 'Material Flow Indicators to Measure Progress Toward Sound Material-Cycle Society', *Journal of Material Cycles and Waste Management*, 9(2): 112–120.

OECD. (2008) 'Measuring Material Flows and Resource Productivity Volume 1'. *The OECD Guide*. Paris: OECD.

OECD. (2011a) *Towards Green Growth*. www.oecd.org/greengrowth

OECD. (2011b) *Towards Green Growth: Monitoring Progress: OECD Indicators*. www.oecd.org/greengrowth

OECD. (2014) *Green Growth Indicators 2014*. OECD Green Growth Studies, OECD Publishing. dx.doi.org/10.1787/9789264202030-en

UNCSD. (2012) *The Future We Want*. www.uncsd2012.org/thefuturewewant.html

UNEP. (2011a) *Towards a Green Economy: Pathways to Sustainable Development and Poverty Eradication*. www.unep.org/greeneconomy/GreenEconomyReport/tabid/29846/language/frFR/Default.aspx

UNEP. (2011b) 'Decoupling Natural Resource Use and Environmental Impacts From Economic Growth', *A Report of the Working Group on Decoupling to the International Resource Panel, UNEP*. www.unep.org/resourcepanel/decoupling/files/pdf/Decoupling_Report_English.pdf

UNEP. (2012) *Measuring Progress Towards an Inclusive Green Economy*. http://www.unep.org/greeneconomy/Portals/88/documents/research_products/Measuring%20Progress%20report.pdf

UNEP. (2014a) 'Managing and Conserving the Natural Resource Base for Sustained Economic and Social Development', *IRP Think-Piece*, issued on 7 February 2014 advocating the embedding of the rational management of the natural resource base of economic and social development in the Post-2015 development agenda and Sustainable Development Goals (SDGs). Paris: UNEP-DTIE. www.unep.org/resourcepanel/Portals/24102/IRP%20Think%20Piece%20Contributing%20to%20the%20SDGs%20Process.pdf

UNEP (2014b). Using Indicators for Green Economy Policymaking. www.unep.org/greeneconomy/Portals/88/documents/GEI%20Highlights/UNEP%20INDICATORS%20GE_for%20web.pdf

UNEP and UNU-IHDP. (2012) *Inclusive Wealth Report 2012: Measuring Progress Toward Sustainability*. Cambridge: Cambridge University Press.

UNESCAP. (2012) Green Growth, Resources and Resilience Environmental Sustainability in Asia and the Pacific. http://www.unep.org/dewa/Portals/67/pdf/G2R2_web.pdf

United Nations (UN), European Union (EU), Food and Agriculture Organisation of the United Nations (FAO), International Monetary Fund (IMF), Organisation for Economic Co-operation and Development (OECD), The World Bank (WB). (2014) *System of Environmental-Economic Accounting 2012 Central Framework*. New York. http://unstats.un.org/unsd/envaccounting/seearev/chapterList.asp?volID=1

Weisz, H., F. Krausmann, N. Eisenmenger, H. Schütz, W. Haas and A. Schaffartzik
(2007) *Economy-Wide Material Flow Accounting. A Compilation Guide.* Luxembourg:
European Commission, Eurostat. circabc.europa.eu/webdav/CircaBC/ESTAT/
envirmeet/Library/meeting_archives_1/meetings_2007_archive/material_
19062007/mfa_guides/MFA_Comp_Guide_final.pdf
World Commission on Environment and Development (WCED) (1987) Report of
the World Commission on Environment and Development: Our Common Future,
www.un-documents.net/wced-ocf.htm

2 Efficiency and fairness of resource use

From a planetary boundary perspective

Satoshi Kojima and Chika Aoki-Suzuki

2.1 Introduction

Human environmental impacts are exponentially increasing along with rapid growth of the scale of economic activities – it has been pointed out that the scale of our economic activities has already surpassed some planetary boundaries (Rockström et al. 2009, Wijkman and Rockström 2012). Figure 2.1 shows global gross domestic product (GDP) and global CO_2 emissions over the last 1,000 years. It is obvious that the exponential growth of the economy and the growth of emissions at a similar pace started around the year 1800, when the industrial revolution gained momentum.

A similar observation applies to the consumption of various resources, including fossil fuels and water, as well as to the extinction rate of species (Hubbert 1993, Pimm and Brooks 2000). Consequently, our environmental impacts have devastated various ecosystems and undermined the very basis of our survival. Nobel Prize laureate Paul Crutzen suggested that we are currently in the "Anthropocene", a new geological age in which humans are altering the global environment, and he pointed out that this situation, where a single species – mankind – not only has rapidly altered the global environment but also has recognised that fact, is unprecedented in the history of the Earth (Crutzen 2002). For example, Vitousek et al. (1997) estimated that around 40 percent of the Earth's land surface has been transformed by human activities. Extensive environmental impacts of mankind such as these may have triggered irreversible and catastrophic destruction of ecosystem services which provide life-supporting services to mankind.

The planetary boundary approach is one which assesses the sustainability of life-supporting ecosystems, identifies biogeophysical processes that serve as an indispensable base for human activities (e.g. atmospheric stabilisation, nitrogen cycle) and assesses human impacts on such processes against the quantified carrying capacity of the Earth (Rockström et al. 2009). The assessment results by Rockström et al. (2009) are shown in Figure 2.2.

Based on the assessment results, two out of ten planetary boundary indicators, i.e. chemical pollution and atmospheric aerosol load, are not yet measured, and three out of the remaining eight indicators, i.e. climate change, nitrogen flow and biodiversity loss, exceed the corresponding planetary boundaries. This

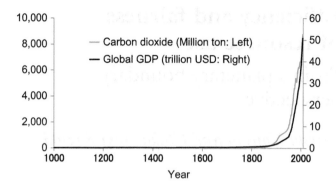

Figure 2.1 Past global GDP and global CO$_2$ emissions

Source: The authors modified the data from Bolt and van Zanden 2013, (GDP) and Boden and Andres 2012 (CO$_2$).

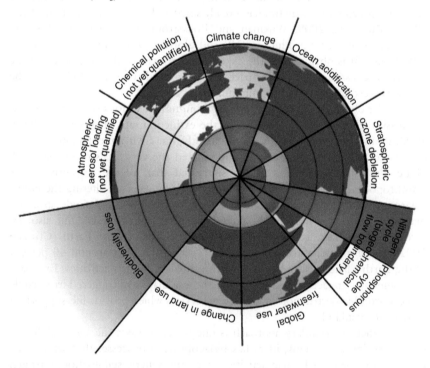

Figure 2.2 Planetary boundaries

Source: Rockström et al. 2009 (credit: Azote Images/Stockholm Resilience Centre)

implies that current economic activities are very likely in overconsumption (or overshoot) and unsustainable. On the other hand, under-consumption problems typified by extreme poverty remain serious despite international efforts such as the Millennium Development Goals (Chen and Ravallion 2010, Batana et al. 2013). Green Economy discussions at Rio+20 in 2012 revealed a serious conflict of views between developed countries, which are facing overconsumption problems from the viewpoint of the carrying capacity of the Earth, and developing and emerging countries, which are facing under-consumption problems (Bouteligier 2013, Marglin 2013). What needs to be done is to achieve sustainable consumption and production in terms of solving under-consumption problems without exceeding planetary boundaries.

While resource efficiency improvement is key to addressing under-consumption problems in developing countries, the International Resource Panel of the United Nations Environmental Programme (UNEP) found that improvements in resource efficiency have not led to a reduction in resource consumption in the member countries of the Organisation for Economic Co-operation and Development (OECD) (UNEP 2011). This phenomenon of an increase in resource consumption as a result of improved resource efficiency is called the rebound effect. The rebound effect implies that improved resource efficiency alone may not be enough to address overconsumption in developed countries and that more advanced or drastic measures, such as capping the total amount of resource consumption, may become necessary.

This chapter first rearticulates the issue of unsustainable consumption as being made up of two problems: one of overconsumption against the carrying capacity of the Earth, and the other of under-consumption to meet the needs of the current generation. This illustrates the importance of equity in resource consumption in addition to resource efficiency improvement.

This chapter is organised as follows: Section 2 clarifies what various indicators of sustainable development and sustainability try to measure by examining the relationship between concrete objectives of sustainable development and these indicators. Section 3 discusses the limits of an improved resource efficiency approach based on the review of existing literature on rebound effects and illustrates the necessity to explicitly reflect environmental constraints such as planetary boundaries. Based on this discussion, Section 4 illustrates the importance of reflecting environmental constraints and equity perspectives in resource productivity indicators. Section 5 provides some conclusions.

2.2   Classification of sustainable development indicators and sustainability indicators

This section provides a framework to discuss sustainable development indicators by clarifying the difference between sustainable development indicators and sustainability indicators. For this purpose we examine the concrete objectives of sustainable development, which is placed as a global policy goal by the Rio Declaration and Agenda 21 adopted at the Rio Earth Summit in 1992, and classify various sustainable development indicators and sustainability indicators in relation to these objectives.

2.2.1   *Sustainable development as a global policy goal*

The most widely cited definition of sustainable development was given in 1987 in a report by the World Commission on the Environment and Development (WCED), commonly referred to as the Brundtland Report, which spurred the

United Nations to organise the Rio Earth Summit in 1992. The Brundtland Report defined sustainable development as "development that meets the needs of the present without compromising the ability of future generations to meet their own needs" (WCED 1987, p.43).

This definition has often been interpreted as simultaneous achievement of intra-generational equity (meeting the needs of the present generation) and inter-generational equity (meeting the needs of future generations), but it is important to recognise that both the Brundtland Report (particularly in Chapter 1) and Principle 6 of the Rio Declaration clearly declared the over-riding priority to satisfy the needs of the current global poor. It was the recognition how serious persistent extreme poverty was that called for the concept of sustainable development (WCED 1987, Lélé 1991). In this sense, sustainable development is primarily about the drastic improvement of conditions for the current poor, not about sustaining the status quo. The primary objective must be realisation of a decent quality of life for all, and it requires that poor countries achieve substantial economic development in order to eradicate material poverty (Kojima 2007).

On the other hand, if meeting the needs of the present generation entails poor countries catching up to developed countries in terms of consumption patterns, then global consumption will surely exceed the carrying capacity of the Earth, and this will cause serious global environmental problems due to disruption of life-supporting ecosystems such as climate stabilisation and water cycles. The expression "without compromising the ability of future generations to meet their own needs" reflects this concern over the potential disruption of life-supporting ecosystems or loss of a survival base for future generations if poor countries follow the development path and consumption patterns of developed countries (Kojima 2007).[1] Inter-generational equity relevant to sustainable development must be interpreted in terms of the conservation of environmental and ecological systems which form the basis of survival for future generations, rather than focusing on the fairness of welfare levels between current and future generations. In this approach, sustainability means the maintenance of life-supporting functions of environmental and ecological systems.[2]

2.2.2 Sustainable development in economics approach

Economics approach, including environmental economics, tends to interpret sustainable development as non-declining (or improving) welfare level across generations. For example, Hanley et al. (1997) is a typical environmental economics textbook which explains that "the general definition of SD [sustainable development] adopted here is that every future generation must have the option of being as well off as its predecessor" (pp. 433–434).

Our discussion in the previous section clarifies that the previous definition of sustainable development within an economics approach focuses on inter-generational equity with respect to welfare level and ignores physical sustainability of environment and ecosystems. This definition would be relevant to sustainable development as a global policy goal only if (1) the needs of the present genera-tion are already met, and (2) the current human impacts are within the carrying capacity of the Earth and there is no concern over disruption of life-supporting ecosystems. If someone is living in a developed country and is enjoying an average quality of life, it is understandable that this person may see that the first condition generally holds. However, it is obvious in poor countries that this is not the case. Whether the latter condition holds is a controversial issue, but at least many have expressed their scepticism against such claims (for example, Rees 2003, MEA 2005, Rockström et al. 2009). Unless these two conditions hold, the definition of sustainable development in economics approach is quite different from what the same word means as a global policy goal.

As part of the theoretical background of sustainable development, discussion of the economics approach, the concept of income proposed by John Hicks (so called "Hicksian income") plays an important role. The Hicksian income is defined as the maximum level of present consumption without compromising the future ability of consumption and production (Hicks 1939). In mainstream economics, the welfare level is assumed to be determined by the consumption level, and consequently the Hicksian income is equivalent to sustainable income in the sense that the current welfare level will be sustained in the future. Once "wealth" is defined as capital stock that underpins the consumption level through production, it is clear that sustainability indicators within an economics approach are derived from the Hicksian income. For example, Genuine Savings (GS) proposed by the World Bank and Inclusive Wealth Index (IWI) proposed by the United Nation University International Human Dimensions Programme (UNU-IHDP) and UNEP are sustainability indicators representing the Hicksian income or sustainability of the current welfare level (Hamilton et al. 1997, Hamilton and Clemens 1999, UNU-IHDP and UNEP 2012).

2.2.3 Classification of indicators of sustainable development and sustainability

It seems useful to classify indicators that monitor the progress of sustainable development into those indicators that monitor the needs satisfaction of the present generation (intra-generational equity indicators), those that monitor sustainability of sound environmental and ecological systems (inter-generational equity indicators), and those that combine these two types. Based on such clas-sification, we further clarify the meaning of sustainability indicators within the economics approach.

a) Intra-generational equity indicators

Intra-generational indicators should address the question, "Do all members of the current generation enjoy decent quality of life?", While gross domestic product (GDP) is the most widely used indicator (or surrogate indicator) of decent quality of life, GDP is an indicator of the scale of economic activities of a nation and not an indicator of decent quality of life – Simon Kuznets, the inventor of GDP, warned that it was not designed for monitoring afflu-ence or the welfare level of a nation (Kuznets 1941, Kuznets 1962). GDP is methodologically well established, and it is an effective indicator of decent quality of life at the lower development stage where material needs are not met, but the low correlation between GDP and welfare level observed in developed countries may be an almost inevitable consequence (Stiglitz et al. 2009, Banerjee et al. 2011).

Against this background, there have been many proposals of alternative indi-cators of decent quality of life or welfare level to GDP (Daly and Cobb 1989, Anand and Sen 1994, Boarini et al. 2006, among others). For example, the Index of Sustainable Economic Welfare (ISEW) proposed by Herman Daly and John Cobb, and its updated version, the Genuine Progress Indicator (GPI), were developed by incorporating environmental and equity aspects to GDP (Daly and Cobb 1989, Cobb et al. 1995). The Human Development Index (HDI) reported by the United Nations Development Programme every year since 1990 is another such attempt.

Methodologies to directly measure subjective happiness or its main deter-minants have also been proposed (Kahneman and Krueger 2006). For example, the Better Life Index (BLI) developed by OECD identifies the main determi-nants of personal happiness in two domains material living conditions domain, including income, employment or settlement, and quality of life domain, including health, education and environment and tries to quantify these deter-minants (OECD 2013).

While these indicators assess whether a representative individual of a country or a specific individual enjoys a decent quality of life or not, intra-generational equity indicators are ultimately expected to assess whether all members of the current generation enjoy decent quality of life or not. In this regard it is remark-able that the Report of the Secretary-General's High-Level Panel of Eminent Persons on the Post-2015 Development Agenda published in May 2013 sug-gested that progress indicators for the Post-2015 Development Goals should ensure that the targets are achieved by all income and social groups, including the most socially marginalised and vulnerable groups, using disaggregated data by income levels and social classes (United Nations 2013).

b)   Inter-generational equity indicators

Inter-generational indicators should address the question, "Does mankind gener-ate environmental impacts leading to the destruction of life-supporting systems on Earth?". Ecological Footprint (EF) and planetary boundaries are primary examples of indicators of sound environmental and ecological systems.

The EF measures ecosystem services required by social and economic systems both to meet resource demands and to assimilate wastes, in terms of productive land area (Global Footprint Network 2013). A certain environmental and ecologi-cal system is sustainable if the EF is smaller than the bio capacity that measures the available ecosystem services in terms of productive land area. If the EF exceeds the bio capacity, it indicates overconsumption (overshoot), and the system is not sustainable.

The planetary boundary takes a different approach from the EF. The planetary boundary approach identifies several ecosystem services (ten ecosystem services in the latest version) that provide life-supporting functions, and sets a respective boundary for each ecosystem service, taking into account mutual influence among different ecosystem services (Rockström et al. 2009).

c)   Economic sustainability indicators

As explained in Section 2.2, GS and IWI are economic sustainability indicators which measure the sustainability of the current welfare level rather than the sustainability of sound environmental and ecological systems. For example, when GS or IWI indicates welfare improvement over time, it cannot guarantee that environmental impacts of mankind will not cause irreversible and catastrophic environmental disruption in the future. Hence GS and IWI are not inter-generational equity indicators in the context of sustainable development as a global policy goal, despite that they measure inter-generational equity with respect to welfare levels across generations. In the context of sustainable development, it would be better to see GS and IWI in relation to decent quality of life. These indicators focus on capital stock or wealth, one of the key determinants of decent quality of life, with extension to natural capital and social capital, and measure how sustainable they are in terms of a lack of decline in extended capital stock over time. It must be noted that these indicators do not directly address the question, "Do all members of the current generation enjoy a decent quality of life?".

d)   Classification of typical indicators of sustainable development and sustainability

We classify major sustainable development indicators and sustainability indicators as shown in Table 2.1.

The previous classification also helps us to understand various integrated indicators. For example, Happy Planet Index (HPI) proposed by the New Economics Foundation is defined as a product of life expectancy and experienced well-being divided by EF, and it is interpreted that the inter-generational equity indicator based on subjective happiness is divided by the sustainability indicator of sound environmental and ecological systems (Marks et al. 2006). Similarly, dashboard type indicators such as OECD's Green Growth Indicators and UNEP's Green Economy Indicators are better understood by classifying the constituent indicators based on Table 2.1.

It is noted that HPI and some constituent indicators of Green Growth Indicators and Green Economy Indicators are efficiency indicators. Efficiency is a useful concept to measure the degree of "cost saving" to achieve certain

Table 2.1 Classification of sustainable development indicators/sustainability indicators

Assessment subject		Sustainable development indicators	Economic sustainability indicators
Intra-generational equity	GDP adjustment approach	GDP, HDI, ISEW/ GPI(Green GDP, GS, IWI as well)	
	Happiness approach	Subjective happiness, BLI	
Intergenerational equity	Sustainability of survival basis	EF, Planetary Boundaries	
	Sustainability of welfare level		Green GDP, GS, IWI

Source: Authors

objectives, but it does not measure how well the objectives were achieved. High HPI, for instance, does not necessarily indicate that the subjects of evaluation enjoy a decent quality of life, neither that their EF is within the carrying capacity of the Earth. Stiglitz et al. (2009) warned not to combine current welfare level and sustainability into one integrated indicator, which is analogous to "a meter that added up in one single number the current speed of the vehicle and the remaining level of gasoline" (p. 17). This is a very important point in developing useful integrated indicators of sustainable development.

2.3   Limits of efficiency approach and environmental constraints

Rio+20 in 2012 highlighted the notion of Green Economy/Green Growth as a means or pathway to achieve sustainable development, and efficiency indicators have gained attention in the Green Economy discussion, as well as in discussions on UNEP's Green Economy Indicators or OECD's Green Growth Indicators. As we pointed out in Section 2.2, efficiency measures the degree of "cost saving" to achieve certain objectives, but in the paradigm which this study labels as the "efficiency approach", it is efficiency improvement itself that is the objective. An efficiency approach is much more popular among politicians and business leaders than a capping approach, which sets an upper limit for resource use and environmental impacts. This is understandable because efficiency improvement is expected to result in better profitability. Furthermore, this approach does not call for painful contraction in economic scale. However, any advantage that this efficiency approach may have is what limits its applicability to sustainable development.

The decoupling argument was pioneered by the Factor Four approach, proposed by Ernst von Weizsäcker in 1990s, and claims that strong decoupling, which means the simultaneous achievement of economic growth (specifically GDP growth) and absolute reduction in resource consumption and environmental impacts, is possible through drastic improvement of resource efficiency (e.g. von Weizsäcker et al. 1997, von Weizsäcker et al. 2009). Strong decoupling seems technically possible, but the International Resource Panel pointed out that strong decoupling has not been achieved in the OECD member countries, even though they have achieved resource efficiency improvement or weak decoupling (UNEP 2011). This phenomenon of an absolute increase in resource uses and environmental impacts under efficiency improvement is called a rebound effect, and has been discussed as early as the nineteenth century when William Jevons argued on coal consumption in England (von Weizsäcker et al. 2009). A common explanation on the mechanism of the rebound effect is that increased benefits due to efficiency improvement induce more consumption (von Weizsäcker et al. 2009). However, there is a possibility that the rebound effect is caused by more serious problems related to the "Dilemma of Growth" as pointed out by Tim Jackson. The dilemma is that economic growth achieved by developed countries may be unsustainable given environmental constraints such as planetary boundaries, while degrowth (negative growth) may destabilise the social and economic system (Jackson 2009). The current social and economic system is designed on the premise of GDP growth, and the mere slowdown, let alone degrowth, of GDP growth could cause problems such as destabilisation of the financial system, collapse of the social security system, increased unemployment, and so on. One example of this GDP growth dependence on the economic system is the very strong correlation between GDP growth rate and lower unemployment in Japan, as shown in Figure 2.3.

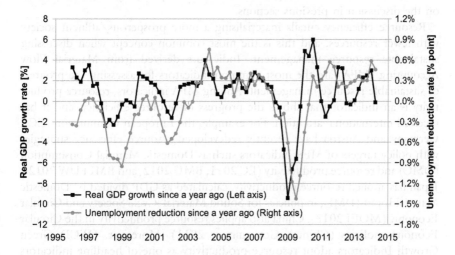

Figure 2.3 Correlation between GDP growth and reduction in unemployment

Source: The authors modified the data from Statistics Bureau, Ministry of Internal Affairs and Communications

As an inevitable consequence of the GDP growth–dependent design of the social and economic system, GDP growth is given the highest priority among policy agendas. Such a society must have not mere positive growth but "robust enough" growth of GDP, which will also be a virtue for that society. Under this very strong incentive to accelerate GDP growth, it is also inevitable that the benefits of efficiency improvement are used to boost GDP growth further. If the rebound effect is in fact caused by this kind of fundamental problem rooted in the current design of the social and economic system, it is highly unlikely that resource consumption and environmental impacts will be reduced in absolute terms through efficiency improvement only.

Inter-generational equity indicators in the context of sustainable development, either in EF or planetary boundary approaches, show that current human environmental impacts exceed the carrying capacity of the Earth (Rockström et al. 2009, Global Footprint Network 2013). Developed countries are associated with huge per capita resource consumption and environmental impacts, and they need to aim for absolute reductions in resource consumption and environmental impacts, even if there must be an adjustment of scale of economy in order to contribute to sustainable development on a global scale.

2.4   Sustainable resource management indicators which reflect planetary boundaries

2.4.1   *Discussion base for indicator development*

This section focuses on the development of sustainable development indicators for sustainable resource management which reflect planetary boundaries based on the discussion in previous sections.

Resource efficiency entails materialising a more prosperous/affluent society with fewer resources, and this is the most common concept when discussing sustainable resource management. Indicators derived from Material Flow Accounting (MFA) are the most common indicators for assessing the progress of sustainable resource management. Among MFA indicators, resource productivity is an indicator that shows the progress of resource efficiency, and it has received international attention. For example, the European Commission (EC), Germany and Austria have recently redeveloped resource efficiency strategies with policy targets of MFA indicators such as Domestic Material Consumption (DMC) and resource productivity (EC 2011, BMU 2012, and BMLFUW 2012). Japan has applied resource productivity, calculated as GDP divided by Domestic Material Input (DMI), in policies for Sound Material–Cycle Society and Circular Economy (MOEJ 2013). China also applies resource productivity in the Circular Economy policies (Chinese Government 2011). Moreover, OECD Green Growth Indicators adopt resource productivity as one of headline indicators (OECD 2011).

However, resource productivity (GDP/resource input or consumption) would have two major challenges to evaluate sustainable resource management from the perspectives of planetary boundaries. First, as argued in discussions on "Beyond GDP", resource productivity may not be able to fully express prosperity because of the limitations of GDP to reflect environmental externality (e.g. Stiglitz et al. 2009, EC 2009 . Second, resource productivity is a relative indicator to show efficiency, not absolute resource consumption. This means that, as discussed in Section 2.2, resource efficiency could not lead to a reduction in resource consumption due to the rebound effect.

As Jackson (2009) discussed, the "Contraction and Convergence" principal needs to be applied to sustainable resource management in the context of the global consumption gap between over-consuming developed countries and under-consuming developing countries. The "Contraction and Convergence" principal was raised in the 1990s to respond to Climate Change issues (Meyer 2000). This principle has been re-raised by Garnaut (2008) as an approach for all countries, that they should converge at the certain level of per capita GHG emissions calculated based on planetary boundary. In the context of sustainable resource management, this principle means that resource consumption would be decreased in over-consuming developed countries and increased in under-consuming developing countries, and consequently would converge to the same resource consumption level within the planetary boundary (Figure 2.4). Kojima et al. (2011) develop a similar argument in the context of promoting Green Economy. They discuss that developed countries are expected to seek social–economic structural change which accommodates environmental capacity and resource constraint, while developing/emerging countries should first address

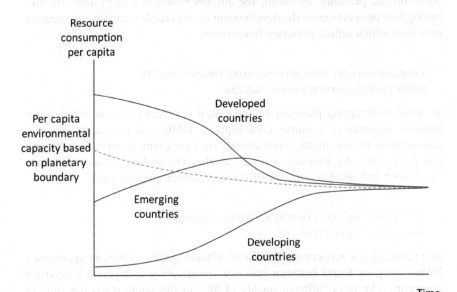

Figure 2.4 Conceptual diagram on Contraction and Convergence
Source: Redeveloped by the authors based on Kojima et al. (2011)

poverty alleviation through improving energy/resource efficiency. They also argue that this principle would contribute to facilitating constructive discussion among countries with different positions.

In this regard, equity issues between developed and developing countries may arise if global convergence is promoted without resolving the growth dilemma. This might cause conflicts over intra-generational equity, one of the crucial issues to achieving sustainable development. Addressing equity of resource consumption and uneven resource distribution is critical in light of human rights for equal achievements of prosperity (Wijkman and Rockström 2012). Utilising resource productivity, a relative indicator between GDP and resource consumption, is one of the most important approaches for developing countries to resolve under-consumption and to achieve material prosperity by improving their high resource efficiency. Conversely, developed countries should recognise their over-consumption as well as the rebound effect induced by seeking efficiency. Developed countries also should reduce their absolute resource consumption and establish a new social system which ensures an affluent quality of life, stabilisation and social prosperity within resource limitations and planetary boundaries. Indicators would be effective tools to discover the level of consumption at which global society should converge in future.

a) *Four crucial perspectives for indicator development*

Based on the previous discussion, the authors would like to propose the following four perspectives on the development of sustainable resource management indicators which reflect planetary boundaries:

I. ABSOLUTE AMOUNT INDICATOR TO MONITOR AN ABSOLUTE
   REDUCTION OF RESOURCE CONSUMPTION

To avoid bankrupting planetary boundaries, it is crucial to assess and monitor absolute amounts of resource consumption. DMC and per capita resource consumption (water, metal, food, energy, etc.) are examples of indicators with this perspective. In addition, analysis on the relationship between planetary boundaries and absolute amount of resource consumption is vital.

II. EXAMINING THE LEVEL OF SERVICE WHICH ENSURES
    AN AFFLUENT QUALITY OF LIFE

By examining the services needed for an affluent quality of life, an appropriate balance may be found between resource consumption and people's need for prosperity. The term "affluent quality of life" in this study refers not only to Basic Human Needs (BHN), which provide minimum consumption and community service, but also to a certain satisfactory level of life where people can enjoy prosperity beyond the BHN.

There are two types of services required for an affluent quality of life. There are services relevant to individual consumption, such as clothing, food and housing; and there are other social system services and infrastructures, such as public transportation, rail/road, water supply/treatment and waste management.

The amount of resources required for these services is not comparable to either over-consumption in some developed countries or under-consumption in developing countries. The level of service is not required to be proportional to the amount of resource consumption.

III. RESOURCE AMOUNTS REQUIRED FOR SERVICES TO SATISFY AN AFFLUENT
     QUALITY OF LIFE AND ITS ASSOCIATED ENVIRONMENTAL IMPACTS

It is necessary to identify what the services for an affluent quality of life are. When this is established, the amount of resources required to implement such services should be estimated to determine the global convergence point of resource consumption. Since resource consumption should not exceed planetary boundaries, it is necessary to simultaneously evaluate the associated environmental impacts of resource consumption. Thus, indicators should clearly express the interrelationship among services, resource consumption and associated environmental impacts. However, it is difficult to determine a single integrated indicator which can show this interrelationship. Thus, a number of indicators relevant to this interrelationship could be employed to facilitate discussion.

IV. DIFFERENCES AMONG COUNTRIES IN RESOURCES, RESOURCE
    CONSUMPTION AND ASSOCIATED ENVIRONMENTAL IMPACTS BOTH
    AT MACRO AND MICRO LEVELS

There is no question that services, resource consumption and associated environmental impacts related to an affluent quality of life are varied and diverse. For example, resources required for air-conditioning systems are likely to be different from region to region. Thus, adjustments must be made to incorporate these differences into resource consumption and environmental impacts to analyse the level of convergence on resource consumption on a global level.

b) Examples of challenges for indicator development

These four perspectives form a basis for the development of sustainable resource management indicators which reflect planetary boundaries. Multi-dimensional evaluation should be conducted with indicators reflecting these four perspectives.

However, there are many challenges that could benefit from more in-depth analysis to identify appropriate concrete indicators.

We would like to take "automobile ownership" as an example of one of these challenges. There are at least three challenges to develop indicators for this example.

First, there are limitations when making substitutions for services (a challenge set out in Perspective ii). Services that serve as benefits for automobile ownership could be replaced by the mobility of owners as well as leisure (recreation) improvement. Mobility services could be substituted by public transportation; however, public transport could not substitute for the leisure provided by automobiles.

Second, there are difficulties in capturing associated impacts due to resource consumption (a challenge set in Perspective iii). Car production and use not only is a matter energy consumption, but also could cause various environmental and social impacts such as traffic congestion, air pollution and impact on ecosystems. The relationship between resource consumption and associated environmental impacts due to implementing the service could consist of complicated multi-hierarchical structures.

Third, the needs of people vary greatly (challenges set out in Perspectives ii and iv). Individual needs for automobiles might show substantial variation, for example, between regions with and without advanced public transportation, or between large and small countries.

c)   Developing international comparable indicators

Sustainable resource management is a global and cross-sectoral issue and should be discussed internationally. However, indicators should be designed carefully so that international comparisons can be conducted for sustainable resource management, recognising the previous four perspectives and their challenges. Setting a top-runner target or showing the average value of indicators is one way to overcome these challenges. There are also increasing trends to evaluate the effects of globalising resource trade using both consumption and production-based indicators (UNU-IHDP and UNEP 2012, OECD 2011). In light of such indicator development trends, further analysis is necessary to establish sustainable resource management indicators which reflect planetary boundaries.

2.5   Conclusions

This chapter clarifies the issues related to sustainable development indicators as well as to economic sustainability indicators, and demonstrates that sustainable development – as a global policy goal advanced by Agenda 21 and the Rio Declaration – primarily calls for intra-generational equity in the sense of needs satisfaction of the present generation (so that all the members of the current generation enjoy a decent quality of life). This may require significant economic growth in developing countries to eradicate acute poverty while achieving intergenerational equity in terms of avoiding serious environmental impacts that would destroy global life-supporting systems. Based on this understanding, we examine sustainable resource management indicators which reflect planetary boundaries as candidates for progress indicators of sustainable development.

Rockström et al. (2009) looked at human impacts in relation to eight quantified planetary boundaries and found that human impacts have already exceeded three of them, i.e. climate change, nitrogen cycle and biodiversity. Developed countries are associated with per capita resource consumption and environmental impacts much larger than world average, meaning that over-consumption (overshoot) is likely to happen in developed countries. On the other hand, the problem of under-consumption represented by absolute poverty is still a serious issue despite international efforts such as the Millennium Development Goals. To promote sustainable resource use against this situation, equity is important, in the sense that resource use of all countries will converge at an appropriate level. This is in addition to the efforts to improve resource efficiency. As a concrete approach, this chapter looks at the "Contraction and Convergence" principle, which has been debated in climate change discussions since 1990s concerning greenhouse gases emissions, and proposes that this principle be applied to an indicator representing both per capita resource consumption and quality of life. Further, this chapter discusses various practical issues associated with the development of such an indicator.

Stiglitz et al. (2009) pointed out that "[w]hat we measure affects what we do; and if our measurements are flawed, decisions may be distorted" (p. 7). We would like to develop indicators which will lead to decisions towards the realisation of a decent quality of life all over the world while maintaining life-supporting ecosystems, and we aim to elaborate on this study in the future.

Notes

1 It must be emphasised here that sustainable development does not mean restrictions to the economic development of developing countries but does mean that the unsustainable way of needs satisfaction in developed countries (life style, consumption patterns) is the central problem. Principle 8 of the Rio Declaration and Chapter 4 of Agenda 21 focus on reduction and eradication of unsustainable consumption in this context.

2 Griggs et al. (2013) redefine sustainable development as "development that meets the needs of the present while safeguarding Earth's life-support system, on which the welfare of current and future generations depends" in the context of Sustainable Development Goals to be adopted by the General Assembly of the United Nations in 2015.

Bibliography

Anand, S., and Sen, A. (1994) *Human development index: methodology and measurement*. New York: Human Development Report Office, United Nations Development Programme.

Banerjee, A., Banerjee, A.V., and Duflo, E. (2011) *Poor economics: a radical rethinking of the way to fight global poverty*. New York: Public Affairs.

Batana, Y., Bussolo, M., and Cockburn, J. (2013) 'Global extreme poverty rates for children, adults and the elderly'. *Economics Letters* 120(3): 405–407.

BMLFUW (Austrian Federal Ministry of Agriculture, Forestry, Environment and Water Management) (2012) *Ressourceneffizienz Aktionsplan* (REAP) [Resource Efficiency Action Plan]. Available at: www.lebensministerium.at/publikationen/umwelt/umweltpolitik_nachhaltigkeit/REAP.html

BMU (Federal Ministry for the Environment, Nature Conservation and Nuclear Safety) (2012) German Resource Efficiency Programme (ProgRess) Programme for the Sustainable Use and Conservation of Natural Resources. Available at: www.bmub.bund.de/en/topics/economy-products-resources/resource-efficiency/german-resource-efficiency-programme-progress/

Boarini, R., Johansson, Å., and d'Ercole, M.M. (2006) *Alternative measures of well-being.* OECD.

Boden, T.A., Marland, G., and Andres, B. (2012) *Global CO₂ emissions from fossil-fuel burning, cement manufacture, and gas flaring.* Oak Ridge, TN: Carbon Dioxide Information Analysis Center, U.S. Department of Energy.

Bolt, J., and van Zanden, J.L. (2013) 'The first update of the Maddison Project: re-estimating growth before 1820'. *Maddison Project Working Paper 4.*

Bouteligier, S. (2013) 'Inequality in new global governance arrangements: the North–South divide in transnational municipal networks'. *The European Journal of Social Science Research* 26(3): 251–267.

Chen, S., and Ravallion, M. (2010) 'The developing world is poorer than we thought, but no less successful in the fight against poverty'. *The Quarterly Journal of Economics* 125: 1577–1625.

Chinese Government. (2011) *Twelfth five-year plan of national economic and social development, China.* Available at: www.gov.cn/2011lh/content_1825838_7.htm

Cobb, C., Halstead, T., and Rowe, J. (1995) *The genuine progress indicator.* San Francisco: Redefining Progress.

Crutzen, P.J. (2002) 'Geology of mankind'. *Nature* 415: 23.

Daly, H.E., and Cobb, J.B. (1989) *For the common good: redirecting the economy toward community, the environment and a sustainable future.* Boston: Beacon Press.

EC (2009) *GDP and beyond: measuring progress in a changing world.* Available at: http://eur-lex.europa.eu/legal-content/EN/TXT/?uri=CELEX:52009DC0433

EC (2011) *Roadmap to a resource efficient Europe.* Available at: http://ec.europa.eu/environment/resource_efficiency/about/roadmap/index_en.htm

Fischer-Kowalski, M., M. Swilling, E.U. von Weizsäcker, Y. Ren, Y. Moriguchi, W. Crane, F. Krausmann, N. Eisenmenger, S. Giljum, P. Hennicke, R. Romero Lankao and A. Siriban Manalang (2011) 'Decoupling Natural Resource Use and Environmental Impacts From Economic Growth', *A Report of the Working Group on Decoupling to the International Resource Panel, UNEP.* www.unep.org/resourcepanel/decoupling/files/pdf/Decoupling_Report_English.pdf

Garnaut, R. (2008) *The Garnaut climate change review final report.* Available at: www.garnautreview.org.au/index.htm

Global Footprint Network (2013) *The national footprint accounts, 2012 edition.* Oakland, CA: Global Footprint Network.

Griggs, D., Stafford-Smith, M., Gaffney, O., Rockström, J., Öhman, M.C., Shyamsundar, P., Steffen, W., Glaser, G., Kanie, N., and Noble, I. (2013) 'Sustainable development goals for people and planet'. *Nature* 495: 305–307.

Hamilton, K., Atkinson, G., and Pearce, D. (1997) 'Genuine savings as an indicator of sustainability'. *CSERGE GEC Working Paper.*

Hamilton, K. and Clemens, M. (1999) 'Genuine savings rates in developing countries'. *The World Bank Economic Review* 13(2): 333–356.

Hanley, N., Shogren, J.F., and White, B. (1997) *Environmental economics: In theory and practice*. Houndmills, UK: Macmillan.

Hicks, J.R. (1939) *Value and capital: An inquiry into some fundamental principles of economic theory*. Oxford: Oxford University Press.

Hubbert, M.K. (1993) 'Exponential growth as a transient phenomenon in human history'. In H.E. Daly and K.N. Townsend (Eds), *Valuing the earth: economics, ecology ethics*. Cambridge, MA: MIT Press: 113–126.

International Labour Office (ILO) (1976) *Employment, growth and basic needs, a report for World Employment Conference in 1976*. Geneva: ILO.

Jackson, T. (2009) *Prosperity without growth? The transition to a sustainable economy*. Sustainable Development Commission. Available at: http://www.sd-commission. org.uk/data/files/publications/prosperity_without_growth_report.pdf

Kahneman, D., and Krueger, A.B. (2006) 'Developments in the measurement of subjective well-being'. *The Journal of Economic Perspectives* 20(1): 3–24.

Kojima, S. (2007) *Sustainable development in water-stressed developing countries: a quantitative policy analysis*. Cheltenham: Edward Elgar.

Kojima, S., Kabaya, K., and Yano, T. (2011) 'Green economy for sustainable development: Japan should lead the policy shift towards global poverty alleviation'. *IGES Policy Brief Vol.12*. Hayama: IGES.

Kuznets, S. (1941) *National income and its composition 1919–1938*. New York: National Bureau of Economic Research.

Kuznets, S. (1962) 'How to judge quality'. *New Republic* 20: 29–32.

Lélé, S.M. (1991) 'Sustainable development: a critical review'. *World Development* 19(6): 607–621.

Marglin, S.A. (2013) 'Premises for a new economy'. *Development* 56(2): 149–154.

Marks, N., Abdallah, S., Simms, A., and Thompson, S. (2006). *The happy planet index*. London: New Economics Foundation.

MEA (Millennium Ecosystem Assessment) (2005) *Living beyond our means: natural assets and human well-being*. Available at: http://www.unep.org/maweb/documents/ document.429.aspx.pdf

Meyer, A. (2000) *Contraction & convergence: the global solution to climate change*. Cambridge, UK: Green Books.

MOEJ (Ministry of the Environment, Japan) (2013) *The 3rd fundamental plan for establishing a sound material-cycle society 2013*. Available at: www.env.go.jp/en/ recycle/smcs/3rd-f_plan.pdf

OECD (2011) *Towards green growth: monitoring progress: OECD indicators*. Available at: http://www.oecd.org/greengrowth

OECD (2013) *How's life? Measuring well-being*. Paris: OECD. Available at: www. oecd-ilibrary.org/economics/how-s-life_9789264121164-en

Pimm, S.L., and Brooks, T.M. (2000) *The sixth extinction: how large, where, and when. Nature and human society: the quest for a sustainable world*. Washington, DC: National Academy Press: 46–62.

Rees, W.E. (2003) 'Is humanity fatally successful?' *Journal of Business Administration and Policy Analysis* 30–31: 67–100

Rockström, J., Steffen, W., Noone, K. Persson, A, Chapin, F.S., Lambin, E.F., Lenton, T.M., Scheffer, M., Folke, C., Schellnhuber, H.J., Nykvist, B., de Wit, C.A., Hughes, T., van der Leeuw, S., Rodhe, H., Sörlin, S., Snyder, P.K., Costanza, R., Svedin, U., Falkenmark, M., Karlberg, L., Corell, R.W., Fabry, V.J., Hansen, J., Walker, B., Liverman, D., Richardson, K., Crutzen, P., and Foley, J.A. (2009) 'A safe operating space for humanity'. *Nature* 461: 472–475

Stiglitz, J., Sen, A., and Fitoussi, J.P. (2009) *Report by the Commission on the Measurement of Economic Performance and Social Progress.* Available at: http://www.stiglitz-sen-fitoussi.fr/documents/rapport_anglais.pdf

United Nations. (2013) 'A new global partnership: eradicate poverty and transform economies through sustainable development' *The Report of the High-Level Panel of Eminent Persons on the Post-2015 Development Agenda.*

UNEP. (2011) 'Decoupling Natural Resource Use and Environmental Impacts From Economic Growth', *A Report of the Working Group on Decoupling to the International Resource Panel, UNEP.* www.unep.org/resourcepanel/decoupling/files/pdf/Decoupling_Report_English.pdf

UNEP. (2012) *Measuring progress towards an inclusive green economy.* Available at: http://www.unep.org/greeneconomy/Portals/88/documents/research_products/Measuring%20Progress%20report.pdf

UNU-IHDP and UNEP (2012) *Inclusive wealth report 2012: measuring progress toward sustainability.* Available at: http://www.unep.org/pdf/IWR_2012.pdf

Vitousek, P.M., Mooney, H.A., Lubchenco, J., and Melillo, J.M. (1997) 'Human domination of Earth's ecosystems'. *Science* 277: 494–499

von Weizsäcker, E., Hargroves, K., Smith, M.H., Desha, C., and Stasinopoulos, P. (2009) *Factor five: transforming the global economy through 80% improvements in resource productivity.* London: Earthscan.

von Weizsäcker, E., Lovins, A.B., and Lovins, L.H. (1997) *Factor 4: doubling wealth, halving resource use.* London: Earthscan.

WCED. (1987) *Our common future.* London: Oxford University Press.

Wijkman, A., and Rockström, J. (2012) *Bankrupting nature: denying our planetary boundaries, an official report to the club of Rome.* London: Routledge.

3 Environmental Kuznets curve

Economic growth and emission reduction

Tetsuya Tsurumi and Shunsuke Managi

3.1 Introduction

The debate over the role economic growth plays in determining environmental quality has been rapidly gaining importance (e.g., Copeland and Taylor, 2004; Stern, 2004; Dasgupta *et al.*, 2006). There are three effects that are key in determining the level of environmental pollution and resource use (see Grossman, 1995; Copeland and Taylor, 2004; Brock and Taylor, 2006). First, an increase in output requires more input and, as a by-product, implies more emissions. Economic growth therefore exhibits a scale effect that has a negative impact on the environment. Second, economic growth also has positive or negative impacts on the environment through a technique effect. Changes in income or preferences may induce changes in policy that in turn lead to changes in production methods and hence emission per unit of output.[1] This suggests that the relationship between income and pollution should vary across pollutants because their perceived damage is different. Third, economic growth has positive or negative impacts on the environment through a composition effect. As income grows, the structure of the economy might change; consequently, there might be an increase in cleaner or dirtier activities. In the case of general industrial pollutants, environmental degradation tends to increase during the structural transformation of an economy from the agricultural to the industrial phase and subsequently starts to fall with the structural change from an energy-intensive economy to a technology-intensive economy based on services and knowledge.

The net of these three effects generates the Environmental Kuznets Curve (EKC).[2] Taking three effects into account, this study analyzes the fundamental characteristics of world pollutants/resource uses. The distinction of the three effects is important for the following two reasons. First, confirmation of the EKC hypothesis does not justify policy inaction. Incentives to reduce pollution/ resource use are provided by the technique effect. The tradeoff between economic growth and environmental quality depends critically on the technique effect. Therefore, estimation of the magnitude and trend of the technique effect would be useful in understanding the size of policy stringency required. If there were no incentive or little incentive to reduce, policymakers would need to implement measures that induce technological change or technological transfer.

It is notable that Dasgupta *et al.* (2001) and Esty and Porter (2005) show that GDP per capita is highly correlated with stringency of environmental regulations, although there is a little heterogeneity. In addition, Esty and Porter (2005) show that all the elements of their indices in regulatory stringency categories show a statistically significant relationship with environmental performance, and this implies that more stringent environmental regulations have a possibility to improve the environment. Therefore, if we find that technique effect does not suffice in reducing emissions, policymakers would need to reconsider whether their environmental policies need to be more stringent. Second, previous EKC studies do not support the existence of a simple, predictable relationship between pollution and per capita income because multiple factors intervene and identification of these effects is required (see Stern, 2004; Copeland and Taylor, 2004). We intend to separate economic growth and industrial structural factors by identifying the scale effect and the composition effect.

In the literature of EKC, parametric functional forms (of quadratic and cubic polynomials) of the relationship between per capita emissions and per capita real GDP have been used to examine the existence of turning points. Although there is an abundant literature on the EKC, its econometric applications have been criticized because of a lack of robust econometric methods (Stern, 2004). Recently, in response to these claims, semi-parametric or nonparametric specifications have been used to reexamine these results because they are more flexible than popular parametric functional forms (see Azomahou *et al.*, 2006, for a recent review). In this study, we use a semi-parametric estimation of generalized additive models. In comparison with the other semi-parametric or nonparametric methods, this technique overcomes the difficulty of including multiple independent variables into specifications.

We use a large and globally representative sample of local and global pollutants[3] and natural resources, including sulfur dioxide (SO_2) emissions, carbon dioxide (CO_2) emissions, and energy use. Our goal in this chapter is to understand the determinants of environmental quality by examining the decomposed factors of scale, technique, and composition effects. This decomposition would help policymakers with understanding the size of policy stringency required.

The remainder of the chapter is organized as follows: in Section 3.2, we briefly review recent studies, whilst in Section 3.3 we describe the research methods and the data. In Section 3.4 the econometric results are presented, whilst Section 3.5 concludes.

3.2   Literature review

A large number of studies have investigated whether the EKC exists both empirically and theoretically. Starting with the influential studies of Grossman and Krueger (1993, 1995) and Selden and Song (1994), a number of empirical studies have investigated this relationship for various pollutants, regions, and time periods. Studies in the literature find an inverted U-shaped relationship, a U-shaped relationship, or a monotonically increasing or decreasing relationship between pollution and rising per capita income levels. Whether greater economic growth hurts the environment or eventually reduces pollution depends on the pollutant (see Dinda, 2004; Stern, 2004; Managi, 2007, for a summary and discussion of the empirical literature).

We focus this review on SO_2, CO_2, and energy use because there are enormous numbers of references to these in the literature. In general, the EKC patterns are more likely to appear for short-term and local impact pollutants than for more global, indirect, and long-term impact pollutants (see Arrow *et al.*, 1995; Cole *et al.*, 1997). Many studies, such as Seldom and Song (1994), Grossman and Krueger (1995), Panayotou (1997), and Torras and Boyce (1998), find an EKC for SO_2. On the other hand, for CO_2 the result is far less conclusive. For example, although Shafic (1994) concludes that CO_2 has a monotonic increasing tendency, Holtz-Eakin and Selden (1995) find an EKC. However, their turning point is excessively high, and therefore the EKC hypothesis cannot be confirmed. However, Schmalensee *et al.* (1998) use the same data as Holtz-Eakin and Selden (1995) and find negative income elasticity at high-income levels within the sample, which supports the existence of the EKC. In comparison with SO_2 and CO_2, there are a limited number of studies concerning energy use. Previous studies for energy use find a monotonous increasing trend instead of an EKC (e.g., Agras and Chapmann, 1997; Suri and Chapman, 1998; Richmond and Kaufmann, 2006).

Recent empirical studies use updated and revised data, and tend to find that common EKC results are highly sensitive to changes in sample, specification, or functional forms. For example, Stern and Common (2001) note the potential sensitivity of the EKC for SO_2 with respect to the country sampled. They suggest that if developing countries are included in the sample, turning point becomes much higher. In addition to this study, Halkos (2003) suggests that choice of econometric method has a large effect on the result for SO_2. In the case of CO_2, Cole (2005) suggests that the EKC peaks at extremely high income for restricted countries. Geleotti *et al.* (2006) also find that both data sampled and estimation method affect an EKC result for CO_2.

The concern that common EKC results are highly sensitive has invoked recent papers using semi-parametric or nonparametric techniques, which test the robustness of previous studies. For example, Millimet *et al.* (2003) estimate semi-parametric models using US state-level panel data and find EKCs for SO_2. Bertinelli and Strobl (2005) also use a semi-parametric regression estimator for a panel of countries for 1950–1990, and for SO_2 and CO_2 they find a positive relationship at low incomes, which flattens out before increasing again at high incomes. Azomahou *et al.* (2006) investigate CO_2 emissions using nonparametric estimation of local linear kernel regressions and find that the relation is rising. Luzzati and Orsini (2009) analyze an EKC for energy use, using fixed effects estimation as a parametric method and generalized additive models as a semi-parametric method. As a result, both estimation results show a monotonic positive relationship. Tables 3.1, 3.2, and 3.3 summarize previous studies concerning SO_2, CO_2, and energy use, respectively.

Table 3.1 Previous studies on EKC applied to SO_2

	Data	Method	Result
Seldon and Song (1994)	1979–1987(30 countries)	Panel regression (Fixed and random effect)	Inverted–U (within-sample peak)
Grossman and Krueger (1995)	1977, 1982, 1988(32 countries)	Panel regression (Random effect) (Time trend)	Inverted–U (within-sample peak)
Panayotou (1997)	1982–1984 (30 countries)	Panel regression (Fixed and random effect) (Time trend)	Inverted–U (within-sample peak)
Torras and Boyce (1998)	1977–1991 (42 countries)	OLS (Location specific dummy)	N-curve (within-sample peak)
Stern and Common (2001)	1960–1990 (73 countries)	Panel regression (Fixed and random effect) (Time fixed effect)	Turning point becomes larger when developing countries are included.
Halkos (2003)	1960–1990 (73 countries)Same data as Stern and Common (2001)	Random coefficient model, Arellano and Bond GMM estimator	Choice of econometric method affects the result.
Millimet et al. (2003)	1929–1994 (US state-level data)	Semi-parametric regression (State and time fixed effect)	Inverted–U (within-sample peak)
Bertinelli and Strobl (2005)	1950–1990 (108 countries)	Semi-parametric regression (Country fixed effect)	Monotonous relation (except for middle income)

Table 3.2 Previous studies on EKC applied to CO_2

	Data	Method	Result
Shafic (1994)	1960–1989 (153 countries)	Panel regression (Fixed and random effect) (Time fixed effect)	Monotonous relation
Holtz-Eakin and Selden (1995)	1951–1986 (130 countries)	Panel regression (Fixed effect) (Time fixed effect)	Inverted–U (outside-sample peak)
Schmalensee *et al.* (1998)	1950–1990 (141 countries)	Nonparametric regression (Linear spline) (Time and country fixed effect)	Inverted–U (within-sample peak)
Bertinelli and Strobl (2005)	1950–1990 (122 countries)	Semi-parametric regression (Country fixed effects)	Monotonous relation (except for middle income)
Galeotti *et al.* (2006)	1960–1997 for OECD, 1971–1997 for non-OECD	Panel regression (Fixed effect) (Time fixed effect)	Result depends on data sampled and estimation method.
Azomahou *et al.* (2006)	1960–1996 (100 countries)	Nonparametric regression (country-specific effect)	Monotonous relation

Table 3.3 Previous studies on EKC applied to energy use

	Data	Method	Result
Agras and Chapman (1997)	1971–1991 (34 countries)	Panel regression (Fixed effect) (Fixed time and country effects)	Inverted–U (outside-sample peak)
Suri and Chapman (1998)	1971–1991 (33 countries)	Panel regression (Feasible GLS) (Fixed time and country effects)	Inverted–U (outside-sample peak)
Richmond and Kaufmann (2006)	1978–1997 (16 countries)	Panel regression (Random coefficient model)	Monotonous relation (except for middle income)
Luzzati and Orsini (2009)	1971–2004 (113 countries)	Panel regression (Feasible GLS) (Fixed country effects) Semi-parametric regression (Generalized additive models)	Panel: Inverted–U (outside-sample peak) Semi-parametric: Monotonous relation

Concerning the literature using parametric estimations that attempt to decompose the determinants of environmental quality into three effects (scale, technique, and composition effect), there are two types of literatures to our knowledge. Panayotou (1997) decomposes determinants of SO_2 concentration into three effects. The study uses GDP/km², GDP per capita, and share of industry in GDP as proxy of scale, technique, and composition effect, respectively.[4] They find the scale effect increases ambient SO_2 concentrations at a diminishing rate, and technique effect decreases the concentration at an increasing rate. Concerning composition effect, they find a peculiar cubic shape with rising portions. Rezek and Rogers (2008) decomposes the determinants of CO_2 emissions into three effects using a panel data of 21 OECD countries from 1971 to 2000. Using an output distance function framework, they find that the technique effect exceeds the scale effect in a few countries.[5]

It is notable that both Millimet *et al.* (2003) and Azomahou *et al.* (2006) reject a parametric specification in favor of their semi-parametric or nonparametric model. However, these semi-parametric and nonparametric analyses only consider per capita income, and therefore the decomposed effects have not been estimated. Our study intends to decompose the determinant of environmental quality into three effects in the framework of a semi-parametric technique.

3.3   Methodology and data

As some EKC studies indicate, the appropriateness of functional forms is problematic (e.g., Dasgupta *et al.*, 2002). We therefore intend to solve this problem using multivariable semi-parametric analysis. Semi-parametric regression analysis relaxes the assumption of linearity and typically substitutes the weaker assumption that the average value of the response is a smooth function of the predictors.

Although several semi-parametric and nonparametric methods can be used to estimate the regression line, there are usually two obstacles. First, as the number of independent variables increases, the sparseness of data inflates the variance of the estimates. This problem of rapidly increasing variance is called the curse of dimensionality. Second, because most of semi-parametric and nonparametric regressions do not provide an equation relating the average response to the independent variables, the result becomes difficult to interpret[6] (see Hastie and Tibshirani, 1990).

These problems led to the development of additive regression models, which have two advantages (Stone, 1985). First, because each of the individual additive terms is estimated using a univariate smoother, the curse of dimensionality is avoided. Second, interpretation of additive models is, therefore, relatively simple because a two-dimensional plot suffices to examine the estimated partial regression function holding the other independent variables constant.

In this study, we use generalized additive models (Hastie and Tibshirani, 1990). We use a cubic spline smoothing[7] iteratively to minimize the partial residuals, which are the residuals after removing the influence of the other variables in the model. In this iteration, the estimation loop stops when the model fit cannot be improved. In this model, a Bayesian approach is used to derive standard errors and confidence intervals.[8]

Table 3.4 shows descriptive statistics and variables used in this study. The data for this study come from several sources. *The Center for Air Pollution*

Table 3.4 Descriptive statistics

Variable	Unit	Obs.	Mean	Std. Dev.	Min	Max
SO_2 emissions per capita	metric tons	3496	0.018	0.038	9.240E-06	0.583
CO_2 emissions per capita	metric tons	3644	3.545	4.939	0.005	40.166
Energy use per capita	kg of oil equivalent	2036	1954.692	1946.534	98.601	11544.480
GDP per capita	real 1996 $ PPP	6599.116	6599.116	6628.066	280.255	44292.240
Capital–labor ratio	$ per worker	3644	22613.940	26014.050	98	159505
Population	person	3644	3.930E+08	1.280E+08	57284	1.260E+09

Impact and Trend Analysis (CAPITA) and Stern (2005) produced a compre-hensive database on SO_2 emissions. Their estimates are considered superior to others in terms of their spatial and temporal resolution and extent (see Stern, 2005). SO_2 is generated mainly from the combustion of petroleum and coal, and is the key pollution for three important environmental problems: local air pollution and smog, acid rain, and dry deposition. It exerts a harmful influence on the respiratory system.

Data on CO_2 emissions and energy use are from *World Development Indicators*. CO_2 emissions are those stemming from the burning of fossil fuels and the manufacture of cement. They include CO_2 produced during con-sumption of solid, liquid, and gas fuels and gas flaring. Whereas SO_2 has local and transboundary impacts, CO_2 is a greenhouse gas and has a global impact. See Cole and Elliott (2003) for more detailed comparisons of each emission.

Because emissions data are often estimated using engineering functions based on inputs, the engineering assumptions may not precisely reflect the true gains from techniques.[9] However, our estimates are able to adequately capture technique effects since each of these estimates considers country- and year-specific information. For example, in the case of SO_2 the sulfur release factor is determined by technology information obtained by country and year from the *International Energy Agency*.[10] The sulfur emissions are calculated as a product of net production of fuels and metals, sulfur content, and the release factor for each country, year, and fuel/metal type (i.e., coal, oil, zinc, copper, and nickel) (see Lefohn *et al.*, 1999). The data for CO_2 is calculated using CO_2 emissions factors for individual fuels, which stem from country- and year-specific estimates of fuel use.[11] Since CO_2 emissions factors cannot be reduced by end-of-pipe technology, they are time-invariant. However, regulations and technology improve fuel efficiency. Therefore, these emissions factors are generally updated over time to allow for changes in technology and regulations (see Marland *et al.*, 2000). Energy use refers to the use of primary energy, such as coal and coal products, oil and petroleum products, natural gas, nuclear, and hydroelectric, before transformation to other end-use fuels.[12] It is notable that, although CO_2 emissions are those stemming from the burning of fossil fuels and the manufacture of cement, fossil fuels are main source of CO_2 emissions. The difference between CO_2 emissions data and energy use data is that the latter takes into consideration not only fossil fuels but also primary energy that emits no CO_2, such as nuclear and hydroelectric. This difference is important when we interpret the estimation result in next section.

Per capita income, which is defined as real GDP per capita measured in 1996 purchasing power parity (chain index), and the capital–labor ratio are obtained from the *Extended Penn World Table*.[13] Population is from *World Development Indicators*. Table 3.5 shows time periods and the number of countries in the sample, whereas the countries for which data are used in each specification are shown in the Appendix.

Table 3.5 Time period and number of countries in the sample

Variable	Time period	Number of countries
SO$_2$ emissions	1963–2000	105
CO$_2$ emissions	1963–2000	112
Energy use	1970–2000	75

3.4 Estimation results

3.4.1 EKC estimation

This study uses the following generalized additive models for EKC:

$$\ln E_{it} = \alpha_1 + f_1(I_{it}) + \mu_{1i} + \nu_{1t} + \varepsilon_{1it}, \tag{1}$$

where E is a per capita environmental index (such as emissions of SO$_2$, CO$_2$, and energy use) for country i in year t, I is income per capita, α_1 is constant term, μ_{1i} is country fixed effect, ν_{1t} is time fixed effect, and ε_{1it} is error term. $f(.)$ is a generic flexible functional form allowing potentially non-linear non-monotonic relationships. We use the normal distribution for estimation. The link function is the identity. The degrees of freedom are controlled by the degree of penalization selected during fitting by the generalized cross validation (GCV).[14] We include a country dummy and year dummy to take into consideration individual and time fixed effects.

The resulting scatter plot in Figure 3.1 shows the predicted contributions to the dependent variable from the independent variables. Figure 3.1 shows the predicted contribution to each pollutant (or resources) from GDP per capita. The central curve represents the estimated result. The upper and lower curves correspond to upper and lower 95% confidence intervals to account for heteroskedasticity and unrestricted correlation over time between observations for a given country. Table 3.6 shows results of a model fit test, which compares the deviance between the full model and the model without each smooth term. We find the term $f_1(I_{it})$ statistically significant. We interpret this term later on.

First, among the three indices, we can explicitly support the EKC hypothesis only in the case of SO$_2$.[15] Second, in the case of CO$_2$, we observe the positive relationship at low and middle incomes, which then flattens out and decreases slightly for high incomes. Although the range of incomes over which we observe a decreasing trend is relatively small, the results support the EKC hypothesis. Third, in the case of energy use, although the slope becomes smoother at high incomes, we find a monotonic increasing relationship at all income levels.

Although most of these results are generally consistent with previous studies, we point out two key distinguishing characteristics. First, the result for CO$_2$ is inconsistent with previous nonparametric studies that generally suggest a monotonic increasing relationship. We should note that if we do not include country dummies, we obtain a monotonic increasing trend for CO$_2$.[16] This implies that

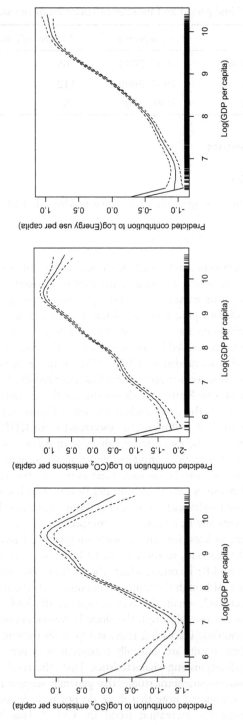

Figure 3.1 Relationship between environmental quality and GDP per capita for SO₂ (left), CO₂ (center), and energy use (right)

Note: The solid curve represents the estimated line and the dashed curves correspond to upper and lower 95% confidence intervals.

Table 3.6 Approximate significance of smooth terms of Equation (1)

F statistics	SO₂	CO₂	Energy use
$f_1(I_{it})$	72.67***	137.1***	181.5***

Note: *, **, and *** indicate "significant" at the 10% level, the 5% level and the 1% level, respectively.

consideration of the country effect has a profound effect on the result. Second, the comparison between the results for CO_2 and energy use provides an important implication. In contrast to the other indices, energy use has an obvious monotonic increasing trend, although the increasing trend diminishes for high incomes. Considering that CO_2 emissions data mainly stems from fossil fuels, while energy use data stems from not only fossil fuels but also carbon-free energy, the main reason why CO_2 emissions have a greater diminishing trend relative to energy use might be changes in carbon intensity, especially in high-income countries. Further analysis in the next subsection provides an explanation of this distinction.

3.4.2 Decomposition of the EKC

A general critique of the EKC papers is that they have few implications for policy making because income is only a proxy variable. To investigate the fundamental factors comprising the income variable, we decompose the income variable into technique, scale, and composition effects. Our empirical model is based on empirical strategy of Antweiler *et al.* (2001). They use GDP per km² as a proxy of scale effect, income per capita as a proxy of technique effect, and capital–labor ratio as a proxy of composition effect. Panayotou (1997) use GDP per km² as a proxy of scale effect, GDP per capita as a proxy of technique effect, and industry share in GDP as a proxy of composition effect. We follow proxies of previous studies for scale, technique, and composition effect.

This study uses the following generalized additive models to decompose the overall effect:

$$\text{In } E_{it} = \alpha + f_1(I_{it}) + f_2(S_{it}) + f_3(k_{it}) + \mu_i + v_t + \varepsilon_{it}, \tag{2}$$

where E is a per capita environmental index such as emissions of SO_2, CO_2, and energy use for country i in year t, I is GDP per capita,[17] a proxy of the technique effect, S is real GDP, a proxy of the scale effect, k is the capital–labor ratio, a proxy of the composition effect, α is a constant term, μ_i is country fixed effect, v_t is time fixed effect, and ε_{it} is an error term.[18] $f(.)$ are generic flexible functional forms allowing potentially non-linear non-monotonic relationships.[19]

The resulting scatter plot in Figure 3.2 shows the predicted contributions to the dependent variable from each of the independent variables. Figure 3.2 shows the three effects for each pollutant, where the results for SO_2, CO_2, and energy use are presented in Figure 3.2(a), (b), and (c), respectively.[20]

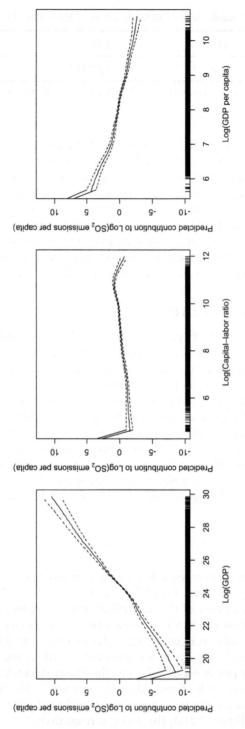

Figure 3.2(a) SO_2: scale effect (left), composition effect (center), and technique effect (right)

Note: The solid curve represents the estimated line and dashed curves correspond to upper and lower 95% confidence intervals.

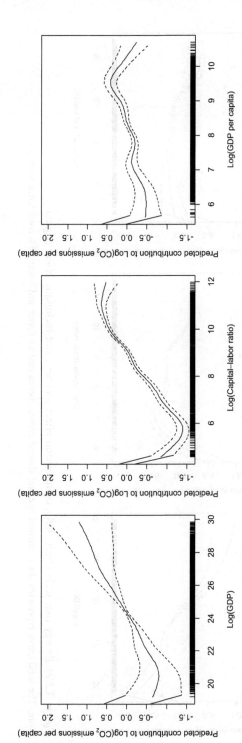

Figure 3.2(b) CO$_2$: scale effect (left), composition effect (center), and technique effect (right)

Note: The solid curve represents the estimated line and dashed curves correspond to upper and lower 95% confidence intervals.

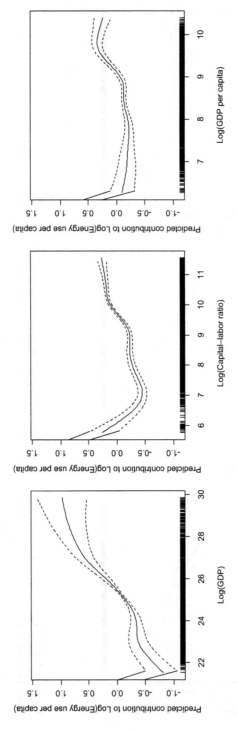

Figure 3.2(c) Energy use: scale effect (left), composition effect (center), and technique effect (right)

Note: The solid curve represents the estimated line and dashed curves correspond to upper and lower 95% confidence intervals.

Table 3.7 Approximate significance of smooth terms of Equation (2)

F statistics	SO_2	CO_2	Energy use
$f_1(I_{it})$	30.40***	14.038***	22.31***
$f_2(S_{it})$	49.36***	4.558***	27.83***
$f_3(K_{it})$	23.82***	51.315***	34.53***

Note: *** indicates "significant" at the 1% level.

The scale effect has a negative impact on the environment, and therefore we expect a positive slope over all income levels. The composition effect reflects the structure of the economy. If higher capital intensity is associated with more pollution-oriented industries, we observe a positive slope. The technique effect reflects the changes in production methods that usually reduce emissions per unit of output, and therefore we expect a negative slope over all income levels. However, if the associated environmental regulations are not implemented or if new technologies are more pollution intensive than previous technologies, we might not be able to identify a negative slope. For the understanding of non-linear pattern, we expect nonparametric method to capture the relationship. Table 3.7 shows results of a model fit test. We find all decomposed three terms statistically significant. We interpret each term below.

Our results show that the scale effects are similar among all three environmental indicators. The positive slopes of the scale effects imply a negative impact of economic expansion on the environment.

On the other hand, the slopes of the composition effects have non-linear relationships, although we find expected increasing slopes in the middle zone of the capital–labor ratio for all environmental indices. In the case of SO_2 and CO_2, it is notable that we can identify a declining tendency at high capital–labor ratio. If a higher capital–labor ratio leads to higher energy efficiency, capital–labor ratio may capture a technique effect, as GDP per capita does. Similarly, if a higher GDP per capita induces structural shifts due to non-homothetic demand (see Echevarria, 2008), which moves demand to cleaner service-type sectors, GDP per capita may have a composition effect. These factors might affect the results. It is also notable that in the case of CO_2 and energy use, we find a declining trend at low capital–labor ratios. This may reflect the use of wood as fuel because the least capital-intensive sector's activity usually depends on wood material and therefore may capture the technique effect. Our results are inconsistent with Cole and Elliott (2003), which show a strong correlation between a sector's capital intensity and its pollution intensity for SO_2 and CO_2.

Additionally, each technique effect shows different characteristics. In light of the significance of the technique effect, it is important to consider why these differences exist. The curve of the technique effect for SO_2 falls more sharply than the other indices, which might be a dominant reason why previous studies tend to observe an EKC for SO_2. It is important to note that SO_2 is the local pollution, and therefore damages are easy to recognize. Two factors seem to reduce pollution intensity. One is adaptation of less sulfur intensive petroleum and coal, and the other is adaptation of desulfurization equipment. Required technologies to reduce pollution already exist in many countries. A consensus now exists that the development of desulfurization equipment has a significant impact on emission reductions. There is, however, some evidence that developing countries tend to avoid incorporating abatement technologies for SO_2 from developed countries, possibly because of higher costs (see Cheremisinoff, 2001). This might be the main reason why the slope of the middle-income area is relatively moderate.

In the case of the slope of the technique effect for CO_2, it is notable that we are not able to find a negative slope except in the high-income area. There seems to be two factors related to a negative slope. One is changes in carbon intensity for primary energy, and the other is development and adaptation of energy-saving technology.[21] On the other hand, the positive slope is thought to stem from the rebound effect or dirtier technology. The rebound effect implies that greater energy efficiency encourages much more energy consumption, so that net energy use actually increases. The resulting slope seems to be the net of these previous factors. It is notable that we are able to find apparent positive slope from \$3,000 to \$11,000, implying a strong rebound effect and/ or dirtier technology. However, above \$11,000 we are able to find a negative slope, implying that the effect of less carbon intensity and/or development and adaptation of energy-saving technology offset the rebound effect and/or dirtier technology, with income increased.

In the case of the slope of the technique effect for energy use, we find relatively moderate slope for the high-income area, compared with that for CO_2 emissions. Considering that the unit of energy use is kg of oil-equivalent, changes in the source of energy play a relatively smaller role in the case of energy use than in the case of CO_2.[22] Therefore, one of the reasons there is a difference in technique effect between CO_2 and energy use at high incomes might be changes in carbon intensity. Tsurumi and Managi (2009) support this argument by using coal intensity in the EKC framework. In their study, they consider two models with generalized additive models. One model includes only GDP per capita, and the other includes not only GDP per capita but also coal share. As a result, whereas the former model shows the declining slope in high-income range, the latter shows a relatively flat slope in that range. This implies that reduction of carbon intensity has a crucial effect on the shape of EKC for CO_2.

In addition, it is important to note that we do not find a declining slope concerning the technique effect for both CO_2 emissions and energy use at the zone of low- and middle-income areas. This implies that technique effect is not sufficient to decrease CO_2 emissions and energy use at this income range. This result is consistent with Rezek and Rogers (2008), where the technique effect exceeds the scale effect only in a few countries.

3.5 Summary and conclusions

In this chapter, we examined the determinants of environmental quality by decomposing the relationship between income and pollution into three effects using a semi-parametric method of generalized additive models, which enables us to use flexible functional forms and to include several independent variables in the model. Using emission data for SO_2 and CO_2 for the period 1963–2000 and data for energy use for the period 1970–2000, we estimated specifications, which include real GDP per capita, real GDP, and the capital–labor ratio, to decompose the overall effect into technique, scale, and composition effects, respectively.

Appendix countries in this study

North America	Bangladesh	Greece	Guinea[b]
Canada	China	Hungary	Guinea Bissau[b]
USA	Hong Kong	Iceland	Kenya
Latin America	India	Ireland	Madagascar[b]
Argentina	Indonesia	Italy	Malawi[b]
Barbados[b]	Japan	Luxembourg[b]	Mali[b]
Bolivia	Korea	Netherlands	Mauritania[b]
Brazil	Malaysia	Poland[b]	Mauritius[b]
Chile	Nepal	Portugal	Moroccob
Colombia	Pakistan	Romania	Mozambique
Costa Rica	Philippines	Spain	Namibia[b]
Dominica[a, b]	Singapore	Sweden	Niger[b]
Dominican Rep.	Sri Lanka	Switzerland	Nigeria[b]
Ecuador	St. Vincent[a, b]	Africa	Rwanda[b]
El Salvador	Thailand	Angola[b]	Senegal
Grenada[a, b]	Middle East	Benin	Seychelles[a, b]
Guatemala	Iran	Botswana[b]	Sierra Leone[b]
Guyana[b]	Israel	Burundi[b]	South Africa
Haiti	Jordan	Cameroon	Tanzania[b]
Honduras	Syria	Cape Verde[b]	Togo
Jamaica	Turkey[a, b]	Central Africa[b]	Tunisia
Mexico	Europe	Chadb	Uganda[b]
Nicaragua	Austria	Congo Dem. Rep.	Zambia
Panama	Belgium	Congo Rep.[a, b]	Zimbabwe
Paraguay	Britain	Cote d'Ivoire[b]	Oceania
Peru	Cyprus	Egypt	Australia
Trinidad and Tobago	Denmark	Ethiopia	Fiji[b]
Uruguay	Finland	Gabon[b]	New Zealand
Venezuela	France	Gambia[a, b]	Papua New Guinea[b]
Asia	Germany[b]	Ghana	

Note:

[a] Not included in SO_2 specification

[b] Not included in energy use specification

Our results of technique effects are decomposed from both production scale and industrial composition, so that the characteristics of its effects provide policymakers with fruitful suggestions as to whether their environmental policies are sufficient to reduce pollution or not. GDP per capita correlates with environmental stringency (Dasgupta *et al.*, 2001), and higher environmental stringency can improve the environment (Esty and Porter, 2005). Thus, if the technique effect does not suffice, environmental policy inaction would not be accepted. The policymakers need to strengthen their environmental policies. In the case of SO_2, we find declining slope, implying that the effect is large. This might be because adaptation of desulfurization equipment suffices to reduce SO_2 emissions. However, in the case of CO_2 and energy use, we do not find a declining slope for low- and middle-income areas. On the other hand, we find declining slope at the high-income area in the case of CO_2 emissions, whereas we find little declining trend in the case of energy use. This difference might be caused by changes in carbon intensity, as we have mentioned in Section 3.4.2.

Our result of the technique effect implies that policies need to be implemented that reduce CO_2 emissions and energy use. It is notable that there is little trend of a negative slope of the technique effect for energy use, even in high-income countries, implying that increased energy efficiency does not lead to the reduction of energy use.

Notes

1 There is a possibility that new technologies are more pollution-intensive than previous technologies. Therefore, the technique effect is not necessarily positive for the environment.
2 Simon Kuznets postulated that economic growth and income inequalities follow an inverted U-curve in 1955 (Kuznets, 1955). The same relation to income has been claimed for environmental quality. The EKC posits an inverted U-shaped relationship between per capita income and environmental quality. The EKC is supported if the income elasticity of environmental degradation turns from positive at lower levels of per capita income to negative at higher levels.
3 Commonly, the atmospheric life of SO_2 is about 1–10 days, whereas the atmospheric life of CO_2 is about 50–200 years. This implies that SO_2 can move 1000 km before decaying and can be a local or transboundary pollutant (see Cole and Elliott, 2003), whereas CO_2 is clearly a global pollutant.
4 As we will explain in Section 3.4.2, we use similar proxies to consider the three effects.
5 They find positive scale effect and negative technique effect, as expected. It is notable that although their sign of composition effect for stochastic frontier analysis (SFA) is positive, the sign of composition effect for deterministic frontier analysis (DFA) is negative.
6 Although we tried to use more flexible nonparametric functions, like a generalized multiplicative model, the results are difficult to interpret.
7 When we used loess function in place of cubic spline function, the results were almost the same.
8 Our estimation technique follows Wood (2004, 2008)

9 On the other hand, concentrations data tend to be affected by site-specific factors. For example, SO_2 gas is produced not only from anthropogenic sources, such as the burning of fossil fuels, but also from natural sources, such as transboundary movement and volcanoes. Whilst concentration data is appropriate if the pollution has a flow externality and only localized effects (i.e., environmental quality is a local public good), concentration data has noise that stems from transboundary movement by wind. In addition, if the emissions have a stock externality, the pollution level is determined by the accumulated emissions that are related to past production as well as to current production. Thus, when we link pollution and economic activity, the emission is considered a better proxy for the environment.

10 Using the cumulative total of thermal generation capacity information by year and the cumulative total of fuel gas desulfurization (FGD) installed capacity by country by year, the percentage of the FGD installed capacity by country by year can be determined (see Lefohn *et al.*. 1999).

11 CO_2 emissions from fossil fuels are calculated following the method of Marland and Rotty (1984). $CO_{2,i} = FC_i \, FO_i \, C_i$, where the three terms represent the net fuel production, the fraction of the fuel oxidized, and the carbon content of the fuel, respectively. i represents solid , liquid, or gaseous fuels. Concerning cement manufacture, an equation analogous to the previous equation is used to calculate CO_2 emissions from calcining $CaCO_3$ with the cement chemistry data.

12 It is equal to indigenous production plus imports and stock changes, minus exports and fuels supplied to ships and aircraft engaged in international transport.

13 See https://sites.google.com/a/newschool.edu/duncan-foley-homepage/home/ EPWT

14 Smoothing parameters are determined to minimize the generalized cross validation (GCV).

15 Although the decreasing trend can be observed at the zone of the low income, its confidence intervals are too wide to interpret.

16 Our result is inconsistent with the previous nonparametric study by Azomahou *et al.* (2006). They used nonparametric estimation of local linear kernel regressions and found that emissions rise, instead of exhibiting an inverted U-shaped relationship. This difference in results might be because we include data that are more recent, where the share of coal in energy use is relatively low, as discussed later on. Although figures are not presented here because of space limitations, our sensitivity analysis shows that the fewer recent years we include in the estimation, the greater the monotonically increasing trend.

17 The technique effect is likely to be associated with a lag (see Antweiler *et al.*, 2001; Cole and Elliott, 2003). Therefore, we also tested lagged GDP per capita. The result with lagged GDP per capita was almost the same as that with the contemporaneous one.

18 We include a country dummy and year dummy to take into consideration individual and time fixed effects.

19 We use the normal distribution for estimation. The link function is the identity.

20 Many studies using parametric functional forms include additional explanatory variables such as trade and institutions (see Stern, 2004; Dasgupta *et al.*, 2006). To check the robustness of our results, we estimate another specification including additional variables in equation (2). These include trade openness and political rights. Trade openness is the ratio of aggregate exports and imports to GDP (which, as in the growth literature, proxies trade openness [or trade intensity; see, e.g., Antweiler *et al.*, 2001; Frankel and Rose, 2005], which is from *World Development Indicators*). The political right is measured on a one-to-seven scale, which is from *Freedom House*. The results of the three effects were almost the same as in Figure 3.2.

21 In the marketplace, carbon abatement technologies such as carbon dioxide absorption or isolation do not exist.
22 If a country changes its main energy source from a carbon-intensive one to a carbon-free one, one could find negative technique effect in the case of CO_2, while one could find little technique effect in the case of energy use because the calorific power of all sources of energy, including carbon-free energy, is converted to oil-equivalent.

Bibliography

Agras, J., and Chapman, D. (1997). Is There an Environmental Kuznets Curve for Energy? An Econometric Analysis. Working Paper, New York State College of Agriculture and Life Sciences, Department of Agricultural, Resource and Managerial Economics.

Antweiler, W., Copeland, B., and Taylor, S. (2001). Is Free Trade Good for the Environment? *American Economic Review*, 91 (4), 877–908.

Arrow, K., Bolin, B., Costanza, R., Folke, C., Holling, C.S., Janson, B., Levin, S., Maler, K., Perrings, C., and Pimental, D. (1995). Economic Growth, Carrying Capacity, and the Environment. *Ecological Economics*, 15, 91–95.

Azomahou, T., Laisney, F., and Van, P.N. (2006). Economic Development and CO_2 Emissions: A Nonparametric Panel Approach. *Journal of Public Economics*, 90 (6–7), 1347–1363.

Bertinelli, L., and Strobl, E. (2005). The Environmental Kuznets Curve Semi-Parametrically Revisited. *Economics Letters*, 88, 350–357.

Brock, W., and Taylor, M.S. (2006). Economic Growth and the Environment: A Review of Theory and Empirics. In Durlauf, S., and Aghion., P. (Eds.), *The Handbook of Economic Growth*. Amsterdam, Elsevier Science Publishers.

Cheremisinoff, N.P. (2001). *Handbook of Pollution Prevention Practices (Environmental Science and Pollution Control Series)*. Cambridge, Marcel Dekker Inc.

Cole, M.A. (2005). Re-Examining the Pollution-Income Relationship: A Random Coefficients Approach. *Economic Bulletin*, 14, 1–7.

Cole, M.A. and Elliott, R.J.R. (2003). Determining the Trade-Environment Composition Effect: The Role of Capital, Labor and Environmental Regulations. *Journal of Environmental Economics and Management*, 46 (3) 363–383.

Cole, M.A., Rayner, A.J., and Bates, J.M. (1997). The Environmental Kuznets Curve: An Empirical Analysis. *Environment and Development Economics*, 2 (4), 401–416.

Copeland, B., and Taylor, S. (2004). Trade, Growth and the Environment. *Journal of Economic Literature*, 42 (1), 7–71.

Dasgupta, S., Hamilton, K., Pandey, K.D., and Wheeler, D. (2006). Environment During Growth: Accounting for Governance and Vulnerability. *World Development*, 34, 1597–1611

Dasgupta, S., Laplante, B., Wang, H., and Wheeler, D. (2002). Confronting the Environmental Kuznets Curve. *Journal of Economic Perspectives*, 16 (1), 147–168.

Dasgupta, S., Mody, A., Roy, S., and Wheeler, D. (2001). Environmental Regulation and Development: A Cross Country Empirical Analysis. *Oxford Development Studies* 29 (2), 173–187.

Dinda, S. (2004). Environmental Kuznets Curve Hypothesis: A Survey. *Ecological Economics*, 49 (1), 431–455.

Echevarria, C. (2008). International Trade and the Sectoral Composition of Production. *Review of Economics Dynamics*, 11, 192–206.

Esty, D.C. and Porter, M.E. (2005). National Environmental Performance: An Empirical Analysis of Policy Results and Determinants. *Environment and Development Economics*, 10 (4), 391–434.

Frankel, J., and Rose, A. (2005). Is Trade Good or Bad for the Environment? Sorting Out the Causality. *Review of Economics and Statistics*, 87 (1), 85–91.

Galeotti, M., Lanza, A, and Pauli, F. (2006). Reassessing the Environmental Kuznets Curve for CO_2 Emissions: A Robustness Exercise. *Ecological Economics*, 57, 152–163.

Grossman, G.M. (1995). Pollution and Growth: What Do We Know?. In Goldin, I. , and Winters, L.A. (Eds.), *The Economics of Sustainable Development* (pp. 19–47). Cambridge, Cambridge University Press.

Grossman, G.M., and Krueger, A.B. (1993). Environmental Impacts of a North American Free Trade Agreement. In Garber, P. (Ed.), *The Mexico-US Free Trade Agreement*. Cambridge, MIT Press.

Grossman, G.M., and Krueger, A.B. (1995). Economic Growth and the Environment. *The Quarterly Journal of Economics*, 110, 353–377.

Halkos, G.E. (2003). Environmental Kuznets Curve for Sulfur: Evidence Using GMM Estimation and Random Coefficient Panel Data Model. *Environment and Development Economics*, 8, 581–601.

Hastie, T.J., and Tibshirani, R.J. (1990). *Generalized Additive Models*. New York, Chapman and Hall.

Holtz-Eakin, D., and Selden, T.M. (1995). Stoking the Fires? CO_2 Emissions and Economic Growth. *Journal of Public Economics*, 57, 85–101.

Kuznets, S. (1955). Economic Growth and Income Inequality, *American Economic Review*, 45, 1–28.

Lefohn, A.S., Husar, J.D., and Husar, R.B. (1999). Estimating Historical Anthropogenic Global Sulfur Emission Patterns for the Period 1850–1990. *Atmospheric Environment*, 33 (21), 3435–3444.

Luzzati, T., and Orsini, M. (2009). Investigating the Energy-Environmental Kuznets Curve. *Energy*, 34, 291–300.

Managi, S. (2007). *Technological Change and Environmental Policy: A Study of Depletion in the Oil and Gas Industry*. Cheltenham, Edward Elgar Publishing Ltd.

Marland, G., Boden, T.A., and Andres, R.J. (2000). Global, Regional, and National Fossil Fuel CO_2 Emissions. In *Trends: A Compendium of Data on Global Change, Carbon Dioxide Information Analysis Center*, Oak Ridge National Laboratory, US Department of Energy, Oak Ridge, TN, USA

Marland, G., and Rotty, R.M. (1984). Carbon Dioxide Emissions from Fossil Fuels: A Procedure for Estimation and Results for 1950–82. *Tellus*, 36(B), 232–261.

Millimet, D.L., List, J.A., and Stengos, T. (2003). The Environmental Kuznets Curve: Real Progress or Misspecified Models? *Review of Economics and Statistics*, 85, 1038–1047.

Panayotou, T. (1997). Demystifying the Environmental Kuznets Curve: Turning a Black Box into a Policy Tool. *Environment and Development Economics*, 2, 465–484.

Rezek, J.P., and Rogers, K. (2008). Decomposing the CO_2-Income Tradeoff: An Output Distance Function Approach. *Environment and Development Economics*, 13, 457–473.

Richmond, A.K., and Kaufmann, R.K. (2006). Energy Prices and Turning Points: The Relationship Between Income and Energy Use/Carbon Emissions. *Energy*, 27(4), 157–180.

Schmalensee, R., Stoker, T.M., and Judson, R.A. (1998). World Carbon Dioxide Emissions: 1950–2050. *Review of Economics and Statistics*, 80, 15–27.

Selden, T.M., and Song, D. (1994). Environmental Quality and Development: Is There a Kuznets Curve for Air Pollution Emissions? *Journal of Environmental Economics and Management*, 27, 147–162.

Shafik, N. (1994). Economic Development and Environmental Quality: An Econometric Analysis. *Oxford Economic Papers*, 46, 757–773.

Stern, D.I. (2004). The Rise and Fall of the Environmental Kuznets Curve. *World Development*, 32, 1419–1439.

Stern, D.I. (2005). Global Sulfur Emissions from 1850 to 2000. *Chemosphere*, 58, 163–175.

Stern, D.I., and Common, M.S. (2001). Is There an Environmental Kuznets Curve for Sulfur? *Journal of Environmental Economics and Management*, 41, 162–178.

Stone, C.J. (1985). Additive Regression and Other Nonparametric Models. *Annals of Statistics*, 13, 689–705.

Suri V., and Chapman D. (1998). Economic Growth, Trade and Energy: Implications for the Environmental Kuznets Curve. *Ecological Economics*, 25 (2), 195–208.

Torras, M., and Boyce, J.K. (1998). Income, Inequality, and Pollution: A Reassessment of the Environmental Kuznets Curve, *Ecological Economics*, 25, 147–160.

Tsurumi, T., and Managi, S. (2009). Economic Growth and Carbon Dioxide Emissions: Use of Energy in Developed Countries. Working Paper, Yokohama National University.

Wood, S.N. (2004) Stable and Efficient Multiple Smoothing Parameter Estimation for Generalized Additive Models. *Journal of the American Statistical Association*, 99, 673–686.

Wood, S.N. (2008) Fast stable direct fitting and smoothness selection for generalized additive models. *Journal of the Royal Statistical Society: Series B*, 70 (3), 495–518.

4 Measuring natural capital use in the global economy

Masahiro Sato

4.1 Introduction

In this ever-globalized world, where the production processes are spreading over the whole planet, we all benefit from water, soil, and forests all over the world. Not only do we eat foods or using raw materials directly transported from other countries, we also consume goods and services that are produced by exploiting ecosystems physically located in those countries, or by emitting carbon dioxides into the atmospheres of those countries. How should we measure and understand this type of natural capital use across borders and its accompanying impacts on the environment?

This chapter discusses the concept, roles, and estimation methods of indicators such as virtual water, virtual land, and embodied carbon, which have been developed to measure indirect natural capital use through international trade. The chapter then quantifies water use embodied in the world trade network by using a multi-regional input–output model and analyzes the interdependency among countries in natural capital use across borders.[1]

4.2 The concept of EEI indicators

Many indicators have been developed, mainly since 1990s, that are designed to capture indirect use of natural capitals across borders. Although there is no fixed generic name for these indicators, we call them in this chapter "embodied environmental-impact indicators" (EEI indicators).

Economic theories have traditionally used the term "embody" in order to describe resources or factors of production that are used as inputs to produce goods or services, especially to produce products traded across borders.[2] For example, the Heckscher–Ohlin theorem, one of the most famous propositions in trade theory (that each country exports goods that use its relatively abundant factor intensively), had drawn considerable attention to the relationship between production factors embodied in international trade and the endowment of these factors in each country.[3]

EEI indicators have adopted this concept of embodiment in measuring natural capital use across borders. They apply it not only to natural resources traded in the markets and physically transported, such as oil, coal, and minerals, but also to a broader range of environmental impacts, including exploitation of natural capitals, such as rainfall, runoff, groundwater, and soil, as well as waste generation, such as carbon emission. Most of these typically have limited or even no markets to trade in and cannot be physically transported across borders.

While the concept of embodiment originally had come from trade literature, EEI indicators can be used in much broader economic contexts than imports or exports between countries. For example, they can be used to measure environmental impacts embodied in consumption or production of specific products, whether or not they are imported or exported. Or they can be used to measure environmental impacts embodied in economic activities of various actors, such as individuals, households, and companies.

However, in order to evaluate the amount of environmental impacts at some aggregate level such as country or region using EEI indicators, it is useful to distinguish between consumption-based and production-based indicators. Consumption-based indicators are the indicators that measure the total environmental impacts occurring both directly in the production of final goods consumed in a country/region and indirectly in the whole supply chain of those goods. The environmental impacts here are not limited to those occurring within the geographic area of the country/region. Therefore, in an open economy, all the impacts on earth need to be included in the calculation as long as the final consumption itself took place in that country/region. But if the final consumption is in other countries, the environmental impacts are excluded even if they occurred inside of the country/region.

On the other hand, production-based indicators are the indicators that measure environmental impacts directly occurring in the production processes located in a country/region. As long as the physical locations of the impacts are in the geographic area of the country, they should be included in the calculation even if the produced goods were exported to other countries.

4.3   Examples of EEI indicators

4.3.1   *Virtual water, water footprint*

"Virtual water" is generally defined as the amount of water directly or indirectly used in the production processes of goods or services. The cross-border transaction of these goods or services is called virtual water trade. Professor Anthony Allan of London University first used the term in the early 1990s. Before that he used to use the term "embedded water" instead of "virtual water" (Allan, 2003).

The reason that Allan, as a geographer who specializes in the Middle East, used this term was to show his idea that the severe water shortage and associated economic and political stress in those areas can be mitigated through global economic process. According to Allan's observation, the Middle East and North Africa (MENA) were importing at least 50 million tons of grain annually. This required 50 km³ of water to produce it, which is the volume of water flowing into Egypt each year down the Nile. By mobilizing virtual water, most of the MENA region's extremely valuable freshwater did not have to be used in food production, which helped MENA to avoid the potential economic inefficiency and political conflicts it would have suffered from .

Water footprint is a concept that Dr. Arjen Hoekstra and his research group at UNESCO-IHE (Institute for Water Education) devised in 2002 from an analogy of ecological footprint in order to measure the total amount of water used in the production of goods and services that were consumed in a nation. Specifically, the water footprint of a nation is calculated as the sum of domestic water use and net virtual water import (Hoekstra and Hung, 2002). The Water Footprint Network (WFN), an international platform for water community founded in 2008, broadened the concept and defined water footprint of an individual, community, or business as the total volume of freshwater used to produce the goods and services consumed by the individual or community or produced by the business.[4] Water use is measured in terms of water volumes consumed (evaporated or incorporated into a product) and/or polluted per unit of time. A water footprint can be calculated for a particular product or for any well-defined group of consumers (for example, an individual, family, village, city, province, state, or nation) or producers (for example, a public organization, private enterprise, or economic sector).

4.3.2 *Virtual land*

Virtual land is a concept that Wichelns (2001) first devised by applying the concept of virtual water to land use.[5] But it was explicitly defined afterwards by Würtenberger et al. (2006) as productive areas hidden in imported or exported agricultural goods.

Land has generally two functions in the economy: physical areas that are occupied by economic activities, and ecosystem assets that provide various ecosystem services. Agricultural products not only occupy land physically, which otherwise would be used for other economic purposes (such as urban facilities or factories), but also utilize ecosystem services that a location provides (such as nutrient cycles for the uptake by crops). Importing agricultural products indirectly uses these functions of lands in other countries.

4.3.3 *Embodied carbon, embedded carbon, carbon footprint, virtual carbon*

The indicators such as embodied or embedded carbon, carbon footprint, and virtual carbon have been devised since the 1990s with the purpose of quantifying CO_2 emission embodied in consumption or trade, although slightly different in exact definitions and scopes, and have been calculated by many researchers (Wyckoff and Roop, 1994; Peters and Hertwich, 2008; Atkinson et al., 2011). Recently, OECD incorporated these ideas into productivity indicators and proposed the concept of production-based CO_2 productivity and demand-based CO_2 productivity in the Green Growth Indicators published in 2011 (OECD, 2011).

Since the 1990s, discussions have been taking place about how emission responsibility should be allocated among countries, considering the presence of international trade. For example, the Kyoto Protocol set binding obligations on industrialized countries to reduce emissions of greenhouse gasses actually emitted within their geographical borders. These are called "territorial emissions" or "production emissions" (Wiedmann et al., 2007; Atkinson et al., 2012). According to this idea, countries can reduce their emissions if they domestically specialize in the production of low carbon-intensive goods and import more carbon-intensive goods from other countries. This can lead to the so-called "carbon leakage" problem – meaning that the total carbon emission of the globe would not decrease, or might even increase, by shifting the emission from developed countries to developing countries, who typically have weaker environmental regulations and governance. On the other hand, "consumption emissions" is an idea that, wherever on the earth actual emission takes place, the final consumer should be responsible for the goods that have been produced by emitting carbon. The EEI indicators, such as embodied carbon, can contribute to these discussions by providing an analytical framework for evaluating countries' responsibilities.

4.4 The roles of EEI indicators

4.4.1 A bridge between global sustainability and national sustainability

Most sustainability indicators, such as genuine savings and inclusive wealth index, have been used to evaluate sustainability at a national level, although they are theoretically not restricted to that. This is not surprising because the principal actors of environmental or development policies are national governments, and these sustainability indicators can be used to evaluate their policies.

However, the causes of most global environmental problems are (geographically and socially) unevenly distributed among and within countries. For example, global warming is caused by greenhouse gasses historically accumulated in the atmosphere in exchange for the high economic growth of developed countries. But its most devastating consequences, such as heavy rain, flood, drought, sea level rise, and desertification are more likely to occur in low-income countries in tropic and arid areas that do not have adequate physical and social infrastructures to guard against them, unlike the countries that have generated the causes of these problems. Especially vulnerable social groups in low-income countries, whose sources of living are highly dependent on local natural capitals such as the ocean, rivers, rain, soil, forest, and coral reefs, are confronting the most serious threads.

The sustainability indicators that evaluate changes of some aggregate or average level of well-being at the national level alone cannot reflect such geographically and socially uneven distribution of damages and responsibilities.

Of course, it is extremely important for global sustainability that developed countries are sustainable at the national level. For example, reducing national CO_2 emission and natural resource use through promoting renewable energy or improving resource efficiency can also mitigate environmental burdens on the entire globe. Also, developed countries can indirectly contribute to the creation of sustainable societies in other countries by leading the development of green technologies or by showing a model of an advanced environmentally friendly society.

However, EEI indicators often reveal the fact that the relatively "clean" economies of rich countries are in part supported by a considerable amount of CO_2 emissions and natural resource use in poor countries. Under such circumstances, the fact that a developed country is judged as sustainable if measured by national-level sustainability indicators has no meaning for global sustainability, or even worsens the burdens of poor countries outside of the scope of national indicators by making the relationship between cause and effect unclear. Thus, EEI indicators discussed in this chapter play a critical role to bridge global and national sustainability by quantifying the interdependency among countries in natural capital use across borders

4.4.2 Sustainable consumption

Sustainable consumption and production (SCP) is one of the policy issues that has been gaining growing attention in the global policy arena. Especially changing the unsustainable patterns of consumption in developed and emerging countries is of vital importance.

One of the reasons that sustainable consumption is essential to achieve sustainable development is the limitation of supply-side efforts. Even if considerable increase of resource productivity and energy efficiency were achieved through technological innovations or process improvements it would not be enough, since the absolute amount of consumption is growing more rapidly especially in emerging nations. Also, there are concerns about so-called "rebound effects," that efficiency benefits of new technologies are offset by the increase of consumption as a behavioral response to the technologies themselves. Therefore, it is necessary to couple with demand-side efforts to change the unsustainable patterns of consumption.

EEI indicators can be powerful tools to raise the awareness of consumers and to change patterns of individual behaviors. They can quantify the amount of environmental burden or resource use related to consumer's behaviors and provide individuals with information in simple sophisticated forms, typically in a single unified index. Furthermore, EEI indicators can be used for policy tools to provide an economic incentive to reduce environmental burdens; for example, to levy a tax on resource use embodied in consumption or to require companies to put a label showing the amount of embodied carbon emission on their products.

4.4.3 Efficiency evaluation

EEI indicators are sometimes used as criteria for evaluating the efficiency of resource use, especially for natural resources that cannot be transported across borders or stored for a long time for later use in large quantities. For example, it is economically almost impossible to transport huge amounts of water needed for irrigation for long distances across the sea and to lift it from coastal area to inland agricultural areas. Also, it is physically impossible to transport land with productive soil or other important ecosystem services. Therefore, countries would have to accept the endowment of their own resources even if exploiting them is extremely inefficient. But if they can import goods that were produced by using much less resources in other countries instead of producing those goods domestically, the corresponding amount of resources can be physically saved in the importing country or even at the global level. Moreover, classical trade theories emphasize that it may also be economically efficient to import goods from countries with higher productivity or abundant resources in a relative sense.

EEI indicators can be used to evaluate the amount of resources saved by international trade. For example, Oki and Kanae (2004) calculated the "global water saving," which measures the amount of water saved by importing agricultural products from countries with higher water productivity to countries with lower productivity. The water productivity of a crop varies greatly by country/region according to the differences in agroclimatic conditions such as temperature, humidity, soil types, or fertilizer inputs, even if the crop belongs to the same variety. Thus, the amount of water actually used to grow the crop, which is calculated by using the productivity of the exporting country, may differ from the amount of water that would have been needed if it were grown domestically, which is estimated by using the productivity of the importing country. The national water saving is calculated by subtracting the latter from the former, and the global water saving is obtained by aggregating national savings (Oki et al., 2003; Yang et al., 2006; Würtenberger et al., 2006; Liu et al., 2009; Wyckoff and Roop 1994; Yang et al., 2011).

4.4.4 Equity evaluation

The geographic distribution of natural capitals such as water, land, and forest are determined by both anthropogenic and natural factors. The former include resource depletion, reforestation, land reclamation, and constructions of dams or canals. But the amount of change that these anthropogenic factors can cause to the distribution is largely constrained by natural factors such as atmospheric circulation, ocean current, water cycle, land topography, and even continental drift before the existence of human beings. In other words, the preconditions of human activities to utilize natural capitals in each country/region are unevenly determined by the planet's structure irrespective of the distribution of socioeconomic factors like population, demand, industry, and technology – nature is fundamentally not fair to the entire humanity.

Of course, we should accept such inequality to a certain degree. It may be neither realistic nor desirable to grow millions of tons of bananas in the Arctic Circle using huge amounts of fossil fuels. However, it is a part of fundamental human rights to ensure basic needs, such as minimum food and nutrients, anywhere in the world. For example, a broad famine that would kill tens or hundreds of thousands of people in African countries should not be left without any international measures, if the scale of the famine is far above the control of the local or national governments.

The fundamental proposition of welfare economic theory argues that with an appropriate redistribution, the markets and prices will bring us to efficient allocations, including more equitable ones. Thus, with regard to natural resources such as coal or minerals that are economically and technically feasible to transport across borders, the equity can theoretically be achieved with sufficient international transfer of wealth, in the form of official development assistance (ODA) or public funds, and international trades, but which is not the case in reality. As for untransferable resources stated above, the equity in this sense is not achievable either theoretically or practically. EEI indicators can be used to evaluate the equity in allocations of such resources. Namely, instead of measuring the amount of resources endowed, we can measure the amount of resource use embodied in consumption of each country.

4.5 Estimation methods of embodied environmental impacts

4.5.1 Advantages and disadvantages of various estimation methods

There are various methods to estimate environmental impacts embodied in production processes across borders, each with both advantages and disadvantages.[6] We focus here on two of these methods: the lifecycle assessment (LCA) approach and the input–output approach.

LCA approach is a bottom-up estimation method that traces environmental impacts occurring in each step of the production process of individual products, from upstream to downstream. Thus, it is sometimes called process-analysis or process-based LCA (Lenzen et al., 2013; Weber and Matthews, 2007). The primary advantage of the LCA approach is that it enables detailed and accurate analysis at a disaggregated level (such as individual products or companies) if relevant data are available. This makes LCA the most popular estimation method not only in academic research but also in business and policy practices. Examples of these practices are the GHG Protocol developed by the World Resource Institute (WRI) and the World Business Council on Sustainable Development (WBCSD), the ISO14064 standard by the International Organization for Standardization (ISO), and the Publicly Available Specifications-2050 (PAS 2050) by the British Standard Institution (BSI)'s (Sato, 2014).

However, LCA cannot capture infinite interaction between intermediate sectors in the whole supply chain. Instead, it sets up an arbitrary system boundary (inter-sectoral cut-off effect (Feng et al., 2011)). For example, making steel requires electricity to power a blast furnace, but generating electricity requires steel to construct a power plant, which in turn requires electricity, and so on. LCA has to stop this iteration somewhere. Thus the calculation is highly dependent on the shape of the arbitrary boundary, ruling out the environmental impacts that have occurred outside the boundary. Another limitation is that of aggregation. In order to evaluate the total environmental impacts at industry or national levels, the impacts of all related products and companies need to be aggregated. But the data used to calculate LCA are too specific to sum up and require considerable degree of coordination or harmonization (Atkinson et al., 2012; Wiedmann et al., 2009; etc.).

Input–output approach is one of the top-down estimation methods that uses an international input–output table constructed by using domestic input–output data of countries and trade flow data. Since each entry of the international input–output table is aggregated at sector or industry level, this approach cannot trace the environmental impacts caused by specific products or companies as LCA approach. However, it can capture the infinite interaction between intermediate sectors through simple matrix algebras using a coefficient matrix. It also enables macro- or meso-scale analysis by using aggregate data at the national or industry level.

Three different models are used in this approach according to the aims and scopes of analysis: the Single-Region Input–Output model (SRIO model), the Bilateral Trade Input–Output model (BTIO model),[7] and the Multi-Region Input–Output model (MRIO model). They differ in terms of range of countries/regions analyzed, assumptions about technology, and the way in which intermediate goods are treated. The SRIO model uses an input–output table of a single country/region and typically aggregates other countries/regions in "the rest of the world (ROW)." Also it assumes identical technologies and environmental-impact intensities both for the country analyzed and the ROW. The BTIO model and the MRIO model use different technologies and environmental-impact intensities for each country/region. However, the BTIO model assumes all imported goods are used for final consumption, and thus it does not expect a situation such that imported goods are used as intermediate inputs in the importing country and re-exported to the exporting country after going through the intermediate sectors of the importing country. The MRIO model distinguishes products imported as final goods and those imported as intermediate inputs so that it can describe complex interactions between different industries across borders, and can capture so called "feedback effect" of re-exported goods.

4.5.2   *Multi-regional input–output (MRIO) model*

This chapter adopts the MRIO model to quantify water use embodied in the world trade network and analyzes the interdependency of countries in natural capital use across borders.

The general idea of the MRIO model, mainly using Peters et al. (2011) and Sato and Nakayama (2014), is as follows: suppose there are m countries with n sectors. Total output vector x^r ($M \times 1$) of country r can be expressed by

$$x^r = Z^{rr}\mathbf{1} + y^{rr} + \sum_s e^{rs},$$

(1)

where Z^{rr} is a $n \times n$ transaction matrix between domestic firms obtained by domestic input–output table, $\mathbf{1}$ is a column vector of 1s ($n \times 1$), y^{rr} is a column vector of domestic purchase of domestic goods ($n \times 1$), and e^{rs} is a column vector of exports of domestic goods to country s ($n \times 1$). Since e^{rs} can be divided into intermediate inputs and final demand, as $e^r = Z^{rs}\mathbf{1} + y^{rs}$, Equation (1) can be transformed into

$$x^r = Z^{rr}\mathbf{1} + y^{rr} + \sum_s \left(Z^{rs}\mathbf{1} + y^{rs} \right).$$

Let A^{rr} be a coefficient matrix of domestic transactions with each technical coefficient of $a_{ij}^{rr} \equiv Z_{ij}^{rr} / x_j^r$, and A^{rs} be a coefficient matrix of transactions from firms in country r to firms in country s with coefficient of $a_{ij}^{rs} \equiv Z_{ij}^{rs} / x_j^s$. Then we get

$$x^r = A^{rr}x^r + \sum_s A^{rs}x^s + y^{rr} + \sum_s y^{rs}.$$

(2)

By defining

$$X \equiv \begin{bmatrix} x^1 \\ x^2 \\ \vdots \\ x^m \end{bmatrix}, \quad A \equiv \begin{bmatrix} A^{11} & A^{12} & \cdots & A^{1m} \\ A^{21} & A^{22} & \cdots & A^{2m} \\ \vdots & \vdots & \ddots & \vdots \\ A^{m1} & A^{m2} & \cdots & A^{mm} \end{bmatrix}, \quad Y \equiv \sum_s \begin{bmatrix} y^{1s} \\ y^{2s} \\ \vdots \\ y^{ms} \end{bmatrix},$$

Equation (2) can also be expressed as

$$X = AX + Y.$$

By rewriting it, we obtain the equilibrium equation of MRIO as

$$X = (I - A)^{-1} Y.$$

(3)

Normally, the data in Z^{rs}, which is necessary to calculate off-diagonal elements of A, are not accessible. Therefore, they should be estimated by using bilateral trade-flow data and domestic input–output tables, assigning the total amount of transaction of each good between the two countries to individual industries in the importing country according to the share of that industry in the total import of that good from the world. It is assumed here that the shares of individual industries in imported goods are the same regardless of exporting countries.

Let c_j^r be the amount of environmental impact per dollar amount of production in industry j in country r. We call this unit amount environmental-impact intensity, such as water intensity, land intensity, or carbon intensity. Let the following be the vectors of environmental-impact intensity.

$$c^r \equiv \begin{bmatrix} c_1^r \\ c_2^r \\ \vdots \\ c_n^r \end{bmatrix}, C \equiv \begin{bmatrix} c^1 \\ c^2 \\ \vdots \\ c^m \end{bmatrix}.$$

The production-based environmental impact can simply be obtained as

$$D_p^r \equiv c^{rT} \cdot x^m = \sum_j c_j^r \cdot x_j^r, \tag{4}$$

where c^{rT} means a transpose of c^r.

The environmental impact embodied in the exports from country r to the world, D^{rw}, can be obtained using (3) as

$$D^{rw} = \hat{C}(I-A)^{-1} F^{rw}, \tag{5}$$

where $\hat{C}$ is a diagonal matrix that has each element of C on the diagonal, and D^{rw} and F^{rw} is defined as following:

$$d_t^{rw} \equiv \begin{bmatrix} d_{t,1}^{rw} \\ d_{t,2}^{rw} \\ \vdots \\ d_{t,n}^{rw} \end{bmatrix}, D^{rw} \equiv \begin{bmatrix} d_1^{rw} \\ d_2^{rw} \\ \vdots \\ d_m^{rw} \end{bmatrix}, F^{rw} \equiv \begin{bmatrix} 0 \\ \vdots \\ \sum_s e^{rs} \\ 0 \\ \vdots \end{bmatrix}.$$

where $d_{t,i}^{rw}$ is the environmental impact embodied in the exports from country r to the world, which occurred in industry i in country t.

Similarly, the environmental impact embodied in the imports from the world to country r, D^{wr}, can be obtained as

$$D^{wr} = \hat{C}(I-A)^{-1} F^{wr}, \tag{6}$$

where D^{wr} and F^{wr} is defined as follows:

$$\mathbf{d}_t^{wr} \equiv \begin{bmatrix} d_{t,1}^{wr} \\ d_{t,2}^{wr} \\ \vdots \\ d_{t,n}^{wr} \end{bmatrix}, \mathbf{D}^{wr} \equiv \begin{bmatrix} \mathbf{d}_1^{wr} \\ \mathbf{d}_2^{wr} \\ \vdots \\ \mathbf{d}_m^{wr} \end{bmatrix}, \mathbf{F}^{wr} \equiv \begin{bmatrix} \mathbf{e}^{1r} \\ \vdots \\ \mathbf{o}^{rr} \\ \vdots \\ \mathbf{e}^{mr} \end{bmatrix}.$$

where $\mathbf{o}^{rr}$ is a column vector of 0s ($M \times 1$).

The value, defined as follows using the results of (5) and (6), is called a balance of trade of consumption-embodied environmental impacts.

$$D_b^r \equiv \sum_t \sum_i d_{t,i}^{rw} - \sum_t \sum_i d_{t,i}^{wr} \tag{7}$$

What does it mean? Let us first consider a case in which transaction into and from the home country occurs not more than once in the same supply chain (case A). There are three patterns, in which the home country is a supplier of raw materials, a supplier of intermediate inputs, or a final consumer (Figure 4.1(a)).

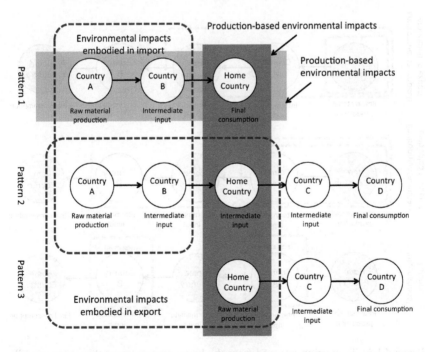

Figure 4.1(a) Transaction into and from the home country not more than once (case A)

As shown in the figure, subtracting the second term from the first term on the right-hand side of Equation (7) eliminates the environmental impacts occurring in the upper stream of the home country in the case of the home country producing intermediate inputs, and gives a value of the difference between the environmental impacts occurring at home in the production process of a good consumed in other countries and those occurring in other countries in the production process of a good consumed at home.

However, in reality, there are cases in which, after a good is exported from home as raw material or intermediate input to the other countries, the intermediate goods or final goods produced by using the first good return to the home country in the downstream of the supply chain, so that the first and second term on the right-hand side of Equation (7) may have double counts. Consider now two other cases in which a transaction into and from home country occurs more than once in the same supply chain: case B, the home country is a final consumer (Figure 4.1(b)), and case C, the home country is not a final consumer (Figure 4.1(c)). In case B, the calculation of Equation (7) eliminates all environmental impacts occurring at home in the supply chain, and leaves those occurring in the other countries in the production process of a good consumed at home as a deficit of the balance of trade. On the other hand, in case C, the environmental impacts occurring in the other countries are eliminated, and only

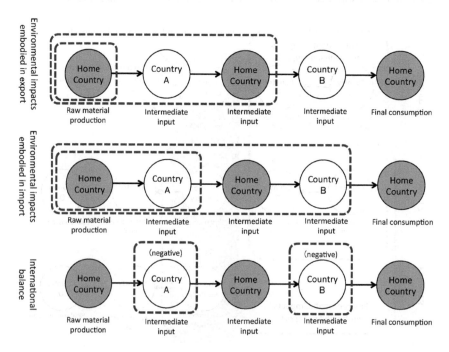

Figure 4.1 (b) Transaction into and from the home country more than once (case B: the home country is a final consumer)

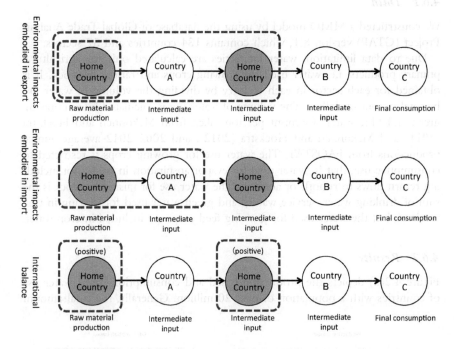

Figure 4.1(c) Transaction into and from the home country more than once (case C: the home country is not a final consumer)

those occurring at home in the production process of a good consumed in the other countries are left as a surplus of the balance of trade.

In sum, in any case Equation (7) gives, as a surplus or deficit of the balance of trade, a value representing the difference between the environmental impacts occurring at home in the production process of a good consumed in other countries and those occurring in the other countries in the production process of a good consumed at home. If the balance is deficit, for example, the environmental services that the home country provides for the other countries' consumption is lower than those which the other countries provide for the home's country's consumption.

Finally, we obtain the consumption-based environmental impact of country r by subtracting the balance of trade from the production-based impact, as follows.

$$D_c^r = D_p^r - D_b^r \tag{8}$$

4.6 Water use embodied in the world trade network

This section quantifies water use embodied in the world trade network by using the MRIO model described in the previous section, and analyzes the interdependency of countries in natural capital use across borders.

4.6.1   Data

We constructed a MRIO model by using the database of Global Trade Analysis Project (GTAP) version 8.1, which contains 134 countries and 57 sectors.

Due to data limitation, water intensities are calculated only for agricultural primary products, i.e. water used for growing crops and raising livestock. It is obtained for each sector in each country by dividing the volume of water use by total output in dollars. The volume of water use is calculated by multiplying green and blue water[8] footprint per ton taken from Mekonnen and Hoekstra (2011) and Mekonnen and Hoekstra (2012), and 2002–2012 average annual productions from FAOSTAT. The water use for growing crops is restricted to consumptive use, that is, water used for evapotranspiration in fields, not including return flows to runoffs or aquifers. The water use for raising livestock is the sum of drinking water, service water,[9] and green water used for grazing in pastureland, but the water used for growing feed crops are included in crop water.

4.6.2   Results

Figure 4.2(a) depicts the production-based and consumption-based water use of countries with a population of over 20 million. Generally, the total amount

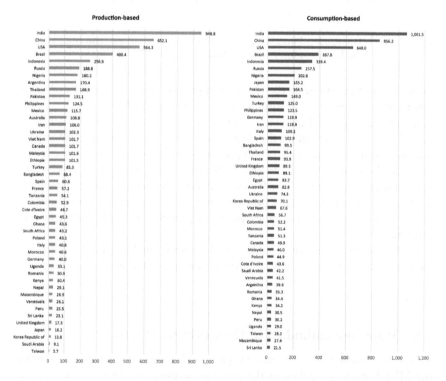

Figure 4.2(a) Production-based and consumption-based water use (country total, km³/year)

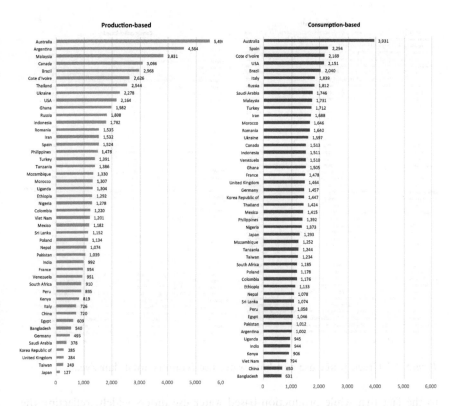

Figure 4.2(b) Production-based and consumption-based water use (ton/year/person)

of water use, both production-based and consumption-based, increases in proportion to population size. Countries with the world's largest populations, such as India, China, the U.S., Brazil, Indonesia, Russia, and Nigeria, are the highest for both indicators. However, some of the relatively high-ranked countries in production-based water use, such as Argentina, Canada, and Malaysia, have much smaller populations and use much less consumption-based water. It indicates that these countries use a large amount of water in water-intensive crops, such as wheat, oil-seed crops, and forage crops, and export them or their processed products. On the other hand, countries such as Bangladesh, Italy, Germany, the U.K., Japan, and South Korea use relatively small amounts of production-based water for their populations. Of these, Italy, Germany, the U.K., Japan, and South Korea have much more consumption-based water compared to their production-based water, with a large part of their water-intensive production process depending on foreign countries.

As shown in Figure 4.2(b), consumption-based water use per capita has larger variations from country to country than production-based water use has. The standard deviation of the latter (530) is about half of that of the former (1083), if only considering countries with populations of over 20 million. This is due

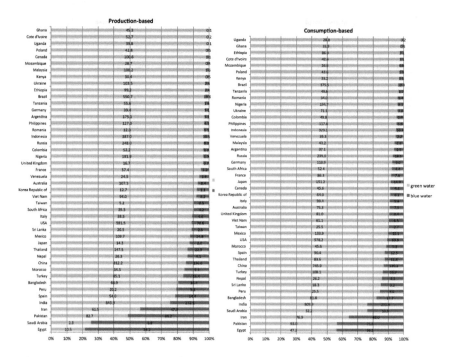

Figure 4.3 Green water use and blue water use (country total, km^3/year)

to the fact that while production-based water use differs widely, reflecting the differences between countries in physical conditions such as water endowments or other agroclimatic factors, consumption-based water use is likely to be, to some extent, leveled over the world through virtual water trades.

In terms of blue and green distinction, most countries use 80 to 90 percent of both production-based and consumption-based water in a green water form as shown in Figure 4.3. But Iran, Pakistan, and Saudi-Arabia obtain more than 40 percent of consumption-based water in a blue water form, and Iran, Pakistan, and Egypt obtain more than 40 percent of production-based water in a blue water form.

Figure 4.4 shows the amount of domestic water use embodied in consumption of other countries, i.e. virtual water export for consumption, and Figure 4.5 is balance of virtual water trade. Again, these figures show only countries with populations over 20 million people. China, the U.S., Brazil, and Argentina are the largest virtual water exporters. With regards to import, in addition to large-population countries such as the U.S. and China, Japan, Germany, Italy, the U.K., Spain, France, and South Korea are large importers. The latter group is in deficit by importing more than they export. Japan especially is the world's largest net importer of virtual water, with its deficit corresponding to about 6.9 percent of gross virtual water trade and 9.2 percent of net virtual water trade of the world, which is embodied in consumption. While most countries with a large population are net exporters, in addition

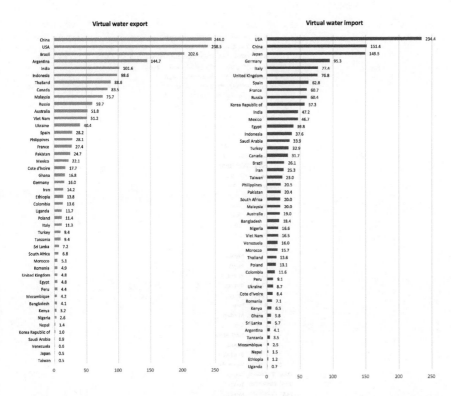

Virtual water export		Virtual water import	
China	244.0	USA	234.4
USA	238.5	China	151.4
Brazil	202.6	Japan	149.5
Argentina	144.7	Germany	95.3
India	101.6	Italy	77.4
Indonesia	98.6	United Kingdom	76.8
Thailand	88.6	Spain	62.8
Canada	83.5	France	60.7
Malaysia	75.7	Russia	60.4
Russia	59.7	Korea Republic of	57.3
Australia	51.8	India	47.2
Viet Nam	51.2	Mexico	46.7
Ukraine	40.4	Egypt	39.8
Spain	28.2	Indonesia	37.6
Philippines	28.1	Saudi Arabia	33.9
France	27.4	Turkey	32.9
Pakistan	24.7	Canada	31.7
Mexico	22.1	Brazil	26.1
Cote d'Ivoire	17.7	Iran	25.3
Ghana	16.8	Taiwan	23.0
Germany	16.0	Philippines	20.5
Iran	14.2	Pakistan	20.4
Ethiopia	13.8	South Africa	20.0
Colombia	13.6	Malaysia	20.0
Uganda	11.7	Australia	19.0
Poland	11.4	Bangladesh	18.4
Italy	11.3	Nigeria	16.6
Turkey	9.4	Viet Nam	16.5
Tanzania	9.4	Venezuela	16.0
Sri Lanka	7.2	Morocco	15.7
South Africa	6.8	Thailand	13.6
Morocco	5.1	Poland	13.1
Romania	4.9	Colombia	11.6
United Kingdom	4.8	Peru	9.1
Egypt	4.8	Ukraine	8.7
Peru	4.4	Cote d'Ivoire	8.4
Mozambique	4.2	Romania	7.1
Bangladesh	4.1	Kenya	6.5
Kenya	3.2	Ghana	5.8
Nigeria	2.6	Sri Lanka	5.7
Nepal	1.4	Argentina	4.1
Korea Republic of	1.0	Tanzania	3.5
Saudi Arabia	0.9	Mozambique	2.5
Venezuela	0.6	Nepal	1.5
Japan	0.5	Ethiopia	1.2
Taiwan	0.5	Uganda	0.7

Figure 4.4 Gross virtual water trade embodied in consumption (country total, km³/year)

to Russia with a slight deficit, Nigeria has a deficit of about 14 billion tons. This is, at the moment, very small compared to Nigeria's huge amount of consumption-based water use, about 203 billion tons. But Nigeria is expected to have the third largest population in the world by 2045, and thus how it will utilize the international food markets in the future is likely to greatly affect the global balance of virtual water trade and the water cycle of the planet.

Table 4.1 shows the world's largest bilateral virtual water trade. In gross terms, exports from China to the U.S., the U.S. to Japan, and Brazil and Argentina to China are the highest trade flows, whilst in net terms exports from the U.S. and China to Japan, and Brazil and Argentina to China are the highest.

Table 4.2 shows the dependency of each country's consumption on foreign water resources from slightly different perspectives. Again, the tables show only countries with populations over 20 million people. The left-hand side of the table shows the ratio of consumption-based water use to domestic water use for own consumption. It expresses how much of consumption-embodied water is supplied by domestic water resources. Since almost all countries, more or less,

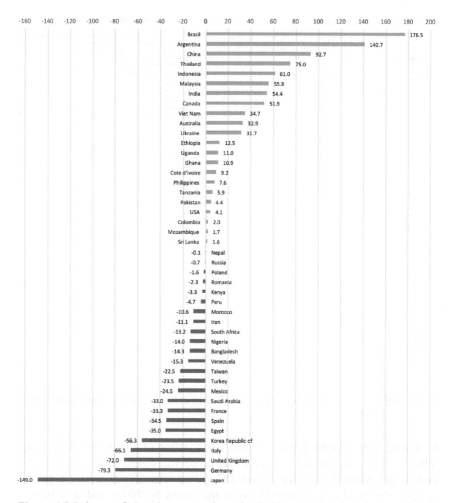

Figure 4.5 Balance of virtual water trade embodied in consumption (country total, km³/year)

import and consume agricultural products from other countries, even big net exporters of virtual water may have dependency of over 100 percent. The median of 46 countries is 130 percent, which indicates they obtain most of their water for consumption from domestic water resources. However, Japan, the U.K., South Korea, Taiwan, Saudi-Arabia, and Germany have ratios of over 400 percent. Japan's ratio of 1051 percent is outstanding. The right-hand side shows the ratio of consumption-based water use to production-based water use. It shows how much of consumption-embodied water could be supplied by domestic water resources, including those currently used for other countries. The median of 46 countries is about 100 percent, which indicates they can theoretically secure sufficient water for domestic consumption by switching the water currently used for exports to

Table 4.1 Bilateral virtual water trade embodied in consumption

Gross export				Net export			
Exporter	Importer	km³/year*		Exporter	Importer	km³/year*	
China	U.S.A.	54.2	(2.5%)	U.S.A.	Japan	32.1	(2.0%)
U.S.A.	Japan	32.2	(1.5%)	China	Japan	31.1	(1.9%)
Brazil	China	29.7	(1.4%)	Brazil	China	27.8	(1.7%)
Argentina	China	26.7	(1.2%)	Argentina	China	26.1	(1.6%)
Canada	U.S.A.	20.3	(0.9%)	Canada	Japan	13.6	(0.8%)
Mexico	U.S.A.	16.3	(0.8%)	Malaysia	China	11.3	(0.7%)
Malaysia	China	14.1	(0.7%)	India	U.S.A.	10.3	(0.6%)
Indonesia	India	13.7	(0.6%)	Russia	Egypt	10.3	(0.6%)
India	U.S.A.	11.5	(0.5%)	Indonesia	India	10.3	(0.6%)
Thailand	U.S.A.	10.9	(0.5%)	Thailand	U.S.A.	9.4	(0.6%)

* The figures in parentheses show the percentages of trade volume in the world total

Table 4.2 Dependency of consumption on foreign water resources

(a) Consumption-based water use/ domestic water use for own consumption		(b) Consumption-based water use/ production-based water use	
Japan	1051%	Japan	1018%
United Kingdom	712%	United Kingdom	515%
Korea Republic of	548%	Korea Republic of	508%
Taiwan	543%	Taiwan	495%
Saudi Arabia	509%	Saudi Arabia	461%
Germany	488%	Germany	296%
Italy	344%	Italy	253%
France	283%	Egypt	172%
Canada	274%	Venezuela	159%
Spain	256%	France	155%
Egypt	190%	Spain	151%
Median of 46 countries with over 20 million people	130%	Median of 46 countries with over 20 million people	100%

domestic use. On the other hand, the ratios of Japan, the U.K., South Korea, Taiwan, Saudi-Arabia, Germany, and Italy are over 200 percent, so that they do not have sufficient water to cover their own consumption even if they use the last drop of domestic water. Again, Japan's ratio of 1018 percent is outstanding.

4.7   Conclusions

EEI indicators can contribute to the achievement of sustainable development in four ways. First, most national-level sustainability indicators cannot reflect the geographically and socially uneven distribution of causes of global environmental problems. EEI indicators can play a critical role to bridge such national-level indicators and global sustainability by quantifying the interdependency among countries in natural capital use across borders. Second, EEI indicators can promote sustainable consumption by raising the awareness of consumers and providing economic incentives to change patterns of individual behaviors. Third, by quantifying the "global savings" of natural capitals that cannot be physically transported across borders, EEI indicators can evaluate the efficiency of use of these natural capitals. Finally, EEI indicators can evaluate the global equity in natural capital use by quantifying the amount of resource embodied in each country's consumption, instead of measuring the amount of their geographical endowments.

There are various methods to estimate environmental impacts embodied in production processes across borders, and each has advantages and disadvantages. The LCA approach enables detailed and accurate analysis at a disaggregated level, such as individual products or companies, but its calculation is highly dependent on the shape of the system boundary it sets arbitrarily in the whole supply chain. Input–output approach cannot trace the environmental impacts caused by specific products or companies, but it enables macro- or meso-scale analysis by using aggregate data at the national or industry levels and can describe complex interactions between different industries across borders.

We quantified water use embodied in the world trade network by using MRIO model. Italy, Germany, the U.K., Japan, and South Korea have much larger consumption-based water use compared to their production-based water use, with a large part of their water-intensive production process depending on foreign countries. Japan especially is one of the world's largest net importers of virtual water, with its deficit corresponding to about 6.9 percent of gross virtual water trade and 9.2 percent of net virtual water trade of the world embodied in consumption. Countries such as India and Nigeria are at the moment highly dependent on their domestic water resources, but how they will utilize the international food markets in the future is likely to greatly affect the global balance of virtual water trade and the water cycle of the planet. The dependency of consumption on foreign water resources is very high in Japan, the U.K., South Korea, Taiwan, Saudi-Arabia, Germany, and Italy, so that they do not have sufficient water to cover the domestic consumption, even if they use the last drop of domestic water resources currently being used.

Notes

1 The estimation here is based on Sato and Nakayama (2014).
2 To embody something means to give a tangible, bodily, or concrete form to an abstract concept (Collins English Dictionary – Complete & Unabridged 2012

Digital Edition), but it originally refers to a philosophical or religious idea of investing a soul or spirit with a physical form.

3 For example, Leamer (1980) proved that if capital is abundant relative to labor in a country, then the capital/labor ratio embodied in production for the country exceeds the capital/labor ratio embodied in consumption (Feenstra, 2004).

4 Water Footprint Network, http://www.waterfootprint.org/

5 A similar concept of "ghost acreage" was already proposed in the 1960s (Borgstrom, 1967).

6 Sato (2014) mapped the scope of different methods in terms of scales of analysis (macro, meso, micro), range of information used, and policy focus.

7 BTIO model is sometimes called, according to types of environmental impacts, Embodied Emissions in Bilateral Trade (EEBT) model or Water Embodied in Bilateral Trade (WEBT) (Sato, 2014; Feng et al., 2011).

8 The concept of green water was first introduced by Falkenmark (1995) to refer to the return flow of water to the atmosphere as evapotranspiration. But lately it has been used generally to refer to the water comes from precipitation, is stored in the unsaturated soils, and subsequently fed back to the atmosphere (Yang et al., 2011). Blue water refers to the water in rivers, lakes, reservoirs, ponds, and aquifers (Rockström et al., 1999).

9 Service water refers to the water used to clean the farmyard, wash the animal, and carry out other services necessary to maintain the environment (Mekonnen and Hoekstra, 2010).

Bibliography

Allan, J.A. (2003) Virtual water-the water, food, and trade nexus. Useful concept or misleading metaphor?, *Water International* 28, 106–113.

Atkinson, G., M. Agarwala, and P. Munoz (2012) Are national economies (virtually) sustainable?: an empirical analysis of natural assets in international trade. In: UNU-IHDP and UNEP (2012) *Inclusive wealth report 2012: measuring progress toward sustainability*, Cambridge: Cambridge University Press.

Atkinson, G., K. Hamilton, G. Ruta, and D. Van Der Mensbrugghe (2011) Trade in "virtual carbon": empirical results and implications for policy, *Global Environmental Change* 21, 563–574.

Borgstrom, G. (1967) *The hungry planet: the modern world at the edge of famine*, New York: The Macmillan Company.

Falkenmark, M. (1995) *Coping with water scarcity under rapid population growth*, Conference of SADC Ministers, Pretoria, 23–24 November 1995.

Feenstra, R.C. (2004) *Advanced international trade: theory and evidence*, New Jersey: Princeton University Press.

Feng, K., A. Chapagain, S. Suh, S. Pfister, and K. Hubacek (2011) Comparison of bottom-up and top-down approaches to calculating the water footprints of nations, *Economic Systems Research* 23, 371–385.

Hoekstra, A.Y., and P.Q. Hung (2002) Virtual water trade, a quantification of virtual water flows between nations in relation to international crop trade. *Value of Water Research Report Series* No. 11, Delft, The Netherland: UNESCO-IHE.

Leamer, E.E. (1980) The Leontief paradox, reconsidered, *The Journal of Political Economy*, 495–503.

Lenzen, M., D. Moran, A. Bhaduri, K. Kanemoto, M. Bekchanov, A. Geschke, and B. Foran (2013) International trade of scarce water, *Ecological Economics* 94, 78–85.

Liu, J., A.J.B. Zehnder, and H. Yang (2009) Global consumptive water use for crop production: the importance of green water and virtual water, *Water Resources Research* 45, W05428, doi:10.1029/2007WR006051.

Mekonnen, M.M., and A.Y. Hoekstra (2010) The green, blue and grey water footprint of farm animals and animal products, *Value of Water Research Report Series* No. 58, Delft, the Netherlands: UNESCO-IHE

Mekonnen, M.M., and A.Y. Hoekstra (2011) The green, blue and grey water footprint of crops and derived crop products, *Hydrology and Earth System Sciences*, 15, 1577–1600.

Mekonnen, M.M., and A.Y. Hoekstra (2012) A global assessment of the water footprint of farm animal products, *Ecosystems*, 15, 401–415.

OECD (2011) *Towards green growth: monitoring progress: OECD indicators*, http://www.oecd.org/greengrowth.

Oki, T., and S. Kanae (2004) Virtual water trade and world water resources, *Water Science and Technology* 49, 203–209.

Oki, T., M. Sato, A. Kawamura, and M. Miyake (2003) Virtual water trade to Japan and in the world, *Value of Water Research Report Series*, No.12, Delft, The Netherlands: UNESCO-IHE, 221–235.

Peters, G.P., and E.G. Hertwich (2008) CO2 embodied in international trade with implications for global climate policy, *Environmental Science & Technology* 42, 1401–1407.

Peters, G.P., R. Andrew, and J. Lennox (2011) Constructing an environmentally-extended multi-regional input-output table using the GTAP database, *Economic Systems Research* 23, 131–152.

Rockström, J., L. Gordon, C. Folke, M. Falkenmark, and M. Engwall (1999) Linkages among water vapor flows, food production, and terrestrial ecosystem services, *Conservation Ecology* 3(2): 5.

Sato, M., 2014, Embodied carbon in trade: a survey of the empirical literature, *Journal of Economic Surveys* 28, 831–861.

Sato, M., and H. Nakayama (2014) Estimation of world virtual water and virtual land using a multi-regional input-output (MRIO) model, *KIER Discussion Paper* 1405, Kyoto: Institute of Economic Research, Kyoto University (Japanese).

Weber, C.L., and H.S. Matthews (2007) Embodied environmental emissions in US international trade, 1997–2004, *Environmental Science & Technology* 41, 4875–4881.

Wichelns, D. (2001) The role of "virtual water" in efforts to achieve food security and other national goals, with an example from Egypt, *Agricultural Water Management* 49, 131–151.

Wiedmann, T. (2009) A review of recent multi-region input–output models used for consumption-based emission and resource accounting, *Ecological Economics* 69, 211–222.

Wiedmann, T., M. Lenzen, K. Turner, and J. Barrett (2007) Examining the global environmental impact of regional consumption activities – part 2: review of input–output models for the assessment of environmental impacts embodied in trade, *Ecological Economics* 61, 15–26.

Würtenberger, L., T. Koellner, and C.R. Binder (2006) Virtual land use and agricultural trade: estimating environmental and socio-economic impacts, *Ecological Economics* 57, 679–697.

Wyckoff, A.W., and J.M. Roop (1994) The embodiment of carbon in imports of manufactured products: implications for international agreements on greenhouse gas emissions, *Energy Policy* 22, 187–194.

Yang, H., J. Liu, A.J.B. Zehnder, and J. Rockström (2011) Ecosystem impacts of virtual water embodied in global trade of agricultural products, In: Koellner, T. (ed.) (2011) *Ecosystem services and global trade of natural resources: ecology, economics and policies*, Oxon: Routledge.

Yang, H., L. Wang, K.C. Abbaspour, and A.J.B. Zehnder (2006) Virtual water trade: an assessment of water use efficiency in the international food trade, *Hydrology and Earth System Sciences Discussions* 10, 443–454.

5 Natural capital and ecosystem accounting

Sana Okayasu and Kei Kabaya

This chapter discusses the importance of considering ecosystem regulating services when measuring the economic value of natural capital and when constructing ecosystem accounts. Some case studies on quantification and valuation of regulating services will also be highlighted to demonstrate current progresses and barriers relevant to such studies.

5.1 Introduction

Human activities rely on the processes and products of ecosystem functioning, ranging from the stable provision of freshwater, thanks to groundwater retention by forests, to the crop harvests that result from pollination by diverse insects, to the regulation of the quality of the air that we breathe daily.

This essential role played by ecosystems is recognized today under the concept of ecosystem services and natural capital. Since the idea of natural capital was introduced by E.F. Schumacher in 1973, it has been defined to different extents by environmental economists such as Costanza, Daly, Farley, Dasgupta, etc., as well as by international organisations promoting this topic. Natural capital is composed of renewable and non-renewable capital acting as stocks from which we obtain a flow of goods through extraction, or services through ecosystem functions (Costanza and Daly, 1992). The goods and services yielded from natural capital can also be understood from the perspective of stock/flow resources, where the stock of natural capital is converted into goods that can be stored or consumed, and fund/service resources, where services are provided from the fund at a given rate and cannot be stored, but can be depleted if consumed at a higher rate (Daly and Farley, 2011).The goods and services obtained from natural capital stocks can also be distinguished according to the type of value they provide, such as use value, option value, and intrinsic value (Dasguputa, 2012). Although the various definitions formulated to date comprise a mix of elements relating to the characteristics or functions of the stock of natural capital itself as well as to the characteristics of the benefits that human society obtains from it, it is generally understood that natural capital constitutes the stock which yields a flow of ecosystem goods and services. Ecosystem services can be categorized broadly into supporting, provisioning, regulating, and cultural services, as outlined further in this chapter.

Today the continued degradation and depletion of natural capital and eco-system services is threatening the sustainability of human activities, the cause of which is attributed mainly to the failure of the current economy and its accounting systems to capture the "bigger picture" of human society's impacts and dependencies on natural capital. Based on the understanding that the sustainable management of ecosystems and the resources they provide requires an appropriate measurement of their stocks and flows, the notion of natural capital has thus been highlighted. By regarding natural capital as an asset on which the economy relies, its active quantification and valuation can be pro-moted as a basis for an appropriate accounting system. Accounting for our dependence on ecosystem services, as well as for the impacts we have on natural capital, will allow the visualisation of the benefits human society obtains from nature and the promotion of investments towards the sustainable management and use of natural capital.

At the Rio + 20 meeting held in Rio de Janeiro in June 2012, the first of its kind since the Rio Earth Summit in 1992, the CEOs of more than 40 financial institutions came together to sign the Natural Capital Declaration as a commit-ment towards considering natural capital within private sector decision-making through their integration into accounting and reporting frameworks by 2020 (UNEP FI and GCP, 2012). This large-scale commitment illustrates the increas-ing international attention on the impacts of ecosystem degradation to the business sector and to the global economy. Since then, the term natural capital has been receiving continued recognition, with the organisation of the World Forum on Natural Capital in Edinburgh in November 2013, which had the participation of 500 delegates from 35 countries, including business leaders, NGOs, academics, experts, and government representatives (Scottish Wildlife Trust, 2013).

5.2   Current progress and barriers of developing ecosystem accounting

5.2.1   *History of SEEA and the experimental ecosystem accounting framework*

One of the main international initiatives for the development of ecosystem accounting is the United Nation's System of Environmental Economic Accounts (SEEA). Under Agenda 21 adopted in 1992 at the Rio Earth Summit, member countries committed to developing an integrated system to account for both the environment and the economy. Based on this com-mitment, the UN introduced the SEEA as a satellite account within the revision of the National Accounts framework in 1993. The SEEA has under-gone revisions since then, in 2003 and 2012. The most recent revision process has resulted in the adoption of the SEEA Central Framework (SEEA-CF) as an international statistical standard for environmental economic accounts in 2012. Subsequently, the SEEA Experimental Ecosystem Accounts (SEEA-EEA) was adopted as an international guideline in 2013, together with the Extensions and Applications to the SEEA (EC et al., 2014, and UN et al., 2014).

The SEEA-CF aims to develop a record of three main aspects, namely the physical flow of materials and energy between the environment and the economy, the stock of environmental assets as well as its variations, and finally, the economic activities related to the environment. The accounting framework consists of the physical and monetary supply and use tables of natural inputs, products, and residuals, the asset account of the stocks of environmental assets and their changes, the series of economic accounts, including depletion-adjusted balancing items, and functional accounts of the transactions related to environmental activities (UN et al., 2014).

Under SEEA-CF, the physical flows between the environment and the economy are recorded as natural inputs (from the environment to the economy), product flows (within the economy) and residuals (from the economy to the environment) (Figure 5.1). The source of natural inputs is regarded as the environmental asset and is recorded from the two perspectives of the physical constituents of the environment and the ecosystem. The environmental constituents include elements such as natural resources, composed of biological resources, minerals, energy

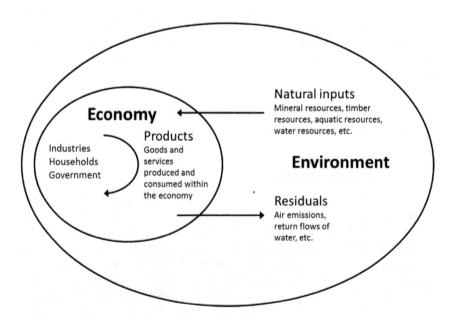

Figure 5.1 Conceptual diagram of physical flows recorded under the SEEA-CF
Source: UN et al., 2014

Table 5.1 Environmental assets covered by the SEEA-CF

Asset category	Sub-category
Mineral and energy resources	Oil resources
	Natural gas resources
	Coal and peat resources
	Non-metallic mineral resources
	(excluding coal and peat resources)
	Metallic mineral resources
Land	
Soil resources	
Timber resources	Cultivated timber resources
	Natural timber resources
Aquatic resources	Cultivated aquatic resources
	Natural aquatic resources
Other biological resources (excluding timber resources and aquatic resources)	
Water resources	Surface water
	Groundwater
	Soil water

Source: UN et al., 2014

resources, soil resources, and water resources (Table 5.1). These environmental assets do not include benefits such as water purification, carbon storage, and flood prevention derived from environmental functions. The non-physical benefits derived from the indirect use of environmental assets are also excluded. Furthermore, the benefits from qualitative elements such as soil fertility are regarded as an intrinsic part of natural resources and are not measured in the asset accounts. The ecosystem perspective is included under the SEEA-EEA.

The SEEA-EEA captures the ecosystem structure and function as ecosystem services and ecosystem assets that provide them. The basic structure of the SEEA-EEA is separated into ecosystem service accounts and ecosystem asset accounts. They are composed of the stock of ecosystem assets and the flow of ecosystem services, as well as the changes in ecosystem assets. Experimentally, the SEEA-EEA also provides methodologies for a monetary evaluation of these assets and services (EC et al., 2014).

The ecosystem services accounts aim to measure the benefits received by human society from the ecosystem's functions. This means that only the final outputs from ecosystems that directly provide benefits to human society are accounted for. As for the flow of services within and between ecosystems, as well as supporting services, they are considered as part of ecosystem assets and are not considered an element of the ecosystem services accounts. The detailed breakdown of ecosystem services follows the Common International Classification of Ecosystem Services (CICES). The CICES is an attempt to streamline the diverse classifications that have been developed since the implementation of the Millennium Ecosystem

Assessment and The Economics of Ecosystems and Biodiversity (TEEB). This classification distinguishes the broad classes of ecosystem services as provisioning, regulating, and cultural services. Provisioning services include the provision of food (crops, meat, dairy, fish, honey, etc.), water, fibres (timber, wool, etc.), fuels, and other products. Regulating services include functions such as water purification, climate regulation, noise buffering, air quality regulation, flood mitigation, and other benefits. Cultural services include a range of non-physical benefits, such as cultural heritages, recreation, and aesthetic enjoyment (EEA, 2013). Elements such as minerals and fossil fuel resources, as well as renewable energy resources such as solar, wind, and wave power, that are already covered by the SEEA-CF are not included within the ecosystem service accounts.

In order to establish the linkage between the ecosystem services accounts and the System of National Accounts (SNA), if the ecosystem service is used as an input within the production process under the SNA, then this service is considered as an SNA service, and if the ecosystem service provides direct benefits to society, then it is considered as a non-SNA service. The SNA services are classified according to the SNA categories of natural biological resources and cultivated biological resources, and can thus be accounted for within the SNA framework.

The ecosystem asset accounts aim to record the spatial area which includes biotic and abiotic elements, as well as other characteristics that function together, in order to capture the condition and the extent of the targeted ecosystems, as well as the ecosystem flows that can be expected from them (Table 5.2). Ecosystem condition provides an overview of the condition of ecosystem assets, and ecosystem extent shows the surface area of these assets. Expected ecosystem service flows measures the total physical quantities of given ecosystem services which are expected to be yielded in the future from the ecosystem asset (Table 5.3). The capacity of the ecosystem asset to yield ecosystem services is generally thought to be dependent on the condition and extent of the ecosystem

Table 5.2 Structure of ecosystem asset accounts (ecosystem condition)

	Ecosystem extent	Characteristics of ecosystem condition
		Relevant aspects of ecosystem condition selected, such as vegetation, biodiversity, soil, water, carbon, etc.
	Area	Relevant indicators of ecosystem condition selected for measurement of previous aspects, such as biomass, species richness, organic matter content, water quality, primary productivity, etc.
Various types of LCEU e.g. forest, agricultural land, wetlands, urban parks, etc.		Values at the end of an accounting period for an EAU

Source: rearranged by authors based on EC et al., 2014

Table 5.3 Structure of ecosystem services accounts

	Expected ecosystem service flows per year
	Relevant types of LCEU within the target EAUe.g. forest, agricultural land, wetlands, urban parks, etc.
Various types of ecosystem services according to CICES (provisioning, regulating, cultural services)	Values at the end of an accounting period for an EAU

Source: rearranged by authors based on EC et al., 2014

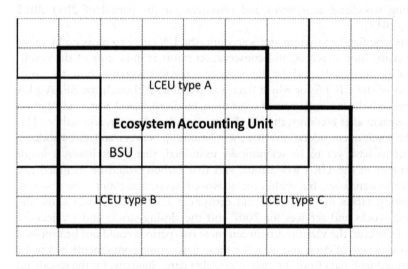

Figure 5.2 EAU, LCEU, and BSU
Source: EC et al., 2014

asset. However, the interrelationships between these are complex, and will thus require diverse metrics for an accurate accounting.

The accounting unit for ecosystem accounts is a spatial unit called the Ecosystem Accounting Unit (EAU), which can coincide with administrative boundaries, environmental management areas, or other features of the landscape. These areas can also be subdivided into Land Cover/Ecosystem Functional Units (LCEU) which serve to distinguish areas based on the type of ecosystems they represent. One EAU would generally extend across different types of LCEUs. The grid on which these units are delineated is made up of Basic Spatial Units (BSU) (Figure 5.2).

5.2.2 *Natural capital accounting at the national level: current achievement and further elaboration*

Parallel to the adoption of the SEEA-CF as an international statistical standard as well as of the SEEA-EEA as an international guideline for ecosystem accounting, a number of countries have already begun piloting these accounting frameworks

100 Sana Okayasu and Kei Kabaya

within their respective contexts, and have been providing valuable input to international discussions.

One of the countries more advanced in the exploration of natural capital and ecosystem accounting is the United Kingdom, which in its 2011 Natural Environment White Paper committed to integrating natural capital into the economy by 2020. In 2012, the Natural Capital Committee was thus established as an independent advisory body to support the government on the various initiatives relating to the sustainable use of natural capital, including the development of accounting frameworks. Based on its Roadmap, the UK began implementing a pilot account in 2013 based on the SEEA-CF and SEEA-EEA frameworks by targeting woodland ecosystems and resources for the period of 2011–2012 (ONS, 2013).

In its woodland ecosystem assets account, the UK chose to measure biomass, biodiversity, human access, and conservation status as indicators of the condition of its woodlands, and for the ecosystem services account chose the components of the CICES for which data was available. Although the SEEA-EEA recommends the five indicators of vegetation, biodiversity, soil, water, and carbon for ecosystem asset accounts, the UK did not include soil, water, and carbon. This was the result of considerations that the relationship between soil and woodland ecosystems have yet to be scientifically examined, that water is not a major constituent of the UK's woodlands, and that carbon would be included not as an ecosystem asset, but within the ecosystem services account. The resulting accounting tables for UK woodland ecosystem assets and services show the opening stocks and services for 2007 and the closing stocks and services for 2012. However, the variations between these two periods could not be captured due to shortage of data, and even for these dates some components had to be substituted with data from the closest available date. Similarly, for the woodland ecosystem services account, data shortages meant that only a few of the 50 or so components within the CICES could be measured as part of this pilot (ONS, 2013).

Apart from the UK, other countries which have been providing concrete inputs to the UN discussions on the development of SEEA-EEA include Australia and Canada. In each of these cases the availability of statistical data creates a considerable limitation to the implementation of currently recommended SEEA-CF and SEEA-EEA frameworks, but pilot studies have been conducted to the extent possible with existing data. As in the case of the UK, some level of adjustment in the selection of accounting components are needed in order to fit the context of each country, as well as the selective use of one-off research results to fill data gaps. Furthermore, as experienced in Australia and Canada, a considerable amount of preparation is required for the establishment of data infrastructure, such as land cover and land use datasets which are fundamental to the development of ecosystem accounts. This entails the mining and consolidation of diverse forms of existing spatial datasets, as well as connecting them with existing and updated statistical datasets.

5.2.3   *Progress towards natural capital accounting in Japan*

With regards to progress within Japan, prior to the development of the SEEA-CF the Japan Research Institute, contracted by the Japanese government, had conducted a study applying the SEEA 1993 framework to Japan (JRI, 1998). There are also a number of individual pilot studies applying this version of the SEEA at prefectural levels within Japan, such as the case studies in Hokkaido, Toyama, Hyogo, Nagasaki, etc. These trials provide insight into the current limitations in developing local level accounts, such as the lack of organised data from which to build the accounts, as well the fact that accounting at prefectural level does not allow the distinction of ecosystem characteristics.

Regarding the SEEA-CF and the SEEA-EEA, no specific trial has been conducted yet, but studies which are of relevance and can input specific data to any future trials do already exist. Although not termed as "ecosystem services" or "natural capital", which have only recently become a central topic of discussions, there have nonetheless been a number of studies and pilot projects aiming to measure natural capital, mainly from the perspective of the multi-functionality, or the public-interest functionality, of ecosystems.

The Forestry Agency of the Ministry of Agriculture, Forestry and Fisheries (MAFF) in 1972 first conducted an assessment of the multi-functionality of Japan's forest resources and valued it at 13 trillion JPY, revising it later in 1991 to a value of 39 trillion JPY, and again in 2000 to 75 trillion JPY (MAFF, 2000). The MAFF also began an assessment of its agricultural lands in 1982, and in 1998 valued them at 7 trillion JPY for farmlands and at 3 trillion JPY for hilly and mountainous areas (MAFF, 1998). In 2001, the Science Council of Japan, in response to a request from the Minister of Agriculture, Forestry and Fisheries, conducted a comprehensive assessment on the multiple functions and values of forests and agricultural land. This assessment demonstrated the important role played by these ecosystems not only in terms of the provisioning services for which they are managed, but also in terms of numerous other ecosystem services such as disaster mitigation and watershed protection (SCJ, 2001).

Additionally, the economic valuation of wetlands conducted under the Ministry of the Environment of Japan (MOEJ) provides a valuable step towards accounting for the economic value of ecosystem assets and services beyond forests and agricultural land. This study covered marshlands and tidal flats which had undergone rapid decline due to land reclamation, and attempted to compile existing data on these areas in order to paint a comprehensive picture of the ecosystem services derived from them, as well as their economic values (MOEJ, 2014) (Table 5.4).

Also relevant to the accounting of ecosystem services, the MOEJ has conducted a pilot study for a comprehensive quantification of ecosystem services in Chiba prefecture. This study has targeted a wide range of ecosystems types, including forest, agricultural land, urban area, freshwater, and coastal ecosystems, and has attempted to provide a tentative measure of the biophysical quantities of various

Table 5.4 Wetland ecosystem services and their values in Japan

Ecosystem services		Annual value (/year)	Unit area value (/ha/year)
Provisioning services	Food production	Approx. 90.7 billion JPY (tidal marshes)	Approx. 1,850,000 JPY (tidal marshes)
Regulating services	Carbon sequestration	Approx. 3.1 billion JPY (wetlands)	Approx. 67,000 JPY (wetlands)
	Carbon storage	Approx. 98.6 billion ~ 141.8 billion JPY (wetlands)	Approx. 4,620,000 ~ 5,320,000 JPY (wetlands)
	Water flow regulation	Approx. 64.5 billion JPY (wetlands)	Approx. 590,000 JPY (wetlands)
	Water purification	Approx. 377.9 billion JPY (wetlands) Approx. 296.3 billion JPY (tidal marshes)	Approx. 3,430,000 JPY (wetlands) Approx. 6,030,000 JPY (tidal marshes)
Supporting services	Habitat and nursery area	Approx. 180 billion JPY (wetlands) Approx. 218.8 billion JPY (tidal marshes)	Approx. 1,630,000 JPY (wetlands) Approx. 4,450,000 JPY (tidal marshes)
Cultural services	Natural scenery	Approx. 104.4 billion JPY (wetlands)	Approx. 950,000 JPY (wetlands)
	Recreation and environmental education	Approx. 10.6 ~ 99.4 billion JPY (wetlands) Approx. 4.5 billion JPY (tidal marshes)	Approx. 96,000 ~ 900,000 JPY (wetlands) Approx. 91,000 JPY (tidal marshes)

Source: rearranged by authors based on MOEJ, 2014

provisioning, regulating, and supporting services obtained from them. Although the study involved a diverse range of methodologies for the quantification of each ecosystem service within each ecosystem type, it focused on the prioritisation of simple methodologies in view of future applications at the governmental level. The results have been provided in the form of per unit area quantities of ecosystem services under each ecosystem type (Table 5.5), as well as in maps representing their distributions within Japan (Kabaya and Okayasu, 2014). These results thus have the potential to be of use in conducting future pilot studies for the development of ecosystem asset and service accounts within Japan.

The policy implications for these studies have been numerous, in particular for the MAFF's assessment of the multi-functionality of forest and agricultural lands. The results of this assessment have served as the foundation for the implementation of new payment for ecosystem services schemes targeting the sustainable use of ecosystem services in agricultural lands. Schemes thus introduced include the "direct payment for the cultivation of hilly and mountainous farmlands" aiming to mitigate abandonment and the related loss of ecosystem

Table 5.5 Trial on the quantification of ecosystem services in Japan

Ecosystem services		Forest	Agricultural land	Urban area	Freshwater	Coastal zone
Provisioning	Food production	71×10^3 t/year (chestnuts) 3.5×10^3 t/year (bamboo shoots)	577×10^3 t/year (rice) 59×10^3 t/year (soy) 104×10^3 t/year (pear)		80 t/year (fish)	>0 t/year (rockfish) >0 t/year (flatfish)
	Freshwater provision				6.1×10^6 m³ (tap water) 878×10^6 m³ (irrigation)	
	Material provision	82×10^3 m³/year (wood)	1.9×10^6 t/year (fodder)			
Regulating	Climate regulation	CO2 sequestration capacity	558×10^3 t-CO2/year	113×10^3 t-CO2/year	2.9×10^3 t-CO2/year	1.5×10^3 t-CO2/year
		Heat latent effect (Evapotranspiration)	1.1×10^9 m³/year	802×10^6 m³/year	589×10^6 m³/year	72×10^6 m³/year	18×10^6 m³/year
	Air quality control	SO2 absorption capacity	25 t/year	235 t/year	193 t/year	3.0 t/year	
		NO2 absorption capacity	708 t/year	707 t/year	672 t/year	7.0 t/year	
	Water regulation	Water flow regulation (Groundwater recharge)	594×10^6 m³/year	1.0×10^9 m³/year	583×10^6 m³/year	65×10^6 m³/year	

(Continued)

Table 5.5 (Continued)

Ecosystem services		Forest	Agricultural land	Urban area	Freshwater	Coastal zone
	Nitrogen removal	5.0 × 10³ t/year	10 × 10³ t/year	1.5 × 10³ t/year	82 t/year	1.2 × 10³ t/year
	Phosphorus removal	75 t/year		22 t/year	74 t/year	513 t/year
Soil conservation	Soil erosion prevention	2.4 × 10⁶ t/year	328 × 10³ t/year			
	Soil fertility Maintenance (Nutrient retention)	222 tN/year 2.5 × 10³ tP/year	37 tN/year 239 tP/year			
Natural hazard mitigation	Flood control	Peak runoff mitigation (calculation of total amount irrelevant to analysis)				
	Landslide mitigation	Increase in safety factor (idem)				
	Wave mitigation	Wave speed reduction (idem)				
Biodiversity and habitats	Habitat and nursery area	187 × 10³ ha	181 × 10³ ha	135 × 10³ ha	13 × 10³ ha	2.7 × 10³ ha
	Maintenance of endangered species and genes	57 plant species	18 plant species		74 plant species 20 fish species	9 plant species 13 fish species
Supporting						

Source: rearranged by authors based on Kabaya and Okayasu, 2014 services in these less productive areas, as well as the "farmland and water conservation and management subsidy" which aimed to promote farmland management practices that enhance the provision of multiple ecosystem services. At the prefectural level, new tax schemes have been introduced for the conservation of the multi-functionality of publicly owned forest ecosystems, highlighting in particular their role in freshwater storage. In over 30 prefectures and cities of Japan similar taxes have been introduced, either as a surcharge to water bills or residential taxes.

Based on the ongoing efforts of countries following the SEEA discussions and conducting their own pilot studies, such as the UK, Australia, and Canada, as well as the previous initiatives within Japan, it is becoming apparent that the establishment of ecosystem accounts will require considerable mining and reorganising of statistical information both at local and national levels. Furthermore, this will need to be accompanied by the development of various methodologies to assess and quantify the level of ecosystem services obtained. This is particularly true for regulating services, as the conventional government statistics already provide some level of information on provisioning services, and for cultural services the general understanding is that most are not quantifiable except for limited components, such as tourism and recreation.

5.3 Challenges in developing natural capital and ecosystem accounts

It will not be an easy task to develop natural capital and ecosystem accounting, which requires vast amount of statistical data and geographic information as well as robust estimates of ecosystem services derived from ecosystem assets. Generally, less information on natural environments is available in comparison with data on socio-economic conditions, and broad uncertainty and stochasticity inherent in ecosystems make it difficult to model the complicated mechanisms of biodiversity and ecosystem services. Although steady progress can be observed, as introduced previously, many conceptual and technical issues to construct ecosystem accounts remain, most of which are addressed in European Commission et al. (2013). Apart from them, two essential issues relevant to ecosystem accounting will be discussed in this section: one is the importance and challenges of accounts for regulating services (e.g. water purification and natural hazard mitigation), and the other is the incorporation of ecosystem accounts into the SEEA-CF.

5.3.1 Importance and challenges of accounts for regulating services

Biodiversity loss and ecosystem degradation have been accelerated due to the economic activities which prioritize land development and resource extraction for tangible and short-term monetary income rather than nature conservation for invisible but sustainable benefits for human livelihoods, mainly represented by regulating services. Conversely, this will imply that visualising benefits from regulating services can halt destructive activities and promote sustainable use of ecosystems services. Such possibilities have motivated environmental economists and nature conservationists to accumulate and share knowledge on the value of ecosystem services, resulting in the TEEB reports, which has illustrated the greater values of regulating services than those of provisioning services in some cases (TEEB, 2010). Since ecosystem accounting is in line with these initiatives, it should be more than the compilation of currently available statistical information on natural resources stocks and flows (e.g. timber and water). It must account for multiple regulating services (not only carbon sequestration) to show the size of comprehensive benefits from ecosystems, as well as for true costs of economic activities, thereby indicating whether the country is on the sustainable development and green economy pathways.

Measuring and estimating individual regulating services is the first step to create the accounts. Spatial approaches have especially gained academic and political attentions recently (Maes et al., 2012), represented by the several GIS-based tools currently available – for example, the Integrated Valuation of Environmental Services and Tradeoffs (InVEST) model (Kareiva et al., 2011). These tools enable us to visualize regulating services on the geographical maps, which will contribute not only to constructing ecosystem accounts requiring geographical information to determine statistical units, but also to formulating landscape plans and environmental policies for better ecosystem conservation. Spatial modelling can also show providers and beneficiaries of ecosystem services, which will be relevant to the following discussion on the incorporation of ecosystem accounts into the SEEA-CF.

However, a number of challenges lie ahead for the accounting of regulating services. For ecosystem accounting, two accounts need to be established, namely, an ecosystem asset and an ecosystem service account expressed both in biophysical and monetary terms (Table 5.6). Based on the understanding that the value of a given asset is determined by the flows of benefits it provides (Tallis et al., 2012), the values of all ecosystem services provided by an ecosystem asset would need to be estimated in order to evaluate the entire value of this ecosystem asset. Meanwhile, this poses another question: how does the

Table 5.6 Information availability and challenges of ecosystem asset and service accounts

	Ecosystem asset (stock)	*Ecosystem service (flow)*
Biophysical quantity	Statistical information available (e.g. forest stock)	Effects of the status of an asset on service provision need to be clarified
Monetary value	Determined by the flow of benefits to provide (i.e. ecosystem service)	Knowledge being accumulated (e.g. de Groot et al. 2012)

condition of an ecosystem asset, or more precisely, its biodiversity, affect the level of service provision from this ecosystem? The effects of biodiversity on some regulating services have been explored (e.g. climate regulation, pest control, and water purification [Balvanera et al., 2014]), but further scientific debate on such linkages will be strongly encouraged (Maes et al., 2012). Accounting for regulating services also needs to pay attention to the demand sides and the double counting (Tallis et al., 2012). Supply that does not benefit people cannot be perceived a service, which could be exemplified by water purification in an uninhabited watershed that flows into the open ocean. Additional accounting for pollination that may have been included in the value of produced crops in the existing accounts can be regarded as double counting. These should be taken into account to avoid overestimation of the values of an ecosystem asset which possibly results in distrust of valuation practices and inefficient decision-making on ecosystem use.

5.3.2 Issues on incorporating of ecosystem accounts into the SEEA framework

Ecosystem accounts are unique among current accounting frameworks in terms of accounting units (i.e. EAU, LCEU, and BAU) and methodologies (e.g. GIS and environmental valuation techniques). Nevertheless, the integration of these accounts into the SNA needs to be explored, since the ultimate purpose of creating ecosystem accounts goes beyond monitoring of ecosystems and into visualising the linkages between ecosystems and economies and thereby providing better pathways to achieve sustainable development and green economy. Several issues that need to be addressed when trying to develop such an accounting framework will be discussed briefly here.

The first question we should ask is who is considered to provide ecosystem services – an ecosystem itself or a relevant sector (e.g. forestry and government [European Commission et al., 2013, p.152])? This is especially important when the trade of ecosystem service matters. An ecosystem itself cannot be an economic entity to receive money in exchange of service provision, and hence payment for ecosystem services cannot be rationalized in the former approach. Given that the practical use of ecosystem accounts to promote economic instruments for ecosystem conservation (e.g. cap and trade) is in mind, the latter approach should be preferable. However, this will impose additional burdens to identify who provides ecosystem services, and thus who can be compensated for such service provision, especially in the case that one LCEU is managed by several sectors individually. The simplest assumption will be that each unit area provides the same level of services, but the more sophisticated ways to allocate them to each sector should be investigated, taking into account the demand of ecosystem services as noted.

Who receives ecosystem services is another important issue to be addressed. Tallis et al. (2012) proposes the concept of "serviceshed" to identify beneficiaries of regulating services. This is defined as the area "where a specific benefit is provided to a specific individual or group of people" and varies by the nature of service and by beneficiary; for instance, the serviceshed of climate regulation is the entire globe, while that of water quality is generally watershed. Identification of beneficiaries can be further complicated in the accounting context, especially considering a sector provisioning ecosystem services. The concept of serviceshed is well applied when regarding an ecosystem as a service provider, but the additional information on the trade of ecosystem services between specific sectors will be required when attributing its provision to an economic sector. However, such information will be extremely difficult to obtain constantly in the case that the serviceshed is large enough to involve multiple ecosystems and economic sectors. For example, consider a factory emitting an air pollutant that disperses far distances but can be filtered by ecosystems. It is clear that the factory enjoys filtration service provided by the sector managing those ecosystems somewhere, but a service provider is changeable depending on the wind direction and the ecological conditions. Put differently, it may be difficult to specify which factory enjoys the air filtration service generated in a specific place.

This complexity of provider and beneficiary of ecosystem services poses another challenge, namely, the national boundary of the accounting framework. Some ecosystem services can be provided to an individual or group of people beyond national boarders (e.g. filtration of air pollutants as shown previously and provision of clean water to the downstream of international rivers), which could be recognized as an export or import of ecosystem services under the national accounting framework. The carbon balance between emission and sequestration within the national territory will exemplify this idea. To record such trades of ecosystem service between countries, bilateral and multilateral cooperation to promote information sharing for securing technical consistency and data accuracy will be required, as is the case of climate change discussion which focuses on measuring six species of greenhouse gases with certain standards. On the basis of the SEEA-EEA, we need further intensive debate on various practical issues, ranging from measurement scopes to estimation techniques and sector specification, to develop an international standard of ecosystem accounting.

Bibliography

Balvanera, P., Siddique, I., Dee, L., Paquette, A., Isbell, F., Gonzalez, A., Byrnes, J., O'Connor, M.I., Hungate, B.A., and Griffin, J.N. (2014) 'Linking biodiversity and ecosystem services: current uncertainties and the necessary next steps', *BioScience*, Vol. 64, No. 1, pp. 49–57.

Costanza, R., and Daly, H. (1992) 'Natural capital and sustainable development', *Conservation Biology*, Vol. 6, No. 1., pp. 37–46.

Daly, H., and Farley, J. (2011) *Ecological economics: principles and applications*, 2nd edition, Washington, DC: Island Press.

Dasgupta, P. (2012) 'Natural capital as economic assets: a review', in UNEP and UNU-IHDP (eds.), *Inclusive wealth report 2012: measuring progress toward sustainability*, Cambridge: Cambridge University Press.

de Groot, R.S., Brander, L., van der Ploeg, S., Costanza, R., Bernard, F., Braat, L., Christie, M., Crossman, N., Ghermandi, A., Hein, L., Hussain, S., Kumar, P., McVittie, A., Portela, R., Rodriguez, L.C., ten Brink, P., and van Beukering, P. (2012) 'Global estimates of the value of ecosystems and their services in monetary units', *Ecosystem Services*, Vol. 1, No. 1, pp. 50–61.

European Commission (EC), Organisation for Economic Co-operation and Development (OECD), United Nations (UN), and World Bank (2014) *System of environmental-economic accounting 2012 experimental ecosystem accounting*. New York: United Nations.

European Environment Agency (2013) *The common international classification of ecosystem services (CICES) Version 4.3*. Available at: http://cices.eu/wp-content/ uploads/2012/07/CICES-V4-3-_-17-01-13.xlsx

Japan Research Institute (1998) *Research on the estimation of integrated environmental economic accounts*. Tokyo: Economic Planning Agency. (in Japanese).

Kabaya, K., and Okayasu, S. (2014) *Unveiling nature's gifts: measuring and visualising ecosystem services*. IGES Research Report No.2014–02. Institute for Global Environmental Strategies

Kareiva, P., Tallis, H., Ricketts, T.H., Daily, G.C., and Polasky, S. (eds.) (2011) *Natural capital: theory and practice of mapping ecosystem services*, Oxford: Oxford University Press.

MAFF (2000) *The monetary value of public interest functions of forests*. Available at: http://www.rinya.maff.go.jp/puresu/9gatu/kinou.html

Maes, J., Egoh, B., Willemen, L., Liquete, C., Vihervaara, P., Schägner, J.P., Grizzetti, B., Drakou, E.G., Notte, A.L., Zulian, G., Bouraoui, F., Paracchini, M.L., Braat, L., and Bidoglio, G. (2012) 'Mapping ecosystem services for policy support and decision making in the European Union', *Ecosystem Services*, Vol. 1, No. 1, pp. 31–39.

Ministry of Agriculture, Forestry and Fisheries (MAFF) (1998) *Results of the valuation of public interest functions of agriculture and farmlands using the replacement cost method*. Available at: http://www.maff.go.jp/primaff/koho/seika/nosoken/ nogyosogokenkyu/pdf/nriae1998-52-4-4.pdf

Ministry of the Environment of Japan (MOEJ) (2014) Assessment of the economic value of wetlands. Available at: http://www.env.go.jp/press/press.php?serial=18162

Office for National Statistics (ONS) (2013) *Measuring UK woodland ecosystem assets and ecosystem services, guidance and methodology*. Available at: http://www.ons. gov.uk/ons/guide-method/user-guidance/natural-capital/index.html

Science Council of Japan (2001) *Report on the valuation of the multiple functions of agricultural lands and forests for the global environment and human society*. Available at: http://www.scj.go.jp/ja/info/kohyo/division-5.html (in Japanese)

Scottish Wildlife Trust (2013) *World forum on natural capital website: 2013 highlights*. Available at: http://www.naturalcapitalforum.com/2013highlights

TEEB. (2010) *The economics of ecosystems and biodiversity: ecological and economic foundations*, edited by P. Kumar, London and Washington: Earthscan.

Tallis, H., Polasky, S., Lozano, J.S., and Wolny, S. (2012) 'Inclusive wealth accounting for regulating ecosystem services', in UNU-IHDP and UNEP (eds.), *Inclusive wealth report 2012: measuring progress toward sustainability*, Cambridge: Cambridge University Press.

United Nations (UN), European Union (EU), Food and Agriculture Organization of the United Nations (FAO), International Monetary Fund (IMF), Organisation for Economic Co-operation and Development (OECD), The World Bank (WB) (2014) *System of environmental-economic accounting 2012 central framework*, New York. Available at: http://unstats.un.org/unsd/envaccounting/seearev/chapterList.asp?volID=1

United Nations Environment Programme Finance Initiative (UNEP FI) and the Global Canopy Programme (GCP) (2012) *The natural capital declaration.* Available at: http://www.naturalcapitaldeclaration.org/about-the-natural-capital-declaration/#

Part 2

Improving sustainability and well-being indicators

6 Inclusive wealth and sustainability indicators

Masayuki Sato

This chapter introduces suggested sustainability indicators from a "capital approach." Various types of capital that act as a source of well-being were measured in the recent research projects. We discuss the pros and cons of the suggested indicators, and how to refine the measures.

6.1 Introduction

When we discuss sustainability, we need to consider environmental and societal factors as well economic factors. This is necessary because of the strong interaction between the economy, the environment, and the state of society. When the economy grows, air and water pollution, resource depletion, ecosystem destruction, and social problems often emerge. Therefore, what constitutes sustainable development and the extent to which our economy and society are sustainable must be considered from multiple perspectives, including economic, environmental, and societal viewpoints (Figure 6.1).

Regarding this point, discussion based on GDP alone is insufficient since, needless to say, it captures only economic factors. However, it is important to note that GDP is a kind of flow indicators. Because sustainability relates to the possibility of sustaining resources at a certain level, we need to focus on the source of the flow (i.e., the stock). This leads to two points to consider in the construction of the sustainability indicator. First, we must move from a solely economic indicator to a more inclusive indictor that includes environmental and societal factors. Second, we must shift from a flow indicator to a stock indicator.

There are many definitions of sustainable development, but the prevailing understanding of the term focuses on well-being not declining in the future due to current development. Well-being is key to understanding the sustainability issue. Well-being means quality of life (Dasgupta, 2004). When we consider the sources that contribute to people's quality of life, there is an extremely varied range of sources, and all should be true in some way. Hence, theoretically or conceptually, the whole stock of goods should be considered as a source of well-being. In the economics literature, the total of the various kinds of stocks has been called inclusive wealth. Human-made capital (economic physical capital), human capital, and natural capital are included in the inclusive

Figure 6.1 Necessity of considering economic, environmental, and societal factors in the concept of sustainable development

wealth, and even social capital, knowledge, institutions, culture, and time can be considered a part of inclusive wealth (Dasgupta, 2009) because all of them can contribute to producing well-being for people.

Obviously, it is impossible or extremely difficult to perfectly measure inclusive wealth. When we try to measure each component of inclusive wealth, there is serious measurement error. Nevertheless, much effort has been poured into better measurement of the various stocks required for the construction of an economic indicator of sustainability.[1]

Because these are pioneering challenges, it is easy to find the limits and problematic points of this approach, especially in terms of the lack of data and the data's incompleteness. However, we should evaluate the direction of this research using the following points. First, these research projects are based on solid economic theory. This means that we can create a better framework for the indicator that builds on the achievement of previous economic theory. In fact, many researchers have been trying to improve the indicators as part of economic and environmental studies (e.g., Fenichel and Abbott, 2014). Second, because of the data contribution of international institutions, available data has become richer in recent years. For example, the database "World Development Indicators" by the World Bank provides data on many kinds of capital, including human-made capital, human capital, and natural capital, as time series data for each country. This development has inspired researchers to tackle the challenges of creating better and wider measures of stocks, and has contributed to the methodological discussion as well. In the next section, we provide an understanding of the basic framework for the measurement and construction of a sustainability indicator, with a particular focus on economic factors.

6.2 The economic framework for constructing a sustainability indicator

Since Pearce and Atkinson (1993) introduced the framework for an indicator of weak sustainability, the theoretical model has become more sophisticated in subsequent studies. Among others, Arrow et al. (2012) and UNU-IHDP and UNEP (2012) provide a basic and clear theoretical framework.

First, we define U_τ as well-being at time τ, and V_t as discounted present value of the well-being at time t. We can write the relationship as (1), with the social discount rate δ.

$$V_t = \int_t^\infty U \cdot e^{-\delta(\tau-t)} d\tau \tag{1}$$

Note that both U and V are produced from inclusive capital. As previously discussed, inclusive capital constitutes any type of capital, which we here express by the vector $\mathbf{K}$. Then we can write V_t in another way as (2). Note that M is the resource allocation mechanism, which represents how efficiently and properly capital K is being used.

$$V_t = V(K_t, M, t) \tag{2}$$

Before defining the indicator, we will define the shadow price in (3), which represents the social value of the capital.

$$P_K = \frac{\partial V_t}{\partial K} \tag{3}$$

By totally differentiating and re-arranging (2), we obtain (4).

$$\frac{dV_t}{dt} = p_K \frac{dK_t}{dt} + \frac{\partial V_t}{\partial t} \tag{4}$$

As we define sustainable development as being "non-declining well-being," the sustainability condition requires that $dV_t/dt \geq 0$ for all t. Therefore, we need to make an indicator to measure the right-hand side (RHS) of (4).

The first term on the RHS of (4) is called genuine savings or adjusted net savings, which represents the temporal change in the value of inclusive capital. If we brush aside the second term on the RHS of (4), this alone can be an indicator of sustainability. The second term on the RHS of (4) is the contribution of time passing, reflecting technological progress, efficiency change, capital gain, and so on. Usually we measure these by using total factor productivity.[2] This model suggests that when we construct a sustainability indicator, we need to measure both the first and second term on the RHS of (4), and then confirm that they do not have non-negative values.

Empirically, the discussion points have focused on what kinds of capital stocks should be measured and how. Previously, Arrow et al. (2012) or UNU-IHDP and UNEP (2012) considered human-made capital, human capital, natural capital, knowledge, and time for measurement. In the next section, we will discuss the contents of each type of capital.

6.2.1 Human-made capital

Human-made capital, such as machinery and social infrastructure, has been measured as an economic statistic in many countries. This measurement has occurred because human-made capital is one of the most important inputs for production of goods and services, and information on the amount of human-made capital is necessary in classical economic models.

In principle, the amount of human-made capital increases through investment and decreases through depreciation. Thus, we can know the change in the amount of human-made capital from the net national investment or net national savings, which can be taken from the national economic accounting system. Though the accurate measurement of the net change in human-made capital is difficult, there are many data sources and studies on its measurement. We can utilize the measurement results for net national investment in constructing sustainability indicators.

6.2.2 Human capital

Since Becker (1964) introduced the concept of human capital, much research has focused on the measurement of human capital. Among others, education has been identified as an important factor for increasing human capital. Because the productivity of labor will improve by education, and the productivity improvement is related to salary, the measurement of human capital often uses data on education effort (e.g., the number of years of education) and wage. However, because accurate estimates are very difficult in many countries due to data availability and precision, proxies can be adopted for human capital accumulation. In the adjusted net savings data of the World Bank, education expenditure has been adopted as a proxy for human capital accumulation. It is no wonder that there are criticisms of this proxy, so improving the measurement of human capital in a realistic way is needed. For example, the Inclusive Wealth Index (IWI) of UNU-IHDP and UNEP tried to take another important factor, health, into account by using the value of statistical life. However, the impact of the health value was quite large in the results, and the health factor almost single-handedly determined the indicator; thus, to date they are omitting the health factor in their model. Overall, human capital is one of the most difficult and challenging components to construct and measure in the sustainability indicator, both in theory and in practice.

6.2.3 Natural capital

Natural capital also contributes to quality of life. Natural resources are necessary for producing goods and services, and a healthy environment is indispensable for human health and a comfortable life. The ecosystem is also essential for human beings; hence it should be included as a part of natural capital.

However, it is quite difficult to measure the amount of natural capital and to evaluate its social value. The reason for this difficulty lies in the presence of externalities and the absence of related indicators of value. Nevertheless, natural capital has attracted especially strong interest since the 1970s, following the publication of *Limits to Growth* by Rome Club and the two oil shocks. Today, the amount of some kinds of natural stocks, e.g., mineral resource and energy resources, are estimated and available in the construction of sustainability indicators. For example, Adjusted Net Savings (ANS) includes tin, gold, lead, zinc, steel, copper, nickel, silver, bauxite, and phosphorus as mineral resources. In addition, energy resources also gather much attention, and there are many estimates of existing energy reserves. We can access the estimates on the remaining coal, oil, and natural gas. Thus, information on these exhaustible natural capitals is relatively rich in the existing sustainability indicators. On the other hand, renewable natural capital is difficult to measure so far due to data availability and prominent externalities. As renewable capital, only forest resources have been taken into account in almost all indicators. However, the measurement is far from ideal estimates. As many researchers suggest, forests have multidimensional value in terms of their ecological value, aesthetic value, and so on. However, timber rent has been used as a proxy for forest value. This is a serious underestimate of forest value. When we use a low accounting price for forest depletion, the indictor will overestimate the status of a country's sustainability. In Section 6.3, we discuss how to estimate such kinds of values.

Furthermore, we need to broaden the coverage of the types of natural capital we measure. For example, fishery resources and natural energy resources are also important natural capital. In addition, water, land, and soil resources are also non-negligible forms of capital. Yang et al. (2015) showed the challenge of broadening the coverage of data capture and put forth a data imputation method. In particular, many researchers are interested in the introduction of ecosystem services, and Fenichel and Abbott (2014) tried to take this into account in sustainability indicators.

In addition, there is more work required to estimate the negative effect of natural capital depreciation, such as air and water pollution. The emission damage of CO_2 has been estimated by ANS and IWI, but challenges remain on how to measure the damage and how to distribute the measurement of damage. Because such environmental damage cannot be accounted for solely within one county and is dispersed all over the world, it must be treated as having the characteristics of a global public good.

6.2.4 *Other capital*

In practice, it can be futile to attempt to incorporate all kinds of capital into the calculation of the indicator. The best way is to select the most important and significant types of capital, while the other types of capitals are treated as error. Of course, as already suggested, the error should be small, and expanding the data coverage will work toward that end. If we can assume the error is small enough, the other types of capital, such as knowledge and institutions, can be measure by estimation of total factor productivity (TFP). If two countries have the same amount of each capital, the differences in the use of that capital will result in differences in the change of inclusive capital. Technology, efficiency, and consumption propensity determine TFP in inclusive capital change. In Chapter 7, we will discuss this in more detail and estimate the impact of TFP on the sustainability indicator.

6.3   Valuation of capital and shadow prices

6.3.1   Rent

The amounts of each type of capital discussed in the previous section have different units of measurement (e.g., tons, hectares, parts per million, etc.). However, when we construct an indicator we need to integrate all types of capital. In this procedure, we need an appropriate weight for adding and deleting each item. The ideal weight is the shadow price as we discussed in the Section 6.2; however, there are many difficulties in finding the accurate shadow price in practice.

Typically, it is convenient to adopt a monetary unit for the shadow price. Estimating environmental value in monetary units is its own field of environmental economics, and good techniques have been developed, such as revealed preference methods and stated preference methods. However, it is costly and time-consuming to estimate the value of the environment. Therefore, there always is incentive to use proxies for the shadow price of natural capital. The shadow prices of mineral, forest, and energy resources, for example, have been proxied by using rent. This is partly because these kinds of capital are traded in the market, and rich data on the transactions and market prices can be considered to reflect the true value. Of course, rent acts as a good proxy in some cases. However, as we discussed, when the capital has externalities it diverges from the true social value. It may be such a case for forest capital. In the end of this section, we will look at some examples from several countries.

6.3.2   Damage cost

Capital such as air quality has no related market price; therefore, rent cannot be used in the calculation. In such cases, we evaluate it by using damage cost. In the ANS of the World Bank, for example, the emission of CO_2 is evaluated by using the damage cost of global warming. What price to apply is subject to debate. The applied damage cost of CO_2 is 20 USD per ton in the ANS and 50 USD per ton in the IWI.

So far, there are few types of capital that we need to value by damage cost, but as we expand the types of capital covered to other forms of air and water pollution in the future, it becomes a bigger problem as to what price we should take as the damage cost.

6.3.3 Willingness to pay

Many types of natural capital, such as the ecosystem, have no market price and cause no specific damage to human beings. For these types of capital, we need some special techniques for their valuation. In studies on environmental economic valuation, willingness to pay (WTP) is a fundamental concept for assigning value to such capital. WTP is based on individual preference (utility) and represents the maximum amount of money a person will pay for a level of quality or change in quantity of the capital. Even for capital that has a market value, WTP can diverge from market price when the capital has externalities. In this sense, WTP is a good estimation of the social value of capital. For example, we suggest that because forest resources have externalities, the use of rent underestimates the value of forest stock. There are many studies that estimate WTP for forest stock, and value other than timber harvesting have been found. Barrio and Loureiro (2010) surveyed many studies on forest valuation, and propose a way to estimate the WTP for forest resources. Based on the results, WTP for uses of forests other than harvesting timber is significantly positive and is related, for example, to GDP. Based on Barrio and Loureiro's regression, the coefficient of GDP on the dependent variable, logarithm of mean WTP, for forest resources is 0.18. From these findings, the impact of adopting WTP instead of timber rent on the sustainability indicator can be seen for the case of India (Figure 6.2).

The top graph in Figure 6.2 represents how much using rent underestimates the valuation of forest depletion. This underestimation results in an overestimation of sustainability (the bottom graph). The impact is not negligible. The sustainability of India is not secure, even before 2000 when India's sustainability was judged to have shifted from sustainable to unsustainable.

6.3.4 Other issues on the shadow prices

In the previous subsection, we consider WTP as an appropriate unit to value capital. Recently, however, doubt about utility theory has been highlighted, and the relationship between subjective well-being and utility has been turned into an object of scientific analysis. If utility is not an appropriate reason to measure the shadow price, we need to adopt a different measurement that is appropriate. One candidate is the happiness or life satisfaction approach. We can find more discussion on these in Chapter 9. Subjective well-being and sustainability are interesting topics also in terms of how to measure the appropriate shadow prices.

Finally, another difficulty that should be pointed out for national indicators is that global public good and ills have spillover effects in other countries. It is difficult to capture this through national indicators because the emissions from one country cause damage to other countries, even if the other countries never emit the pollution. In this case, the other countries' sustainability actually become worse, but we cannot find the effect in the countries' indicator. One idea provided by the IWI is to sum up the damage by emissions all over the world, then to distribute the damage to each country. However, this method produces

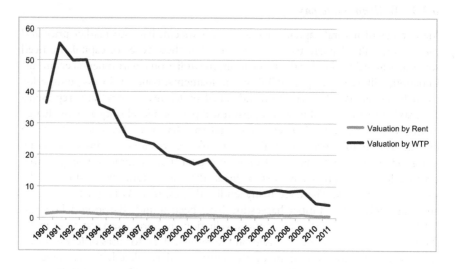

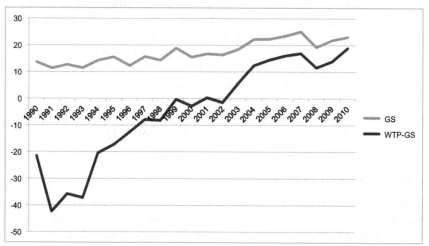

Figure 6.2 The valuation of forest depletion and sustainability indicator in India

another problem on how to distribute the damage costs. To make sustainability indicators more sophisticated, we need to appropriately consider international relationships in countries' sustainability.

6.4   Conclusion and remarks

In this chapter, we looked at the economic framework for constructing a sustainability indicator and discussed the empirical challenges in the measurement of various kinds of capital. Basically, the theoretical framework is sophisticated, but consideration of international dependency and the valuation of each type of capital are needed in future theoretical work.

Meanwhile, empirical studies should be conducted as first steps toward constructing a sustainability indicator. However, as shown by ANS and IWI, the accumulated data are becoming richer and the areas needing improvement are being recognized. One way to construct a better indicator is to maximally utilize the available data and complement the missing data by adequate statistical methods. In the next chapter, we demonstrate one idea on how to empirically improve the indicator with the data available today.

Notes

1 For example, the Inclusive Wealth Index (IDI) of UNU-IHDP and UNEP and the Adjusted Net Savings (ANS) of the World Bank are two excellent achievements. We will discuss the pros and cons of these previous studies later.
2 We will discuss this in detail in Chapter 7.

Bibliography

Arrow, K., Dasgupta, P., Goulder, L., Daily, G., Ehrlich, P., Heal, G., Levin, S., Mäler, L.G., Schneider, S., Starrett, D., and Walker, B. (2004) 'Are We Consuming Too Much?', *Journal of Economic Perspectives* 18(3): 147–172.

Arrow, K., Dasgupta, P., Goulder, L., Munford, K., and Oleson, K. (2012) 'Sustainability and the Measurement of Wealth', *Environment and Development Economics* 17: 317–353.

Arrow, K., Dasgupta, P., and Mäler, K.-G. (2003). 'Evaluating Projects and Assessing Sustainable Development in Imperfect Economies', *Environmental and Resource Economics* 26(4): 647–685.

Barrio, M., and M. L. Loureiro (2010) 'A meta-analysis of contingent valuation forest studies', *Ecological Economics* 69: 1023–1030.

Becker, G. (1964) *Human Capital: A Theoretical and Empirical Analysis, with Special Reference to Education*, New York, National Bureau of Economic Research.

Dasgupta, P., (2004) *Human Well-Being and the Natural Environment*, New York, Oxford University Press.

Dasgupta, P. (2009) 'The Welfare Economic Theory of Green National Accounts', *Environmental and Resource Economics* 42: 3–38.

Fenichel, E.P., and Abbott, J.K. (2014) 'Natural Capital: From Metaphor to Measurement', *Journal of the Association of Environmental and Resource Economists* 1(1): 1–27.

Hamilton, K. (2012) 'Comments on Arrow et al., "Sustainability and the measurement of wealth"', *Environment and Development Economics* 17: 356–361

Pearce, D.W., and Atkinson, G.D. (1993) 'Capital Theory and the Measurement of Sustainable Development: An Indicator of "Weak" Sustainability', *Ecological Economics* 8(2): 103–108.

United Nations University and International Human Dimensions Programme on Global Environmental Change and United Nations Environmental Program (2012) *Inclusive Wealth Report*, Cambridge, Cambridge University Press.

Yang, J., Sato, M., andManagi, S. (2015) 'National Sustainability Assessment: Measurement of Sustainable Index by Multiple Imputations', *Environmental Economics and Policy Studies*, forthcoming.

7 Growth of inclusive wealth

Masayuki Sato

This chapter discusses how the temporal movement of inclusive wealth paths can be estimated as an indicator of sustainability, with a focus on the adjustment for total factor productivity (TFP). We adjust the indicator to capture more inclusive capital and residuals. This chapter presents the methodology for estimating inclusive wealth-based TFP, which thus considers both technological progress and efficiency change, and evaluates the contribution of TFP to sustainable development.

7.1 Introduction

As introduced in Chapter 6, a promising economic approach for assessing sustainability is based on the evaluation of inclusive wealth (IW). The amount of IW is calculated by a weighted summation of all types of capital using their shadow prices, while the difference in wealth over time is referred to as genuine savings (GS).[1]

The theoretical basis of GS is the extension of the macroeconomic growth model, although it has also been used to examine sustainable development. In this regard, total factor productivity (TFP) is one of the most important topics. TFP is considered to be a residual, namely the remainder of the output change explained by inputs such as capital and labor. TFP thus accounts for changes in technological progress efficiency change and other economic parameters, such as social institutions and individual preferences.

TFP has been suggested to play an important role in the assessment of sustainability using GS (Arrow et al., 2004). However, few empirical studies have analyzed the contribution of TFP to GS. For example, although Arrow et al. (2004, 2012) incorporate TFP into their GS calculations, they estimate TFP using traditional growth accounting techniques (i.e., using capital and labor as inputs and GDP as an output). Such a GDP-based calculation of TFP ignores the effects derived from the utilization of human capital and natural capital, which are the key variables in their capital approach.

By contrast, because the essence of GS as an indicator of sustainability lies in its inclusiveness, the combination of human-made capital, human capital, and natural capital is crucial in its calculation. Xepapadeas and Vouvaki (2009) find that the externalities of natural capital are considerable in TFP estimations, which has the effect of driving traditional TFP downward. Because Xepapadeas and Vouvaki focus on the production of GDP, however, their externality-adjusted TFP calculations cannot be used in the direct adjustment of GS.

To focus on the effects derived from IW utilization and the temporal change in the amounts, we estimate TFP in this chapter using GS as an output and human-made capital, human capital, and natural capital as inputs. We assume a correspondence between capital assets and GS and emphasize the concept of IW. This approach is based on the observation that countries may have different levels of performance based on their GS indicators, despite having the same capital assets. In other words, we examine why the ability to realize sustainable development (i.e., non-negative GS) differs between countries despite them having identical productive bases. An important hypothesis in this regard is that the way in which capital assets are used and combined differs from one country to the next. Some countries efficiently use their endowed capital, with appropriate technological advancements and future-oriented stock consumption schemes, whereas others may inefficiently use their valuable capital. These differences can affect the countries' respective TFP and TFP-adjusted GS indicators. In this chapter, we discuss a framework for estimating a more elaborate version of TFP. Then we compare the IW–TFP-adjusted indicator to the GDP–TFP-adjusted indicator. Finally, we discuss the implication of considering TFP with respect to the literature on sustainability indicators.

7.2   Total factor productivity and using inclusive wealth or genuine savings as indicators of sustainability

7.2.1   *Methodology*

Technological progress and efficiency change are usually measured in the economic growth literature by using TFP. However, for sustainable development indicators like GS, only annual data are available. As suggested by Arrow et al. (2004), TFP should have a non-negligible effect when assessing sustainability; thus it is important to estimate the TFP along with the annual indicators.

Arrow et al. (2004) recognized that traditional TFP does not account for the contribution of natural capital, and as a result the study merges the TFP data on human-made capital and human capital of Collins and Bosworth (1996) and Klenow and Rodriguez-Clare (1997) with the output (consumption) elasticities of the two types of capital. Arrow et al. (2004) mentions the possibility of the misspecification of TFP and the capital elasticities as a result of neglecting natural capital. Overestimating the contribution of TFP in wealth accounting is suggested accordingly.

In this chapter, we critically consider the handling of TFP in the previous studies and extend the consideration of IW. For example, in actuality important technological progress and efficiency improvements have been made in the use of natural capital (e.g., technology for energy savings and CO_2 emission reductions), which should contribute to the sustainability indicator. From another perspective, reductions in consumption should contribute to conserving natural capital; hence, reduced consumption should contribute to increasing sustainability indicators. In both cases, GDP-based TFP fails to measure the contributions of technological progress and efficiency changes because the changes in natural capital are not considered.

These examples imply that countries have differing abilities to produce sustainable well-being from a given amount of IW. Even if two countries have the same amount of IW, a country with higher environmental technology can produce more sustainable well-being than another country without such technology.

Our focus in this chapter is to estimate IW-based TFP. This estimation enables more suitable adjustment of the annual indicator of sustainability.

Against this background, we consider the mapping from the input (IW data) and the output (GS data), and term this IW-based TFP. Because manufactured goods are closely related to the depletion of natural capital, it is possible for GDP-based TFP to indicate good performance in sustainability and IW-based TFP to indicate poor performance.[2] In such a case, as Arrow et al. (2004) point out, the adjustment of the GDP-based TFP may lead to an overestimation of sustainability performance for certain countries. In this regard, when the residual is used to adjust GS rather than GDP, we must also consider consumption. For example, let us assume that two countries both have the same amount of capital stock (IW) and the same output (GDP). If one country has a relatively low level of consumption and high investment, its GS should thus be higher than the other. Because our focus lies in the sustainable use of capital assets, and because GS is calculated using capital stock change, we should measure the ability of a country to gain GS by measuring the shift from capital assets to GS. In this sense, IW-based TFP is particularly suited for the adjustment of GS,[3] including changes in consumption propensity, and it reflects improvements in capital stock usage toward sustainability. For comparison, we present the empirical results for IW-based and GDP-based TFP.

Moreover, we adopt the Malmquist index as a measurement of TFP in order to investigate the mapping from capital assets to wealth changes. The Malmquist index is suitable for assessing the connection between inputs and outputs under multivariate input inefficiency. By considering IW as an input, we inevitably need to specify the estimation model with multivariates. In addition, the inefficiency of resource use and technological progress should also be estimated. For these purposes, the Malmquist index is chosen as the simplest and best-suited index. Using distance function specification, our problem can be formulated as follows:

$$T(t) \equiv \left\{ (x_t, y_t) : x_t \text{ can produce } y_t \right\} \tag{1}$$

Let $x = (x^1, \ldots x^M) \in R_+^M$ and $y = (y^1, \ldots y^N) \in R_+^N$ be the vectors of inputs and outputs, respectively. The technology set, which is defined by (1), consists of all feasible input vectors x_t and output vectors y_t at time t, and satisfies certain axioms, which are sufficient to define meaningful distance functions. The distance function is defined as

$$d_{T(t)}(x_t, y_t) = \min\{\delta; (x_t, y_t / \delta) \in T(t)\}, \tag{2}$$

where δ is the maximal proportional amount that y_t can be expanded given technology $T(t)$. This formulation produces an output-oriented distance function. Data envelopment analysis (DEA) is used to estimate the distance function under constant returns to scale (CRS) by solving the following optimization problem (Managi, 2003):

$$d_{T(t)}(x_t, y_t) = \max_{\delta, \lambda} \delta$$
$$s.t. \quad \Upsilon_t \lambda \geq \frac{y_i^t}{\delta} \tag{3}$$
$$X_t \lambda \leq x_i^t$$
$$\lambda \geq 0,$$

where δ is the measure of efficiency for country i in year t, λ is an N × 1 vector of weights, and Υ_t and X_t are the vectors of outputs y_t and inputs x_t. To estimate productivity changes over time, several distance functions are used for the input–output vector for period $t + 1$ and technology in period t. The Malmquist index (M_0) is defined as (4), with several distance functions:

$$M_O(y_t, x_t, y_{t+1}, x_{t+1}) = \left[\frac{d_O^t(y_{t+1}, x_{t+1})}{d_O^t(y_t, x_{tt})} \times \frac{d_O^{t+1}(y_{t+1}, x_{t+1})}{d_O^{t+1}(y_t, x_t)} \right]^{1/2} \tag{4}$$

where d_O represents the geometric distance to the frontier, which is the best available technology in the correspondence from the given inputs to outputs.

Hence, a country on the frontier can be considered as the most sustainable under the prevailing resource constraints. Similarly, the distance to the frontier represents the inefficiency of resource use. The rationale for this is that another country (i.e., a country at or closer to the frontier) can perform better under the same resource constraints.

The estimation of this index is done using DEA, a non-parametric estimation method. M_0 can be divided into two components. The first ratio represents efficiency changes and the second represents technological changes. Based on this formulation, we estimate the Malmquist index in the mapping from capital assets to GS as follows:

$$f : \{P_M M, P_H H, P_N N\} \rightarrow GS \tag{5}$$

In some cases, countries have the same levels of capital assets but different levels of sustainability because of the ways that they use capital assets or their different saving rates. This difference is captured by the Malmquist index, which, for this purpose, is reformulated as

$$
M_O\left(GS_t, P_M M_t, L_t, P_N N_t, GS_{t+1}, P_M M_{t+1}, L_{t+1}, P_N N_{t+1}\right)
$$
$$
= \left[\frac{d_O^t\left(GS_{t+1}, P_M M_{t+1}, L_{t+1}, P_N N_{t+1}\right)}{d_O^t\left(GS_t, P_M M_t, L_t, P_N N_{t+1}\right)}\right.
$$
$$
\left. \times \frac{d_O^{t+1}\left(GS_{t+1}, P_M M_{t+1}, L_{t+1}, P_N N_{t+1}\right)}{d_O^{t+1}\left(GS_t, P_M M_t, L_t, P_N N_t\right)}\right]^{1/2} \tag{6}
$$

Based on this reformulation, in this chapter we discuss the potential increase in GS in each country. Because this index is measured as the difference between two years, a value greater than (or less than) one means an improvement (reduction) in TFP. Using this index allows us to examine the contribution of TFP to GS by country.

For comparison, we estimate GDP-based TFP and observe the differences between the two types of TFP. Equation 7 is estimated based on the reformulated Malmquist index:

$$
M_O\left(GDP_t, P_M M_t, L_t, GDP_{t+1}, P_M M_{t+1}, L_{t+1}\right)
$$
$$
= \left[\frac{d_O^t\left(GDP_{t+1}, P_M M_{t+1}, L_{t+1}\right)}{d_O^t\left(GDP_t, P_M M_t, L_t\right)} \times \frac{d_O^{t+1}\left(GDP_{t+1}, P_M M_{t+1}, L_{t+1}\right)}{d_O^{t+1}\left(GDP_t, P_M M_t, L_t\right)}\right]^{1/2} \tag{7}
$$

This equation indicates the feasible technology of producing goods with fewer inputs. It is thus possible that GDP-based TFP differs from IC-based TFP because the GS in TFP may increase for all types of capital in IW.

7.2.2 *Data*

For estimating IW-based TFP, we rely on the GS values for 208 countries and regions from 1970 to 2009 in the World Development Indicators (WDI) database.[4] As previously noted, GS in the WDI database is defined as the sum of human-made capital investment (e.g., net national savings: dM_t/d_t), human capital investment (e.g., education expenditure: dH_t/d_t), and the damage to or degradation of certain natural resources (e.g., energy depletion, mineral depletion, forest depletion, and CO_2 emissions: dN_t/d_t).[5]

As both stock and flow data are involved, we next create datasets for capital stock in each country and each year. In this chapter, the stock calculation starts with the results presented by Kunte et al. (1998), which provides an estimation of per capita capital stock in 1994, valued in 1990 US dollars. In particular, the estimation includes data for subsoil stock and timber and non-timber forest stock. Based on these stock data, we calculate the annual amount of stocks using flow data from the WDI database (i.e., depletion of energy resources, minerals, and forests, and damage caused by CO_2 emissions).

The data for subsoil stock presented in Kunte et al. (1998) correspond to the sum of energy and mineral depletion derived from the WDI. The data for timber and non-timber forest stock correspond to forest depletion (or accumulation) from the WDI database. Based on these data, we calculate the values of each year's capital stock. Note that we calculate all variables in 2000 US dollars using 1990 and 2000 deflators.[6] We calculate IW-based TFP for only countries that have a complete panel dataset.

7.3   Results

Based on the estimate procedure explained in Section 7.2.1, we estimate each country's IW-based TFP for all years in the dataset. Then by averaging each year's IW-based TFP, we observe the rough effect of using IW-based TFP on the sustainability indicator (Table 7.1).

Using the estimates of the IW-based TFP estimation, we proceed to calculate the growth rates of per capita IW. Here, we follow the same process as that in Arrow et al. (2004), with the exception of the use of TFP growth from Collins and Bosworth (1996), which was based on GDP output. The result of the calculation is presented in Table 7.2.

Table 7.1 Ranking and summary of estimated TFP

1	Mexico	1.4517	2	United States	1.1333			
3	Pakistan	1.0979	4	Japan	1.0534	5	Thailand	1.0412
6	Venezuela, RB	1.0383	7	Canada	1.0226	8	Australia	1.0182
9	Ecuador	1.0159	10	Botswana	1.0149	11	Bolivia	1.0147
12	Mauritania	1.0139	13	United Kingdom	1.0125	14	Malaysia	1.0112
15	Portugal	1.0107	16	Greece	1.0103	17	Belgium	1.0101
18	Guatemala	1.0095	19	Nicaragua	1.0092	20	Honduras	1.0083
21	Rwanda	1.0082	22	France	1.0071	23	Dominican Rep.	1.0068
24	Senegal	1.0065	25	Ghana	1.0060	26	Netherlands	1.0047
27	Turkey	1.0043	28	Jamaica	1.0033	29	Finland	1.0024
30	Sri Lanka	1.0014	31	Spain	1.0009	32	Sweden	0.9998
33	Norway	0.9994	34	Philippines	0.9993	35	Benin	0.9990
36	China	0.9981	37	Austria	0.9973	38	Ireland	0.9917
39	Denmark	0.9917	40	Korea, Rep.	0.9857	41	Morocco	0.9768
42	India	0.9724	43	Kenya	0.9252			

All countries	TFP in GS	Efficiency Change in GS	Technological Change in GS
1970s	1.0284	1.0275	1.0089
1980s	1.0414	1.0651	0.9872
1990s	0.9975	0.9571	1.0482
2000s	1.0138	1.0443	0.9847

Table 7.2 Growth rates of per capita IW-based TFP

Country	GS per GNI (1)	Growth Rate of Unadjusted Genuine Wealth (2)	Population Growth Rate (3)	Growth Rate of Per Capita Genuine Wealth (Before Adjusted TFP) (4)	TFP Growth Rate (5)	Growth Rate of Per Capita Genuine Wealth (After TFP Adjustment) (6)
1 Australia	7.2549	1.7292	1.3434	0.3858	2.7413	3.1271
2 Austria	13.6654	1.9678	0.2785	1.6892	0.3395	2.0287
3 Belgium	13.8743	2.6183	0.2261	2.3922	1.7085	4.1007
4 Benin	0.4443	0.0115	3.1947	-3.1832	0.0443	-3.1389
5 Bolivia	-2.0251	0.5407	2.2559	-1.7153	0.7102	-1.0051
6 Botswana	28.1134	1.2954	2.5422	-1.2469	-0.1059	-1.3527
7 Canada	9.7347	2.4631	1.1911	1.2720	4.2694	5.5415
8 China	15.7264	1.2460	1.3200	-0.0740	9.1296	9.0556
9 Denmark	11.3874	1.5924	0.2569	1.3355	0.3785	1.7140
10 Dominican Rep	13.1614	0.9328	2.0085	-1.0756	0.4054	-0.6702
11 Ecuador	-7.1698	1.1150	2.3060	-1.1910	0.1278	-1.0632
12 Finland	12.9313	1.1568	0.3781	0.7787	0.6385	1.4172
13 France	13.6412	2.2584	0.5052	1.7532	1.1935	2.9467
14 Ghana	2.0095	0.0298	2.6281	-2.5983	0.2045	-2.3938
15 Greece	14.2537	1.7052	0.6854	1.0198	0.9632	1.9830
16 Guatemala	2.4897	0.2751	2.4294	-2.1544	0.0056	-2.1488
17 Honduras	14.0405	0.2110	2.9879	-2.7769	-0.0773	-2.8542
18 India	10.2321	0.5854	2.0083	-1.4229	1.0627	-0.3602
19 Ireland	14.7483	2.6853	0.9521	1.7332	0.2752	2.0084
20 Jamaica	9.1327	0.1972	1.0120	-0.8147	0.1644	-0.6503

21	Japan	19.1053	23.6921	0.5771	23.1150	2.1735	25.2884
22	Kenya	12.5420	0.1216	3.2436	-3.1220	3.1936	0.0717
23	Korea, Rep.	22.2910	2.8993	1.1859	1.7134	1.2038	2.9173
24	Malaysia	13.4488	1.6793	2.4701	-0.7908	0.9132	0.1224
25	Mauritania	-17.3458	0.7089	2.5638	-1.8548	0.1184	-1.7364
26	Mexico	4.8379	0.6814	2.0521	-1.3707	165.7486	164.3780
27	Morocco	14.5214	1.0958	2.0334	-0.9375	-0.1483	-1.0858
28	Netherlands	16.1763	3.3185	0.6391	2.6794	0.3015	2.9809
29	Nicaragua	-7.9548	-0.0059	2.4566	-2.4625	0.0321	-2.4304
30	Norway	14.0762	3.0169	0.4939	2.5230	0.6574	3.1804
31	Pakistan	9.1019	0.4778	2.7293	-2.2516	1.8454	-0.4062
32	Philippines	15.0021	0.8702	2.3767	-1.5065	0.4109	-1.0956
33	Portugal	9.2816	0.6521	0.5952	0.0569	0.8032	0.8601
34	Rwanda	5.6369	0.3948	2.6083	-2.2135	-0.0815	-2.2950
35	Senegal	-0.4151	-0.0680	2.7137	-2.7817	0.1813	-2.6005
36	Spain	12.2155	1.7027	0.6762	1.0265	0.9035	1.9300
37	Sri Lanka	14.8434	0.4356	1.3563	-0.9208	-0.0157	-0.9364
38	Sweden	16.1993	2.4656	0.3180	2.1475	0.4843	2.6319
39	Thailand	19.7857	1.0142	1.6390	-0.6248	7.1610	6.5362
40	Turkey	15.2429	0.0202	2.0663	-2.0461	1.1121	-0.9340
41	United Kingdom	8.3496	1.9964	0.2053	1.7911	2.1913	3.9824
42	United States	8.7533	2.3784	1.0556	1.3227	8.3258	9.6485
43	Venezuela, RB	-3.1724	0.1491	2.6329	-2.4838	14.4187	11.9349

Note: The TFP growth rate (column 5) is calculated as IC-based TFP growth × 1.73 for the purpose of comparison with Arrow et al. (2004).

1. The average for all sample countries is 5.61. This implies the tendency of the whole sample in this chapter to be judged as sustainable. However, it should be noted that there is considerable variation among countries. Attention should therefore be paid to the interdependency among them, and care should be taken when drawing general conclusions about global sustainability.

Contrary to the findings presented by Arrow et al. (2004), we demonstrate that many countries have positive TFP growth rates even though the respective values of their natural capital have been taken into account.

Using the same methodology, we next calculate GDP-based TFP, which can serve as a measure of productivity based on how many economic goods and services are produced using the same types of capital as inputs. As Table 7.3

Table 7.3 Comparison of IC-based TFP and GDP-based TFP adjustment

	IC-based TFP growth rate	GDP-based TFP growth rate	IC-based TFP adjusted IW growth	GDP-based TFP adjusted IW growth
Australia	2.7413	0.0203	3.1271	0.4060
Austria	0.3395	0.1746	2.0287	1.8638
Belgium	1.7085	0.2589	4.1007	2.6511
Benin	0.0443	0.1846	−3.1389	−2.9986
Bolivia	0.7102	0.2183	−1.0051	−1.4970
Botswana	−0.1059	0.1491	−1.3527	−1.0977
Canada	4.2694	0.1007	5.5415	1.3727
China	9.1296	−0.0905	9.0556	−0.1645
Denmark	0.3785	0.1226	1.7140	1.4581
Dominican Rep	0.4054	0.0185	−0.6702	−1.0571
Ecuador	0.1278	0.2135	−1.0632	−0.9774
Finland	0.6385	0.3037	1.4172	1.0824
France	1.1935	0.1643	2.9467	1.9175
Ghana	0.2045	−0.3157	−2.3938	−2.9140
Greece	0.9632	0.4449	1.9830	1.4647
Guatemala	0.0056	0.2021	−2.1488	−1.9522
Honduras	−0.0773	0.1709	−2.8542	−2.6060
India	1.0627	−0.3871	−0.3602	−1.8100
Ireland	0.2752	0.1606	2.0084	1.8938
Jamaica	0.1644	0.9465	−0.6503	0.1318
Japan	2.1735	0.7033	25.2884	23.8182
Kenya	3.1936	0.4161	0.0717	−2.7059
Korea. Rep.	1.2038	0.2017	2.9173	1.9151
Malaysia	0.9132	0.3210	0.1224	−0.4698
Mauritania	0.1184	0.0611	−1.7364	−1.7937
Mexico	165.7486	0.3336	164.3780	−1.0371
Morocco	−0.1483	0.4411	−1.0858	−0.4964
Netherlands	0.3015	0.0437	2.9809	2.7231

Nicaragua	0.0321	0.4469	−2.4304	−2.0156
Norway	0.6574	0.1768	3.1804	2.6999
Pakistan	1.8454	6.4999	−0.4062	4.2483
Philippines	0.4109	0.0121	−1.0956	−1.4944
Portugal	0.8032	0.5224	0.8601	0.5793
Rwanda	−0.0815	3.2663	−2.2950	1.0528
Senegal	0.1813	0.3170	−2.6005	−2.4647
Spain	0.9035	0.2826	1.9300	1.3091
Sri Lanka	−0.0157	−0.2191	−0.9364	−1.1399
Sweden	0.4843	0.0502	2.6319	2.1978
Thailand	7.1610	0.1741	6.5362	−0.4508
Turkey	1.1121	0.3114	−0.9340	−1.7347
United Kingdom	2.1913	0.1727	3.9824	1.9637
United States	8.3258	0.1105	9.6485	1.4333
Venezuela. RB	14.4187	−0.1228	11.9349	−2.6066

Table 7.4 Comparison results

	This study		Arrow et al. (2004)	
	Before TFP adjustment	After TFP adjustment	Before TFP adjustment	After TFP adjustment
India	−1.42	−0.36	−0.57	0.54
Pakistan	−2.25	−0.41	−1.35	0.59
China	−0.07	9.06	2.06	8.33
United Kingdom	1.79	3.98	1.30	2.29
United States	1.32	9.65	0.72	0.75

Note: The values of this study are derived from Table 7.2.

shows, the IW- and GDP-based TFP values are quite different. This reflects that GDP-based TFP does not include technological advancements and efficiency change in the utilization of natural capital or frugality in consumption. Table 7.3 also suggests that the evaluation of sustainability can be altered by the adoption of TFP. As the concept of GS includes not only human-made capital but also human and natural capital, in addition to the consumption rate it is more plausible to use IW-based TFP when we assess sustainability using the GS indicator.

Now we compare the calculation of the sustainability indicator in this chapter based on IW-based TFP and that of Arrow et al. (2004) in five countries (Table 7.4).

For instance, Arrow et al. (2004) suggest that the wealth growth of India and Pakistan is not conducted in a sustainable manner. However, when using the TFP growth rate, it appears that both countries are on a sustainable development path. Yet this study suggests that this is not true, even if the TFP growth rate is considered. The results in Table 7.4 indeed suggest that the previous adjustment using GDP-based TFP leads to an overestimation of the growth rate of per capita wealth.

For China, this study suggests that before the TFP adjustment, its path for wealth growth can be evaluated as not sustainable. Although we find the opposite result when the TFP growth rate is considered, both studies suggest sustainable development paths for the UK and the US. Other countries cannot be compared to the previous study to examine TFP effect; however, adjusting the change in IW by using IW-based TFP should be a better indicator for assessing sustainability.

7.4   Implications and discussions

In this chapter we calculated IW-based TFP as a Malmquist index using multiple data sources, including the WDI database. We stress that IW-based TFP can be very different than GDP-based TFP, as the former considers both human and natural capital in addition to the human-made capital primarily considered in the latter. Compared with previous studies that have used GDP-based TFP, our results suggest that the respective sustainability values could be inflated. Specifically, we find that certain countries such as India and Pakistan are not sustainable, in contrast to the findings of previous researchers.

Overall, TFP is found to be significantly different among the investigated countries, reflecting their varied levels of technological development and efficiency of resource use. In conclusion, we recommend adopting IW-based TFP to assess sustainable development from the perspective of wealth accounting, including the use of GS indicators. GDP-based TFP may lead to either overestimation or underestimation due to the exclusion of natural capital.

Although this chapter provided an alternative TFP concept and estimation methodology, future research should aim to analyze factors that contribute to sustainable development, such as consumption. When societies consume less and invest more in future generations, the sustainability level (i.e., GS) should improve. Another scholarly challenge is to identify the consumption effect. In this chapter, consumption did not have significant effect on IW-based TFP. However, consumption level is directly related to the sustainability of development because it identifies how much investment is being done. The effect of consumption on sustainability should always be kept in mind.

For more sophisticated sustainability studies, an expanded dataset is also needed. However, we acknowledge the complexity of including factors that were omitted from previous studies, such as ecological stock in natural capital and health in human capital.

Notes

1   GS is also called genuine investment (Arrow et al., 2003), inclusive investment (Dasgupta, 2007), and adjusted net savings (World Bank's World Development Indicators). All these terms indicate a change in wealth as a source of well-being.

A recent research project by the United Nations Environment Programme developed an IW index and stressed the difference between this concept and GS in theoretical assumptions and empirical techniques (see United Nations University-International Human Dimensions Programme and United Nations Environment Program, 2012). However, because we need complete panel data for the estimation of TFP in this chapter, we use data provided by the World Bank.

2 For instance, in the case of technological progress that is economically beneficial but environmentally harmful, GDP-based TFP is good, but IW-based TFP may not be. In the empirical examination in this chapter, we confirm whether these two TFP values are different.

3 It may be misleading to use IW-based TFP because this concept includes not only production but also output use. Because we follow the same procedure for estimation, however, we use the term TFP.

4 http://databank.worldbank.org/

5 In the analysis presented, we use GS data without CO_2 emissions damage data. If we had included such damage, our sample size would have become very small because most CO_2 emissions data are unavailable.

6 Hence, our dataset evaluates all variables in 2000 US dollars.

Bibliography

Arrow, K., P. Dasgupta, L. Goulder, G. Daily, P. Ehrlich, G. Heal, S. Levin, K-G. Mäler, S. Schneider, D. Starrett, and B. Walker (2004), 'Are we consuming too much?', *Journal of Economic Perspectives*, 18(3): 147–172.

Arrow, K., P. Dasgupta, L. Goulder, K. Munford, and K. Oleson (2012), 'Sustainability and the measurement of wealth', *Environment and Development Economics*, 17: 317–353.

Arrow, K., P. Dasgupta, and K.-G. Mäler (2003), 'Evaluating projects and assessing sustainable development in imperfect economies', *Environmental and Resource Economics*, 26(4): 647–685.

Collins, S., and B. Bosworth (1996), 'Economic growth in East Asia: accumulation versus assimilation', *Brookings Paper on Economic Activity*, 2: 135–203.

Dasgupta, P. (2007), *Economics: a very short introduction*, New York: Oxford University Press.

Klenow, P.J., and A. Rodriguez-Clare (1997), 'The neoclassical revival in growth economics: Has it gone too far?', In B. Bernanke and J. Rotemberg (eds.), *NBER macroeconomics annual 1997*, Cambridge, MA: MIT Press.

Kunte, A, K. Hamilton, J. Dixon, and M. Clemens (1998), 'Estimating national wealth: methodology and results', *World Bank Discussion Paper*, Washington, D.C.

Managi, S. (2003), 'Luenberger and Malmquist productivity indices in Japan, 1955–1995', *Applied Economics Letters*, 10: 581–584.

United Nations University-International Human Dimensions Programme and United Nations Environment Program (2012), *Inclusive wealth report 2012*, Cambridge: Cambridge University Press.

Xepapadeas, A., and D. Vouvaki (2009), 'Total factor productivity growth when factors of production generate environmental externalities', *Fondazione Eni Enrico Mattei Working Papers*, 281: 1–31.

8 The Better Life Index and measurement of well-being

Hideyuki Mizobuchi

8.1 Introduction

Per capita GDP has long been used as a proxy measure of well-being. However, it is now widely recognized that income data provide a partial perspective on the array of factors that affect people's lives. Given the issues with using GDP per capita as a measure of well-being, many researchers have been searching for alternative measures. In particular, the importance of incorporating a wider range of socio-economic conditions rather than income alone is now widely recognized.

Research over the last two decades has substantially improved our understanding of these conditions. The OECD has actively led this line of research, seeking an alternative measure of well-being. On the OECD's fiftieth anniversary, which was held under the theme 'Better Policies for Better Lives', the organization launched the OECD Better Life Initiative. They identified 11 dimensions as essential to well-being and released 24 headline indicators which capture distinct aspects of well-being (OECD, 2011). The dimensions cover material living conditions, such as income and wealth, as well as quality of life (QOL) factors, such as community, environment, and work–life balance.

The web-based tool *Your Better Life Index*, a key instrument of the OECD Better Life Initiative, profiles the 34 OECD member countries and 2 non-member countries across the 11 well-being indicators.[1] Each well-being indicator whose range is between 0 and 10 aggregates multiple headline indicators classified under the corresponding dimension. In this chapter, the OECD Better Life Index (BLI) refers to 11 well-being indicators and 24 headline indicators.

Each dimension of well-being is explored and analysed in detail in OECD (2011). However, evaluating overall well-being by summarizing the 11 individual indicators is the responsibility of the users of the statistics.[2] In this chapter, we illustrate two approaches to measuring and analysing overall well-being based on a comprehensive set of indicators covering multiple aspects of people's lives. Although we use the OECD BLI, our approaches are applicable to any comprehensive well-being dataset.

The first approach is to aggregate individual headline indicators that capture a specific socio-economic aspect of life into a single composite indicator. Among a number of construction techniques of the composite indicator, the 'benefit of the doubt' approach (BOD) has received increased attention from researchers, as it avoids subjectivity in the determination of weights (Cherchye et al., 2004;

Cherchye et al., 2007; Despotis 2005a, 2005b; Mahlberg and Obersteiner, 2001; and OECD 2008). Under BOD, the weights are country-specific and are endogenously determined such that they maximize the value of each country's resulting composite indicator. Thus, larger weights are given to the individual indicators (topics of well-being) on which each country performs well. The core idea is that a good relative score of a country on an individual indicator shows that it considers that individual indicator as relatively important. Therefore, a country cannot make excuses for lower composite indicator scores by pointing out a harmful or unfair weighting scheme under the international comparison based on BOD.

The second approach is to use subjective well-being among headline indicators as a measure of overall well-being.[3] In this approach, investigating the relationship between subjective well-being and the remaining headline indicators enables us to assess the sources of differences in subjective well-being across countries. By using a comprehensive set of headline indicators, we can fully explain cross-country variations.[4] It explains what makes some countries rich and others poor.[5] The study shows that non-material aspects of people's lives, such as social relations with family and friends, in addition to material aspects, such as income and jobs, are important for determining subjective well-being. Frey (2008) surveys the effect of various factors on subjective well-being.

This chapter is presented as follows. Section 8.2 explains data released by the OECD Better Life Initiative. Section 8.3 explains the approach based on the composite well-being indicators and presents empirical findings based on this approach. Section 8.4 explains the approach based on subjective well-being and presents empirical findings based on this approach. Section 8.5 concludes.

8.2 OECD Better Life index

The search for measures of a well-being alternative to GDP per capita has received growing attention. The Commission on the Measurement of Economic Performance and Social Progress, appointed by former French president Nicholas Sarkozy in 2008, discusses previous studies and unresolved issues with measuring well-being.

Drawing upon the recommendations of the commission (Stiglitz et al., 2009), in 2011 the OECD's Better Life Initiative released multiple indicators to evaluate people's lives in each member country based on 11 socio-economic dimensions identified as essential to well-being. We call these indicators the OECD BLI. The data were updated in 2012 and 2013 to include the latest data with additional indicators. The present study adopts the latest version of the data, which was released in 2013. These data cover 36 countries, including Brazil and Russia.

As mentioned previously, the BLI consists of two types of indicators: 11 well-being indicators and 24 headline indicators. The 24 headline indicators evaluate the socio-economic conditions of people in each country on dimensions such as air quality, water quality, and students' test scores. These are classified under 11 more general socio-economic dimensions, such as *environment* and *education*. Thus, each dimension of well-being is characterized by multiple headline indicators, which are expressed in different units such as dollars, years, and number of people. Table 8.1 reports the descriptive statistics for the 24 headline indicators

Table 8.1 Summary statistics of variables and their correlations with subjective well-being

Variables	Unit	Mean					Std. Dev.	Correlation[a]
		Total	Male	Female	High	Low	Total	Total
Housing								
Dwellings without basic facilities	%	2.3					3.2	−0.47
Housing expenditure	%	20.8					3.0	0.10
Rooms per person	%	1.6					0.4	0.60
Income								
Household net adjusted disposable income	current PPP US$	22,383			43,877	8,778	6,943	0.56
Household net financial wealth	current PPP US$	36,710					27,426	0.42
Gini coefficient for disposable income[b]	[0, 1]	0.3					0.1	0.34
Jobs								
Employment rate	%	66.1	72.5	59.8	81.6	45.4	7.2	0.71
Job security	%	10.6	10.6	10.5			4.8	0.04
Long-term unemployment rate	%	3.1	3.2	3.1	1.8	5.5	2.6	−0.58
Personal earnings	current US$	33,402	36,192	29,527	43,137	20,140	12,371	0.58
Community								
Quality of support network	%	89.6	89.0	90.2	92.9	84.5	5.7	0.54
Education n								
Educational attainment	%	74.0	74.8	73.3			17.0	0.19
Student skills	standardized score	493.3	488.7	497.9	544.4	446.2	30.3	0.15
Years of education	years	17.4	17.1	17.8			1.2	0.12

Indicator	Unit							
Environment								
Air pollution	micrograms per m²	20.8					9.3	−0.19
Water quality	%	83.0	82.3	83.7	84.8	84.1	10.9	0.65
Civic engagement								
Consultation on rule-making	standardized score	7.1					2.7	0.24
Voter turnout	%	71.9	72.3	71.6	78.3	67.8	11.9	0.36
Health								
Life expectancy	years	79.6	76.7	82.4			3.1	0.43
Self-reported health	%	67.7	70.5	65.4	78.4	59.6	14.5	0.63
Life satisfaction								
Cantril ladder of life satisfaction	[0, 10]	6.6	6.5	6.6	7.1	6.2	0.9	1.00
Safety								
Assault rate	%	4.1	4.5	3.7			2.3	0.01
Homicide rate	cases per 100000	3.0	4.9	1.2			5.1	0.01
Work-life balance								
Employees working very long hours	%	9.9	13.3	5.7			9.9	−0.16
Time devoted to leisure and personal care	hours	14.6	14.8	14.4			0.8	0.23

a) The correlation between each indicator and life satisfaction (= subjective well-being). Both refer to the national average of total populations.

b) The Gini coefficient of disposable income is a part of the OECD Income Distribution database. All other variables are underlying data for the OECD Better Life Index.

along with the Gini index.[6] According to the file released by the OECD Better Life Initiative, the data years of the underlying detailed indicators are from around 2009. Thus, the 11 well-being indicators and 24 headline indicators capture the life circumstances of people in each country around this period.

Each well-being indicator aggregates multiple headline indicators classified under its own topic. This aggregation process takes two steps. First, each headline indicator under the same topic is normalized according to a standard formula which converts the original values into numbers between 0 and 10 as follows: $\dfrac{value\,to\,convert - minimum\,value}{maximum\,value - minimum\,value} \times 10$ Second, within each topic the normalized headline indicators are averaged with equal weights. For example, while the topic of environment is constructed using two secondary indicators – water quality and air pollution – their scores are first normalized in a range between 0 and 10. Then they are aggregated into a well-being indicator of *environment* as follows: $\dfrac{water\,quality\,score + air\,pollution\,score}{2}$. Thus, 11 well-being indicators are constructed so that their values are also between 0 and 10.

Figure 8.1 shows 11 well-being indicators relative to GDP per capita. The positive relationship between these indicators and per capita income is evident, except for *work–life balance*. This indicates that as the economy grows, people's lives improve in many aspects. Among these 11 well-being indicators, the first 3 topics – *housing, income,* and *jobs* – are categorized under material living conditions, and the remaining 8 topics are categorized under QOL. Similarly, while the headline indicators classified under the first three topics capture the material living standards of average people in each country, headline indicators classified under the remaining topics capture their QOL.

One of the 24 headline indicators classified under life satisfaction is national average of reported life satisfaction, based on the Cantril Ladder question by the Gallup World Poll on a 0–10 scale. The remaining 23 headline indicators are categorized under 10 dimensions of well-being. The reliability of reported life satisfaction as a measure of subjective well-being is widely accepted, and it has been widely reported that subjective well-being is affected by various factors associated with people's lives (Frey and Stutzer, 2002; Frey, 2008). Thus, we can assume that the subjective well-being of each country reflects the socio-economic conditions of the country as characterized by the remaining 23 headline indicators and the Gini index.

In addition to a national average of indicators, the OECD Better Life Initiative releases headline indicators for different population groups within each country. Table 8.1 also reports the descriptive statistics for these indicators. Life circumstances for males and females are similar on many dimensions. Females have a slightly higher subjective well-being on average than males have by about 0.1 on a 0–10 scale. On the other hand, high-income earners enjoy better lives than low-income earners on all dimensions except for the *environment* dimension, which is characterized by water quality.[7] High-income earners report significantly higher

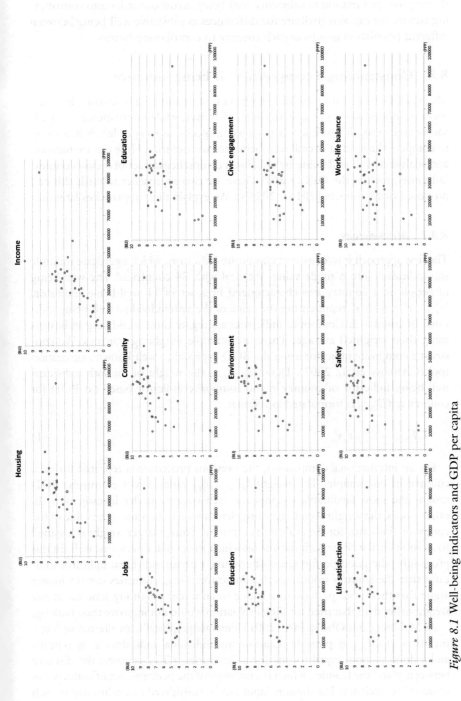

Figure 8.1 Well-being indicators and GDP per capita

Note: Constructed from Your Better Life Index (http://www.oecdbetterlifeindex.org) and Penn World Table 7.0. BLI: Better Life Index.

subjective well-being than low-income earners by about 1 on a 0–10 scale. As we decompose the variation in subjective well-being across countries into contributing factors, we can also attribute the differences in subjective well-being between different population groups in each country to contributing factors.

8.3   Constructing a composite well-being indicator

The OECD BLI compares life circumstances of different countries in many socio-economic aspects of a 'better life'. However, while international comparison of well-being is possible when assessing specific aspects of life, it is difficult to compare the level of overall well-being across countries. How can we measure and analyse overall well-being by utilizing a comprehensive set of socio-economic indicators, such as the OECD BLI? There are two approaches towards this end proposed by Mizobuchi (2014a, 2014b). We explain these approaches later on.

8.3.1   *Methodology*

The first approach is to construct composite indicators, which aggregate multiple sub-indicators into a single value. We deal with 34 countries.[8] The well-being of people in a country k is characterized by a set of 11 well-being indicators $\left(y_1^k,...,y_{11}^k\right)$, with y_m^k representing the value of the mth individual well-being indicator of country k. Composite indicators aggregate these well-being indicators using their weighted average. There are multiple weighting schemes. We construct a composite indicator using the BOD approach, a well-known aggregation tool (Cherchye et al., 2007). Denoting μ_m^c as the weight of the mth individual well-being indicator of country c, the composite indicator based on BOD for country c, CI_{BOD}^c, is formulated as follows:

$$CI_{BOD}^c = \Sigma_{m=1}^{11}\mu_m^c y_m^c \tag{1}$$

For an international comparison, the previous procedure is repeated for each country in our sample. The weight $\left(\mu_1^c,...,\mu_{11}^c\right)$ varies across countries. BOD assigns the most favourable weights for each country under investigation. In other words, the weight is endogenously determined to maximize the value of the composite indicator for the evaluated country c. Thus, a larger weight is assigned to an individual well-being indicator on which the country performs well. In this procedure, the good performance of country c on an individual indicator indicates that the country prioritizes that indicator. Thus, countries can no longer argue that their poor performance is due to an unfair weighting scheme, as any weight other than that used for their evaluation would not improve their ranking.

As Mahlberg and Obersteiner (2001) illustrate graphically, an alternative interpretation of CI_{BOD}^c is possible. Considering individual indicators y^c as outputs and a dummy input equal to one for all countries, CI_{BOD}^c captures the distance between y^c and the frontier, which is a measure of the performance of country c in terms of its efficiency. The dummy input can be considered as a helmsman in each country, which is intended to guarantee the people a better life; this is reflected by the values of the 11 well-being indicators.[9]

Although BOD is widely used in many applications, its assumption of invariant input is problematic. This is particularly salient when constructing a composite well-being indicator, as this assumption dismisses the fact that each country is faced with different conditions for providing a better life or higher levels of well-being for its people. As Dasgupta (2001) and Arrow et al. (2004) advocate, it is widely believed that the productive base of economies, which consists of a variety of assets and a social infrastructure, determines people's well-being. When we consider individual well-being indicators as outputs, it is appropriate to consider the productive base as corresponding inputs and differentiate the levels of productive base across countries.

Countries endowed with larger productive bases have an advantage in being able to guarantee their people better life circumstances compared with those endowed with smaller ones. As BOD does not differentiate the size of the productive bases, it overestimates countries with larger productive bases and underestimates those with smaller ones. Reasonable performance measures in terms of providing well-being should evaluate countries' capabilities for converting their productive bases to well-being indicators.

BOD's estimation procedure for composite indicators or efficiency is rooted in data envelopment analysis (DEA; Charnes et al., 1978). The original DEA is an established tool for measuring the efficiency of decision-making units based on the comparison of combinations of inputs and outputs across units in a sample. Thus, it differentiates the amounts of outputs as well as inputs. An efficiency score obtained under DEA is the weighted average of outputs of the evaluated country and, thus, it also defines the composite indicator. By applying DEA to the aggregate of individual well-being indicators along with the productive bases, we can construct an alternative composite indicator $CI_{DEA}^{c} = \Sigma_{m=1}^{11} \mu_m^c y_m^c$, which becomes a more appropriate performance measure for country c.

We consider the case in which each country k is bestowed with a productive base characterized by a set of three types of wealth $\left(x_1^k, x_2^k, x_3^k\right)$, with x_n^k the value of nth wealth in country k.[10] Countries' individual well-being indicators are considered as being produced from this wealth vector. DEA shares the flexible weighting scheme with the BOD procedure. Under the construction based on DEA, the weights assigned to well-being indicators are also endogenously determined to maximize the value of the composite indicator for each country. However, there are additional constraints for this optimization problem, which are as follows:

$$\Sigma_{m=1}^{11} \mu_m^c y_m^k \leq \Sigma_{n=1}^{3} \nu_n^c x_n^k \text{ for } k = 1,\ldots,34 \tag{2}$$

There are 34 countries in a sample. Thus, 34 constraints are introduced. DEA selects country-specific weights that maximize the composite indicator for the evaluated country c under BOD evaluation. The constraints (2) require application of favourable weights $\left(\mu_1^c,\ldots,\mu_{11}^c\right)$ for country c to other countries, and the resulting composite indicators of other countries are under the upper bounds $\Sigma_{n=1}^{3} \nu_n^c x_n^k$. It is noteworthy that the constraint varies across countries. As with the weights assigned to individual indicators, the weights assigned to the wealth vector $\left(v_1^c, v_2^c, v_3^c\right)$ are also optimally chosen for the evaluated country c. Thus, if the evaluated country c has a smaller productive base, the upper bound $\sum_{n=1}^{3} v_n^c x_n^k$ becomes greater and relaxes the constraint of the optimization problem for constructing a composite indicator. It leads to making CI_{DEA}^c greater than CI_{BOD}^c. On the other hand, if the evaluated country c has a larger productive base, the upper bound $\sum_{n=1}^{3} v_n^c x_n^k$ becomes smaller and tightens the constraint of the optimization problem for constructing a composite indicator. It leads to making CI_{DEA}^c smaller than CI_{BOD}^c. Thus, DEA solves the problem with BOD of underestimating countries with smaller productive bases and overestimating those with larger productive bases.

8.3.2 *Empirical results*

We compute two composite indicators, CI_{BOD} and CI_{DEA}, which aggregate 11 well-being indicators based on the approaches of BOD and DEA. CI_{DEA} measures countries' performances by differentiating the countries' productive bases in a sample, while CI_{BOD} assumes that they are constant across countries. The data on countries' productive bases are obtained from the comprehensive wealth accounts which the World Bank has been developing (World Bank, 2011). We explain Mizobuchi's (2014a) empirical result based on CI_{BOD} and CI_{DEA} later on.

Table 8.2 presents the full empirical results, containing the scores of composite indicators CI_{BOD} and CI_{DEA} and their corresponding rankings along with the existing human development index (HDI) and GDP per capita. To ensure comparability, we rescale CI_{BOD}, CI_{DEA}, and HDI scores so that their maximum values are 1. We compare composite indicators with these two measures, as GDP per capita has long been used as a measure of well-being and HDI is one of the most popular alternative measures of well-being. Composite indicators and HDI fail to completely discriminate among all the countries in our sample, and some countries are ranked equally. In particular, a larger number of countries are equally ranked as the highest in CI_{BOD} and CI_{DEA}. However, comparing the number of countries equally ranked (19 out of 34 for CI_{BOD} and 10 for CI_{DEA}), the discriminative power of CI_{DEA} improves compared to CI_{BOD} by also incorporating information about the productive base.

By construction, CI_{BOD} becomes higher than HDI for countries which achieve high scores on socio-economic dimensions rather than *income, education* and *health*, which are incorporated by HDI. For example, the scores of Luxembourg, the UK, and Spain are 1, which is the highest possible under CI_{BOD}, while they are ranked relatively low among OECD countries in terms of HDI.[11] The well-being of people in the UK is close to the highest level on multiple dimensions, such as *community, environment,* and *safety*. Luxembourg records decent well-being scores on all dimensions except for *education*, leading to a lower evaluation under HDI. While Spain records lower scores of well-being in terms of *income* and *education*, the level of well-being in terms of *safety* and *work–life balance* is close to the highest. On the other hand, countries with higher scores in *education*

Table 8.2 Composite indicators of Better Life Index, Human Development Index, and GDP per Capita

	BOD		DEA		HDI		GDP per capita	
Australia	1.0000	(1)	0.6836	(26)	0.9841	(2)	47566	(3)
Austria	0.9894	(20)	0.7232	(23)	0.9341	(18)	41063	(7)
Belgium	1.0000	(1)	0.8680	(15)	0.9384	(16)	38580	(11)
Brazil	0.7877	(31)	1.0000	(1)	0.7524	(33)	10521	(34)
Canada	1.0000	(1)	0.8099	(16)	0.9596	(7)	40023	(9)
Chile	0.7053	(33)	1.0000	(1)	0.8480	(30)	13689	(31)
Czech Republic	0.9450	(22)	1.0000	(1)	0.9171	(22)	25553	(25)
Denmark	1.0000	(1)	0.4716	(33)	0.9469	(13)	37377	(12)
Finland	1.0000	(1)	0.5692	(30)	0.9320	(19)	34765	(17)
France	0.9236	(28)	0.7308	(21)	0.9352	(17)	34385	(18)
Germany	1.0000	(1)	0.7510	(18)	0.9564	(8)	36226	(14)
Greece	0.9418	(23)	0.6631	(27)	0.9171	(22)	30201	(22)
Hungary	0.9260	(27)	0.8888	(13)	0.8618	(27)	18001	(29)
Iceland	1.0000	(1)	0.4784	(32)	0.9532	(11)	40096	(8)
Ireland	1.0000	(1)	0.5481	(31)	0.9617	(5)	35878	(15)
Israel	0.9391	(25)	1.0000	(1)	0.9394	(15)	28452	(23)
Italy	0.9148	(29)	0.7925	(17)	0.9245	(21)	30895	(20)
Japan	1.0000	(1)	0.7289	(22)	0.9511	(12)	35011	(16)
Korea	0.9455	(21)	0.9124	(12)	0.9447	(14)	26675	(24)
Luxembourg	1.0000	(1)	0.6014	(29)	0.9171	(22)	93388	(1)
Mexico	0.7043	(34)	1.0000	(1)	0.8098	(31)	12887	(32)
Netherlands	1.0000	(1)	0.7414	(19)	0.9617	(5)	44583	(5)
New Zealand	1.0000	(1)	0.6071	(28)	0.9628	(3)	30797	(21)
Norway	1.0000	(1)	0.3393	(34)	1.0000	(1)	56499	(2)
Poland	0.9895	(19)	1.0000	(1)	0.8576	(28)	18366	(28)
Portugal	0.8528	(30)	0.8685	(14)	0.8555	(29)	22339	(26)
Russia Federation	0.9368	(26)	1.0000	(1)	0.7938	(32)	15704	(30)
Slovak Republic	0.9406	(24)	1.0000	(1)	0.8810	(26)	21414	(27)
Spain	1.0000	(1)	0.7228	(24)	0.9288	(20)	30908	(19)
Sweden	1.0000	(1)	0.7008	(25)	0.9543	(10)	39295	(10)
Switzerland	1.0000	(1)	0.7386	(20)	0.9554	(9)	44375	(6)
Turkey	0.7617	(32d)	1.0000	(1)	0.7333	(34)	10886	(33)
United Kingdom	1.0000	(1)	0.9207	(11)	0.9139	(25)	37001	(13)
United States	1.0000	(1)	1.0000	(1)	0.9628	(3)	45614	(4)
Mean	0.9472		0.7900		0.9131		33206	
Std. Dev.	0.0857		0.1852		0.0641		15595	

BOD: benefit of the doubt approach; DEA: data envelopment analysis; HDI: Human Development Index.

Table 8.3 Correlations among composite indicators

	BOD	DEA	HDI	GDP per capita
Correlation coefficient				
BOD	1.0000	−0.5424	0.7859	0.6314
DEA		1.0000	−0.6348	−0.6144
HDI			1.0000	0.6604
GDP per capita				1.0000
Spearman rank correlation coefficient				
BOD	1.0000	−0.6367	0.7689	0.8136
DEA		1.0000	−0.5918	−0.6422
HDI			1.0000	0.7790
GDP per capita				1.0000

BOD: benefit of the doubt approach; DEA: data envelopment analysis; HDI: Human Development Index.

or *health* but relatively low scores on other dimensions of QOL lose their ranking largely by switching from HDI to CI_{BOD}. France and Israel are such examples.

Table 8.3 shows the correlation of composite indicators with HDI scores and GDP per capita. It shows that CI_{BOD} and HDI, which share a similar pattern of distribution, are highly correlated with each other. CI_{BOD} is also strongly positively correlated with GDP per capita. As Figure 8.1 suggests, greater GDP per capita induces higher individual well-being indicators, leading to the larger composite indicator CI_{BOD}. Therefore, the significant correlation between CI_{BOD} and GDP per capita is straightforward.

On the other hand, CI_{DEA} is distributed in a considerably different manner. Whereas the correlations between CI_{BOD} and HDI and between CI_{BOD} and GDP per capita are 0.7859 and 0.6314, respectively, the correlations between CI_{DEA} and HDI and between CI_{DEA} and GDP per capita are − 0.6348 and − 0.6144, respectively. Interpreting the negative correlation between CI_{DEA} and GDP per capita is not as intuitive. It is worth noting that all the countries in the low-income group, except Hungary, are ranked the highest under CI_{DEA}. High-income countries can afford to invest a variety of assets that are accumulated into their large productive bases. However, these countries are likely to fail in providing a level of well-being commensurate with their large productive bases. Thus, this leads to countries' lower performances in terms of well-being as measured by CI_{DEA}. In the end, there are strong negative correlations between CI_{DEA} and GDP per capita.

However, the large negative correlation between CI_{DEA} and GDP per capita does not necessarily imply that their country rankings are in reverse order. In particular, the US, which has one of the largest GDP per capita, is also ranked highest under CI_{DEA}. Countries with the lowest GDP per capita also have the smallest productive bases. Although the large productive base, which stems from the US having the

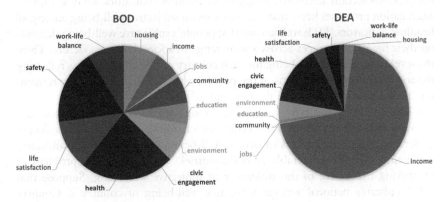

Figure 8.2 Average weight for composite indicators

Note: BOD: benefit of the doubt approach; DEA: data envelopment analysis.

highest GDP per capita, is advantageous, people in the US enjoy a better life than is expected given their large productive base, leading to a higher evaluation of performance measured by CI_{DEA}. Similarly, Belgium and the UK, which have relatively high GDP per capita, leading to comparably large productive bases, are also ranked relatively high under CI_{DEA}. This indicates that they also succeed in providing their people with high well-being corresponding with their large productive bases. On the other hand, there are countries, such as Greece, Hungary, and Portugal, which have very low GDP per capita and correspondingly low productive bases, but which are also ranked lower under CI_{DEA}. The level of well-being enjoyed by their people is very low and it is not justifiable by their lower productive bases.

CI_{BOD} and CI_{DEA} choose the country-specific weights that maximize the resulting composite indicator score of each country under evaluation. Therefore, higher weights are assigned to the individual indicators on which each country performs well. Thus, it is possible to conclude that the composite indicators reflect the policy priority of each country on country-specific weights. Figure 8.2 shows the average weight for both individual indicators CI_{BOD} and CI_{DEA}. Widely distributed weights indicate that policy priority encompasses a spectrum covering 11 dimensions, revealing the importance of increasing dimensions in measuring countries' performance. A clear distinction in relative weights found between CI_{BOD} and CI_{DEA} indicates that neglecting the productive base distorts the inference of countries' policy priorities.

8.4 Measuring sources of difference in average subjective well-being across countries

8.4.1 *Methodology*

In this section, we explain the second approach to measuring and analysing overall well-being by using a comprehensive set of socio-economic indicators. While the previous section attempted to aggregate multiple indicators, we deal with no aggregation processes here. Instead, we focus on subjective well-being among all headline indicators.[12] It is well known that people's subjective well-being depends on their life circumstances across a wide range of socio-economic factors. Thus, the level of subjective well-being for each country can be considered as reflecting the socio-economic conditions of the people, which are captured by the remaining 23 headline indicators and the Gini index.[13]

Using countries' subjective well-being, along with 23 headline indicators and the Gini index (hereafter 24 socio-economic variables), we can acquire a deeper understanding of the sources of overall well-being. National average subjective well-being differs considerably across countries. We consider the problem of identifying the source of this difference in subjective well-being. Suppose that SWB^c indicates national average subjective well-being of country c. Country c's socio-economic vector y^c consists of its 24 socio-economic variables so that $y^c = \left(y_1^c, \ldots, y_{24}^c\right)$. As 24 socio-economic variables are classified under 10 well-being topics, we represent this with 10 sub-vectors so that $y^c = \left(y_1^c, \ldots, y_{10}^c\right)$.

Each topic captures a distinct socio-economic condition. Thus, each socio-economic condition is characterized by a vector consisting of multiple indicators, as Table 8.1 suggests. The relationship between SWB^c and y^c is summarized by a happiness function H as follows:

$$SWB^c = \theta^c H\left(y^c\right) \tag{3}$$

By assuming a macroeconomic happiness function H which is common to all the countries, we can attribute differences in subjective well-being across countries to differences in y. However, individuals who share the same life circumstances do not necessarily draw the same level of subjective well-being. This is because socio-economic vector y does not cover more personal aspects of people's subjective well-being, such as personality, demography, and culture.[14] Thus, some individuals are intrinsically happier than others, even though their life conditions are identical. Similarly, people in one country might have higher subjective well-being than people in another country, even though the two countries have identical socio-economic conditions.

Rather than identifying such uncovered factors in further detail and measuring their respective contributions, we introduce an overarching concept called *sensitivity of happiness* θ to capture these influences on national average subjective well-being. It is constructed so that $0 \leq \theta \leq 1$. The maximum value of 1 indicates that a country is sensitive to its socio-economic conditions. A smaller value of θ indicates a less sensitive or more insensitive country. For example, given any socio-economic vector y, a larger share of individuals who are intrinsically happy in a country raises its national average subjective well-being beyond the level expected based on its socio-economic status $H(y)$, leading to a larger θ.

Once we formulate a country's subjective well-being with the happiness function H and the sensitivity term θ, we can decompose the cross-country variations in subjective well-being into multiple factors. Multilateral comparison requires a reference country. We analyse the likely reasons why the subjective well-being of each country is higher or lower than a hypothetical reference country. We construct a hypothetical reference country characterized by the sensitivity term and the socio-economic vectors which are averaged over all 36 countries so that $\bar{\theta}=(1/36)\Sigma_{k=1}^{36}\theta^k$ and $\bar{y}=(1/K)\Sigma_{k=1}^{36}y^k=\left(\bar{y}_1^k,...,\bar{y}_{10}^k\right)$. The subjective well-being of people in the reference country is expressed by $\bar{\theta}H(\bar{y})$. This is the level of happiness which we expect people to experience when they face the average life circumstances across countries in every socio-economic aspect and when they are characterized by average sensitivity of happiness. We can attribute the difference between SWB^c and $\bar{\theta}H(\bar{y})$ to the difference in the sensitivity term and the 10 contributing socio-economic factors between country c and the reference country using Equation (4).[15]

$$\underbrace{\frac{SWB^c}{\bar{\theta}H(\bar{y})}}= \underbrace{\frac{\theta^c}{\bar{\theta}}}_{sensitivity}\times\underbrace{\frac{H(y^c)}{H(\bar{y}_1,y_2^c,...,y_{10}^c)}}_{1st\ factor}\times\cdots\times\underbrace{\frac{H(\bar{y}_1,...,\bar{y}_9,y_{10}^c)}{H(\bar{y})}}_{10-th\ factor} \tag{4}$$

In the previous equation, the contribution of each socio-economic factor is captured by the increase in subjective well-being associated with the difference in a corresponding socio-economic condition between country c and the reference country, holding all other socio-economic conditions fixed. For example, the contribution of the *environment* factor indicates the extent to which subjective well-being increases when the headline indicators classified only under the *environment* aspect improve.

8.4.2 *Empirical results*

Once we estimate the happiness function from the 24 socio-economic variables, we can fully decompose the differences in countries' average subjective well-being between each country in a sample and the reference country into 10 socio-economic factors and a sensitivity term. There are multiple estimation approaches, and we explain the empirical results based on DEA by Mizobuchi (2014b) later on.

Figure 8.3 reports the decomposition of the differences in subjective well-being between each country and the reference country.[16] It shows the extent to which each country's well-being is greater than that of the reference country and where the difference comes from by quantifying the contribution of each factor on a percentage scale. Each country has its own reason why its average subjective well-being exceeds or falls below the level of the reference country. Switzerland and Norway have the largest and second largest subjective well-being ratings, respectively. While Switzerland's subjective well-being is attributed mainly to *income* and *health* factors, Norway's is attributed mainly to *housing* and *work–life balance* factors. Similarly, while the *heath* factor significantly reduces subjective well-being in both countries, factors which positively

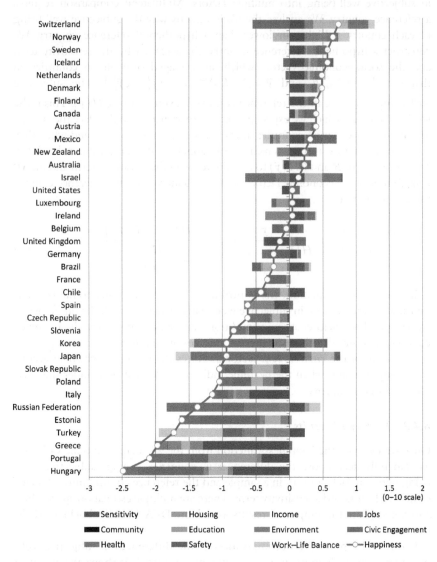

Figure 8.3 Explaining differences in subjective well-being relative to reference country (0–10 scale)

Note: Drawn from Mizobuchi (2014b)

affect countries' subjective well-being differ between Japan and Korea; the *income* factor positively affects Japan's subjective well-being and *civic engagement* positively affects Korea's.

A sensitivity term certainly explains differences in subjective well-being in many countries. In particular, lower sensitivity is found in countries with low subjective well-being. The largest sensitivity terms are found in Greece and Hungary, which are characterized by the lowest and the third lowest values of subjective well-being. Thus, their subjective well-being is lower than would be expected based on socio-economic status. While life circumstances are poor in both countries, subjective well-being is much lower than would be suggested by socio-economic status. Australia is an exceptional country which has high subjective well-being and good life circumstances but shows lower sensitivity of happiness. This means that while Australians' socio-economic status is good, their subjective well-being is not as high as expected.

From the decomposition results of each country in Figure 8.3, we can identify the main drivers of the differences in subjective well-being among countries. The average difference in subjective well-being and each factor's average contribution depends on the selection of the reference country. Thus, for the purpose of understanding the relative contribution of factors in generating the variation in subjective well-being, it is more appropriate to compare the standard deviations between factors across countries rather than the means. Figure 8.4 reports standard deviations for each factor.

Among all the factors, the *health* factor considerably influences the cross-country differences in subjective well-being, with the largest standard deviation of 20.03%. The sensitivity term also plays an important role in generating the differences in subjective well-being, with a standard deviation of 18.59%, which is comparable to the largest *health* factor. The second largest socio-economic factor is *civic engagement* at 13.93%. On the other hand, *safety* and *community* factors hardly contribute to the cross-country variation in subjective well-being.

We also consider the overall impact of material living standards, as well as QOL, along with the separate role of each factor. We sum up the standard

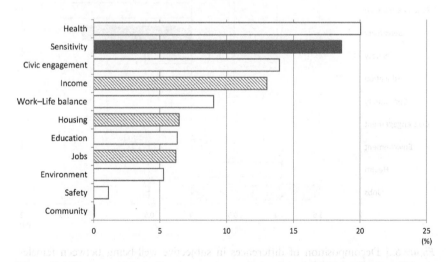

Figure 8.4 Decomposition of cross-country variation in subjective well-being (%)

deviations of factors in each domain so that the factors classified under material living standards add up to 25.66% and the factors classified under QOL add up to 55.75%. Cross-country differences in socio-economic conditions categorized under QOL explain more than half of the total variation in subjective well-being across countries.

Although coverage of indicators is limited, a set of underlying indicators for different population groups is also made available by the OECD Better Life Initiative.[17] Following the same methodology, we can investigate why subjective well-being of one group is higher than that of another group within each country. While females' subjective well-being is on average higher than that of males, high-income earners' subjective well-being is on average higher than that of low-income earners. We explain the reasons for such gaps between different population groups later on.

By setting males in each country as the reference country, we can decompose the ratio of females' subjective well-being to males' subjective well-being in each country.[18] Figure 8.5 reports the average contributions of each factor. Females' subjective well-being is lower than males' by 1.33% on average. For understanding the relative contribution of factors in generating the differences of subjective well-being between females and males, it is more appropriate to compare the means between contributing factors rather than to compare the standard deviations.

Among eight socio-economic factors, half raise females' subjective well-being compared to that of males, whereas the remaining half lower it. In particular, *work–life balance* and *safety* factors considerably raise females' subjective well-being, showing averages increased by 1.56% and 0.54%, respectively.

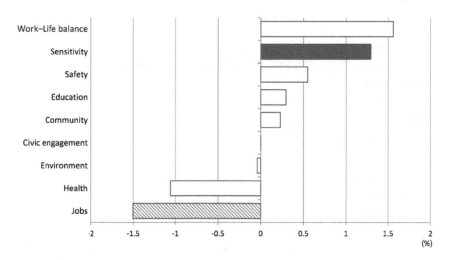

Figure 8.5 Decomposition of differences in subjective well-being between females and males (%)

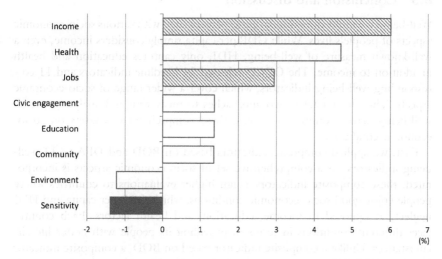

Figure 8.6 Decomposition of differences in subjective well-being between high- and low-income groups (%)

On the other hand, the *jobs* factor significantly lowers females' subjective well-being, with an average of −1.50%. Clearly, the sensitivity term also plays a key role in raising females' subjective well-being, with an average of 1.29%, which is comparable to the largest *work–life balance* and *jobs* factors in terms of magnitude.

In a similar manner, setting low-income earners in each country as the reference country, we can decompose the ratio of high-income earners' subjective well-being to low-income earners' subjective well-being in each country.[19] Figure 8.6 reports the average contribution of each factor. We note that high-income earners' subjective well-being is higher than that of low-income earners' well-being by 15.01% on average. To understand the relative contribution of factors in generating the differences in subjective well-being between high- and low-income earners, we compare the means between contributing factors rather than the standard deviations.

Most socio-economic factors raise high-income earners' subjective well-being in comparison to that of low-income earners', except for the *environment* factor. The *environment* factor lowers high-income earners' subjective well-being with an average of −1.22%. It means that high-income earners are more dissatisfied with the water quality than are low-income earners, and thus the factor lowers high-income earners' subjective well-being relative to low-income earners'.[20] The sensitivity term also plays a key role for lowering high-income earners' subjective well-being relative to that of low-income earners' subjective well-being, with an average of −1.39%. This negative sensitivity term means high-income earners' subjective well-being is not as high as expected given their socio-economic conditions.

8.5   Conclusion and discussion

Well-being is a multi-dimensional concept associated with various socio-economic aspects of people's lives. While GDP per capita simply considers income, even a well-known measure of well-being, HDI, only captures education and health in addition to income. The OECD released 24 headline indicators and 11 corresponding well-being indicators, which cover a wider range of socio-economic aspects. This chapter takes two approaches to measuring and analysing overall well-being across countries by using these comprehensive datasets on socio-economic conditions.

First, we applied composite indicators based on BOD and DEA to 11 well-being indicators. As a comprehensive set of socio-economic aspects is incorporated, these composite indicators assign higher evaluations to countries where people enjoy good socio-economic conditions, which GDP per capita and HDI neglect, as opposed to income, education, and health factors. Each country faces different conditions in terms of providing its people with better life circumstances. Unlike a composite indicator based on BOD, a composite indicator based on DEA differentiates countries' productive base. Countries that provide their people a level of well-being that matches their productive base are highly evaluated under a composite indicator based on DEA.

Second, we explored the relationship between subjective well-being and 24 socio-economic variables, consisting of 23 headline indicators and the Gini index. Based on the estimated happiness function, we decomposed the variation in countries' average subjective well-being into 10 socio-economic factors and a sensitivity term. The *health* factor and sensitivity term made the largest contributions. In addition, following the same methodology, we could decompose the differences in subjective well-being between different population groups in each country. On average, females' subjective well-being was slightly higher than males' and that of high-income earners was considerably higher than that of low-income earners. While females were happier than expected based on their socio-economic situations, high-income earners were happier than were low-income earners, but not as happy as would be expected based on their better socio-economic situations.

Here we briefly discuss what is missing in our analysis. The first approach is based on composite indicators evaluating countries' performance in providing their people with better socio-economic conditions. The second approach considers how these people draw satisfaction from their different socio-economic conditions. As this chapter adopts two approaches and conducts its examinations from both sides, it provides a broader perspective on measuring and analysing overall well-being. However, our adoption of these two approaches independently is not satisfactory. Given a country's productive base, what are the possible combinations of socio-economic situations? Among these feasible combinations, which socio-economic condition maximizes subjective well-being of the people? A way to answer these questions together is not clear at this point. The two approaches explained in this chapter are the first step for providing plausible policy recommendations based on a comprehensive set of socio-economic indicators in the future.

Appendix A

Definition of composite well-being indicators

The composite indicator based on BOD for country c, $CI_{BOD,c}$, is formulated as follows:

$$CI_{BOD,c} = \max_{\mu_1^c,\dots,\mu_{11}^c} \left\{ \begin{array}{l} \Sigma_{m=1}^{11}\mu_m^c y_m^c : \Sigma_{m=1}^{11}\mu_m^c y_m^k \le 1 \text{ for } k=1,\dots,34; \mu_m^c \\ \ge 0 \text{ for } m=1,\dots,11 \end{array} \right\} \tag{5}$$

For an international comparison, the previous procedure is repeated for each country in our sample. The weight $\left(\mu_1^c,\dots,\mu_{10}^c\right)$ is endogenously determined to maximize the value of the composite indicator for country c. Thus, a larger weight is assigned to an individual indicator on which the country performs well.

On the other hand, the composite indicator based on BOD for country c, $CI_{BOD,c}$, is formulated as follows:

$$CI_{DEA}^c = \max_{\mu_1^c,\dots,\mu_{10}^c,\nu_1^c,\nu_2^c,\nu_3^c} \left\{ \begin{array}{l} \Sigma_{m=1}^{11}\mu_m^c y_m^c : \Sigma_{m=1}^{11}\mu_m^c y_m^k \le \Sigma_{n=1}^{3}\nu_n^c x_n^k \text{ for } k=1,\dots,34; \\ \Sigma_{n=1}^{3}\nu_n^c x_n^c = 1; \mu_m^c \ge 0 \text{ for } m=1,\dots,11; \nu_n^c \ge 0 \\ \text{for } n=1,2,3 \end{array} \right\} \tag{6}$$

Both DEA and BOD select country-specific weights that maximize the composite indicator for each country under evaluation. However, there is a difference in constraint between DEA and BOD in Equations (5) and (6). The constraints in Equations (5) and (6) state that when we apply favourable weights to the evaluated country c, the resulting composite indicators of other countries are bounded by the upper bounds. While Equation (5) sets 1 as the upper bound across countries, Equation (6) sets the variable upper bound $\Sigma_{n=1}^{3}\nu_n^c x_n^k$ for each country k. Weights $(\nu_1 c,\dots,\nu_{Nc})$ are optimally chosen for the evaluated country c under the assumption that $\Sigma_{n=1}^{3}\nu_n^c x_n^k = 1$. Thus, if the evaluated country c has a relatively small productive base, the upper bound of the constraint for many countries becomes greater than 1 so that $\Sigma_{n=1}^{3}\nu_n^c x_n^k > 1$. It relaxes the constraint of the optimization problem and makes it possible for the composite indicator of the evaluated country c to be greater than 1.

Notes

1 The number of countries covered was 34 in 2011. The revised dataset, released in 2012, includes 36 countries, incorporating Brazil and Russia.
2 *Your Better Life Index* (http://www.oecdbetterlifeindex.org/) was designed as an interactive tool that allows users to assign the importance of each of the 11 topics and to track the performance of countries.
3 Data on the subjective well-being of a country indicate the national average subjective well-being of people in the country. In this chapter, we call it countries' subjective well-being or simply subjective well-being.

4 Helliwell and Wang (2012, 2013) also investigate socio-economic factors and cross-country variation in subjective well-being by using individual survey data rather than countries' averages.

5 The terms 'happiness', 'subjective well-being', and 'life satisfaction' are used interchangeably, as is common in the literature.

6 As Diener et al. (1995) and Ferrer-i-Carbonell and Ramos (2013) advocate, there has been an accumulation of empirical evidence indicating that people dislike income equality. Thus, when analysing the sources of subjective well-being, which is one of headline indicators, we incorporate the Gini index along with the remaining 23 headline indicators.

7 This does not mean that high-income earners live in more polluted areas. The BLI measure of water quality depends on survey questions querying respondents' water satisfaction. It is likely that high-income earners set a higher standard for water quality.

8 Originally, the OECD BLI covered 36 countries. As the comprehensive wealth accounts of the World Bank – which we utilize later – reports data of 34 countries among the 36, we focus on these 34 countries.

9 This interpretation is rooted in Lovell et al. (1995).

10 Three types of wealth in the productive base corresponds to the classification in the comprehensive wealth accounts of World Bank (2011): x_1^k is produced capital consisting of machinery, structures, and equipment; x_2^k is natural capital consisting of agricultural land, protected areas and forests, and subsoil assets; and x_3^k is intangible capital.

11 See also Mahlberg and Obersteiner (2001) and Zaim et al. (2001).

12 Since the Cantril ladder of life satisfaction is the most common measure of subjective well-being, we simply call it subjective well-being.

13 We have already explained the rationale for incorporating the Gini index in note 7.

14 De Neve et al. (2012) investigate the role of personality types, and Oishi (2010) discusses the role of cultural differences in explaining differences in people's subjective well-being.

15 Equation (4) starts from $H(\mathbf{y})$ and approaches $H(\bar{\mathbf{y}})$ by changing each socio-economic variable of country c, x_n^c to the cross-country average $\bar{y}_n$ in the order from the first socio-economic aspect to the tenth, one by one. However, it is possible to start from $H(\bar{\mathbf{y}})$ and approach $H(\mathbf{y})$ by changing from the cross-country average of each socio-economic vector $\bar{y}_n$ to that of country c. Strictly speaking, the following empirical result adopts the average of these two decomposition results.

16 We note that countries' subjective well-being is lower than that of the reference country on average, reflecting the relatively high level of subjective well-being of the reference country, characterized by $\bar{\theta}$ and $\bar{\mathbf{y}}$.

17 Because of data limitations, we can only use eight socio-economic factors for comparing males and females and seven socio-economic factors for comparing high- and low-income earners.

18 In the previous analysis on the variation in national average subjective well-being, the same reference country is used for each country. However, in the decomposition of the differences in subjective well-being between females and males, a different reference is used for each country. Moreover, the happiness function is constructed over 72 data points, which comprise males and females in 36 countries.

19 As with the case of comparing males and females, the happiness function is constructed over 72 data points, which comprise high- and low-income earners in 36 countries.

20 See note 8.

Bibliography

Arrow, K., Dasgupta, P., Goulder, L., Daily, G., Ehrlich, P., Heal, G., Levin, S., Mäler, K., Schneider, S., Starrett, D., and Walker, B. (2004). 'Are We Consuming Too Much?' *Journal of Economic Perspectives*, Vol. 18, No. 3, pp. 147–172.

Charnes, A., Cooper, W.W., and Rhodes, E. (1978). 'Measuring the Efficiency of Decision Making Units.' *European Journal of Operational Research*, Vol. 2, No. 6, pp. 429–444.

Cherchye, L., Moesen, W., Rogge, N., and Van Puyenbroeck, T. (2007). 'An Introduction to "Benefit of the Doubt" Composite Indicators.' *Social Indicators Research*, Vol. 82, No. 1, pp. 111–145.

Cherchye, L., Moesen, W., and Van Puyenbroeck, T. (2004). 'Legitimately Diverse, Yet Comparable: On Synthesizing Social Inclusion Performance in the EU.' *JCMS: Journal of Common Market Studie*, Vol. 42, No. 5, pp. 919–955.

Dasgupta, P. (2001). *Human Well-Being and the Natural Environment*, Oxford: Oxford University Press.

De Neve, J.-E., Christakis, N.A., Fowler, J.H., and Frey, B.S. (2012). 'Genes, Economics, and Happiness.' *Journal of Neuroscience, Psychology, and Economics*, Vol. 5, No. 4, pp. 1–27.

Despotis, D. K. (2005a). 'A Reassessment of the Human Development Index via Data Envelopment Analysis.' *Journal of the Operational Research Society*, Vol. 56, No. 8, pp. 969–980.

Despotis, D.K. (2005b). 'Measuring Human Development via Data Envelopment Analysis: The Case of Asia and the Pacific.' *Omega*, Vol. 33, No. 5, pp. 385–390.

Diener, E., Diener, M., and Diener, C. (1995). 'Factors Predicting the Subjective Well-Being of Nations.' *Journal of Personality and Social Psychology*, Vol. 69, No. 5, pp. 851–864.

Ferrer-i-Carbonell, A., and Ramos, X. (2013). 'Inequality and Happiness.' *Journal of Economic Surveys*, Vol. 28, No. 5, pp. 1016–1027.

Frey, B.S. (2008). *Happiness: A Revolution in Economics*, Cambridge, MA: The MIT Press.

Frey, B.S., and Stutzer, A. (2002). *Happiness and Economics*, Princeton, NJ: Princeton University Press.

Lovell, C.A.K., Pastor, J.T., and Turner, J.A. (1995). 'Measuring Macroeconomic Performance in the OECD: A Comparison of European and Non-European Countries.' *European Journal of Operational Research*, Vol. 87, No. 3, pp. 507–518.

Mahlberg, B., and Obersteiner, M. (2001). 'Remeasuring the HDI by Data Envelopement Analysis.' *IIASA Interim Report IR-01-069*.

Mizobuchi, H. (2014a). 'Measuring World Better Life Frontier: A Composite Indicator for OECD Better Life Index.' *Social Indicators Research*, Vol. 118, No. 3, pp. 987–1007.

Mizobuchi, H. (2014b). 'Socioeconomic Factors and Sensitivity of Happiness.' *Discussion Paper Series, Faculty of Economics, Ryukoku University*, No.14–01.

Oishi, S. (2010). 'Culture and Well-Being.' In E. Diener, J. F. Helliwell, and D. Kahneman, eds., *International Differences in Well-Being*, New York, NY: Oxford University Press, pp. 34–69.

Organization for Economic Cooperation and Development (2008). *Handbook on Constructing Composite Indicators: Methodology and User Guide*, Paris: OECD Publishing.

Organization for Economic Cooperation and Development (2011). *How's Life?*, Paris: OECD Publishing.

Stiglitz, J.E., Sen, A., and Fitoussi, J.-P. (2009). *Report by the Commission on the Measurement of Economic Performance and Social Progress*, Available at: http://www.stiglitz-sen-fitoussi.fr/documents/rapport_anglais.pdf.

World Bank (2011). *The Changing Wealth of Nations*, Washington, DC: World Bank Publications.

Zaim, O., Färe, R., and Grosskopf, S. (2001). 'An Economic Approach to Achievement and Improvement Indexes.' *Social Indicators Research*, Vol. 56, June, pp. 91–118.

9 A monetary evaluation of life
Life satisfaction approach

Tetsuya Tsurumi, Hideyuki Mizobuchi, and Shunsuke Managi

9.1 The OECD's BLI indices

Over the last several decades, a large number of papers have considered the concept of quality of life (QOL). In a pioneering study, Campbell et al. (1976) discuss the effects of various factors, such as economic situation, employment, health, home life, community, housing, and leisure, on QOL. Since then, various studies have attempted to define QOL (e.g., Peck and Stewart, 1985; Richards et al., 2007). In 2011, the Organisation for Economic Co-operation and Development (OECD) introduced the Better Life Index (BLI) to compare well-being across countries using 11 dimensions related to material living conditions and quality of life (OECD, 2011). These include (1) Housing Conditions, (2) Income and Wealth, (3) Jobs and Earnings, (4) Social Connections, (5) Education and Skills, (6) Environmental Quality, (7) Civic Engagement and Governance, (8) Health Status, (9) Subjective Well-Being, (10) Personal Security, and (11) Work and Life Balance.

Of the 11 indices, life satisfaction tends to be considered the index most closely related to QOL. Many researchers have examined the relationship between life satisfaction and various indices. For example, concerning Housing Conditions, Peck and Stewart (1985) find that an increase in housing satisfaction has a large impact on life satisfaction, and more recent papers suggest similar results (Oswald et al., 2003; Westaway, 2006; Das, 2008; Zebardast, 2009; Lee and Park, 2010; Ibem and Amole, 2013). Lee and Park (2010) conducted a survey of Korean people living in the U.S. state of Michigan and found similar results. Ibem and Amole (2013) conducted a survey of people living in urban areas in Nigeria. They considered 31 housing factors and found that housing size affects life satisfaction most and that utilities such as water, sewer systems, and electricity have the second-largest impact on life satisfaction.

Concerning (2) Income and Wealth, in a seminal paper Easterlin (1974) suggested the "Easterlin Paradox," the possibility that an increase in average income does not necessarily lead to an increase in average life satisfaction. The cause of this paradox tends to be explained in one of two ways. The first involves the relative income hypothesis, according to which people's life satisfaction tends to decrease when they compare their income with the incomes of others, and the adaptation income hypothesis, according to which people adapt their income. The second is the idea that the factors that decrease life satisfaction (e.g., decreased social capital, increased stress, and the degradation of the environment) occur simultaneously with economic development (Bartolini and Bonatti, 2003). However, recent papers have suggested a robust positive relationship between life satisfaction and income. Stevenson and Wolfers (2008) found a positive relationship using both between-country and within-country datasets. Deaton (2008) found similar results using a dataset from the Gallup World Poll that includes a survey of individuals in 132 countries. Kahneman and Deaton (2010) used a different dataset from the Gallup World Poll, the Gallup-Healthways Well-Being Index (GHWBI). In this dataset, life satisfaction data are obtained using Cantril's Self-Anchoring Scale, where 0 means the worst possible life and 10 means the best possible life. This index is affected more by the incomes of others.[1] They find positive relationships between income and life satisfaction and between emotional satisfaction (a comparison of positive and negative attitudes) and income, although the latter ceases to be positive when income exceeds $75,000. Stevenson and Wolfers (2013) also find a positive relationship. However, few studies have been conducted concerning assets.[2]

With regard to (3) Jobs and Earnings, Pouwels et al. (2008) found that working hours has a negative impact on life satisfaction using German Socio-Economic Panel data. Booth and Van Ours (2008) investigated whether gender or having children is related to the effect of working hours on satisfaction (working hours satisfaction, job satisfaction, and life satisfaction). The results indicate that women with jobs (except for jobs over 40 hours per week) have higher levels of life satisfaction than other women: women with full-time jobs tend to have the highest level of life satisfaction, while women with part-time jobs (fewer than 15 hours per week) tend to have the second-highest life satisfaction. On the other hand, men with full-time jobs (including jobs over 40 hours per week) have higher levels of life satisfaction than other men. Previous studies suggest that unemployment has a robust strong negative relationship with life satisfaction. Clark and Oswald (1994) found that unemployment has a stronger negative effect on life satisfaction than divorce or marital separation. They also suggest that highly educated people's life satisfaction decreases more due to unemployment than that of others, and that unemployed people adapt to their situation over time. Gerlach and Stepahan (1996) found that the shock resulting from unemployment is weaker for young people and elderly people than for middle-aged people. Di Tella et al. (2001) also found a negative effect of unemployment on life satisfaction using data for 12 European countries from 1975 to 1991, taken from the Euro-Barometer Survey Series. Clark et al. (2006) suggested that men tend to suffer more severe effects from unemployment than women do.

Various studies have been conducted on (4) Social Connections. Most studies explore the effect of social capital on life satisfaction.[3] Inglehart and Kingemann (2000) focused on social capital measured by confidence in others and found that its average value in a country has a positive relationship with subjective well-being. Bjørnskov (2003) focused on social capital measured by confidence in others and citizen participation, and found that the effect of social capital on subjective well-being is larger than income, at least in developed countries. Furthermore, Helliwell and Putnam (2004) considered social capital measured by connections with family, friends, neighbors, and coworkers, citizen participation, and confidence in others, and found that this factor has direct and indirect (through health) positive effects on subjective well-being and life satisfaction. A number of studies focus on volunteer activity as social capital. Early studies indicated that volunteer activity has good effects on subjective well-being in life after retirement (Havighurst et al., 1968; Maddox, 1968; Ward, 1979; Fengler, 1984). Following these studies, various studies have used longer-term datasets and a variety of control variables, such as demographics, economic situation, health, lifestyle, social support, and religious and personality indices, to confirm estimation robustness. Binder and Freytag (2013) investigated the effects of various types of social capital, such as volunteer activity, marriage, frequency of meeting friends or family, and frequency of talking with neighbors, using British Household Panel Survey data. The results indicated that volunteer activity has good effects on life satisfaction; these positive effects are explained using "role theory." For example, Moen et al. (1992) found that women tend to cultivate social networking, status, repute, resources, and emotional satisfaction by playing multiple roles, which include volunteer activity, which leads to healthier situations.[4]

(5) Education and Skills opens opportunities for people and has effects on economic situations, social capital, and crime rates (OECD, 2011). Therefore, education may have indirect effects on life satisfaction through the other BLI factors. However, some recent studies have investigated the direct effect of education on life satisfaction. Salinas-Jiménez et al. (2011) found that education has a positive effect on life satisfaction after controlling for the effect of income using a dataset taken from the World Values Survey. Cuñado and Pérez de Gracia (2012) also showed that education has not only indirect effects but also direct effects on life satisfaction. They found that education has effects on income and job status and, after controlling for these indirect effects, that education increases life satisfaction.[5]

Concerning (6) Environmental Quality, Welsch (2002) was the first study to examine the relationship between pollution and life satisfaction. Welsch used a country-level dataset of air pollution and life satisfaction for 54 countries in the late 1990s. The results indicated that nitrogen dioxide (NO_2), which is a substance that contributes to acid rain and respiratory disease, causes a statistically significant decrease in the level of life satisfaction. Using a panel dataset for 50 countries, Tsurumi et al. (2013) suggested that particulate matter (PM10) and sulfur dioxide (SO_2) cause statistically significant decreases in the level of life satisfaction.[6] In addition, there is a possibility that aspects of the surrounding environment have effects on life satisfaction, including noise (Bernard et al., 2005; Rehdanz and Maddison, 2008), climate (Maddison and Rehdanz, 2011), and nature (Ambley and Fleming, 2011, 2013; MacKerron and Mourato, 2013). For example, Ambley and Fleming (2011) investigated the relationship between house-to-park distance and life satisfaction using Australian data and found that having a park nearby increases life satisfaction. Ambley and Fleming (2013) used the ratio of green coverage obtained from the Geographic Information System as an index of the amount of green space, and found that in urban areas in Australia the ratio of green space around one's residence has positive effects on life satisfaction.

Concerning (7) Civic Engagement and Governance, a number of papers have examined the effects of political systems on national subjective well-being. Frey and Stutzer (2000, 2002) investigated the effect of direct democracy in Switzerland on life satisfaction and found a positive relationship between them. Dorn et al. (2007) found that democracy increases life satisfaction using panel data for 28 countries from 1988 to 1999. Helliwell and Huang (2008) showed that the governance index of the World Bank has a stronger relation with life satisfaction than does per capita income using World Values Survey data.

With regard to (8) Health Status, previous studies have identified its robust positive effects on life satisfaction. Ferrer-i-Carbonell and van Praag (2002) examined the effects of specific diseases on subjective well-being using a large German dataset. They found that hearing impairment is equivalent to a 20 percent decrease in income and that a heart or blood disorder is equivalent to a 47 percent decrease in income. Other papers use subjective indices of health (e.g., Powdthavee, 2005).

Concerning (10) Personal Security, Powdthavee (2005) was the first study to examine crime victims' life satisfaction. The results indicate that crime victims tend to have lower life satisfaction than non-victims. The results also suggest that non-victims have lower life satisfaction if they live in an area where the crime rate is relatively high. Ambley et al. (2013) showed that the number of thefts in a residential area causes a statistically significant decrease in life satisfaction.

Finally, concerning (11) Work and Life Balance, Pouwells et al. (2008) showed that the effects of income on life satisfaction are underestimated in cases of prolonged work. This suggests when we estimate the effects of income on life satisfaction, we should include an index of prolonged work; if we do not include it, the effects of income are underestimated by 12 percent in for women and by 25 percent for men.

9.2   Survey analysis

We use data derived from an Internet survey conducted November 27–30, 2013, that targeted people residing in Japan. The survey selected respondents based on prefectural demographics such as population, sex, and age ratios. There were 2,921 valid responses, which formed the basis for our subsequent analysis. We also obtained data on environmental factors, such as air pollution, green coverage rate (park and forest), and crime. Table 9.1 shows the indices we adopted as a better life index that is appropriate for Japan.

First, concerning (1) Housing Conditions, we adopted floor area per capita as a proxy of quality of housing rather than HOI (number of rooms per person in a dwelling). In Japan, many people are concerned about their limited land area because of heavy population concentrations in urban areas. Thus, it seems better to consider the floor area rather than the number of rooms. With regard to ho1 (Housing cost overburden rate), we adopted the proportion of dwelling expenses

Table 9.1 Indices adopted

BLI topics	Indices adopted	Target concept	Calculation methods
(1) Housing conditions	Floor area per capita (m²) ※HOI (Number of rooms per person in a dwelling)	Quality of housing	Floor area (m²)/Number of people in a dwelling
	Proportion of dwelling expenses of household income (%) ※ho1 Housing cost overburden rate	Affordability of housing	Proportion of dwelling expenses to household income excluding tax (%) = (dwelling expenses/household income excluding tax) × 100 Dwelling expenses (yen): How much are dwelling expenses per month (including house loan or house rent, heating and electricity charges, house insurance, fixed asset tax, and ground rent)?Household income excluding tax (yen): See below ((2) Income and Wealth)
(2) Income and Wealth	Household income excluding tax (million yen) ※IWI Household net adjusted disposable income	Current and future consumption possibilities	Household income excluding tax (million yen): How much is your estimated household income excluding tax, including bonuses and pensions, in 2014? Note 1: Includes aid from the federal and local governments and income from financial assets and real estate. Note 2: Tax: income tax, tax on property, cost of social security (pension, health insurance, etc.), inhabitant tax. Note 3: Excludes the sale value of financial assets and real estate.
	Assets (million yen) ※IWII Household net financial wealth		Assets (million yen) = Financial assets + non-financial assets. • Financial assets: savings, insurance products (total direct deposit) excluding non-refundable insurance, equity and equity investment trusts (actual value), claims (value), and bond investment trusts (actual value). • Non-financial assets: assessed value of house and property excluding the house and property in a company's name.

(*Continued*)

Table 9.1 (Continued)

BLI topics	Indices adopted	Target concept	Calculation methods
(3) Jobs and Earnings	Length of unemployment (months) ※JE1 Employment rate, JE11 Long-term unemployment	Quantity of jobs	Length of unemployment (months)
	Length of job contract (year) ※je2 Employees working on temporary contracts	Quality of jobs	Length of job contract (years) Options: • Permanent employee, self-employed = 40 years (hypothesized) • Employee working on a temporary contract = 1, 2, 3, 5 years (length of job contract) • Part-time employee = 1 year (hypothesized)
(4) Social Connections	Reliable people (people) ※SC1 Social network support	Personal relationships	Reliable people (people): If you were in trouble, how many people could you count on to help you whenever you needed them among your family, relatives, friends, neighbors, and coworkers? ※Options: 0, 1, 2, 3, 4, 5, 6, 7, 8, 9, or more than 10 people.
	Participation in community activities (days/year) ※sc1 Frequency of social contract sc2 Time spent volunteering	Community relationships	Participation in community activities (day/year). ※Community activity: neighborhood community association, women's society, young men's association, etc.
(5) Education and Skills	Years of education (years) ※ES1 Educational attainment es1 Education expectancy	Quantity of education	Years of education (years): Academic background Junior high school graduate = 0 High school graduate = 3

			Vocational school, specialized vocational high school, junior college = 5
			University degree = 7
			Master's degree = 9
			Doctoral degree = 11
			※Definition: years of education after compulsory education.
(6) Environmental Quality	Suspended particulate matter (SPM) concentrations (µg/m³) ※daily maximum	Quality of the environment	Suspended particulate matter (SPM) concentrations (µg/m³).
			※Source: Atmospheric Environmental Regional Observation System (AEROS)
			※Maximum one-hour value in the survey period in the monitoring point nearest respondents' residence.
	※ENI Air quality		※Using Geographical Information System (GIS).
	Proportion of park area (%) ※en3 Access to green spaces	Subjective perceptions of the environment	Proportion of park area (%): proportion of park area within a radius of 1,500 meters from respondents' residence.
			※Source: Japan's Ministry of Land, Infrastructure, Transport and Tourism (http://nlftp.mlit.go.jp/ksj/gml/datalist/KsjTmplt-L03-b-u.html).
			※Using Geographical Information System (GIS).
			※We hypothesize a 1,500-meter walking sphere.
	Proportion of forest area (%) ※en3 Access to green spaces		Proportion of forest area (%): proportion of forest area within a radius of 1,500 meters from respondents' residence.
			※Source: Japan's Ministry of Land, Infrastructure, Transport and Tourism (http://nlftp.mlit.go.jp/ksj/gml/datalist/KsjTmplt-L03-b-u.html).
			※Using Geographical Information System (GIS).
			※We hypothesize a 1,500-meter walking sphere.

(Continued)

Table 9.1 (Continued)

BLI topics	Indices adopted	Target concept	Calculation methods
(7) Civic Engagement and Governance	Not adopted		※We judge this index to be unsuitable for individual-level analysis.
(8) Health Status	Self-reported health status (-) ※HSII Self-reported health status	Morbidity in its different dimensions	Self-reported health status (-): How is your health in general? ※Rating on a scale of 0 to 10 (poor = 0; very good = 10)
(9) Subjective Well-Being	Life satisfaction (-) ※SWI Life satisfaction	Evaluation of life	Life satisfaction (-): All things considered, how satisfied are you with your life as a whole these days? Use a 0 to 10 scale, where 0 is dissatisfied and 10 is satisfied.
(10) Personal Security	Number of crimes per 1,000 members of the population (number/1,000 people) ※PSI Intentional homicidesps2 Feeling of security	Opportunities to live in a safe environment	Number of crimes per 1,000 members of the population within the municipality where respondents live (number/1,000 people). ※Source: e-Stat (portal site of the official statistics of Japan) (http://www.e-stat.go.jp/SG1/chiiki/Welcome.do).
(11) Work and Life Balance	Long working hours (hours/week) ※WLI Employees working more than 50 hours per week Time spent on leisure and personal care (hours/week) ※WLII Time in leisure and personal care	Work–life balance	Long working hours (hours/week): working hours exceed 50 hours per week ※Long working hours = average working hours per week − 50 (long working hours = 0 if average working hours per week are 50 hours or less). Time spent on leisure and personal care (hours/week): time spent on leisure and personal care per week.

to household income excluding tax, which follows the BLI policy. However, we did not adopt HOII (lack of access to basic sanitary facilities: absence of indoor housing toilets and/or a bathroom (bath or shower)) because in contrast to developing countries, most residences in Japan have good sanitation. We also did not adopt ho2 (satisfaction with housing) because we are considering objective indices rather than subjective indices for the purpose of determining policy implications.

Next, concerning (2) Income and Wealth, we adopted household income (excluding tax) as a proxy of IWI (household net adjusted disposable income). We also adopted assets (financial and non-financial assets) as a proxy of IWII (household net financial wealth). We did not adopt the other indices the OECD proposed because they are secondary or subjective.

With regard to (3) Jobs and Earnings, we adopted length of unemployment, which corresponds to the quantity of jobs, as a proxy of JEI (employment rate) and JEII (long-term unemployment). We also adopted the length of job contracts as a proxy of je2 (employees working on temporary contracts), which corresponds to the quality of jobs.

Concerning (4) Social Connections, we adopted the number of reliable people as a proxy of SCI (social network support). We also adopted participation in community activities as a proxy of sc1 (frequency of social contract) and sc2 (time spent volunteering).

With regard to (5) Education and Skills, we adopted years of education as a proxy of ESI (educational attainment) and es1 (education expectancy). On the other hand, we did not adopt ESII (students' cognitive skills) or es3 (civic skills) because it is difficult to measure these skills with our survey data.

Concerning (6) Environmental Quality, we adopted suspended particulate matter (SPM) concentrations as a proxy of ENI (air quality) and proportions of park area and forest area as proxies of en3 (access to green spaces). The indices the OECD proposed are subjective; our contribution is the development of objective indices. We did not adopt en1 (environmental burden of disease) because it is difficult to distinguish disease caused by environmental pollution from disease caused by other factors. We also did not adopt en2 (satisfaction with local environment) because it is subjective.

We consider (7) Civic Engagement and Governance unsuitable for individual-level analysis.

For (8) Health Status, we adopted self-reported health status as a proxy of HSII (self-reported health status), but did not adopt HSI (life expectancy at birth) or hs1 (infant mortality) because our survey is conducted with individuals.

Concerning (9) Subjective Well-Being, we adopted life satisfaction as a proxy of SWI (life satisfaction) because we consider its determinants in this study.

With regard to (10) Personal Security, we adopted the number of crimes per 1,000 people within a municipality in which respondents live as a proxy of PSI (intentional homicides) and ps2 (feeling of security).

Finally, concerning (11) Work and Life Balance, we adopted long working hours as a proxy of WLI (employees working more than 50 hours per week) and time spent on leisure and personal care as a proxy of WLII (time in leisure and personal care).

Table 9.2 Descriptive statistics

	N	Average	S.D.	Min.	Max.
Floor area per capita (m²)	2921	39.71	27.23	1.67	200
Proportion of dwelling expenses of household income (%)	2921	32.92	50.12	0.31	720
Household income excluding tax (million yen)	2921	0.46	2.94	0.50	20
Assets (million yen)	2921	24.70	29.80	1	200
Length of unemployment (months)	2921	0.36	1.98	0	12
Length of job contract (years)	2921	18.03	19.60	0	40
Number of reliable people (people)	2921	5.00	3.19	0	10
Participation in community activities (days/year)	2921	7.16	30.55	0	365
Years of education (year)	2921	5.25	2.20	0	12
Suspended particulate matter (SPM) concentration (µg/m³)	2921	28.76	13.13	0	240
Proportion of park area (%)	2921	2.74	3.79	0	72.88
Proportion of forest area (%)	2921	10.90	15.96	0	94.36
Self-reported health status (-)	2921	6.126	2.15	0	10
Life satisfaction (-)	2931	5.70	2.28	0	10
Number of crimes per 1,000 members of the population (number/1,000 people)	2921	13.82	7.47	0	107.60
Long working hours (hours/week)	2921	1.92	5.93	0	55
Time spent on leisure and personal care (hours/week)	2921	55.06	22.16	0	133
Age	2921	46.53	14.44	13	85
Sex dummy	2921	0.57	0.50	0	1
Marriage dummy	2921	0.66	0.47	0	1

Table 9.2 shows the descriptive statistics. To control for individual attributes, we use data on age, a sex dummy (Men = 1, Women = 0), and a marriage dummy (married = 1, not married = 0). We show the distributions of each index in Appendix A.

9.3   Life Satisfaction Approach

What aspects of daily life are highly valued? The Life Satisfaction Approach (LSA), which evaluates various aspects of daily life in terms of life satisfaction, may provide an answer. The basics of the LSA approach are shown in Figure 9.1. Here, we assume an individual whose dwelling environment has just improved: the green coverage of his/her residential area increases by 1 percent. We assume,

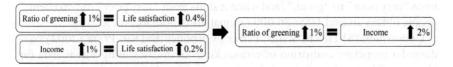

Figure 9.1 The Life Satisfaction Approach

with all other factors remaining the same, that a 1 percent increase in green coverage leads to a 0.4 percent increase in the person's life satisfaction. We also assume, with all other factors remaining the same, that a 1 percent increase in the person's income leads to a 0.2 percent increase in the person's life satisfaction. In this case, a 1 percent increase in green coverage is equal to a 2 percent increase in the person's income in terms of life satisfaction, as shown in Figure 9.1. More specifically, if the person's income is 5 million yen, then a 2 percent increase in income corresponds to 100 thousand yen, so the monetary value of a 1 percent increase in green coverage corresponds to 100 thousand yen.

Usually, the relationships between life satisfaction and other aspects of daily life are statistically estimated by multiple regression, which can estimate the relationship between two factors while the other factors remain constant. The details of this methodology are given in Appendix B. To obtain robust estimation results, we also conduct DEA, as shown in the previous chapter, to estimate individual monetary values. The details of DEA are given in Appendix B.

9.4 Literature on the Life Satisfaction Approach

A large number of studies have investigated the monetary value of environmental condition ((6) Environmental Quality), while others have addressed (4) Social Connections, (7) Civic Engagement and Governance, (8) Health Status, and (10) Personal Security.

Powdthavee (2008) focused on (4) Social Connections using (a) frequency of meeting with friends or relatives and (b) frequency of talking with neighbors as proxies. Using survey data for Great Britain, the results suggest the following: the results for (a) indicate that a person who meets with friends or relatives once or twice a month obtains a monetary value of around US$70,000[7] (annual household income), a person who meets with them once or twice a week obtains around US$100,000 (annual household income) and a person who meets with them every day obtains around US$130,000 (annual household income) compared with a person who never meets with them. The results for (b) indicate that a person who talks with neighbors once or twice a week obtains around US$48,000 (annual household income), and that a person who talks with them every day obtains around US$84,000 (annual household income) compared with a person who does not talk with them. Powdthavee (2008) also conducted estimations for unemployment ((3) Jobs and Wealth) that suggest that a person who is unemployed loses around US$140,000 (annual household income). In addition, he found that for self-reported health ((8) Health Status), people obtain around

US$500,000 (annual household income) when a self-reported evaluation shifts from "very poor" to "good,", and when it shifts from "very poor" to "excellent," people obtain around US$630,000 (annual household income).

Concerning (8) Health Status, Ferrer-i-Carbonell and van Praag (2002) conducted a monetary evaluation of various kinds of diseases using survey data for Germany. The results suggested that the monetary value ranges between 10 percent and 80 percent of household income.

There are many studies on (6) Environmental Quality. Of previous studies on air pollution, studies on PM10 are dominant. PM10 corresponds to particles less than 10 micrometers in diameter that cause respiratory disease or heart disease. PM10 stems from dust in factories and construction sites, the combustion of oil, automobile emissions, and soil particles carried by wind. World Development Indicators (2013) has found that the annual global average is 40.88 µg/m^3. The annual average for the high-income group is 22.14 µg/m^3, and for the upper-middle-income group it is 44.97 µg/m^3, for the lower-middle-income group it is 51.94 µg/m^3, and for the low-income group it is 53.84 µg/m^3. While the environmental criteria for PM10 vary by country, the WHO (2006) lists 50 µg/m^3 (24-hour average) and 20 µg/m^3 (annual average) as guideline values. Ferreira and Moro (2010) used survey data in Ireland (The Urban Institute of Ireland's National Survey on Quality of Life) and suggested that a 1 µg/m^3 increase in PM10 has an annual household income equivalent of around US$1,500.[8] Menz and Welsch (2010) used data for 25 OECD countries and showed that a 1 µg/m^3 increase in PM10 has an annual household income equivalent of US$133 to US$250.[9] Menz (2011) used data for 48 countries from 1990 to 2006 and showed that a 1µg/m^3 increase in PM10 has an annual household income equivalent of US$162 in the short term and of US$5,368 in the long term.[10] Levinson (2012) used data from the General Social Survey in the United States from 1984 to 1996 and shows that a 1µg/m^3 increase in PM10 has an annual household income equivalent of US$497 to US$964.[11] Ambley and Fleming (2013) evaluated the monetary value of greenery in Australia's main cities (public parks, community gardens, cemeteries, sports fields, national parks, and wilderness areas) and show that a 1 percent increase in greenery (1 percent = 143 m^2) has an annual household income equivalent of US$1,149.[12]

With regard to (10) Personal Security, Ambley et al. (2013) suggested a one-person decrease in the number of annual property crime victims per 1,000 members of the population in New South Wales in Australia has an annual household income equivalent of A$3,135.[13] Cohen (2014) used data for the United States from 1993 to 2004 and showed that property crime victims' damage has an annual household income equivalent of around US$114,990.

9.5   The monetary value of various aspects of life: results

Table 9.3 shows the estimation results for monetary values in terms of their annual household income equivalents. We assume an exchange rate of 100 yen to the dollar. We find ranges of monetary values among the three estimation methods. However, as mentioned in Appendix B, it is difficult to determine which

Table 9.3 Estimated monetary values in terms of annual household income equivalents

BLI topics	Indices	Units	Ordered probit regression	Stochastic frontier regression	Data envelopment analysis
(1) Housing Conditions	Dwelling expenses in household income	US$/%	–	–	332
	Floor area per capita	US$/m2	570	716	1,761
(2) Income and Wealth	Assets	US$/US$	9	9	66
(3) Jobs and Earnings	Length of unemployment	US$/month	7,439	9,497	3,898
	Length of job contract	US$/year	500	638	407
(4) Social Connections	Reliable people	US$/person	6,711	8,142	3,936
	Participation in community activities	US$/day/ year	501	471	2,270
(5) Education and Skills	Years of education	US$/year	–	–	1,252
(6) Environ-mental Quality	Suspended particulate matter (SPM) concentrations	US$/ (μg/m3)	–	–	0.18
	Proportion of park area	US$/%	2,832	3,051	21,317
	Proportion of forest area	US$/%	–	–	10,905
(8) Health Status	Self-reported health status	US$/1 point	42,893	48,899	5,582
(10) Personal Security	Number of crimes per 1,000 members of the population	US$/ (number)	–	–	27
(11) Work and Life Balance	Long working hours	US$/ (hours/ week)	2,328	2,228	60
	Time spent on leisure and personal care	US$/ (hours/ week)	763	895	123

Note: Blank cells correspond to results that are not statistically significant.

estimation result is most reliable, so we have to interpret the estimation results under a range of estimates.

Concerning "Dwelling expenses in household income" in (1) Housing Conditions, we obtain a statistically significant result only for DEA, which shows an annual household income equivalent of US$332. For "Floor area per capita," we find that the annual household income equivalent ranges from US$570/m² to US$1,761/m².

Concerning "Assets" in (2) Income and Wealth, we find that a US$1 increase in assets corresponds to an annual household income equivalent ranging from US$9 to US$66. With regard to "Length of unemployment" in (3) Jobs and Earnings, we find that a one-month increase in the period of unemployment has an annual household income equivalent ranging from US$3,898 to US$9,497, which is above Japan's average monthly income. This implies that the impact of unemployment is relatively high, as mentioned in Clark and Oswald (1994). Concerning "Length of job contract" in (3) Jobs and Earnings, we find that a one-year increase in the length of the contract has an annual household income equivalent between US$407 and US$638.

Concerning (4) Social Connections, we find that a one-person increase in "Reliable people" has an annual household income equivalent ranging from US$3,936 to US$8,142, which is almost the same as our estimated monetary values for an additional month of unemployment. With regard to "Participation in community activities" in (4) Social Connections, we find an annual household income equivalent ranging from US$471/day/year to US$2,270/day/year. With regard to "Years of education" in (5) Education and Skills, we find a statistically significant result only for DEA, which suggests that a one-year increase in years of education has an annual household income equivalent of US$1,252.

Next, concerning SPM concentrations in (6) Environmental Quality, we could only find a statistically insignificant impact of SPM concentrations in both approaches of ordered profit and SFA. Moreover, WTP of a decrease of one µg/m³ in SPM concentrations estimated by DEA is an tiny amount equivalent to US$0.18 in an annual household income, which is extremely lower than the result of Menz and Welsch's (2010) of US$133 to US$250 for 25 OECD countries.[14] With regard to "Proportion of park area" in (6) Environmental Quality, we find an annual household income equivalent ranging from US$2,832/percentage point to US$21,317/percentage point, which is higher than Ambley and Fleming's (2013) finding for Australia. This may be because the definition of greenery in Ambley and Fleming (2013) includes not only parks but also community gardens, cemeteries, sports fields, national parks, and wilderness areas. Concerning "Proportion of forest area" in (6) Environmental Quality, we find a statistically significant result only for DEA, which identifies an annual household income equivalent of US$10,905/percentage point. This is also higher than Ambley and Fleming's (2013) finding.

With regard to "Self-reported health status" in (8) Health Status, a one-point increase has an annual household income equivalent ranging from US$5,582 to US$48,899. Concerning "Number of crime per 1,000 members of the population" in (10) Personal Security, we find a statistically significant result only for DEA, which has an annual household income equivalent of US$27/crime. This is lower than the finding of Ambley et al. (2013) for Australia. With regard to "Long working hours" in (11) Work and Life Balance, we find an annual household income equivalent ranging from US$60/hour/week to US$2,328/hour/week. Concerning "Time spent on leisure and personal care" in (11) Work and Life Balance," we find an annual household income equivalent ranging from US$123/hour/week toUS$895/hour/week.

Using the coefficients estimated from probit regression and stochastic frontier regression, we consider the relative impacts among our BLI indices. We consider a 1 percent change in each index, which we define as the difference between the maximum value of the index and the minimum value of the index. Figure 9.2 shows the relative impact of all the statistically significant indices on life satisfaction, where we assume the overall impact of our BLI indices to be 100 percent. Figure 9.2 shows that "Self-reported health status" has the largest impact on life satisfaction in terms of the 1 percent change between the minimum and maximum values. This result is consistent with the result of Powdthavee (2008). We find that "Proportion of park area" has the second-largest impact on life satisfaction – it is larger than economic indices such as "Household income" and "Assets." It is also notable that "Participation in community activities" is equal to those economic indices. In summary, we find that health conditions, park areas, and social community are relatively important for people in Japan.

In addition, as mentioned previously, with DEA we can calculate individual monetary values. Figure 9.3 shows the estimated individual marginal monetary values for our BLI indices. In this figure, the horizontal axis corresponds to our

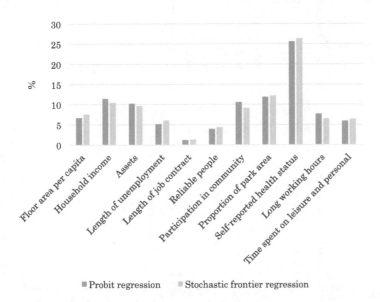

■ Probit regression ■ Stochastic frontier regression

Figure 9.2 Relative impact of our BLI indices on life satisfaction

Note: We assume that the overall impact of our BLI indices that are statistically significant is 100%.

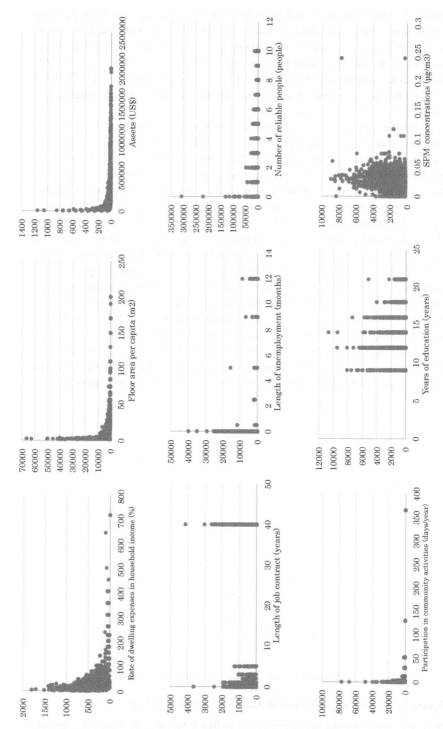

Figure 9.3 Distributions of individual monetary values

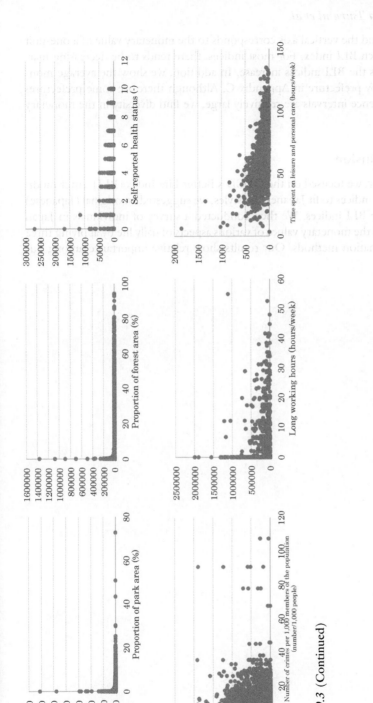

Figure 9.3 (Continued)

BLI indices and the vertical axis corresponds to the monetary value of a one-unit increase in each BLI index. For most indices, there tends to be decreasing marginal utility as the BLI indices increase. In addition, we show the average monetary values by prefecture in Appendix C. Although there are some prefectures whose confidence intervals are relatively large, we find diversity in the monetary values.

9.6   Conclusion

In this chapter, we focused on the OECD's Better Life Index (BLI). After modifying the BLI indices to fit Japanese lifestyles, we suggested an original (Japanese) version of the BLI indices. We then conducted a survey of individuals in Japan and evaluated the monetary values of various aspects of daily life by applying three kinds of estimation methods. Our results show relative importance among our BLI indices.

Appendix A

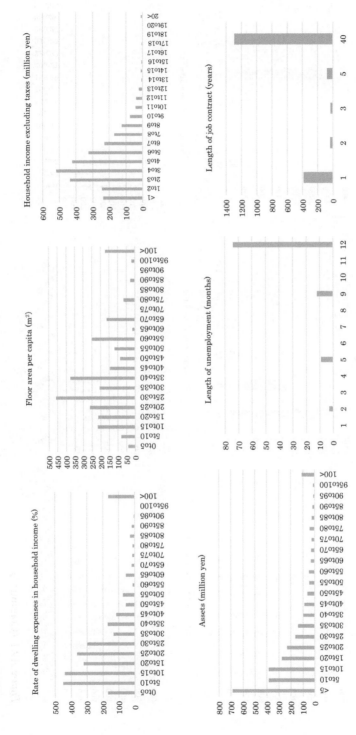

Figure A9.1 Distribution of each index

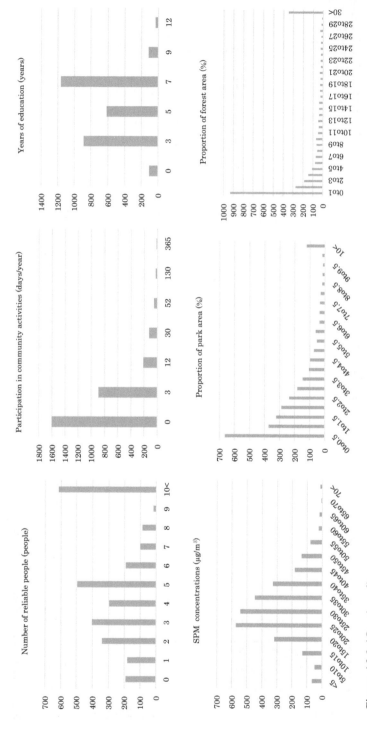

Figure A9.1 (Continued)

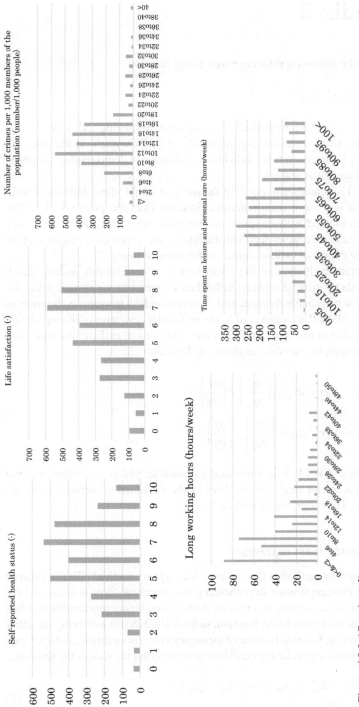

Figure A9.1 (Continued)

Appendix B

We consider the following subjective well-being function.

$$SWB^k = f\left(x^k, y^k, z^k\right) \tag{1}$$

Here, SWB^k refers to individual k's subjective well-being. $x^k = \left(x_1^k, \ldots, x_M^k\right)$ refers to individual k's various aspects of life, y^k is k's household income, and $z^k = \left(z_1^k, \ldots, z_N^k\right)$ corresponds to individual attributions (demographic variables) such as marriage status and sex.

Equation (1) includes any possible factors that could affect individual well-being; thus, it is a more comprehensive function than the previous one. This implies that compared with the previous literature using LSA, which takes only limited explanatory variables into consideration, our estimation results capture more accurate effects of various aspects of life on well-being.[15]

The monetary evaluation of life environment m corresponds to how much income y needs to increase to keep individual k's well-being constant if the life environment m marginally changes, and it corresponds to marginal willingness to pay (MWTP). MWTP is represented as the first-order derivative of the well-being function f, as shown in Equation (2). In addition, we can evaluate the monetary values of demographic variables as shown in Equation (2):

$$MWTP_m = -dy \,/\, dx_m = \left(\frac{\partial f}{\partial x_m}\right) \Big/ \left(\frac{\partial f}{\partial y}\right)$$

$$MWTP_n = -dy \,/\, dz_n = \left(\frac{\partial f}{\partial z_n}\right) \Big/ \left(\frac{\partial f}{\partial y}\right) \tag{2}$$

In estimating MWTP, it is important to consider which estimation method should be used. In this study, we use three kinds of estimation methods to obtain robust results. Hereafter, we explain each type.

B.1   Ordinary least squares

The first estimation method is the ordinary least squares method. We use ordered probit model estimation when hypothesizing the functional form as linear and the distribution of the error term as a normal distribution. Under this condition, when there is one common well-being function, individual subjective well-being can differ from the well-being function because of measuring errors or omitted variables. Coefficients are determined under the condition of minimizing the sum of the residuals.

$$SWB^k = \alpha_0 + \Sigma_{m=1}^{M} \alpha_m x_m + \beta y + \Sigma_{n=1}^{N} \gamma_n z_n + v^k$$

$$v^k \overset{iid}{\sim} N\left(0, \sigma^2\right) \tag{3}$$

After estimating Equation (3), we can determine the first-order derivative concerning x_m, y, and z_n, and we can obtain the following MWTPs.

$$MWTP_m = \alpha_m / \beta$$
$$MWTP_n = \gamma_n / \beta \tag{4}$$

Almost all the previous literature on LSA adopt the above multiple regression method. One of the problems with this method is the hypothesis that all people's well-being can be described by one well-being function. In other words, this method does not consider each person's feeling of well-being. People in the same living environment or demographic situation do not necessarily feel the same degree of life satisfaction. This is because of character differences among people, which are thought to affect individuals' sensitivity of well-being. The error term in Equation (3) includes both the part where sensitivity is reflected and the measuring error. Therefore, we cannot clearly identify the measured well-being function because we cannot identify what kind of character the person has.

B.2 Stochastic frontier regression

Stochastic frontier regression was developed by Aigner et al. (1977) and is widely applied to firm-level and industry-level analysis. This method separates the reason why firm production is separated from the production function into the difference of efficiency and the measurement error. It can then estimate the production function (production frontier) of the most efficient firm.

In our analysis, we use this estimation method to estimate the well-being function. We separate the difference from the individual well-being function into two factors: the difference from well-being sensitivity and other factors such as measurement errors. Finally, we estimate the well-being of individuals whose well-being function is the highest. While this functional form is the same as Equation (3), it includes the term of well-being sensitivity.

$$SWB^k = \alpha_0 + \Sigma_{m=1}^{M} a'_m x_m + \beta y + \Sigma_{n=1}^{N} \gamma_n z_n + v^k - u^k$$
$$v^k \overset{iid}{\sim} N\left(0, \sigma_v^2\right) \tag{5}$$
$$u \overset{iid}{\sim} N_+\left(0, \sigma_u^2\right)$$

where v^k corresponds to the error term, which is mainly reflected by the measurement error and which follows the standard normal distribution with mean zero. u^k refers to the scalar represented with well-being sensitivity with a positive value, which scale 0 for people who tend to be sensitive, and the score increases in reverse proportion to sensitivity. Here, v^k and u^k are independently distributed. As Aigner et al. (1977) suggest, we can derive the likelihood function under the above assumption and identify the coefficients of Equation (5) with the maximum–likelihood method. We can then estimate the monetary values concerning various aspects of daily life or demographics using Equation (4).

When we use an ordinary least squares method, the coefficients are determined as fitted to a combination of all people's well-being, life environment, and demographics ($\{x^k, y^k, z^k\}_{k=1}^{K}$), as possible. However, the estimated function tends to have large values when the stochastic frontier method is used because we estimate the well-being function of a person who has the most sensitive responsiveness to well-being. This is why the estimated coefficients of Equation (3) and Equation (5) are different.

B.3   Data envelopment analysis

Data envelopment analysis (DEA) was developed by Charnes et al. (1978) and is widely applied to firm-level and industry-level efficiency and to productivity analysis along with the stochastic frontier method.[16] By this estimation method, we can estimate the production function under consideration of the difference between firms' efficiency, just as with the stochastic frontier method. What is different from the ordinary least squares method and the stochastic frontier method is that DEA does not consider an error term resulting from a measurement error. In other words, it regards the gap from the production function as difference in efficiency among firms. We therefore consider that all gaps between each person's life satisfaction and the well-being function stem from the difference of responsiveness to well-being.

The application of DEA consists of two stages. First, we ignore the information of each person's demographics and regard the well-being function as having only variables concerning life environment.[17] Under this condition, we estimate the well-being function ($g(x^k, y^k)$) and responsibility against well-being (v^k).

$$SWB^k = g\left(x^k, y^k\right) \cdot v^k$$
$$v^k \geq 0 \tag{6}$$

In DEA, responsibility against well-being (v^k) is formulated as a problem of linear programming as follows:

$$1 / v^k = \max \left\{ \begin{array}{l} \varphi : \Sigma_{j=1}^{J}\lambda^j x_m^j \geq x_m^k \ for\ m = 1,\ldots, M; \\ \Sigma_{j=1}^{J}\lambda^j y^j \geq y^k; \Sigma_{j=1}^{J}\lambda^j z_n^j \geq z_n^k \ for\ n = 1,\ldots, N; \\ \Sigma_{j=1}^{J}\lambda^j y^j \leq y^k; \lambda^j \geq 0 \ for\ j = 1,\ldots, J \end{array} \right\} \tag{7}$$

Since we ignore the demographic variables, which should affect the well-being function, differences in responsibility for well-being among people are thought to be reflected by their demographics and characteristics. We therefore estimate these effects with the following regression model.

$$\log\left(v^k\right) = \gamma_n + \Sigma_{n=1}^{N}\gamma_n z_n + \varepsilon^k$$
$$\varepsilon^k \overset{iid}{\sim} N\left(0, \sigma_\varepsilon^2\right) \tag{8}$$

The error term ε^k corresponds to differences of responsibility for well-being, which stem from each person's characteristics. The other terms capture the effects of demographic changes on well-being. To summarize the above two steps, the well-being function is reformulated as follows:

$$SWB^k = g\left(x^k, y^k\right) \cdot h\left(z^k\right) \cdot \exp\left(\varepsilon^k\right) \tag{9}$$

Using Equation (9), we can calculate the first derivative ($\partial f / \partial z_n$) along with the ordinary least squares and stochastic frontier methods. However, since we estimate $g\left(x^k, y^k\right)$ by DEA, we cannot calculate the first derivative concerning income and life environment. We therefore cannot estimate the monetary values using Equations (2) and (5), so we conduct an approximate calculation as follows:

$$\left(\frac{\partial f}{\partial x_m}\right) \approx \frac{\Delta SWB}{\Delta x_m} = \frac{\left(g\left(x, y\right) - g\left(\overline{x}_m, x_{-m}, y\right)\right) h\left(z\right)}{x_m - \overline{x}_m} \tag{10}$$

$$\left(\frac{\partial f}{\partial y}\right) \approx \frac{\Delta SWB}{\Delta y} = \frac{\left(g\left(x, y\right) - g\left(x, \overline{y}\right)\right) h\left(z\right)}{y - \overline{y}} \tag{11}$$

After determining the criterion values concerning x_m and y, we calculate the increment from the criterion values ($\overline{x}_m$ and $\overline{y}$), following the increment of well-being. We then obtain the ratio. We approximate the marginal change of well-being by this ratio. If we can approximate the first derivative as in Equations (10) and (11), we can determine the monetary value concerning life environment by assigning it to Equation (2).

DEA does not consider the error term from the measurement error and therefore has the problem that estimated results are largely affected, even if there are only a few error outliers in the observation data. However, DEA has an advantage in that we can determine the well-being function more specifically since DEA does not impose functional form restrictions. In addition, as is clear from Equations (10) and (11), the first derivatives vary by life environment, income, and demographic variables. For instance, a person who lives in an area in which the green coverage is remarkably low is expected to have a larger increase in well-being from an increase in green coverage than a person who lives in an area in which the green coverage is extremely high. In addition, this increase in well-being is expected to vary by income and by age. When we apply DEA, by calculating Equations (10) and (11), the estimated monetary values vary by individual according to each person's life environment, income, and demographics. Thus, DEA has an advantage that it can calculate each person's monetary value.

In Appendix B, we compared three estimation methods: the ordinary least squares method, the stochastic frontier method, and DEA. It is notable that each method has strengths and weaknesses, and it is difficult to determine which is most reliable. We therefore show all the estimation results of the three estimation methods.

Appendix C

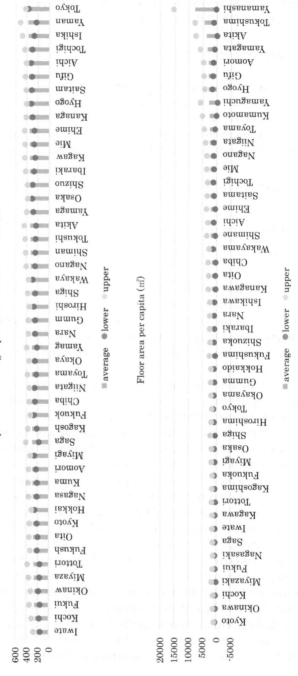

Proportion of dwelling expenses of household income (%)

■ average ● lower ● upper

Floor area per capita (㎡)

■ average ● lower ● upper

Figure A9.2 Average monetary values by prefecture in Japan

Notes: The vertical axis corresponds to the monetary value (US$) of a one-unit change in each index. The upper and lower correspond to the 95% confidential intervals.

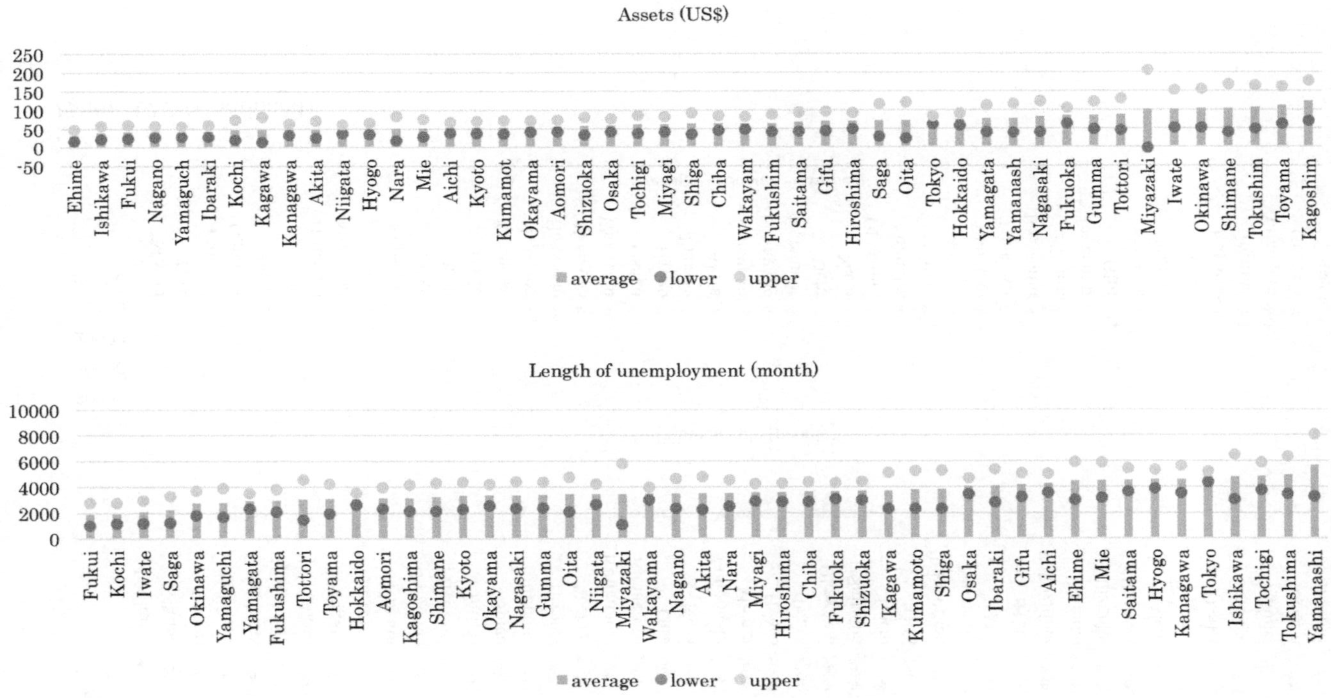

Assets (US$)

average ● lower ● upper

Length of unemployment (month)

average ● lower ● upper

Figure A9.2 (Continued)

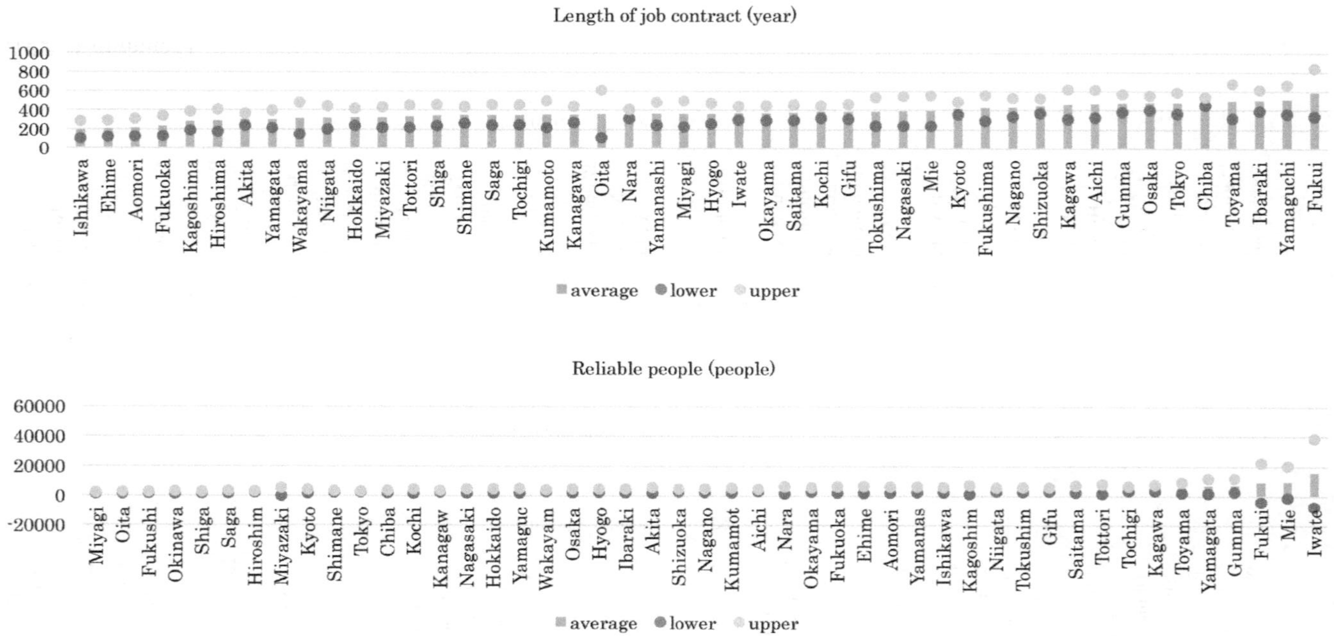

Length of job contract (year)

Fukui
Yamaguchi
Ibaraki
Toyama
Chiba
Tokyo
Osaka
Gunma
Aichi
Kagawa
Shizuoka
Nagano
Fukushima
Kyoto
Mie
Nagasaki
Tokushima
Gifu
Kochi
Saitama
Okayama
Iwate
Hyogo
Miyagi
Yamanashi
Nara
Oita
Kanagawa
Kumamoto
Tochigi
Saga
Shimane
Shiga
Tottori
Miyazaki
Hokkaido
Niigata
Wakayama
Yamagata
Akita
Hiroshima
Kagoshima
Fukuoka
Aomori
Ehime
Ishikawa

1000
800
600
400
200
0

■ average ● lower ● upper

Reliable people (people)

Iwate
Mie
Fukui
Gunma
Yamagata
Toyama
Kagawa
Tochigi
Tottori
Saitama
Gifu
Tokushim
Niigata
Kagoshim
Ishikawa
Yamanas
Aomori
Ehime
Fukuoka
Okayama
Nara
Aichi
Kumamot
Nagano
Shizuoka
Akita
Ibaraki
Hyogo
Osaka
Wakayam
Yamague
Hokkaido
Nagasaki
Kanagaw
Kochi
Chiba
Tokyo
Shimane
Kyoto
Miyazaki
Hiroshim
Saga
Shiga
Okinawa
Fukushi
Oita
Miyagi

60000
40000
20000
0
-20000

■ average ● lower ● upper

Figure A9.2 (Continued)

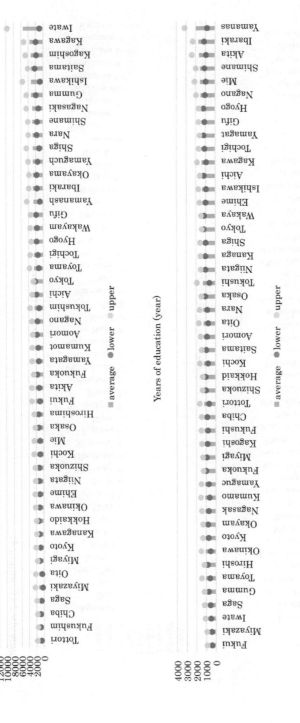

Figure A9.2 (Continued)

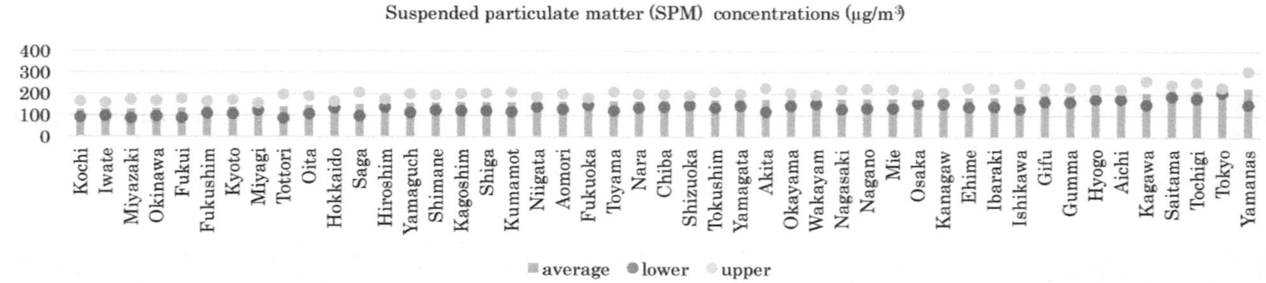

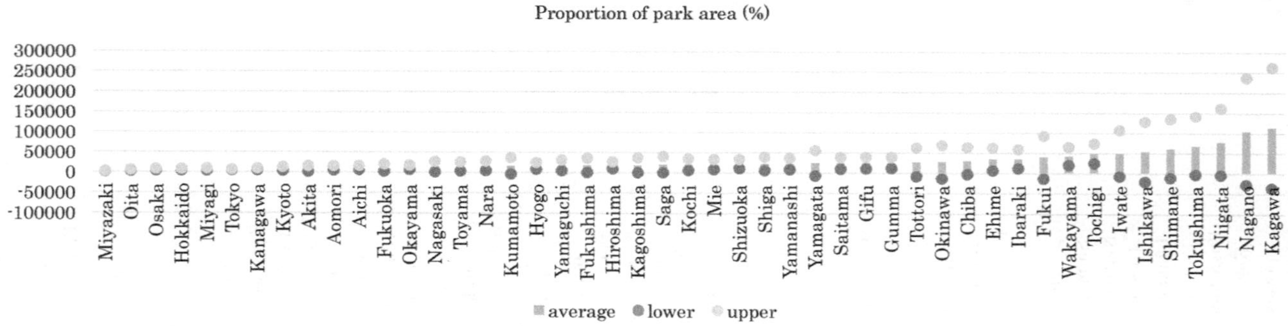

Suspended particulate matter (SPM) concentrations (μg/m³)

400
300
200
100
0

Yamanas
Tokyo
Tochigi
Saitama
Kagawa
Aichi
Hyogo
Gumma
Gifu
Ishikawa
Ibaraki
Ehime
Kanagaw
Osaka
Mie
Nagano
Nagasaki
Wakayam
Okayama
Akita
Yamagata
Tokushim
Shizuoka
Chiba
Nara
Toyama
Fukuoka
Aomori
Niigata
Kumamot
Shiga
Kagoshim
Shimane
Yamaguch
Hiroshim
Saga
Hokkaido
Oita
Tottori
Miyagi
Kyoto
Fukushim
Fukui
Okinawa
Miyazaki
Iwate
Kochi

■ average ● lower ● upper

Proportion of park area (%)

300000
250000
200000
150000
100000
50000
0
-50000
-100000

Kagawa
Nagano
Niigata
Tokushima
Shimane
Ishikawa
Iwate
Tochigi
Wakayama
Fukui
Ibaraki
Ehime
Chiba
Okinawa
Tottori
Gumma
Gifu
Saitama
Yamagata
Yamanashi
Shiga
Shizuoka
Mie
Kochi
Saga
Kagoshima
Hiroshima
Fukushima
Yamaguchi
Hyogo
Kumamoto
Nara
Toyama
Nagasaki
Okayama
Fukuoka
Aichi
Aomori
Akita
Kyoto
Kanagawa
Tokyo
Miyagi
Hokkaido
Osaka
Oita
Miyazaki

■ average ● lower ● upper

Figure A9.2 (Continued)

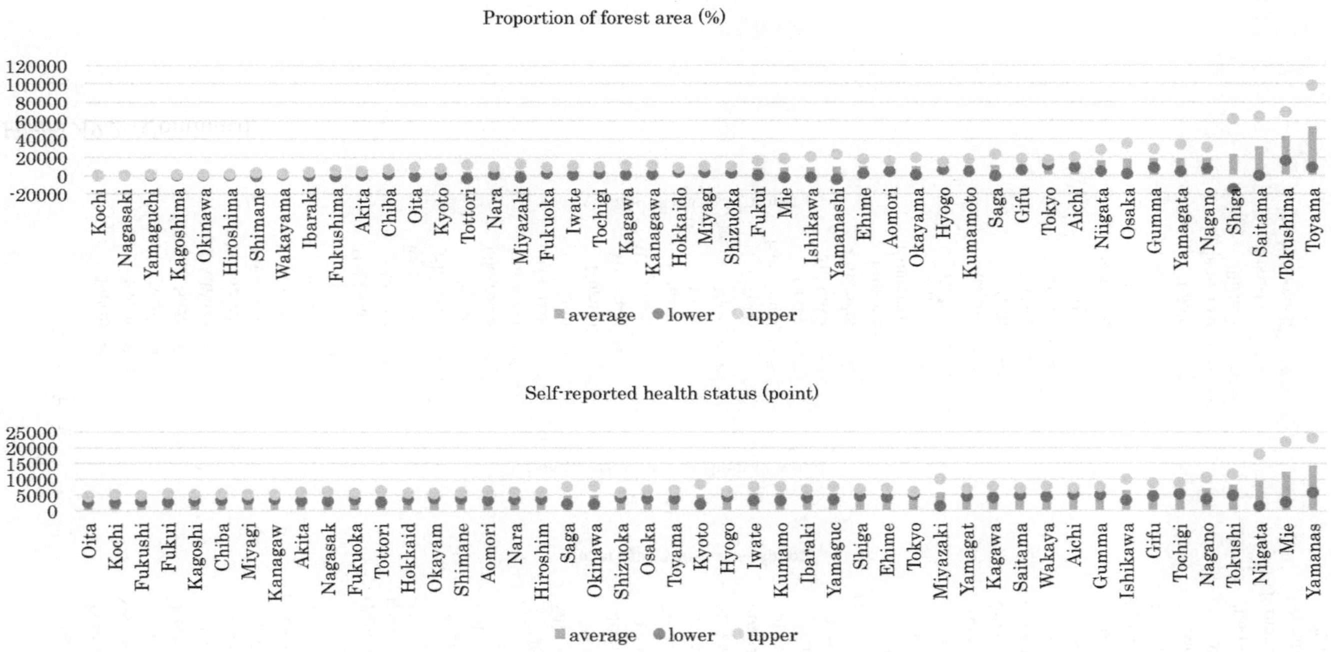

Proportion of forest area (%)

■ average ● lower ● upper

Toyama, Tokushima, Saitama, Shiga, Nagano, Yamagata, Gumma, Osaka, Niigata, Aichi, Tokyo, Gifu, Saga, Kumamoto, Hyogo, Okayama, Aomori, Ehime, Yamanashi, Ishikawa, Mie, Fukui, Shizuoka, Miyagi, Hokkaido, Kanagawa, Kagawa, Tochigi, Iwate, Fukuoka, Miyazaki, Nara, Tottori, Kyoto, Oita, Chiba, Akita, Fukushima, Ibaraki, Wakayama, Shimane, Hiroshima, Okinawa, Kagoshima, Yamaguchi, Nagasaki, Kochi

120000, 100000, 80000, 60000, 40000, 20000, 0, -20000

Self-reported health status (point)

■ average ● lower ● upper

Yamanas, Mie, Niigata, Tokushi, Nagano, Tochigi, Gifu, Ishikawa, Gumma, Aichi, Wakaya, Saitama, Kagawa, Yamagat, Miyazaki, Tokyo, Ehime, Shiga, Yamaguc, Ibaraki, Kumamo, Iwate, Hyogo, Kyoto, Toyama, Osaka, Shizuoka, Okinawa, Saga, Hiroshim, Nara, Aomori, Shimane, Okayam, Hokkaid, Tottori, Fukuoka, Nagasak, Akita, Kanagaw, Miyagi, Chiba, Kagoshi, Fukui, Fukushi, Kochi, Oita

25000, 20000, 15000, 10000, 5000, 0

Figure A9.2 (Continued)

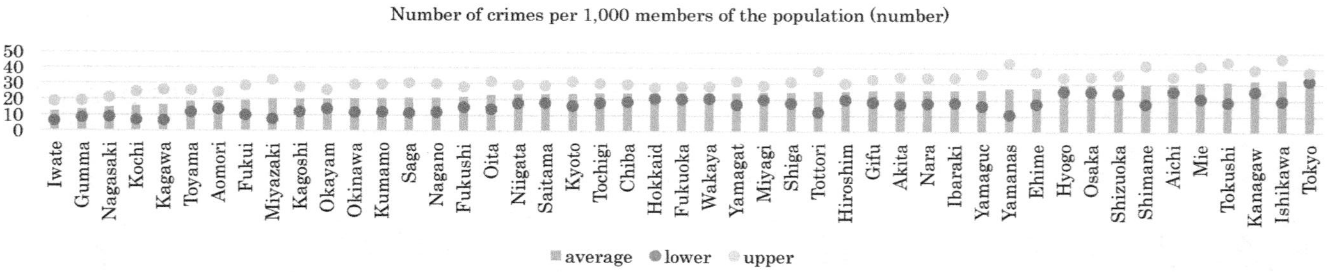

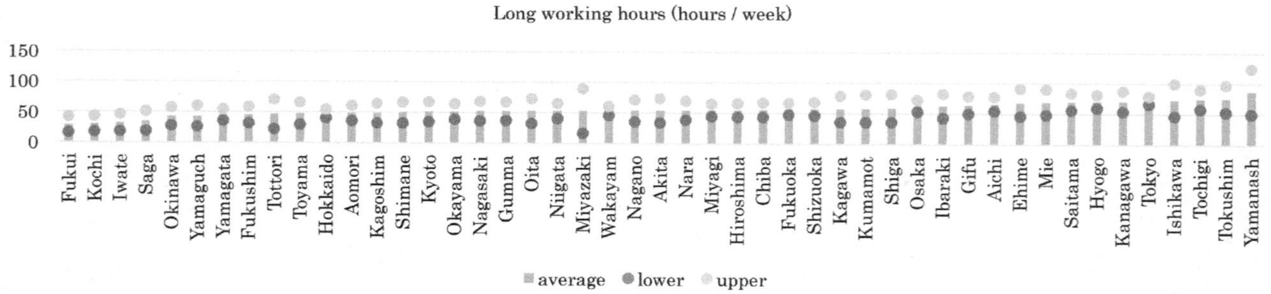

Number of crimes per 1,000 members of the population (number)

Tokyo · Ishikawa · Kanagaw · Tokushi · Mie · Aichi · Shimane · Shizuoka · Osaka · Hyogo · Ehime · Yamanas · Yamaguc · Ibaraki · Nara · Akita · Gifu · Hiroshim · Tottori · Shiga · Miyagi · Yamagat · Wakaya · Fukuoka · Hokkaid · Chiba · Tochigi · Kyoto · Saitama · Niigata · Oita · Fukushi · Nagano · Saga · Kumamo · Okinawa · Okayam · Kagoshi · Miyazaki · Fukui · Aomori · Toyama · Kagawa · Kochi · Nagasaki · Gunma · Iwate

■ average ● lower ● upper

50
40
30
20
10
0

Long working hours (hours / week)

Yamanash · Tokushim · Tochigi · Ishikawa · Tokyo · Kanagawa · Hyogo · Saitama · Mie · Ehime · Aichi · Gifu · Ibaraki · Osaka · Shiga · Kumamot · Kagawa · Shizuoka · Fukuoka · Chiba · Hiroshima · Miyagi · Nara · Akita · Nagano · Wakayam · Miyazaki · Niigata · Oita · Gunma · Nagasaki · Okayama · Kyoto · Shimane · Kagoshim · Aomori · Hokkaido · Toyama · Tottori · Fukushim · Yamagata · Yamaguch · Okinawa · Saga · Iwate · Kochi · Fukui

■ average ● lower ● upper

150
100
50
0

Figure A9.2 (Continued)

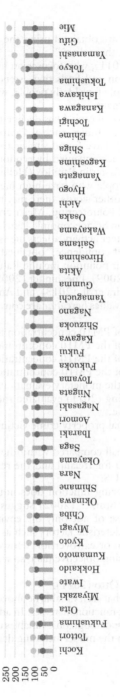

Time spent on leisure and personal care (hours / week)

■ average ● lower ● upper

Figure A9.2 (Continued)

Notes

1 Usually life satisfaction data are obtained using the question "How satisfied are you with your life as a whole these days?"
2 A related study is Plagnol (2011), who focuses on income and assets as determinants of economic satisfaction and finds that assets have a positive relationship with economic satisfaction only for elderly people, whereas income has a positive relationship for people of all ages.
3 Putnam (2000) found that social capital has declined over the last several decades in the United States, and other studies, such as Paxton (1999), Rothstein (2001), and Costa and Kahn (2003), have found similar trends in European countries. The decline of social capital accompanied by economic growth is thought to be one factor that explains the Easterlin Paradox (Helliwell, 2003; Pugno, 2009).
4 There is a possibility that people who have high life satisfaction may tend to do more volunteer activities. In other words, there may be a reverse causality problem between life satisfaction and volunteering. Meier and Stuzer (2008) considered this problem by using German Socioeconomic Panel data: they controlled for this problem and find that volunteer activity affects life satisfaction.
5 They call this direct effect "self-confidence," obtained by knowledge accumulation.
6 Other papers that consider air pollution include Rahdanz and Maddison (2008), MacKerron and Mourrato (2009), Luechinger (2009, 2010), Ferreira and Moro (2010), Menz (2011), Ferreira et al. (2013), and Ambrey et al. (2014).
7 In this chapter, all monetary values hereafter are converted in US$ 2013 using the CPI-U.
8 The sample annual average of PM10 concentration is $20.8 \ \mu g/m^3$.
9 The sample annual average of the PM10 concentration is $29.2 \ \mu g/m^3$.
10 The sample annual average of the PM10 concentration is $36.29 \ \mu g/m^3$.
11 The sample annual average of the PM10 concentration is $30.4 \ \mu g/m^3$. Menz and Welsch (2012) summarized the monetary evaluations of SO_2 and NO_2.
12 Although Ambley and Fleming (2011) evaluated the monetary value of scenery, the scenery index is subjective.
13 The average number of annual property crime victims per 1,000 members of the population was 59.7.
14 Their estimation is rather small compared with other studies: Ferreira and Moro (2010) of around US$1,500 for Ireland and the results by Levinson (2012) of US$497 to US$964 for the US.
15 It is notable that our well-being function does not include all the factors that affect well-being. Frey and Stutzer (2002) suggest that subjective well-being differs among people because of not only life environment factors and demographic factors but also characteristic factors such as self-confidence, autogenous suppression, and introversion or extroversion. However, it is difficult to capture these characteristic factors using objective data, so we do not include them in our model.
16 Please refer to Bogetoft and Otto (2011).
17 To apply DEA, it is necessary that each variable be above zero, and variables should be transformed as the well-being function increases. In addition, variables are preferred not to be zero. However, most demographic variables do not meet this requirement, so we cannot apply DEA with the model including demographic variables.

Bibliography

Aigner, D., Lovell, C.A.K., and Schmidt, P. (1977). Formulation and Estimation of Stochastic Frontier Production Function Models, *Journal of Econometrics*, 6: 21–37.

Ambrey, C., and Fleming, C. (2011). Valuing Scenic Amenity Using Life Satisfaction Data, *Ecological Economics* 72: 106–115.

Ambrey, C., and Fleming, C. (2013). Public Greenspace and Life Satisfaction in Urban Australia, *Urban Studies,* 1–32.

Ambrey, C., Fleming, C.M., and Chan, A.Y.C. (2014). Estimating the Cost of Air Pollution in South East Queensland: An Application of the Life Satisfaction Non-Market Valuation Approach, *Ecological Economics,* 97: 172–181.

Ambrey, C., Fleming, C., and Manning, M. (2013). The Life Satisfaction Approach to Estimating the Cost of Crime: An Individual's Willingness-to-Pay for Crime Reduction, *Griffith Business School Discussion Papers Economics.* No. 2013–01.

Bartolini, S., and Bonatti, L. (2003). Endogenous Growth and Negative Externalities, *Journal of Economics,* 79: 123–144.

Binder, M., and Freytag, A. (2013). Volunteering, Subjective Well-Being and Public Policy, *Journal of Economic Psychology,* 34: 97–119.

Bjørnskov, C. (2003). The Happy Few: Cross-Country Evidence on Social Capital and Life Satisfaction, *Kyklos,* 56: 3–16.

Bogetoft, P., and Otto, L. (2011). *Benchmarking with DEA, SFA, and R* (Vol. 157, p. 351). New York: Springer. doi:10.1007/978-1-4419-7961-2

Booth, A.L. and van Our, J.C. (2008). Job Satisfaction and Family Happiness: The Part-Time Work Puzzle, *Economic Journal,* 118: 77–99.

Campbell, A., Converse, P.E., and Rodgers, W.L. (1976). *The Quality of American Life: Perceptions, Evaluations, and Satisfactions.* New York: Russell Sage Foundation.

Charnes, A., Cooper, W.W., and Rhodes, E. (1978). Measuring the Efficiency of Decision Making Units, *European Journal of Operational Research,* 2(6): 429–444. doi:10.1016/0377-2217(78)90138-8

Clark, A., Diener, E., Georgellis, Y., and Lucas, R. (2006). Lags and Leads in Life Satisfaction: A Test of the Baseline Hypothesis. *Working paper,* CNRS and DELTA-Federation Jourdan.

Clark, A., and Oswald, A. (1994). Unhappiness and Unemployment, *Economic Journal* 104(424): 648–659.

Cohen, M.A. (2014). The Effect of Crime on Life Satisfaction, *Journal of Legal Studies,* 37(2): S325-S353.

Costa, D., and Kahn, M. (2003). Understanding the American Decline in Social Capital, 1952–1998, *Kyklos,* 56: 17–46.

Juncal Cuñado, J., and Gracia, F. (2012). Does Education Affect Happiness? Evidence for Spain, *Social Indicators Research,* 108: 185–196.

Das, D. (2008). Urban Quality of Life: A Case Study of Guwahati, *Social Indicator Research,* 88(2): 297–310.

Deaton, A. (2008). Income, Health and Wellbeing Around the World: Evidence from the Gallup World Poll, *Journal of Economic Perspective,* 22(2): 53–72.

Di Tella, R., MacCulloch, R.J., and Oswald, A.J. (2001). Preferences over Inflation and Unemployment: Evidence from Surveys of Happiness. *American Economic Review,* 91(1): 335–341.

Dorn, D., Fischer, J.A.V., Kirchgässner, G., and Sousa-Poza, A. (2007). Is It Culture or Democracy? The Impact of Democracy and Culture on Happiness, *Social Indicators Research,* 82(3): 505–526.

Easterlin, R. (1974). Does Economic Growth Improve the Human a Lot? Some Empirical Evidence. In P.A. David and M.W. Reder (Eds.), *Nations and Households in Economic Growth: Essays in Honor of Moses Abramovitz.* New York: Academic Press.

Fengler, A.P. (1984). Life Satisfaction of Subpopulations of Elderly, *Research on Aging*, 6: 189–212.

Ferreira, S., Akay, A., Brereton, F., Cunado, J., Martinsson, P., Moro, M., and Ningal, TF. (2013). Life Satisfaction and Air Quality in Europe, *Ecological Economics*, 88: 1–10.

Ferreira, S., and Moro, M. (2010). On the Use of Subjective Well-Being Data for Environmental Valuation, *Environmental and Resource Economics*, 46: 249–273.

Ferrer-i-Carbonell, A., and van Praag, B.M.S. (2002). The Subjective Costs of Health Losses Due to Chronic Diseases. An Alternative Model for Monetary Appraisal, *Health Economics*, 11: 709–722.

Frey, B.S., and Stutzer, A. (2000). Happiness, Economy, and Institution, *Economic Journal*, 110: 918–938.

Frey, B.S., and Stutzer, A. (2002). *Happiness and Economics: How the Economy and Institutions Affect Well-Being*. Princeton, NJ: Princeton University Press.

Gerlach, K., and Stephan, G. (1996). A Paper on Unhappiness and Unemployment in Germany, *Economic Letters*, 52(3): 325–330.

Havighurst, R.J., Neugarten, B.L., and Tobin, S.S. (1968). Disengagement and Patterns of Aging. In B.L. Neugarten (Ed.), Middle Age and Aging: A Reader in Social Psychology. Chicago: University of Chicago Press.

Helliwell, J.F. (2003). How's Life? Combining Individual and National Variables to Explain Subjective Wellbeing, *Economic Modelling*, 20: 331–360.

Helliwell, J.F., and Huang, H. (2008). How's Your Government? International Evidence Linking Good Government and Well-Being, *British Journal of Political Science*, 359: 1435–1446.

Helliwell, J.F., and Putnam, R.D. (2004). The Social Context of Well-Being. *Philosophical Transactions of the Royal Society* B, 359: 1435–1446.

Ibem, E.O., and Amole, D. (2013). Subjective Life Satisfaction in Public Housing in Urban Areas of Ogun State, Nigeria, *Cites*, 35: 51–61.

Inglehart, R., and Klingemann, H.D. (2000). Genes, Culture, Democracy, and Happiness. In E. Diener and E.M. Suh (Eds.), *Culture and Subjective Well-Being*. Cambridge: MIT Press.

Jiménez, M.M.S., Artés, J., and Salinas-Jiménez, J. (2011). Education as a Positional Good: A Life Satisfaction Approach, *Social Indicators Research*, 103: 409–426.

Kahneman, D., and Deaton, A. (2010). High Income Improves Evaluation of Life but Not Emotional Well Being, *PNAS*, 107(38): 16490–16493.

Lee, E., and Park, N.K. (2010). Housing Satisfaction and Quality of Life Among Temporary Residents in the United States, *Housing and Society*, 37(1): 43–67.

Levinson, A. (2012). Valuing Public Goods Using Happiness Data: The Case of Air Quality, *Journal of Public Economics*, 96: 869–880.

Luechinger, S. (2009). Valuing Air Quality Using the Life Satisfaction Approach, *Economic Journal* 119: 482–515.

Luechinger, S. (2010). Life Satisfaction and Transboundary Air Pollution, *Economic Letters*, 119: 482–515.

MacKerron, G., and Mourato, S. (2009). Life Satisfaction and Air Quality in London, *Ecological Economics* 68: 1441–1453.

MacKerron, G., and Mourato, S. (2013). Happiness is Greater in Natural Environments, *Global Environmental Change*, 68: 1441–1453.

Maddison, D., and Rehdanz, K. (2011). The Impact of Climate on Life Satisfaction, *Ecological Economics*, 70: 2437–2445.

Maddox, G.L. (1968). Persistence of Life Style Among the Elderly: A Longitudinal Study of Patterns of Social Activity in Relation to Life Satisfaction. In B.L. Neugarten (Ed.), *A Reader in Social Psychology* (pp. 181–183). Chicago: University of Chicago Press.

Meier, S., and Stutzer, A. (2008). Is Volunteering Rewarding in Itself?, *Economica*, 75: 39–59.

Menz, T. (2011). Do People Habituate to Air Pollution? Evidence from International Life Satisfaction Data, *Ecological Economics* 71: 211–219.

Menz, T., and Welsch, H. (2010). Population Aging and Environmental Preferences in OECD Countries: The Case of Air Pollution, *Ecological Economics*, 69: 2582–2589.

Menz, T., and Welsch, H. (2012). Life-Cycle and Cohort Effects in the Valuation of Air Quality: Evidence from Subjective Well-Being Data, *Land Economics*, 88(2): 300–325.

Moen, P., Dempster-McClain, D., and Williams, R.M., Jr. (1992). Successful Aging: A Life-Course Perspective on Women's Multiple Roles and Health, *American Journal of Sociology*, 97: 1612–1638.

OECD (2011). *How's Life?: Measuring Well-Being*. Paris: OECD Publishing.

Oswald, F., Wahl, H.W., Mollenkopf, H., and Schilling, O. (2003). Housing and Life-Satisfaction of Older Adults in Two Rural Regions in Germany, *Research on Aging*, 25(2): 122–143.

Paxton, P. (1999). Is Social Capital Declining in the United States? A Multiple Indicator Assessment, *American Journal of Sociology*, 105: 88–127.

Peck, C., and Stewart, K.K. (1985). Satisfaction with Housing and Quality of Life, *Home Economics Research Journal*, 13(4): 363–372.

Pouwels, B., Siegers, J., and Vlasblom, J.D. (2008). Income, Working Hours, and Happiness, *Economics Letters*, 99: 72–74.

Powdthavee, N. (2005). Unhappiness and Crime: Evidence from South Africa, *Economica*, 72: 531–547.

Powdthavee, N. (2008). Putting a Price Tag on Friends, Relatives, and Neighbours: Using Surveys of Life Satisfaction to Value Social Relationships, *Journal of Socio-Economics*, 37: 1459–1480.

Plagnol, A.C. (2011). Financial Satisfaction Over the Life Course: The Influence of Assets and Liabilities, *Journal of Economic Psychology*, 32: 45–64.

Pugno, M. (2009). The Easterlin Paradox and the Decline of Social Capital: An Integrated Explanation, *The Journal of Socio-Economics*, 38: 590–600.

Putnam, R.D. (2000). *Bowling Alone*. New Cork: Simon & Schuster.

Rehdanz, K., and Maddison, D. (2008). Local Environmental Quality and Life-Satisfaction in Germany, *Ecological Economics*, 64: 787–797.

Richards, R., O'Leary, B., and Mutsunziwa, K. (2007). Measuring Quality of Life in Informal Settlements in South Africa, *Social Indicators Research*, 81: 375–388.

Rothstein, B. (2001). Social Capital in the Social Democratic Welfare State, *Politics and Society*, 29: 207–241.

Salinas-Jimenez, M.D.M., Artes, J., and Salinas- Jimenez, J. (2011). Education as a Positional Good: A Life Satisfaction Approach, *Social Indicators Research*, 103: 409–426.

Stevenson, B., and Wolfers, J. (2008). Economic Growth and Subjective Well-Being: Reassessing the Easterlin Paradox. Brookings Papers on Economic Activity, Economic Studies Program, *The Brookings Institution*, 39(1): 1-102.

Stevenson, B., and Wolfers, J. (2013). Social Capital and Subjective Wellbeing in Europe: A New Approach on Social Capital. Brookings Papers on Economic Activity, *Social Indicator Research,* 114: 493–511.

Tsurumi, T., Kuramashi, K., and Managi, S. (2013). Determinants of Happiness: Environmental Degradation and Attachment to Nature. In S. Managi (Ed.), *The Economics of Biodiversity and Ecosystem Services.* New York: Routledge,.

van Praag, B.M.S., and Baarsma, B.E. (2005). Using Happiness Surveys to Value Intangibles: The Case of Air Port, *Economic Journal,* 114: 224–246.

Ward, R.A. (1979). The Meaning of Voluntary Association Participation to Older People, *Journal of Gerontology,* 34, 438–445.

Welsch, H. (2002). Preferences over Prosperity and Pollution: Environmental Valuation Based on Happiness Surveys, *Kyklos,* 55(4): 473–494.

Westaway, M.S. (2006). A Longitudinal Investigation of Satisfaction with Personal and Environmental Quality of Life in an Informal South African Housing Settlement, Doornkop, Soweto, *Habitat International,* 30: 175–189.

World Health Organization. (2006). *WHO Air Quality Guidelines for Particulate Matter, Ozone, Nitrogen Dioxide and Sulfur Dioxide: Global Update 2005.* Geneva: WHO Press.

Zabardast, E. (2009). The Housing Domain of Quality of Life and Life Satisfaction in the Spontaneous Settlements on the Tehran Metropolitan Fringe, *Social Indicators Research,* 90: 307–324.

Part 3

Towards green growth

Analysis and actions

10 Effects of disasters on markets

Yutaka Ito and Shunsuke Managi

10.1 Introduction

The world has witnessed an alarming increase in the frequency and severity of disasters. According to the report of Emergency Events Database (ED-MAT),[1] a total of 196 natural disasters occurred in 2012 that killed about 10,783 people and affected over 104 million people in the world. The estimated amount of economic damage was US$290 billion. In most disasters, the bulk of immediate damage is caused by destroyed assets, such as buildings, infrastructure, inventories, and growing crops. Disasters also generate short- and long-term losses in economic activity and income in the affected area, as people and companies lose their means of production and access to markets.

There is accumulating evidence regarding the relationship between fatalities or damage from disasters and mitigation measures. For example, using data from 73 countries from 1980 to 2002, Kahn (2005) found that countries with high gross domestic product (GDP) per capita suffer fewer deaths from natural disasters compared with countries with low GDP per capita. Similarly, using data from 151 countries from 1960 to 2003, Toya and Skidmore (2007) found that the economic damage resulting from disasters in wealthy countries is less than the damage incurred in poor countries. Kellenberg and Mobarak (2008) showed that the relationship between GDP per capita and death tolls is an inverted U-shape, which is similar to the environmental Kuznets curve hypothesis (Grossman and Krueger, 1995). In addition, Anbarci et al. (2005) showed that GDP per capita and inequity have negative and positive influences on fatalities resulting from disasters based on the analysis of 269 earthquakes from 1960 to 2002. Escaleras et al. (2007) obtained the same results in line with the literature. These previous studies indicate that an increase in GDP per capita in developed countries leads to a decrease in natural disaster damage.

In addition to this research, there are also papers that have conducted the estimation for the changes of market prices in response to natural disasters, which we introduce later. If the stock market could rapidly provide information on the true impact of disasters on the economy, that might be a convenient tool for decision-making in order to recover such damage. Thus, in this chapter we analyze the responses of stock market price to natural disasters using an event study approach by taking the Great Hanshin Earthquake and the Great East Japan Earthquake as examples.

The remainder of this chapter is organized in the following manner. Section 10.2 provides the information about the Great East Japan Earthquake and the Great Hanshin Earthquake. Section 10.3 shows an analysis of the previous literature regarding using an event study analysis. Sections 10.4 and 10.5 describe the empirical methodology and data, respectively. Section 10.6 presents and discusses the empirical results, and Section 10.7 summarizes and concludes the chapter.

10.2   The Great East Japan Earthquake and the Great Hanshin Earthquake

On Friday, March 11, 2011, Japan experienced the world's fourth-largest earthquake in recorded history (Japan Meteorological Agency, 2011), with a magnitude of 9.0.[2] This devastating earthquake, called the Great East Japan Earthquake, caused catastrophic damage to Japan. The National Police Agency (2011) reported 15,636 people dead and 5,699 injured. In addition, 4,808 people are still reported missing. In both the Tohoku district and in other regions electricity, gas, and water were disconnected. Roads, railways, airports, and other transportation infrastructure were also severely damaged by the earthquake and the subsequent destructive tsunami. Nuclear accidents at the Fukushima Dai-ichi nuclear plant began on March 12, 2011, with a series of equipment failures, nuclear meltdowns, and releases of radioactive materials occurring at this nuclear power plant following the earthquake and tsunami. These effects have continued to worsen and have created uncertainty in the Japanese economy.

From a financial perspective, the ability of the market to function after the shock of a disaster is based on effective resource allotment. Hence, we analyze the market's reaction to the effect of two devastating earthquakes in Japan, the Great East Japan Earthquake and the Great Hanshin Earthquake. The Great Hanshin Earthquake, which occurred on January 17, 1995, created the third-largest amount of human damage (Kinki Construction Association, 2005), with 6,433 deaths and 512,882 damaged buildings. In our study, we compare the market's reaction to each disaster.

Figure 10.1 shows the daily returns of the Nikkei Stock Price Average for 30 transaction days before and after both the Great Hanshin Earthquake and the Great East Japan Earthquake (i.e., the disaster occurred on transaction day 0). Table 10.1 provides the summary of the daily average returns and the standard deviation of the Nikkei Stock Price Average before and after the day of the event.

Compared to the daily returns on the average price before the event, the value after the event was approximately 0.4% and 0.2% lower for the Great Hanshin Earthquake and the Great East Japan Earthquake, respectively. In particular, in the case of the Great East Japan Earthquake, the daily returns declined by 10%

on the transaction day after the earthquake occurred. In addition, the standard deviation after each event was 1.0 and 1.8 points higher than the value before the two disasters, respectively. Thus, we consider these market fluctuations and their magnitudes as a process of adjustment to economic damage, and we examine how the market reacts to these unanticipated and devastating disasters. As explained in the following section, the event study analysis is employed to investigate the shock of the stock prices from the disaster in the literature.

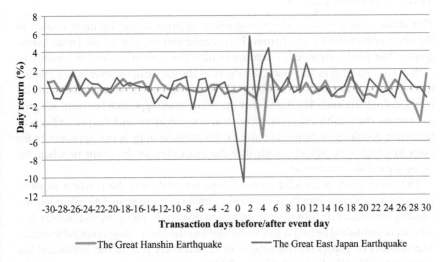

Figure 10.1 Daily return of Nikkei Stock Average before and after event day

Table 10.1 Daily return and standard deviation of Nikkei Stock Average before and after event day

Event		Transaction days before/after the event (day)	
		– 30 to – 1 *(Before the event)*	*0 to 30* *(After the event)*
The Great Hanshin Earthquake	Daily return (%)	0.099	– 0.391
	St. Dev	0.637	1.624
The Great East Japan Earthquake	Daily return (%)	0.016	– 0.187
	St. Dev	1.04	2.809

Because the sample size is relatively small, there may be a bias in the industrial sector for earlier studies. These earlier studies may be effective for understanding a localized event; however, the Great East Japan Earthquake and the subsequent nuclear power plant disaster extensively affected not only the Tohoku area but also the entirety of Japan and the world. Hence, it is important to consider this disaster on a more comprehensive scale. For these reasons, we use a large sample of stock prices to compare the effects of the catastrophic earthquake on the Japanese industrial sectors.

10.3 Previous studies

This study analyzes the stock-price reaction of firms in the Japanese market in the aftermath of the Great Hanshin Earthquake and the Great East Japan Earthquake. The study attempts to determine how the market reacted differently to each event. To analyze the financial effects of the catastrophic events, we employ the event study approach. MacKinlay (1997) describes the characteristics of this methodology in detail. He shows that the event study approach has been adopted to examine the wealth effects of mergers and acquisitions and the price effects of financing decisions by firms. The use of this methodology is not appropriate for cases in which it is difficult to identify the exact date of the event or when the event is partially anticipated.

The event study is a useful methodology for analyzing the reaction of stock prices to a particular event. In the field of finance, more than 565 event studies (dealing with share distributions, earnings or dividends, mergers, and massive lay-offs) were published between 1974 and 2000 in the five leading financial journals. The number of papers on this subject increased every year in the 1980s and has remained stable (Kothari and Warner, 2006).

In addition to the financial literature, empirical studies investigate the relationship between environmental and financial performances. Takeda and Tomozawa (2008) and Yamaguchi (2008) analyzed how stock prices react to the announcements of environmental ratings in Japan using the event study method. Martin and Dominic (2007) examined whether corporate financial performance is affected by the public endorsement of environmental and social performances in the U.K. market. This literature estimates the market's reaction to positive announcements from companies, such as environmentally friendly efforts.

There are also several studies that examine the effects of negative announcements on stock prices. For instance, Klassen and McLaughlin (1996) and Rao (1996) investigated whether pollution accidents cause stock prices to decrease. Gunther and Laguna (2010) examined the stock market's reaction to 64 explosions in the petrochemical industry.

Similarly, a few studies have examined the financial implications of natural disasters. These studies examine the relationship between the returns to the stock market and a variety of unexpected catastrophic events, such as airline crashes (Barrett, Heuson, Kolb, and Schropp, 1987; Davidson, Chandy, and

Cross, 1987; David and Betty, 2004), hurricanes (Lamb, 1995, 1998; Angbazo and Narayanan, 1996; Hanabusa, 2010), and earthquakes (Shelor, Anderson, and Cross, 1991, 1992). A few studies have examined nuclear accidents, such as the Three Mile Island accident (Bowen, Castanias, and Daley, 1983; Hill and Schneeweis, 1983) and the Chernobyl nuclear meltdown (Kalra, Henderson, and Raines, 1993; Fields and Janjigian, 1989). We employ the event study approach to examine the effects of two catastrophic events on the stock prices of Japanese industries.[3]

10.4   Event study methodology

We performed a daily event study, as implemented by MacKinlay (1997), to examine stock price behavior related to the disaster. The change in the equity value associated with the disaster is taken as an unbiased estimate of the total financial consequences of the event. The first task in conducting the event study is to define the event of interest and the period over which the share prices of the firms involved are examined (i.e., the event window). It is common to use a larger event window than the specific period of interest. That is, the window runs from a few days before to a few days after the event to capture the changes in the stock prices over the long term. In our study, the event window is the period of [0: 30] (i.e., 30 transaction days after the day the event occurred).

The market model is applied to describe the behavior of the asset returns and to separate the changes in the value of the overall market effects caused by the disaster. The normal relationship between the observed returns of a given stock i at time t, $R_{i,t}$, and the market returns at the same time, $R_{m,t}$, is given by Equation (1):

$$R_{i,t} = \alpha_i + \beta_i R_{m,t} + \varepsilon_{i,t}. \tag{1}$$

The term $\beta_i R_{m,t}$ is the portion of the return to the security i on the day that is due to market-wide factors. The parameter α_i measures the effects of the average daily returns on the stock that are not due to market movements. Finally, $\varepsilon_{i,t}$ measures the effects of the change in the value of the stock of firm i on day t that is not due either to movement in the market or to the firm's average daily return, and assumes that the error terms (i.e., the abnormal returns) are *iid*. This means that the stock has an expected return of zero and a constant variance of σ^2. On the day of an event (here, the Great Hanshin Earthquake on Tuesday, January 17, 1995, and the Great East Japan Earthquake on Friday, March 11, 2011), the deviation in an individual stock's daily return from what is expected is based on Equation (1). That is, the prediction error is taken as an unbiased estimate of the financial effects of the event. The abnormal return (*AR*) is calculated as follows in Equation (2):

$$AR_{i,t} = R_i - \hat{\alpha}_i - \hat{\beta}_i R_{m,t}. \tag{2}$$

Equation (2) represents the abnormal return or the prediction error, where $\hat{\alpha}_i$ and $\hat{\beta}_i$ are the estimates of α_i and β_i, respectively. Abnormal returns are computed given the market model parameters estimated with the ordinary least squares method through the period $[-246: -1]$ in the event time (i.e., the estimation window). We set the estimation window for each event at 246 transaction days prior to the day of the disaster.

We calculate the average abnormal daily return (AAR) of the two events in the 32 categories of the Japanese industry to compare the reaction of each industrial stock price. The average abnormal returns across N companies are calculated using Equation (3):

$$AAR_{i,t} = \frac{1}{N}\sum_{1}^{N} AR_{i,t}. \tag{3}$$

Moreover, we examine the average cumulative abnormal return ($ACAR$) through the period $[0: 30]$ (i.e., the event window) to verify the trend of the abnormal returns in each industry after the event and calculated it using Equation (4):

$$ACAR_{i,t} = \sum_{t=0}^{t} AAR_{i,t}. \tag{4}$$

Following MacKinlay (1997), we calculate the standard t-statistic for each industrial average abnormal return and the average cumulative abnormal return for each event to determine whether the market reacted efficiently to the shock of the disaster (i.e., the null hypothesis is H0: $AAR=0$ ($ACAR=0$)).

10.5   Data

To investigate the market's reaction to the devastating earthquake, we obtain the daily closing stock price for the companies listed in the first section of the Tokyo Stock Exchange and the Nikkei Stock Average index from the Yahoo! Finance website. In Tables 10.2 and 10.3, we summarize this data for the case of the Great Hanshin Earthquake and for the case of the Great East Japan Earthquake using the criteria of the middle classification of the Tokyo Stock Exchange.

We eliminate the firms with missing returns. The number of the sample is 603 for the Great Hanshin Earthquake and 1,019 for the Great East Japan Earthquake. In Table 10.4, we present the date of the estimation window, the event day, and the event window for each event. The estimation window and the event window are 246 and 31 transaction days, respectively.

10.6   Results and discussion

In this section, we provide the empirical results for the events studied and discuss the reaction of the Japanese industry to these two disasters. The results are

Table 10.2 Summary of stock price in each sector before/after the Great Hanshin Earthquake

Sector	Before the event (Jan. 14, 1994, to Jan. 13, 1995)				After the event (Jan. 17 to Feb. 28, 1995)				Sample
	Average (%)	St. Dev	Max (%)	Min (%)	Average (%)	St. Dev	Max (%)	Min (%)	
Fishery, Agriculture & Forestry	0.025	1.81	10.50	-5.68	-0.39	2.53	8.71	-10.76	3
Mining	0.031	1.90	11.19	-7.27	-0.34	1.94	4.94	-6.94	3
Construction	-0.049	1.70	17.58	-19.80	0.16	3.74	21.76	-18.69	48
Foods	0.005	1.92	19.23	-16.13	-0.33	2.35	12.20	-10.66	32
Textile & Apparels	0.061	1.96	17.32	-8.89	-0.40	2.71	17.21	-15.74	19
Pulp & Paper	0.085	1.75	11.91	-9.47	-0.55	2.05	6.06	-7.80	6
Chemicals	0.062	1.94	16.60	-10.15	-0.39	2.41	10.28	-11.43	68
Pharmaceutical	-0.014	1.59	11.40	-17.70	-0.22	1.90	9.84	-8.99	15
Oil & Coal Products	0.003	1.53	9.76	-6.47	-0.46	2.45	6.14	-7.38	2
Rubber Products	0.046	1.62	11.53	-7.77	-0.40	2.65	17.54	-7.04	7
Glass & Ceramics Products	0.030	1.96	11.28	-10.48	-0.26	2.76	11.00	-11.34	18
Iron & Steel	0.086	2.03	24.43	-11.86	-0.37	2.80	18.94	-11.20	23
Nonferrous Metals	0.029	1.67	16.36	-7.60	-0.47	2.57	11.36	-9.98	15
Metal Products	-0.022	1.86	14.76	-17.34	-0.40	2.94	9.15	-16.67	9
Machinery	0.081	1.97	17.94	-13.49	-0.48	2.66	22.69	-11.47	48
Electric Appliances	0.045	1.95	35.56	-10.91	-0.48	2.48	31.87	-20.00	83
Transport Equipment	0.065	1.80	16.00	-10.56	-0.54	2.08	10.33	-8.02	31
Precision Instruments	0.036	1.85	19.61	-10.75	-0.35	2.36	15.38	-8.99	11

(Continued)

Table 10.2 (Continued)

Sector	Before the event (Jan. 14, 1994, to Jan. 13, 1995)				After the event (Jan. 17 to Feb. 28, 1995)				Sample
	Average (%)	St. Dev	Max (%)	Min (%)	Average (%)	St. Dev	Max (%)	Min (%)	
Other Products	0.041	2.01	13.49	-11.99	-0.41	2.82	18.85	-12.13	17
Electric Power & Gas	-0.059	1.18	9.07	-6.29	-0.19	2.17	9.41	-11.79	12
Land Transportation	-0.009	1.38	13.22	-7.46	-0.23	1.89	9.38	-7.06	19
Marine Transportation	0.061	1.83	14.56	-8.85	-0.53	2.45	10.75	-11.44	6
Air Transportation	-0.004	1.67	5.26	-6.00	-0.10	2.86	10.43	-7.21	2
Warehousing and Harbor transportation	-0.020	1.78	13.21	-6.59	-0.44	3.05	16.29	-8.71	6
Information & Communication	0.055	2.03	13.21	-16.60	-0.53	2.42	12.99	-10.84	10
Wholesale Trade	0.050	2.13	21.05	-18.60	-0.49	2.64	16.39	-10.50	30
Retail Trade	-0.013	1.88	12.59	-13.79	-0.66	2.56	7.14	-15.75	17
Banks	0.015	1.57	8.70	-6.14	-0.24	2.13	10.70	-9.41	17
Securities & Commodity Futures	0.021	2.35	18.54	-11.11	-0.47	3.34	14.29	-8.87	6
Other Financing Business	-0.002	1.88	11.76	-8.60	-0.54	2.58	8.57	-11.59	6
Real Estate	0.012	2.03	15.38	-7.43	-0.21	3.65	18.42	-10.11	8
Services	-0.004	1.72	11.54	-8.59	-0.30	2.39	8.44	-6.89	6
Total	0.032	1.87	35.56	-19.80	-0.37	2.63	31.87	-20.00	603

Table 10.3 Summary of stock price in each sector before/after the Great East Japan Earthquake

Sector	Before the event (Mar. 9, 2010, to Mar. 10, 2011)				After the event (Mar. 11 to Apr. 25, 2011)				Sample
	Average (%)	St. Dev	Max (%)	Min (%)	Average (%)	St. Dev	Max (%)	Min (%)	
Fishery, Agriculture & Forestry	0.012	1.19	5.52	-5.16	-0.38	3.21	8.92	-15.21	4
Mining	0.011	2.09	8.51	-9.42	0.42	6.26	22.86	-23.36	3
Construction	0.015	2.16	32.14	-14.71	0.67	7.57	82.61	-26.50	65
Foods	-0.019	1.40	23.95	-8.93	-0.15	3.71	19.23	-23.42	48
Textile & Apparels	0.064	2.46	44.12	-12.96	-0.24	5.04	26.83	-25.35	27
Pulp & Paper	0.027	1.71	14.17	-7.44	-0.20	4.76	24.32	-21.74	8
Chemicals	0.041	1.94	31.91	-16.57	-0.07	4.83	27.56	-28.25	90
Pharmaceutical	0.004	1.48	26.76	-9.92	-0.15	3.40	15.64	-20.72	27
Oil & Coal Products	0.115	1.65	6.39	-6.32	0.21	4.09	12.39	-21.63	3
Rubber Products	0.064	1.87	12.86	-6.01	-0.25	3.92	15.55	-20.67	9
Glass & Ceramics Products	0.091	2.65	38.33	-20.90	0.14	5.84	32.97	-27.59	23
Iron & Steel	0.041	2.46	46.67	-26.19	0.06	5.64	32.17	-25.81	27
Nonferrous Metals	0.057	2.27	21.92	-13.73	0.08	5.54	37.97	-25.00	18
Metal Products	0.018	2.43	27.68	-13.89	0.40	6.46	75.00	-25.81	22
Machinery	0.087	2.48	46.00	-13.60	-0.02	5.49	69.44	-33.33	88
Electric Appliances	0.062	2.96	50.00	-33.33	-0.10	5.49	52.94	-50.00	122
Transport Equipment	0.075	2.10	27.21	-14.07	-0.21	4.19	18.95	-25.50	44
Precision Instruments	0.012	2.08	18.18	-14.20	-0.19	4.43	30.77	-20.41	15

(Continued)

Table 10.3 (Continued)

Sector	Before the event (Mar. 9, 2010, to Mar. 10, 2011)				After the event (Mar. 11 to Apr. 25, 2011)				Sample
	Average (%)	St. Dev	Max (%)	Min (%)	Average (%)	St. Dev	Max (%)	Min (%)	
Other Products	0.002	2.14	22.13	-15.60	0.10	5.19	38.17	-34.43	31
Electric Power & Gas	-0.024	0.94	4.33	-7.76	-0.81	4.94	23.53	-24.68	13
Land Transportation	-0.027	1.30	10.96	-12.98	-0.25	3.24	14.29	-21.05	27
Marine Transportation	-0.049	2.01	7.54	-8.09	-0.48	4.80	23.08	-27.78	6
Air Transportation	0.233	2.69	19.74	-15.91	-0.09	5.58	20.32	-18.10	3
Warehousing and Harbor Transportation	0.022	1.59	15.56	-5.84	-0.20	3.71	11.65	-15.92	9
Information & Communication	0.025	2.02	32.65	-20.36	-0.33	4.37	22.41	-23.92	40
Wholesale Trade	0.120	4.62	100.00	-50.00	-0.08	5.16	33.33	-40.00	69
Retail Trade	0.019	2.06	36.36	-17.86	-0.14	4.86	33.33	-32.53	51
Banks	-0.013	1.58	12.54	-15.38	-0.26	3.46	13.69	-25.37	52
Securities & Commodity Futures	-0.027	2.58	34.48	-16.25	-0.44	4.99	23.86	-34.55	11
Other Financing Business	0.064	3.79	55.56	-33.33	-0.34	5.74	20.00	-28.36	14
Real Estate	0.090	4.60	100.00	-50.00	-0.51	5.14	35.29	-50.00	21
Services	0.052	2.36	41.67	-16.67	-0.05	5.91	37.97	-34.92	29
Total	0.043	2.54	100.00	-50.00	-0.10	5.16	82.61	-50.00	1019

Table 10.4 Summary of event window, event day, and estimation window

Event	Estimation window	Event day	Event window	The number of sample
The Great Hanshin Earthquake	Jan. 14, 1994, to Jan. 13, 1995 246 transaction days	Jan. 17, 1995	Jan. 17, 1995, to Feb. 28, 1995 31 transaction days	603
The Great East Japan Earthquake	Mar. 9, 2010, to Mar. 10, 2011	Mar. 11, 2011	Mar. 11, 2011, to Apr. 25, 2011	1019

reported in Tables 10.5 to 10.8. In Tables 10.5 and 10.6, we report the results of the average abnormal returns and the average cumulative abnormal returns for the case of the Great Hanshin Earthquake. Similar to the case of the Great Hanshin Earthquake, we provide the results for the Great East Japan Earthquake in Tables 10.7 and 10.8. The results of the average abnormal returns and the average cumulative abnormal returns are presented in Tables 10.7 and 10.8.

The reactions to the two disasters are illustrated by the significance of their *t-statistics*. In addition, we show the results of the event study in Figures 10.2 through 10.5.[4] Figures 10.2 and 10.3 show the results of the Great Hanshin Earthquake, and Figures 10.4 and 10.5 show the results of the Great East Japan Earthquake. In each case, the first figure shows the result of the average abnormal return, and the second figure shows the average cumulative abnormal return for each event. In these tables and figures, we omit the category that did not indicate a significance level under 10%.

In our study, we show the responses to the disaster in both the short term and long term in comparison to the effects of the disasters on the Japanese market. This chapter mainly discusses the results of the average cumulative abnormal returns. We choose the event window of the period $t = 0$ to $t = 5$ (short term) and $t = 10, 20,$ and 30 (long term).

10.6.1 *The Great Hanshin Earthquake*

First, we show the market reaction to the Great Hanshin Earthquake. From the results in Table 10.5, there are nine sectors that were significantly affected during the short term or long term (i.e., $t = 0$ to 5 or $t = 10, 20,$ and 30). In the case of the *Construction* sector, the results indicate that the dates from 0 to 2, 5, and 10 are positive and statistically significant. The results for the *Pulp & Paper* sector are not statistically significant except for $t = 0$ (i.e., the day the Great Hanshin Earthquake occurred). The results for the *Rubber Product* sector are not statistically significant except for when $t = 3$. The *Glass & Ceramics Products* sector has a positive and statistically significant measurement at $t = 4$ and 20, but it is negative

Table 10.5 The results of average abnormal return (AAR) after the Great Hanshin Earthquake

Sector	t = 0	t = 1	t = 2	t = 3	t = 4	t = 5	t = 10	t = 20	t = 30
Construction	0.178***	0.769***	0.044***	-0.16	-0.544	0.632***	0.144*	-0.194	0.238
Pulp & Paper	-0.513*	-0.016	-0.318	-0.256	-0.825	0.505	-0.161	-0.334	0.527
Rubber Products	-0.266	-0.344	-0.491	-0.692*	-1.328	0.355	0.291	-0.263	0.262
Glass & Ceramics Products	-0.056	0.155	-0.122	-0.021	0.718***	-0.182	-0.021	0.104***	-0.05*
Iron & Steel	-0.371**	0.41**	0.226***	-0.317	0.147**	0.017	-0.068	-0.281	-0.033*
Transport Equipment	-0.118	-0.274*	-0.329	-0.394	-0.424	0.291	-0.147	-0.31	0.244
Electric Power & Gas	-0.261	0.192	-0.72***	-0.226	-2.731***	1.64***	0.376*	-0.43	0.243
Retail Trade	-0.351*	-0.453**	-0.499*	-0.404	-2.027***	0.267	0.018	-0.707***	0.254
Securities & Commodity Futures	0.458***	-0.605*	0.628***	0.728***	1.435***	-1.378***	-0.569	0.688***	0.341

Note: */**/*** indicates t-statistic is significant at 10%/5%/1% level.

Table 10.6 The results of average cumulative abnormal return (ACAR) after the Great Hanshin Earthquake

Sector	t = 0	t = 1	t = 2	t = 3	t = 4	t = 5	t = 10	t = 20	t = 30
Construction	0.178***	0.932***	0.976***	0.816***	0.283***	0.915***	2.706***	2.175***	1.437***
Pulp & Paper	-0.513*	-0.529	-0.848	-1.103	-1.928	-1.423	-1.816	-2.523	-4.851
Rubber Products	-0.266	-0.61	-1.102	-1.794**	-3.122**	-2.768**	-1.873	-3.064	-4.334
Glass & Ceramics Products	-0.056	0.099	-0.024	-0.044	0.673***	0.491**	-0.16	-0.722	-0.358*
Iron & Steel	-0.371**	0.039	0.264**	-0.053	0.094**	0.111**	-1.632	-2.039	-2.694
Transport Equipment	-0.118	-0.385	-0.714	-1.108*	-1.532	-1.241	-1.787	-3.322**	-4.688**
Electric Power & Gas	-0.261	-0.069	-0.789	-1.015	-3.746***	-2.106*	-1.148	-0.253	-0.046*
Retail Trade	-0.351*	-0.763**	-1.262***	-1.666***	-3.693***	-3.426***	-4.231***	-5.133***	-8.292***
Securities & Commodity Futures	0.458***	-0.147	0.482	1.21***	2.645***	1.267**	-2.875	1.617**	3.844***

Note: */**/*** indicates t-statistic is significant at 10%/5%/1% level.

Table 10.7 The results of average abnormal return (AAR) after the Great East Japan Earthquake

Sector	t = 0	t = 1	t = 2	t = 3	t = 4	t = 5	t = 10	t = 20	t = 30
Construction	-0.11	-0.108**	-2.118	0.696	-0.098	0.75	0.319	0.255	-0.07
Foods	-0.416	-3.191	-5.537***	2.901**	0.138	1.882*	0.351	0.339	0.012
Pharmaceutical	-0.72	-3.535	-6.191***	3.352*	1.179***	1.35	0.251	0.287	-0.375**
Glass & Ceramics Products	0.036	0.977**	1.211***	-0.352*	-0.345	-0.635	0.164	-0.157	-0.05
Iron & Steel	-0.014	0.722**	1.055***	-0.838***	-0.177	-0.287	0.039	-0.122	0.049
Nonferrous Metals	-0.077	0.469	0.29*	0.057	0.087	-0.297	-0.093	-0.202	-0.233
Machinery	-0.079	-0.053***	-0.046***	-0.211***	0.02	-0.061	-0.139**	0.052	-0.091
Electric Appliances	0.803***	-1.067	0.954***	-0.075***	0.15	-1.164***	0.088	0.07	-0.071
Transport Equipment	-0.13	-0.388	-0.276**	0.025**	-0.086	0.053	-0.089	-0.046	-0.078
Electric Power & Gas	-0.851	-4.862*	-10.482***	3.646***	2.66***	1.946	-0.704**	2.555***	-0.101
Land Transportation	-0.421	-2.758	-4.724**	2.981*	0.298	1.71	0.471	0.278	-0.099
Air Transportation	-1.359	-5.812	-7.285	5.243	-0.047	4.032	-1.871***	0.16	0.275
Information & Communication	-0.42	-3.29	-3.759	2.975**	-0.077	0.953	-0.029	0.115	0.19*
Wholesale Trade	-0.727	-4.254***	-5.098***	4.551***	-0.195*	1.197	-0.145*	-0.591***	0.186**
Retail Trade	-0.721	-4.173***	-5.16***	3.557***	0.678**	1.374	0.176	0.233	0.018
Banks	-0.57	-2.935	-3.139	1.849	-0.078	1.457	0.674***	-0.188	-0.155
Services	-0.468	-3.417	-4.655***	2.215	0.97**	1.216	0.26	0.04	-0.061

Note: */**/*** indicates *t-statistic* is significant at 10%/5%/1% level.

Table 10.8 The results of average cumulative abnormal return (ACAR) after the Great East Japan Earthquake

Sector	$t=0$	$t=1$	$t=2$	$t=3$	$t=4$	$t=5$	$t=10$	$t=20$	$t=30$
Construction	-0.11	-0.219*	-2.336*	-1.64	-1.738	-0.988	0.566*	-0.844	-1.361
Foods	-0.416	-3.607*	-9.144***	-6.243***	-6.105***	-4.223**	-1.509	-1.41	-1.53
Pharmaceutical	-0.72	-4.255**	-10.446***	-7.094***	-5.915**	-4.565**	-2.567	-2.046	-2.998
Glass & Ceramics Products	0.036	1.013***	2.223***	1.871***	1.525***	0.89**	1.463	-0.044	-1.248
Iron & Steel	-0.014	0.708**	1.763***	0.925***	0.748***	0.462**	0.409	-0.197	-0.477
Nonferrous Metals	-0.077	0.392*	0.682**	0.738**	0.825**	0.528*	-0.394	-1.67	-1.984
Machinery	-0.079	-0.132***	-0.178***	-0.389***	-0.369***	-0.43***	-0.102	-1.391	-2.084
Electric Appliances	0.803***	-0.264***	0.69***	0.615***	0.765***	-0.398***	-0.634	-0.819	-0.102***
Transport Equipment	-0.13	-0.518*	-0.794**	-0.768**	-0.854*	-0.802	-0.811	-1.704	-2.475
Electric Power & Gas	-0.851	-5.713**	-16.195***	-12.549***	-9.888***	-7.942***	-8.679***	-13.235***	-20.247***
Land Transportation	-0.421	-3.18	-7.904*	-4.923*	-4.625*	-2.915	-0.885	-2.142	-3.208
Air Transportation	-1.359	-7.17	-14.455*	-9.212*	-9.259*	-5.227	-3.605	-8.773*	-9.652
Information & Communication	-0.42	-3.71*	-7.469**	-4.494	-4.571*	-3.617	-2.165	-3.229	-3.963
Wholesale Trade	-0.727	-4.981***	-10.08***	-5.528***	-5.723***	-4.526***	-2.821**	-3.936***	-5.086***
Retail Trade	-0.721	-4.895***	-10.055***	-6.498***	-5.82***	-4.446***	-2.75	-2.661	-2.842
Banks	-0.57	-3.505*	-6.644*	-4.795**	-4.873**	-3.416	-1.592	-1.952	-2.266
Real Estate	-0.351	-4.44**	-6.31	-5.203*	-5.216*	-4.857**	-5.045**	-6.138***	-6.923***
Services	-0.468	-3.885*	-8.539**	-6.325***	-5.354**	-4.138*	-1.505	-2.637	-2.918

Note: */**/*** indicates *t-statistic* is significant at 10%/5%/1% level.

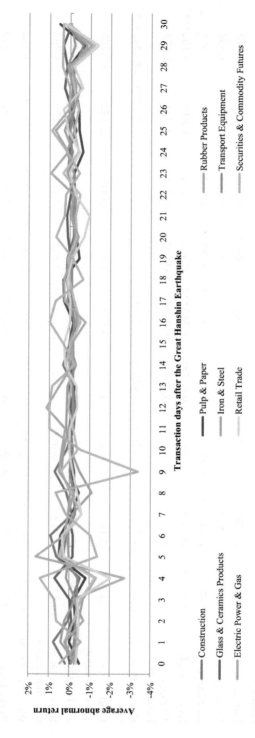

Figure 10.2 The results of average abnormal return (AAR) after the Great Hanshin Earthquake

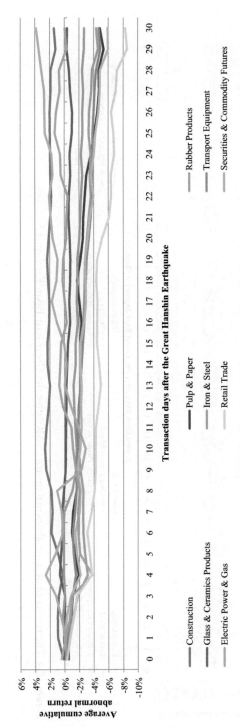

Figure 10.3 The results of average cumulative abnormal return (ACAR) after the Great Hanshin Earthquake

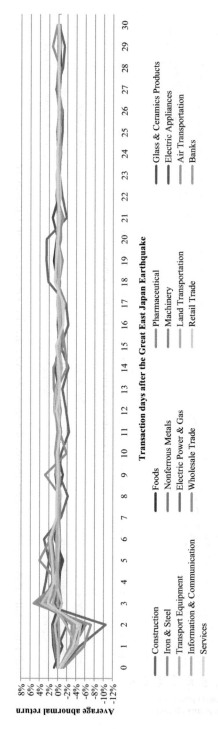

Figure 10.4 The results of average abnormal return (AAR) after the Great East Japan Earthquake

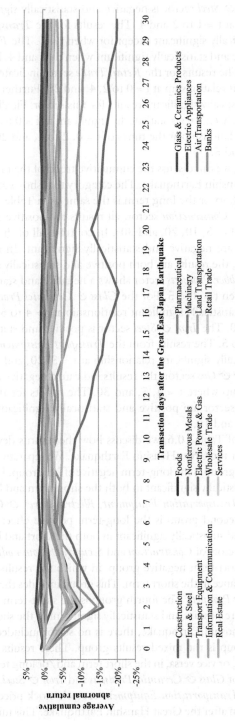

Figure 10.5 The results of average cumulative abnormal return (ACAR) after the Great East Japan Earthquake

at t = 30. The *Iron & Steel* sector is negative and statistically significant at t = 0 and 30 and positive at t = 1 to 2 and 4. The results for the *Transport Equipment* sector are not statistically significant except for when t = 1. The *Electric Power & Gas* sector is negative and statistically significant when t = 2 and 4, but it is positive when t = 5 and 10. The results for the *Retail Trade* sector indicate a negative and statistically significant relationship at t = 0 to 2, 4, and 20. Furthermore, there are no positive and statistically significant results for this sector. Finally, the sector of *Security & Commodity Futures* is statistically significant at t = 0 to 5, and 20, and it shows a positive relationship at the times of t = 0, 2 to 4, and 20, and negative results when t = 1 and 5.

Using Table 10.6, we can discuss the cumulative trend of the market's reaction toward the Great Hanshin Earthquake. The category that shows statistical significance in either the short or the long term is the same as in Table 10.5.

In the case of the *Construction* sector, all results are positive and statistically significant (i.e., t = 0 to 5, 10, 20, and 30). In contrast, all of the results for the *Retail Trade* sector are negative and statistically significant. In the case of the *Pulp & Paper* sector, the results are both positive and statistically significant only when t = 0. The *Rubber Products* sector shows a negative and statistically significant relationship when t = 3 to 5. For the *Glass & Ceramics Products* sector, we find a positive and statistically significant relationship at t = 4 to 5 and a negative relationship at t = 30. The *Iron & Steel* sector is positive and statistically significant at t = 2 and 4 to 5. The results from the *Transport Equipment* sector show a negative and statistically significant relationship at t = 3, 20, and 30. In the case of the *Electric Power & Gas* sector, the results indicate a negative and statistically significant relationship where t = 4, 5, and 30. The results for the *Securities & Commodity Futures* sector are positive and statistically significant for all results except for t = 1 to 2 and 10.

From the results of Table 10.6, we discuss how the returns deviated from the expected returns after the Great Hanshin Earthquake. We separate the sectors into five groups. The first group is the long-term negative effect group. Here, the results are negative and statistically significant in both the short term and long term. This group includes the *Transportation Equipment, Electric Power & Gas*, and *Retail Trade* sectors. The second group is the long-term positive effects group. These results are positive and statistically significant in both the short and long term. This group includes the sectors of *Construction* and *Security & Commodity Futures*. The third group is the short-term negative group, in which the results show negative and statistical significance in the short term. This group includes the sectors of *Pulp & Paper* and *Rubber Products*. The fourth group is the short-term positive group, in which the results are positive and statistically significant in the short term. In the case of the Great Hanshin Earthquake, there is no sector included in the fourth group. The fifth group is the mixed results group. These results are statistically positive and negative, or vice versa, in the short term and/or long term. This group includes the sectors of *Glass & Ceramics Products* and *Iron & Steel*.

First group: The *Transportation Equipment* sector's stock price reacted negatively in the long term after the Great Hanshin Earthquake. This might be because there was an expectation that there would be a decrease in the amount of transport equipment produced. The earthquake damaged, delayed, or stopped the operation of a manufacturing plant and caused vehicle production to decrease to 40,000 (Asahi Shinbun Company, 1995a). Therefore, the results for the *Transportation Equipment* sector are statistically negative in the long term.

The result for the *Electric & Gas* sector indicates a statistically negative trend for the long term. According to Asahi Shinbun Company (1995b), the total damages to the facility of the Kansai Electric Company and Osaka Gas are estimated to be approximately 200 billion yen. These costs might be the result of the negative trend in the *Electric & Gas* sector. The *Retail Trade* sector has a statistically negative trend. Asahi Shinbun Company (1995c) reported the results of an interview survey of 450 retail seller firms conducted by Himeji Chamber of Commerce and Industry. The report shows that over 65% of retail sellers had a transaction relationship with firms that were damaged by the Great Hanshin Earthquake, and these retail sellers were concerned about the deteriorating economy in Japan. Therefore, the market indicates a negative trend in the *Retail Trade* sector.

Second group: From the results in Table 10.6, the *Construction* sector shows a statistically positive trend in both the short term and long term. There were 639,686 buildings damaged due to the Great Hanshin Earthquake (Goto, 2011). These results might indicate that the demand for construction increased and caused the stock prices in the *Construction* sector to increase in the short term and the long term. The *Securities & Commodity Futures* sector shows a similar trend. The Daiwa Securities Group (2006) reported that the amount of commission revenue accounted for approximately 50% of the profit in the securities industry. This may be because the income of the commission was increased due to the accrual trade of financial goods caused by the earthquake. Therefore, the stock price might indicate a positive trend in the *Securities & Commodity Futures* sector.

Third group: The *Pulp & Paper* sector is statistically negative at only t = 0 (i.e., the day of the Great Hanshin Earthquake). This might be due to the market preventing the decrease in demand in the *Pulp & Paper* sector associated with the damage of the earthquake. The result of the *Rubber Products* sector shows a statistically negative trend in the short term. In 1995, the amount of rubber production in Hyogo prefecture was 10% (Economic Planning Agency of Japan, 1995). Therefore, the market can be considered to have reacted negatively when analyzing the reduction of rubber production.

Fifth group: The *Glass & Ceramics Products* sector indicates a statistically positive relationship in the short term and a negative relationship in the long term. The market can be considered to have reacted positively to the earthquake because of the expectation of an increase in construction demand. The *Iron & Steel* sector shows a statistically negative relationship when t = 0 and a positive relationship when t = 2, 4, and 5. The earthquake damaged several iron industry plants (Asahi Shinbun Company, 1995b). Therefore, the stock price of the *Iron & Steel* sector indicates a negative effect at t = 0. However, these materials are important to construction. Hence, the market might indicate a positive trend after the event. In the long term, the *Iron & Steel* sector might not be statistically significant for these mixed effects.

10.6.2   *The Great East Japan Earthquake*

Next, we discuss the market reaction to the Great East Japan Earthquake. From the results in Table 10.7, we find that 17 sectors indicate a statistically significant level in either the short term or the long term.

In the case of the *Construction* sector, the results are statistically significant and negative at t = 1. The results for the *Foods* sector are negative and statistically significant at t = 2 and positive and statistically significant when t = 3 and 5. The results of the *Pharmaceutical* sector are negative and statistically significant at t = 2 and 30 and positive at t = 3 to 4. In the case of the *Glass & Ceramics Products* and *Iron & Steel* sectors, we find a positive and statistically significant result at t = 1 to 2 and a negative and statistically significant result at t = 3. The results for the *Nonferrous Metals* sector show a positive and statistically significant result only at t = 2. In the case of the *Machinery* sector, the results are negative and statistically significant at t = 1 to 3 and 10. The results of the *Electric Appliances* sector are positive and statistically significant at t = 0 and 2 and negative and statistically significant at t = 3 and 5. In the case of the *Transportation Equipment* sector, the results are negative and statistically significant at t = 2 and positive and statistically significant when t = 3. The results for the *Electric Power & Gas* sector are negative and statistically significant when t = 1 to 2 and 10, and positive and statistically significant when t = 3 to 4 and 20. In the case of the *Land Transportation* sector, we find a statistically significant and negative result at t = 2 and a positive result when t = 3. From our results, the *Air Transportation* sector is statistically significant and negative when t = 10. The results of the *Information & Communication* sector show statistically positive significance when t = 3 and 30. In the case of the *Wholesale Trade* sector, it is statistically significant and negative at t = 1 to 2, 4, 10, and 20, and positive when t = 3 and 30. The results of the *Retail Trade* sector are negative and statistically significant when t = 1 to 2 and positive at t = 3 to 4. In the case of the *Banks*, the results are statistically significant and positive only when t = 10. The results of the *Services* sector are statistically significant and negative at t = 2 and positive at t = 4.

As in the case of the Great Hanshin Earthquake, we show the results of the aggregated trend of market reaction due to the Great East Japan Earthquake in Table 10.8. Eighteen sectors are significant. From the results in Table 10.8, only the *Construction* sector and the *Electric Appliances* sector show statistically significant mixed results. In the case of the *Construction* sector, the result is statistically significant and negative when t = 1 to 2 and positive at t =10. The results of the *Electric Appliances* sector are statistically significant and positive at t = 1 and 2 to 4 and negative when t = 1, 5, and 30.

The results of the sectors including *Glass & Ceramics Products*, *Iron & Steel*, and *Nonferrous Metals* have the same trend. These sectors indicate a positive and statistically significant trend at t = 1 to 5, and there is no negative result. In contrast, as shown in Table 10.8, the other categories do not show positive and statistically significant results. The *Foods, Pharmaceutical, Machinery, Retail Trade,* and *Services* sectors have a similar trend of being negative and statistically significant at t = 1 to 5. In the case of the *Transport Equipment* and *Banks* sectors, the results are negative and statistically significant at t = 1 to 4. The *Land Transportation* and the *Air Transportation* sectors show similar trends, except when t = 20. These two results are negative and statistically significant at t = 1 to 4. In the case of the *Air Transportation* sector, the trend is negative and statistically significant when t = 20.

The *Electric Power & Gas* and *Wholesale Trade* sectors show a similar trend. These results are negative and statistically significant at t = 1 to 5, 10, 20, and 30. The results for the *Real Estate* sector are similar to those for the *Electric Power & Gas* and *Wholesale Trade* sectors, except when t = 2. In the case of the *Information & Communication* sector, the results are negative and statistically significant at t = 1 to 2, and 4.

Using these results, we can discuss what makes the returns deviate from the expected return after the Great East Japan Earthquake. When t =0, there are no sectors that have a statistically significant result except for the *Electric Appliance* sector. This is because the devastating earthquake occurred at 14:46 JST (05:46 UTC) on Friday, March 11, 2011, and the tsunami warning was issued at 14:59 on the same day. The market in Japan closes at 15:00. Therefore, the market did not have enough time to react and anticipate the damage of the earthquake and subsequent tsunami. As in the case of the Great Hanshin Earthquake in Table 10.8, we separate the sectors into five groups.

The first group includes the *Electric Power & Gas, Air Transportation, Wholesale Trade,* and *Real Estate* sectors. From the results in Table 10.8, there are no sectors included in the second group. The third group includes the *Foods, Pharmaceutical, Machinery, Transport Equipment, Land Transportation, Information & Communication, Retail Trade, Banks,* and *Service* sectors. The fourth group includes the sectors of *Glass & Ceramics Products, Iron & Steel,* and *Nonferrous Metals.* Finally, the fifth group includes the *Construction* and *Electric Appliances* sectors.

First group: It might appear that the Fukushima Dai-ichi nuclear accidents are the main contributors to the results for the *Electric Power & Gas* sector. In particular, the explosion in Units 1 through 4 and the subsequent release of radioactive materials and power shortages caused economic damage, including the undetermined compensation of the electric companies, especially of Tokyo Electric Power Company. The results of Table 10.8 and Figure 10.5 for the *Electric & Gas* sector are negative and statistically significant over both the short term and the long term.

The results for the *Air Transportation* sector illustrate a negative and statistically significant trend in both the short term and the long term. Narita Airport (2011) reported that the number of international air passengers from April 28 to May 8, 2011, decreased to 50% compared with the same period from the previous year. These results might indicate a decrease in travel demand and apprehension regarding the earthquake and the effects of radioactive material due to the Fukushima Dai-ichi nuclear accidents. These accidents caused the *Air Transportation* sector's stock price to have a negative trend in the market.

The National Police Agency (2011) reported that 110,427 buildings were completely destroyed in Japan, particularly in the Tohoku area, as a result of the Great East Japan Earthquake. The loss of these buildings caused decreases in profit from rent over both the short term and the long term. Therefore, the *Real Estate* sector indicates a negative and statistically significant result for both time periods.

In the case of the *Wholesale Trade* sector, the results show a negative and statistically significant result for both the short and long term. This might be due to the damage to suppliers and vendors in Japan, especially in the Tohoku area. In addition, the damage to shipping infrastructures, such as road, sea, and air transportation, hinders the interaction between wholesale trade companies and suppliers (and/or vendors). Therefore, the market in Japan showed a downward trend in the profit margins of the *Wholesale Trade* sector, especially in the Tohoku area, from the disaster.

Third group: The *Land Transportation* sector in Japan was severely damaged by the disaster. The East Japan Railway Company (2011a) reported 1,200 damages related to ground installations for the bullet train line and 4,400 damages to the conventional lines, with a projected cost of 58.7 billion yen to recover these damages (East Japan Railway Company, 2011b). In addition to the number of damaged buildings, the National Police Agency (2011) reported that 3,559 roads and 77 bridges were damaged as a result of the earthquake and tsunami. Therefore, both the flow of passengers using the railroad or expressway buses and the commodity distribution were disrupted. The market indicates a statistically significant and negative sign for the *Land Transportation* sector.

With the exception of the *Land Transportation* sector, the results for the remaining sectors may be explained by mixed factors, such as a decrease in demand, the effect of the Fukushima Dai-ichi nuclear accidents, or the collapse of the manufacturing plant that produced goods, materials, or parts for each sector due to the Great East Japan Earthquake. For instance, the results for the *Foods* sector might be affected by the release of radioactive materials. According to the Food Safety Commission (2011), radioactive materials over the provisional regulation standard were detected in several kinds of food (e.g., in the case of raw milk, 28 samples out of 128 exceeded the provisional regulation value). Furthermore, harmful rumors following the Fukushima Dai-ichi nuclear accidents decreased the demand for food (The Mainichi Daily News, 2011).

As in the *Foods* sector, the results for the *Transport Equipment* sector are negative and statistically significant in the short term. The Bank of Tokyo-Mitsubishi UFJ (2011) reported that the reduction of production due to the Great East Japan Earthquake in eight automotive industries was approximately 359,000 vehicles (e.g., the report showed that all of Honda's automobile manufacturing plants shut down until April 3, 2011). The results of these sectors do not indicate statistical significance in the long term because the companies in these sectors changed their suppliers from companies that were damaged due to the Great Tohoku Earthquake and/or tsunami to companies that were undamaged.

Ministry of Economy, Trade and Industry (2011) reported the summary of the survey of the effect on supply chain to manufacturing, retail, and service sectors in Japan. In this result, 80% of the processing industry and 60% of the material production industry are expected to recover the supply chain. Therefore, these sectors, except for *Land Transportation*, might be relatively easier to adjust the disaster compared to the sectors of the first group.

Fourth group: The sectors related to resources (i.e., *Glass & Ceramics Products*, *Iron & Steel*, and *Nonferrous Metals*) that might be needed to construct not only buildings but also infrastructure, such as roads, bridges, or railways, are positive and statistically significant.

Fifth group: Last, we discuss the fifth group. In the *Construction* sector, the number of the damaged buildings is lower than in the case of the Great Hanshin Earthquake. In addition, the manufacturing plants that produce materials such as timber or wooden chips might be severely damaged. Therefore, the sector of *Construction* might indicate statistically negative trends in the short term. On the other hand, in the long term, it might be considered that the companies included in the *Construction* sector adjust the demand of construction by changing to a supplier that is not damaged.

10.7 Conclusions

In this chapter, we examined how natural disasters affected the stock prices of the Japanese industry using an event study methodology. We found that the damage from the disasters had a statistically significant impact on the stock prices of several sectors. The results show that in 9 sectors and 18 sectors, the effects are statistically significant for the Great Hanshin Earthquake and the Great East Japan Earthquake, respectively. We also found that these sectors could be sepa-rated into five groups using the empirical results. That is, these sectors could be separated based on the effects of the damage to the stock price, whether statisti-cally significant, negative or positive, and whether the effects were short term (i.e., t = 0 to 5) or long term (i.e., t = 10, 20, and 30). We summarize the results of these five groups after each disaster.

In the case of the Great Hanshin Earthquake, three sectors are included in the first group (i.e., negative impact in the long term): *Transport Equipment, Electric Power & Gas*, and *Retail Trade*. The *Construction* and *Security & Commodity Futures* sectors are included in the second group (i.e., positive impact for long term). The *Pulp & Paper* and *Rubber Products* sectors are classified into the third group (i.e., negative impact for the short term). There are no sectors included in the fourth group (i.e., positive impact for the short term). The *Glass & Ceramics Products* and *Iron & Steel* sectors are included in the fifth group (i.e., positive and negative impact).

In the case of the Great East Japan Earthquake, the *Electric Power & Gas, Air Transportation, Wholesale Trade*, and *Real Estate* sectors are included in the first group. There are no sectors included in the second group. There are nine sec-tors classified in the third group: *Foods, Pharmaceutical, Machinery, Transport Equipment, Land Transportation, Information & Communication, Retail Trade, Banks*, and *Service*. There are three sectors in the fourth group: *Glass & Ceramics*

Products, Iron & Steel, and *Nonferrous Metals*. The fifth group includes the *Construction* and *Electric Appliances* sectors.

We found that the *Electric & Gas* sector was included in the first group for both events.[5] The market might expect a decrease in electricity and gas production, which causes the profits from this sector to decrease. However, the reasons for a decrease in electricity and gas production may differ for the two events. In the case of the Great Hanshin Earthquake, the decrease in the demand for electricity and gas may be due to the damage to the manufacturing plants in the other sectors. In the case of the Great East Earthquake, there might be additional reasons. For instance, there is uncertainty regarding the compensation cost by the electric power company and/or the government because the effect of the release of radioactive material on humans and on the other sectors is unknown in the long term.

The remaining sectors are not included in the same group for both disasters. Hence, a market will effectively react to economic conditions even if the disaster is unanticipated and devastating. Additionally, several sectors do not indicate statistically significant results for either event. For example, the *Marine Transportation, Oil & Coal Products, Chemicals*, and *Textile & Apparels* sectors do not indicate statistically significant results. This finding implies that, on average, the stock prices for these sectors did not deviate from the expected returns. Therefore, the stock prices of these sectors are less sensitive to the events of an earthquake.

Finally, we conclude from these empirical results that a disaster affects the stock prices of several sectors in the Japanese market through the actions of the investors. The results show different effects on the stock prices of the Japanese industrial sectors. Thus, the market has adjusted to the economic conditions.

Appendix

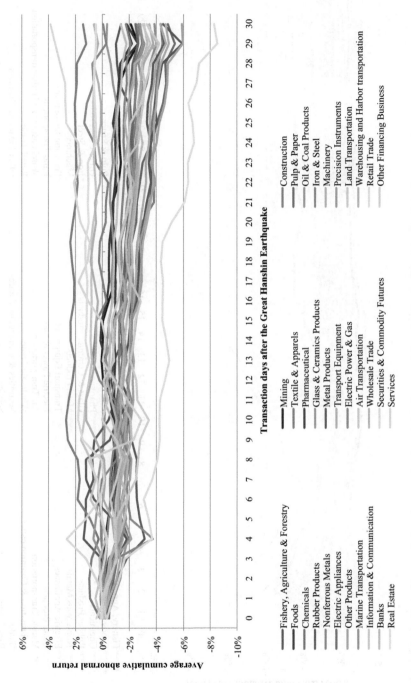

Figure A10.1 Average cumulative abnormal return in each sector after the Great Hanshin Earthquake

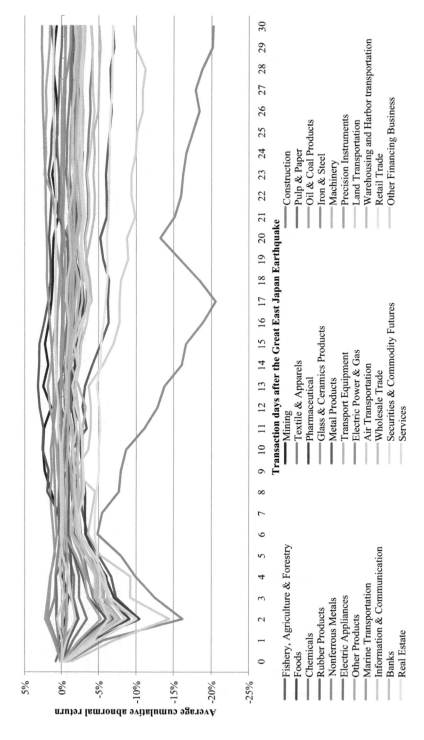

Figure A10.2 Average cumulative abnormal return in each sector after the Great East Japan Earthquake

Notes

1 The ED-MAT is provided on the website of the Centre for Research on the Epidemiology of Disasters: http://www.emdat.be/
2 The previous three largest earthquakes occurred on May 22, 1960, in Chile, March 28, 1964, in Alaska, and December 26, 2004, in the west coast of northern Sumatra.
3 Because the nuclear accidents following the earthquake and tsunami occurred during the weekend, the effects are analyzed from the Monday market as a combined effect of the earthquake, in the case of the Great East Japan Earthquake.
4 In the appendix, Figures A-1 and A-2 show the results of the average cumulative returns, which include all of the sectors.
5 From a financial point of view, this result is interesting because the companies included in the *Electric & Gas* sector are usually classified as a relatively low-risk investment commodity. Therefore, the risk of the stock price in the *Electric & Gas* sector might be slightly higher if the damage from the disaster is considered.

Bibliography

Anbarci, N., Escaleras, M., and Register, C. A. (2005) Earthquake fatalities: the interaction of nature and political economy. *Journal of Public Economics*, 89, 1907–1933.
Angbazo, L. A., Narayanan, R. (1996) Catastrophic shocks in the property-liability insurance industry: evidence on regulatory and contagion effects. *Journal of Risk and Insurance*, 63, 619–637.
Asahi Shinbun Company. (1995a) *The reduction of vehicle production is 40 thousand caused from the Great Hanshin Earthquake*, February 18. <http://www.asahi.com/english/?iref=com_gnavi>
Asahi Shinbun Company. (1995b) *Special topic in Osaka*, February 17. <http://www.asahi.com/english/?iref=com_gnavi>
Asahi Shinbun Company. (1995c) *The damage of the Great Hanshin Earthquake to logistics*, January 28. <http://www.asahi.com/english/?iref=com_gnavi>
Bank of Mitsubishi-Tokyo UFJ. (2011) *Tokai economic report*, March 29. (In Japanese) <http://www.bk.mufg.jp/report/ecomon2011/report_tokai_1103.pdf>
Barrett, B. W., Heuson, A. J., Kolb, R. W., and Schropp, G. H. (1987) The adjustment of stock prices to completely unanticipated events. *Financial Review*, 22, 345–354.
Barros, C. P., Managi, S., and Matousek, R. (2011) The technical efficiency of the Japanese banks: non-radial directional performance measurement with undesirable output. *Omega – The International Journal of Management Science*, 40 (1), 1–8.
Bowen, R. M., Castanias, R. P., and Daley, L. A. (1983) Intra-industry effects of the accident at Three Mile Island. *The Journal of Financial and Quantitative Analysis*, 18, 87–111.
Daiwa Securities Group. (2006) *The changing in Securities Sector in Japan, annual report*. <http://www.daiwa-grp.jp/japanese/pdf/ar2006/ar2006_02.pdf>
David. A. C., and Betty. J.S. (2004) The market's reaction to unexpected, catastrophic events: the case of airline stock returns and the September 11th attacks. *The Quarterly Review of Economics and Finance*, 44, 539–558.
Davidson, W. N., III, Chandy, P. R., and Cross, M. (1987) Large losses, risk management, and stock returns in the airline industry. *Journal of Risk and Insurance*, 54, 162–172.
East Japan Railway Company. (2011a) *The damage of ground installation and its restorative condition*, April 1. <http://www.jreast.co.jp/press/2011/20110401.pdf>

East Japan Railway Company. (2011b) *The effect of the Great East Japan Earthquake on earning estimate*, April 27. <http://www.jreast.co.jp/investor/financial/2011/pdf/kessan_03.pdf>

Economic Planning Agency of Japan. (1995) *Economic survey in Japan*. Cabinet Office, Government of Japan (In Japanese).

Escaleras, M., Anbarci, N., and Register, C.A. (2007). Public sector corruption and major earthquakes: a potentially deadly interaction. *Public Choice*, 132, 209–230.

Fields, A., and Janjigian, V. (1989) The effect of Chernobyl on electric-utility stock prices. *Journal of Business Research*, 18, 81–88.

Food Safety Commission. (2011) *Summary of the effect of radioactive materials on foods*, March 29. <http://www.fsc.go.jp/sonota/emerg/emerg_torimatome_20110329.pdf>

Goto, Y. (2011) The effect of the Great East Japan Earthquake on Japanese Market, *Prism of Economy*, 92 (In Japanese). <http://www.sangiin.go.jp/japanese/annai/chousa/keizai_prism/backnumber/h23pdf/20119102.pdf>

Grossman, G., and Krueger, A. (1995). Economic growth and the environment. *Quarterly Journal of Economics,* 110 (2), 353–377.

Gunther, C.B., and Laguna, M.A. (2010) How does the stock market respond to chemical disasters? *Journal of Environmental Economics and Management*, 59, 192–205.

Hallstrom, D.G., and Smith, V.K. (2005). Market responses to hurricanes. *Journal of Environmental Economics and Management*, 50, 541–561.

Hanabusa, K. (2010) Effects of foreign disasters on the petroleum industry in Japan: a financial market perspective. *Energy*, 35, 5455–5463.

Hill, J., and Schneeweis, T. (1983) The effect of Three Mile Island on electric utility stock prices: a note. *Journal of Finance*, 38, 1285–1292.

Hyogo Prefecture (2008) *Status report on restoration and reconstruction after the Great Hanshin-Awaji Earthquake* (In Japanese). <http://web.pref.hyogo.jp/contents/000171409.pdf>

Intergovernmental Panel on Climate Change. (2007) Impacts, adaptation and vulnerability. *Working Group II Report*. April 6.

Japan Meteorological Agency (2011) *The magnitude of the Great East Japan Earthquake*, March 13. <http://www.jma.go.jp/jma/press/1103/13b/201103131255.html>

Kahn, M.E. (2005). The death toll from natural disasters: the role of income, geography, and institutions. *The Review of Economics and Statistics*, 87 (2), 271–284.

Kalra, R., Henderson, G.V., and Raines, G.A. (1993) Effects of the Chernobyl nuclear accident on utility share prices. *Quarterly Journal of Business and Economics*, 32, 52–78.

Kellenberg, D.K., and Mobarak, A.M. (2008). Does rising income increase or decrease damage risk from natural disasters? *Journal of Urban Economics*, 63, 788–802

Kinki Construction Association. (2005) *Following the step to recovery from the Great Hanshin Earthquake*. Ministry of Land, Infrastructure, Transport, and Tourism (In Japanese).

Klassen, R.D., and McLaughlin, C.P. (1996) The impact of environmental management on firm performance. *Management Science*, 42 (8), 1199–1214.

Kothari, S., and Warner, J. (2006) Econometrics of event studies, in: E. Eckbo (Ed.), *Handbook of corporate finance. Empirical corporate finance*. Amsterdam, Elsevier-North-Holland.

Kunihiro, H. (2010) Effects of foreign disasters on the petroleum industry in Japan: a financial market perspective. *Energy*, 35, 5455–5463.

Lamb, R. P. (1995) An exposure-based analysis of property-liability insurer stock values around Hurricane Andrew. *Journal of Risk and Insurance*, 62, 111–123.

Lamb, R. P. (1998) An examination of market efficiency around hurricanes. *Financial Review*, 33, 163–172.

MacKinlay, A. C. (1997) Event studies in economics and finance. *Journal of Economic Literature*, 35, 13–39.

The Mainichi Newspapers. (2011) *Compensation of harmful rumor in Ibaraki*, July 21. (In Japanese). <http://mainichi.jp/area/ibaraki/news/20110721 ddlk08040004000c.html>

Martin, M. C., and Dominic, M. (2007) Impact of the FTSE4Good Index on firm price: an event study. *Journal of Environmental Management*, 82, 529–537.

Ministry of Economy, Trade and Industry. (2011) *The survey to the supply chain damage due to the Great East Japan Earthquake*, April 26. <http://www.meti.go.jp/press/ 2011/04/20110426005/20110426005-1.pdf>

Narita Airport. (2011) *The estimate of international air passenger in golden week*, April 25. <http://www.naa.jp/jp/press/2011/0425_688.html>

National Police Agency. (2011) *The damage due to the Great East Japan Earthquake and its measure*, July 27. <http://www.npa.go.jp/archive/keibi/biki/higaijokyo.pdf>

Rao, S. M. (1996) The effect of published reports of environmental pollution on stock prices. *Journal of Financial and Strategic Decisions*, 9 (1), 25–32.

Shelor, R. M., Anderson, D. C., and Cross, M. L. (1991) The impact of the California earthquake on real estate firms' stock value. *Journal of Real Estate Research*, 5, 335–340.

Shelor, R. M., Anderson, D. C., and Cross, M. L. (1992) Gaining from loss: property-liability insurer stock values in the aftermath of the 1989 California earthquake. *Journal of Risk and Insurance*, 59, 476–488.

Takeda, F., and Tomozawa, T. (2008) A change in market responses to the environmental management ranking in Japan. *Ecological Economics*, 67, 465–72.

Toya, H., and Skidmore, M. (2007). Economic development and the impacts of natural disasters. *Economic Letters*, 94, 20–25.

West, C. T., and Lenze, D. G. (1994). Modeling the regional impact of natural disaster and recovery: a general framework and an application to Hurricane Andrew. *International Regional Science Review*, 17 (2), 121–150.

Yamaguchi, K. (2008) Reexamination of stock price reaction to environmental performance: a GARCH application. *Ecological Economics*, 68, 345–352.

11 Environmental impact of mega events

*Cao Huijuan, Hidemichi Fujii
and Shunsuke Managi*

11.1 Introduction

Beijing organized the 2008 Olympic Games with the slogan, "Green Olympics, Hi-tech Olympics and People's Olympics". This slogan illustrates the determination of the Chinese government to offer an environmentally friendly yet impressive Olympic event. To improve air quality during the 2008 Summer Olympics (August 8–24) and the Paralympic Games (September 9–17), the Beijing government implemented various aggressive measures, both in Beijing and in the surrounding area. These temporary measures mainly focused on the industrial sector and traffic control and were considered to be effective by the Chinese government.

A specific industrial pollution control policy was enforced in 2008. Power plants were required to reduce their emissions by 30 per cent from their levels in June. This reduction was required even for plants that had already met the Chinese emission standards. Moreover, certain heavily polluting factories were ordered to reduce their operating capacities, whereas others were completely shut down (Liu et al., 2012). To strictly control air pollutant emissions, the Beijing municipal government announced an "Air Quality Guarantee Plan for the 29th Olympic Games in Beijing". In this plan, similar control measures were extended to five surrounding provinces, including Tianjin, Hebei, Shanxi, Inner Mongolia, and Shandong[1] (Wang et al., 2010b). In Tianjin and Hebei, this policy was compulsorily and strictly implemented. However, for Shanxi, Inner Mongolia, and Shandong, the plan was only implemented if air conditions became extremely serious. Wang et al. (2010b) found that in June 2008 the daily emissions of sulphur dioxide (SO_2), nitrogen dioxide (NOx), and particulate matter (PM10) in Beijing totalled 103.9, 428.5, and 362.7 tons, respectively. During the Olympic Games, the daily emissions of SO_2, NOx, and PM10 in Beijing were reduced to 61.6, 229.1, and 164.3 tons, which were 41, 47, and 55 per cent lower than the respective June 2008 emission levels. Additionally, factory closures reduced the SO_2 emissions by 85 per cent in the industrial sector (Wang et al., 2010b).

To reduce the emissions of NOx, and PM10, traffic control measures were also enforced in Beijing in 2008. First, from July 1 to September 20, all

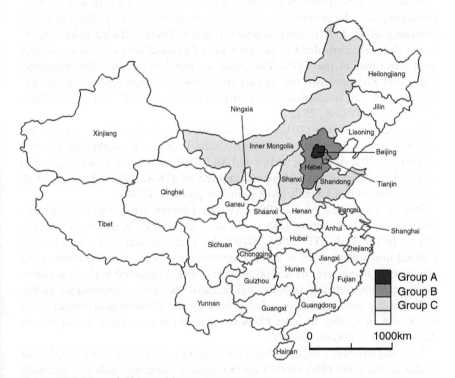

Figure 11.1 Map of China with group areas

Note 1: Group A: Beijing, Group B: Tianjin and Hebei, Group C: Shanxi, Inner Mongolia, and Shandong. Note 2: In this study, Xinjiang, Tibet, Hong Kong, Macau, and Taiwan are not included due to missing data.

on-road vehicles (including trucks and passenger cars) that failed to meet the Euro I emissions standards were banned from Beijing's roads. Second, mandatory restrictions that limited the use of government vehicles were implemented from July 20 to September 20. Additionally, the number of personal vehicles in use was reduced by 50 per cent. Personal vehicles were allowed on roads only on alternate days based on license plate numbers, such that odd-numbered vehicles could drive on odd-numbered days and even-numbered vehicles could drive on even-numbered days (Liu et al., 2012). According to Wang et al. (2010b) and Song et al. (2012), most manufacturers of construction materials were shut down, and all construction activities ceased temporarily. This measure was taken because most of the dust emitted was from the construction sector.

Long-term national policies on air pollution control were also in effect, as opposed to the above policies, which were created to be temporary and specific for the Olympic Games. During the 10th Five-Year Plan (FYP) period (2001–2005), the Chinese government established SO_2 emission targets for specific industrial sectors in heavily polluting regions. Most of the sectors involved heavily polluting industries, e.g., oil refineries and steelmaking factories.

To address atmospheric SO_2 emissions and the resulting health and environmental impacts, the government established an environmental policy framework consisting of an array of environmental policies. These included policy instruments that were embedded in various types of national laws and environmental goals described in the FYPs. The plans are not law but describe economic, social, and environmental targets that are imposed through agreements, performance incentives, or existing laws (Guttman and Song, 2007; Fujii et al., 2013; Schreifels and Wilson, 2012).

Schreifels and Wilson (2012) noted that these targets were largely aspirational and not strictly enforced. As a result, China became the world's largest SO_2 emitter in 2005. According to You and Xu (2010), economic losses due to acid rain and acid deposition in China amounted to 176.42 billion Yuan in 2000, or 1.97 per cent of China's gross domestic product (GDP).

Due to the failure of the 10th FYP, the Chinese government put greater emphasis on SO_2 reduction goals in the subsequent FYP (Schreifels and Wilson, 2012). In the 11th FYP (2006–2010), this emphasis included a novel set of political instruments, such as binding agreements with provincial governors and managers of major state-owned power companies, a modified evaluation system for government officials, political and financial incentives, performance audits, and stronger enforcement of existing laws by the Chinese government. As a result, the air quality in most Chinese cities did not continue to deteriorate despite rapid economic growth.

Arne and Maennig (2012) analysed the regional economic impact on the labour market of the 2006 FIFA World Cup in Germany using regionally and sectorally disaggregated data. They used the difference-in-differences (DD) approach and found a small but statistically significant positive employment effect on the hospitality sector. Similarly, our study also uses the DD approach to analyse the environmental impact of the 2008 Olympic Games on air quality in its host city, Beijing, and comparisons are made with other cities in China. All previous analyses applied an engineering method without particular attention to other regions, and thus the actual effect of the Olympics on air quality is not clear. We aim to clarify whether temporary measures for air quality improvement in Beijing and the surrounding areas were more effective than the typical national polices, also by considering substitution effects from Beijing to surrounding areas of emission. In this research, panel data at the city level for air pollution during the 2003–2010 period was used. This dataset covers 29 capital cities all around China.

11.2   Background

Wang et al. (2010b) observed that the daily emissions of SO_2, NOx, and PM10 in Beijing were significantly reduced during the 2008 Olympic Games. Schleicher et al. (2012) found that the temporary measures to reduce air pollution at the 2008 Beijing Olympic Games had a large impact over a short time frame. These measures mainly focused on factory closures and traffic control. In the study by Schleicher et al. (2012), weekly samples of fine particulate matter (PM2.5 and PM10) were collected continuously from October 2007 to February 2009.

The results indicated that the PM2.5 and PM10 concentrations were comparatively lower during the 2008 Olympic Games.

Cai and Xie (2011) observed that the traffic control policy implemented was effective for air quality improvement in the short term. They conducted a modelling assessment on the effects of the odd- and even-day traffic restriction scheme (TRS) on traffic-related air pollution during the 2008 Olympic Games and noted that this temporary measure improved the air quality in the urban area of Beijing over the short term. Gao et al. (2009) and Schreifels and Wilson (2012) studied the SO_2 pollution control policies in China and found that these policies were ineffective during the 2001–2005 period, and thus, SO_2 emissions increased. However, after 2005, when air pollution control policies were implemented more strictly, SO_2 emissions were significantly reduced. Fujii et al. (2013) analysed air pollution abatement in 10 industrial sectors from 1998 to 2009 in China, and concluded that air pollution was reduced significantly at the national level over those years.

All of the previous studies on air pollution control during the Olympic Games focused on the local level in Beijing and demonstrated that the temporary measures used were effective in the short term (i.e. several months during the Olympic season). On the other side, the studies on air pollution at the national level indicated that air pollution control policies were effective in the long term (i.e. one decade), as air pollution was significantly reduced over longer time frames. However, no previous study has indicated whether air quality was relatively improved in Beijing compared to improvements in other areas of China. In fact, the air quality in many areas which were not influenced by the Olympic Games also improved after the year 2008. It is resulted from some national environmental policies.

Many carefully provided studies only focus on Beijing itself and conclude that air quality was improved after the Olympic Games. However, there is no previous study comparing Beijing with other non-Olympic–related areas. Therefore, without the comparison, we do not know whether the improvement of air quality in Beijing resulted from the environmental impact of the Olympic Games, or whether it resulted from other national environmental policies. As mentioned above, "Air Quality Guarantee Plan for the 29th Olympic Games in Beijing" not only covered Beijing, but also covered five surrounding provinces. In this paper, we estimate the effect of specific measures for the Olympic Games and aim to clarify whether there is some environmental impact after the Olympic Games in the mid term (i.e. several years). The relative comparison between Olympic-related areas and non-related areas in China indicates the Olympic impact of the air quality on host city Beijing and its surrounding area.

11.3 Methodology and data

11.3.1 Difference-in-differences approach

The DD approach was established to identify treatment effects that occur at a particular location after a specific period. The DD approach is used to compare the differences in outcome between a treatment and control group (the affected and unaffected group) and also to compare the differences before, during, and after a specific period. This approach can be used to evaluate the impact of a mega-sports event. According to Hotchkiss et al. (2003) and Jasmand and Maennig (2008), the DD approach can be used to isolate the impact of an event from pure macroeconomic shocks, and the use of additional geographic units as a control group is suggested.

In this study, temporary measures are defined as those measures that started during the preparation for the Olympic Games and that ended shortly after the Olympic Games ended. Air quality improvement due to a change in environmental policy was the studied outcome. The study used the host city, Beijing, and its surrounding areas as its treatment group; other parts of China constituted the control group. The specific environmental impact of the Olympic Games is the difference in air quality between the treatment and control groups outlined above.

The DD approach is consistent with our research objective (see, e.g., Dachis et al. [2011]) and can be used to clarify the environmental impact of the 2008 Olympic Games on air quality in its host city, Beijing. Let t denote time, with $t = 2008$ as the intervention point, $t < 2008$ denotes the period before the 2008 Beijing Olympic Games, and $t > 2008$ denotes the period after it. Let i denote the location. The two indicators, based on the time dimension t and spatial dimension i, can be defined as:

$$X^P = \begin{cases} 1 & if \quad t \geq 2008 \\ 0 & else \end{cases} \qquad (1)$$

$$X^V = \begin{cases} 1 & if \quad i \in v \\ 0 & else \end{cases} \qquad (2)$$

In Equation (1), X^P denotes the period during or after the 2008 Beijing Olympic Games.[2] In Equation (2), X^V denotes the areas belonging to the treatment group (Beijing and the surrounding area) or the control group (the other areas in China).

According to Dachis et al. (2011), this function (see Equation 3) can be broken down into five parts: (1) the function l (i, t), which has a latent effect on air quality improvement that is continuous in time i and location t; (2) the air quality improvement that occurs after the 2008 Beijing Olympic Games, as γX^P; (3) a jump in the air quality improvement that occurs in the host city, Beijing, and the surrounding area, as βX^V; (4) an interaction effect on time and location, as $\lambda X^P X^V$; and (5) a mean-zero error term.

$$e\,(i, t) = \gamma X^P + \beta X^V + \lambda X^P X^V + \epsilon\,(i,t) \qquad (3)$$

Most papers that employ the DD approach use many years of data and focus on serially correlated outcomes, but ignore that the resulting standard errors are inconsistent. It is because failing to cluster standard error in the DD model is known to significantly underestimate the size of the standard error and to make coefficients falsely appear to be statistically significant. According to the literature, computing standard errors that are robust to serial correlation appears relatively easy to implement in most cases. Researchers suggest that it should become standard practice in applied work, even when the sample size is small.[3] Following these studies, we use fixed effect regression, and the standard errors are reported as robust and clustered with each city-level data.[4]

11.3.2 Data

Several types of air pollutants are established as dependent variables, whereas "time term", "location term", and "interaction term of time and location" are defined as independent variables. In this study, city-level data were used for air pollution for the 2003–2010 period. This dataset consisted of 29 cities, all of which were provincial capital cities for 29 different provinces in China.[5] Datasets used included the concentration of SO_2, PM10, and NOx, indicating the annual average level of each type of air pollutant.

The statistical data cover data for entire station data instead of sampled data from plant. The data are collected as daily averages of the year. The benefit of using average data is being able to capture overall data instead of particular time, but it lacks particularly high periods of concentration, which is also important for health reasons. Managi and Kaneko (2009, 2010) provide discussion on the accuracy of statistical data in China. Though there are many potential problems associated with the data, these are the best available data in China. We cited their study and add this discussion in revised draft.

11.4   Results and discussion

In order to clarify the environmental impact of the Beijing Olympic Games, we first compare the Olympic-related area with the non-related areas on air pollution before and after the year 2008 with the DD approach (see Figure 11.2). In this estimation, the Olympic-related area is Beijing and surrounding area. This is because in order to improve the air quality in Beijing, specific environmental protection policies were not only implemented in Beijing but also in the surrounding area of Beijing. Moreover, the surrounding area is the main producing region of coal in China and has a large number of high-polluting energy industries.

In DD approach, the "after term" indicates the percentage of air pollution reduction in the whole country, compared with the term before and after the Olympic Games in 2008. Moreover, air pollution reduction in both the Olympic-related area and non-related areas are included in this term. The "interaction term of time and location" indicates how much air pollution was reduced after year 2008 only in the Olympic-related area, which is compared with the term of 2003–2007. If the coefficient of interaction term is negative and statistically significant, it is explained as the environmental impact of the 2008 Beijing Olympic Games.

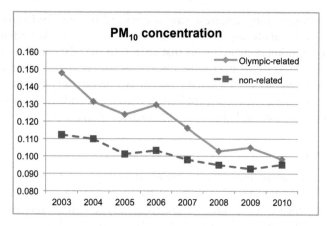

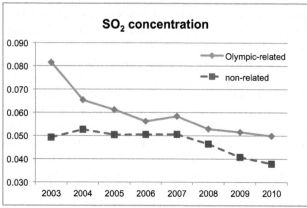

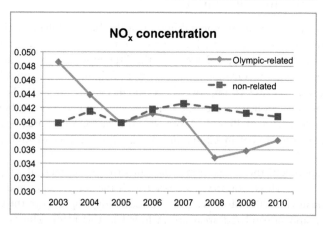

Figure 11.2 Trend of emission concentration before and after 2008 Beijing Olympics

Note 1: The linear line shows the trend of concentration in Olympic-related areas, which are host city Beijing and its surrounding areas. The dotted line shows that of Olympic non-related areas.

Note 2: unit: ug/m³

Table 11.1 Effects on emission after 2008 Beijing Olympics

| | Compare Olympic-related area with non-related area | | | | | |
| | SO_2 | | PM10 | | NOx | |
	coef.	P-value	coef.	P-value	coef.	P-value
After	–8.959	0.002	–10.617	0.000	0.261	0.838
(Robust Std.Err.)	**(2.581)		***(1.994)		(1.263)	
Related	(omitted)		(omitted)		(omitted)	
After*Related	–4.152	0.354	–17.038	0.011	–6.994	0.002
(Robust Std.Err.)	(4.400)		**(6.214)		**(2.050)	
Obs.	232		232.		232	
R^2		0.17		0.35		0.09

Note: Std. Err. is adjusted for 29 clusters in city. "Related" is omitted because of collinearity with fixed effect. *,**,*** indicates significance at the 90%, 95% and 99% confidence levels, respectively. The unit of concentration is ug/m^3.

The result of the DD approach, expressing the relative change of pollution concentration after the 2008 Olympic Games, is shown in Table 11.1. The result shows a statistically significant expected sign of interaction effect for time and location (i.e. "after*related" term). The concentration of PM10 and NOx exhibited an interaction effect for time and location, with statistical significance. Moreover, the interaction effect for the SO_2 concentration was not statistically significant.

This improved air quality may be related to the 2008 Beijing Olympic Games, as this event led the local government of Beijing to implement temporary measures for air quality improvement, which mainly focused on the industrial sector and traffic control.

A specific industrial pollution control policy was enforced in 2008 (see Appendix 1) through the "Air Quality Guarantee Plan for the 29th Olympic Games in Beijing". This plan was also extended to surrounding areas, including Tianjin, Hebei, Shanxi, Shandong, and Inner Mongolia (Wang et al., 2010b). In Tianjin and Hebei, both of which are in Group B, this policy was implemented compulsorily and strictly. However, in Shanxi, Inner Mongolia, and Shandong, all of which were in Group C, this policy was implemented only if air quality became extremely serious. The plan was implemented as a temporary measure, only starting shortly before and lasting throughout the 2008 Beijing Olympic Games. The results from the DD approach indicate that those temporary measures had an effect on air pollution control. As a result, the concentration level for each of these air pollutants, PM10 and NOx, was significantly decreased in Beijing and the surrounding areas compared with other non-Olympic–related areas.

However, as discussed, a traffic control measure was also enforced in Beijing in 2008. This measure mainly focused on reducing the number of vehicles on the road, especially emphasizing heavily polluting vehicles. According to Wang et al. (2010b), emission control measures for mobile sources, including high-emitting vehicle restrictions, government vehicle limitations, and alternate-day driving rules for Beijing's 3.3 million private cars, reduced NOx by 46 per cent from the traffic sector. According to the above results, it is clear that the impact of the interaction effect on the three types of pollutants was different, even within the same year. This difference is mainly due to the difference in air pollutants originating from various emitters. According to Wang et al. (2010b), the industrial sector emitted most of the SO_2, whereas vehicles emitted only PM10 and NOx. Given the above results, the temporary air quality control measures in the host city, including factory closures and traffic control, had a significant effect after the Olympic Games.

A discussion of the post-evaluation term is provided below. In each case, every post-evaluation term of SO_2 and PM10 exhibited statistical significance. Additionally, the coefficient of each "post-evaluation" is negative. However, every post-evaluation term of NOx exhibited an insignificant result, indicating that the concentration of SO_2 and PM10 decreased during the 2003–2010 period, whereas NOx did not decrease significantly at the national level.

The result of the post-evaluation term for the concentrations of SO_2 and PM10 is consistent with the implementation of environmental measures during the 10th and 11th FYPs. These post-evaluation terms indicate that the SO_2, soot, and dust from the industrial sector were reduced significantly during the implementation of the pollution reduction policies. Some specific measures for SO_2 reduction were mentioned in the 10th FYP that mainly focused on the industrial sector. In the 11th FYP, some specific measures for soot, dust, and NOx reduction in urban areas were also mentioned, although the focus was still mainly on SO_2. The concentration of NOx did not change significantly, possibly due to the rapid increase in vehicles throughout the country. It is suggested that specific measurements for NOx be implemented more strictly at the national level.

Xu et al. (2013) noted that this area suffers from severe air pollution, which is consistent with the results of this study. Wind-blown dust, coal combustion, vehicular emissions, and industry activities all contribute to the poor air quality. The air quality is particularly poor for several reasons. First, the tertiary industries in Beijing, Tianjin, and Hebei contribute 75.5, 45.3, and 35.2 per cent of the local GDP, respectively. Moreover, the industrial sectors in Tianjin and Hebei contribute approximately 53.0 per cent and 52.0 per cent of the local GDP, respectively, in 2009. Second, the stock of vehicles in the two mega-cities, Beijing and Tianjin, increased exponentially in the past 10 years, reaching 5 million in Beijing and 1.8 million in Tianjin in 2011. Third, in 2009 the coal consumption in this area amounted to 333 million tons, accounting for 10.3 per cent of the total national consumption.

Pollution emissions in Beijing and the surrounding areas from the industrial sector were reduced due to technological progress leading to pollution reduction and the shutting down of factories nationwide. However, after the 2008 Olympic Games, pollution reduction did not exhibit any significant effects in Beijing and the surrounding area compared to the national level. It can be inferred that the reduction in air pollution in Beijing may have resulted mainly from traffic control during the Olympic Games. Considering that the industrial sector is one of the main air pollution emitters, progressive new technologies for pollution reduction should be introduced in the industrial sector to reduce air pollution in the long term.

Table 11.2 Substitution of emissions after 2008 Beijing Olympics

	Compare host city Beijing with its surrounding area					
	SO_2		PM10		NOx	
	coef.	P-value	coef.	P-value	coef.	P-value
After	–11.933**	0.044	–27.88**	0.015	–5.04***	0.000
(Robust Std.Err.)	(4.456)		(7.731)		(0.443)	
Host	(omitted)		(omitted)		(omitted)	
After*Host	–7.067	0.174	1.347	0.869	–10.16***	0.000
(Robust Std.Err.)	(4.456)		(7.731)		(0.443)	
Obs.	48		48		48	
R^2	0.16		0.48		0.41	

Note: Std. Err. is adjusted for 29 clusters in city. "Host" is omitted because of collinearity with fixed effect. *,**,*** indicates the significance at the 90%, 95% and 99% confidence levels, respectively. The unit of concentration is ug/m^3.

In case the Olympic Games may have forced industries to shift their production activities from Beijing to other locations, we also test the substitution effects of pollutants from the host city to its surrounding areas.

In this test, we compared the host city Beijing and its surrounding area on air pollution concentration, and the results are shown in Table 11.2. In the interaction term on "after " and "host", only the result of NOx shows statistical significance. It indicates that in the Beijing city, the concentration of NOx is 10.16 per cent less than the surrounding area. The result of NOx shows the existence of substitution effect, which is from Beijing to its surrounding area. Moreover, the "after * host" term of SO_2 and PM10 did not show any statistical result, which means there is no substitution effect.

11.5 Conclusion

To the best of our knowledge, this is the first paper that has quantified the environmental impact of the Olympic Games on air quality in Beijing compared to air quality improvements in other areas in China. This study used air pollution panel data at the city level for the 2003–2010 period.

The results indicate that air quality improved in Beijing, but that these improvements were only short term after the 2008 Olympic Games. This temporary reduction was due to several temporary measures, mainly factory closures and traffic control. However, there is no evidence to support the notion that air pollution measures related to the Olympics reduced the concentration of SO_2. The study also provides evidence of substitution for NOx emission from Beijing to surrounding areas. One issue that deserves further attention is that we used only city-level data, which covered only 29 cities. Future research should cover additional areas over the long term.

Appendix

Table A11.1 Air pollution control policy in China during 2001–2008

National level		Local level	
Year	Environmental regulations	Period	Measures on air quality improvement
2001	Emissions standard of air pollutants for coal-burning, oil-burning, and gas-fired boiler		
2002	State council approves plotting programs for acid rain control region and SO_2 control region		
2002	Technology policies on SO_2 emissions control from coal combustion		
2003	Cleaner production promotion law		
2003	State council issues the regulations on pollution levy		
2003	Vehicle emission standards Euro II for light-duty vehicles and heavy-duty diesel engines		
2004	Emissions standard of air pollutants for cement industry		
2005	Air quality reporting system in 113 cities		
2007	Comprehensive working plan of energy conservation and emission reduction		
2008 March	Vehicle emission standards Euro IV for light-duty vehicles	2008 Feb. 27	Air quality guarantee plan for the 29th Olympics in Beijing
2008 July	Vehicle emission standards Euro IV for heavy-duty diesel engines	2008 Jul. 7	Vehicle restrictions based on license plate numbers
		2008 Jul. 28	Emergency measures for extreme air conditions

Table A11.2 Summary of data at provincial level, among 29 capital cities in China

Variable	Data	Unit
Concentration		
SO_2	SO_2 concentration[a]	ug/m³
PM10	PM10 concentration[a]	ug/m³
NOx	NOx concentration[a]	ug/m³
Emission		
SO_2	amount of SO_2 emitted from industrial sector[b]	10 thousand tons
Dust	amount of dust emitted from industrial sector[b]	10 thousand tons
Soot	amount of soot emitted from industrial sector[b]	10 thousand tons
GDP	GDP[a] at provincial level (deflated to 2005 price level)	100 million Yuan
Emission adjusted by economic scale		
SO_2	amount of SO_2 emitted from industrial sector per GDP	100 ton per Yuan
Dust	amount of dust emitted from industrial sector per GDP	100 ton per Yuan
Soot	amount of soot emitted from industrial sector per GDP	100 ton per Yuan

Notes

1: [a]Data source: China Statistical Year Book
[b]Data source: China Environmental Statistical Year Book

2: In this study, Xinjiang, Tibet, Hong Kong, Macau, and Taiwan are not included due to missing data. Also, soot emitted in 2005 was not included due to missing data.

3: All of these 29 capital cities belong to 29 provinces in China.

Notes

1 In this study, Beijing was defined as Group A. The "surrounding area", Tianjin and Hebei, were defined as Group B. Shanxi, Inner Mongolia, and Shandong were defined as Group C (see Figure 11.1).
2 Due to some temporary measures starting from 2007, this study also discussed the change after 2007 in the results as an alternative specification.
3 In this study, sample size is 232, which means 29 city-level data of air pollutants for the 2003–2010 period.
4 These are obtained using the "xtreg" command with the "fe vce (cluster id)" option in Stata.
5 Xinjiang, Tibet, Hong Kong, Macau, and Taiwan are not included due to missing data.

Bibliography

Arne, F., and Maennig, W. (2012). Sectoral labour market effects of the 2006 FIFA World Cup. *Labour Economics*, *19*(6), 860–869. http://dx.doi.org/10.1016/j. labeco.2012.07.006

Bazmi, A.A., and Zahedi, G. (2011). Sustainable energy systems: role of optimization modeling techniques in power generation and supply – a review. *Renewable and Sustainable Energy Reviews*, *15*(8), 3480–3500. doi:http://dx.doi.org/10. 1016/j.rser.2011.05.003

Cai, H., and Xie, S. (2011). Traffic-related air pollution modeling during the 2008 Beijing Olympic Games: the effects of an odd-even day traffic restriction scheme. *Science of The Total Environment*, *409*(10), 1935–1948. doi:http://dx.doi.org/ 10.1016/j.scitotenv.2011.01.025

Dachis, B., Duranton, G., and Turner, M.A. (2011). The effects of land transfer taxes on real estate markets: evidence from a natural experiment in Toronto. *Journal of Economic Geography*, *12*(2), 327–354. doi:10.1093/jeg/lbr007

Diehla, T. (2012). The Dark Energy Survey Camera (DECam). *Physics Procedia*, *37*(0), 1332–1340. doi:http://dx.doi.org/10.1016/j.phpro.2012.02.472

Fujii, H., Managi, S., and Kaneko, S. (2013). Decomposition analysis of air pollution abatement in China: empirical study for ten industrial sectors from 1998 to 2009. *Journal of Cleaner Production*, *59*(15), 22–31. http://www.sciencedirect. com/science/article/pii/S0959652613004629

Gao, C., Yin, H., Ai, N., and Huang, Z. (2009). Historical analysis of SO_2 pollution control policies in China. *Environmental Management*, *43*(3), 447–457. doi:10.1007/s00267-008-9252-x

Guttman, D., and Song, Y. (2007). Making central-local relations work: comparing America and China environmental governance systems. *Frontiers of Environmental Science and Engineering in China*, *1*(4), 418–433

Hotchkiss, J.L., Moore, R.E., and Zobay, S.M. (2003). The impact of the 1996 Summer Olympic Games on employment and wages in Georgia. *Southern Economic Journal*, *69*(3), 691–704. http://www.jstor.org/stable/1061702

Jasmand, S., and Maennig, W. (2008). Regional income and employment effects of the 1972 Munich Summer Olympic Games. *Regional Studies*, *49*(7), 0–24. http:// www.tandfonline.com/doi/abs/10.1080/00343400701654095

Liu, Y., He, K., Li, S., Wang, Z., Christiani, D.C., and Koutrakis, P. (2012). A statistical model to evaluate the effectiveness of PM2.5 emissions control during the Beijing 2008 Olympic Games. *Environment International*, *44*(0), 100–105. doi:http://dx.doi.org/10.1016/j.envint.2012.02.003

Managi, S., and Kaneko, S. (2009). Environmental performance and returns to pollution abatement in China. *Ecological Economics*, *68*(6), 1643–1651. http:// dx.doi.org/10.1016/j.ecolecon.2008.04.005

Managi, S., and Kaneko, S. (2010). *Chinese economic development and environment.* Cheltenham, UK, Edward Elgar Publishing Ltd.

Parameshwaran, R., Kalaiselvam, S., Harikrishnan, S., and Elayaperumal, A. (2012). Sustainable thermal energy storage technologies for buildings: a review. *Renewable and Sustainable Energy Reviews*, *16*(5), 2394–2433. doi:http://dx.doi.org/10. 1016/j.rser.2012.01.058

Saidur, R., Islam, M.R., Rahim, N.A., and Solangi, K.H. (2010). A review on global wind energy policy. *Renewable and Sustainable Energy Reviews*, *14*(7), 1744–1762. doi:http://dx.doi.org/10.1016/j.rser.2010.03.007

Schleicher, N., Norra, S., and Chen, Y. (2012). Efficiency of mitigation measures to reduce particulate air pollution – a case study during the Olympic Summer Games 2008 in Beijing, China. *Science of The Total Environment,* (427–428), 146–158. http://dx.doi.org/10.1016/j.scitotenv.2012.04.004

Schreifels, J.J., Fu, Y., and Wilson, E.J. (2012). Sulfur dioxide control in China: policy evolution during the 10th and 11th Five Year Plan and lessons for the future. *Energy Policy,* 48(0), 779–789. doi:http://dx.doi.org/10.1016/j.enpol.2012.06.015

Shunze, W., Yuantang, L., Jinnan, W., Yao, L., and Zhizhong, Z. (2007). Analysis and suggestion on distortion of environmental protection investment in China. *China Population, Resources and Environment,* 17(3), 112–117. doi:10.1016/S1872-583X(07)60016-3

Song, S., Wu, Y., Jiang, J., Yang, L., Cheng, Y., and Hao, J. (2012). Chemical characteristics of size-resolved PM(2.5) at a roadside environment in Beijing, China. *Environmental Pollution (Barking, Essex : 1987),* 161, 215–221. doi:10.1016/j.envpol.2011.10.014

Wang, L., Jang, C., Zhang, Y., Wang, K., Zhang, Q., Streets, D., Fu, J., et al. (2010a). Assessment of air quality benefits from national air pollution control policies in China. Part I: Background, emission scenarios and evaluation of meteorological predictions. Part II: Evaluation of air quality predictions and air quality benefits assessment. *Atmospheric Environment,* 44(28), 3442–3457. doi:10.1016/j.atmosenv.2010.05.051

Wang, S., Zhao, M., Xing, J., Wu, Y., Zhou, Y., Lei, Y., He, K., et al. (2010b). Quantifying the air pollutants emission reduction during the 2008 Olympic games in Beijing. *Environmental Science and Technology,* 44(7), 2490–2496. doi:10.1021/es9028167

Xu, J., Wang, X., and Zhang, S. (2013). Risk-based air pollutants management at regional levels. *Environmental Science & Policy,* 25, 167–175. doi:10.1016/j.envsci.2012.09.014

Xu, X., Deng, F., Guo, X., Lv, P., Zhong, M., Liu, C., Wang, A., et al. (2012). Association of systemic inflammation with marked changes in particulate air pollution in Beijing in 2008. *Toxicology Letters,* 212(2), 147–156. doi:10.1016/j.toxlet.2012.05.014

You, C.F., and Xu, X.C. (2010). Coal combustion and its pollution control in China. *Energy,* 35(11), 4467–4472. doi:http://dx.doi.org/10.1016/j.energy.2009.04.019

Zhou, M. (2011). Intensification of geo-cultural homophily in global trade: evidence from the gravity model. *Social Science Research,* 40(1), 193–209. doi:10.1016/j.ssresearch.2010.07.002

12 Voluntary industrial toxics program and performance

Hidemichi Fujii, Shunsuke Managi
and Hiromitsu Kawahara

12.1 Introduction

Improved productivity is the main driver of economic growth, but rapid growth can increase pollutant emissions due to the greater use of resources.[1] Consequently, there is a conflict between economic growth and environmental concerns. In research on growth theory, analyses of economic growth and the environment have shown the importance of productivity increases and found that improved productivity decreases the input demand for lower pollution levels (Akao and Managi, 2007). Thus, emission reductions should be considered for continuous productivity progress. This study analyzed productivity by considering environmental policies on the provision and dissemination of environmental information in the United States (U.S.) and Japan.

The provision and dissemination of environmental information can complement traditional policy instruments for controlling environmental performance (Tietenberg and Wheeler, 2001). The provision of information is a quasi-regulatory mechanism because consumers, investors, and other stakeholders can use it to pressure firms to change their environmental behaviors (Arora and Cason, 1996; Lyon and Maxwell, 2004). For example, a provision that requires firms to provide specific environmental information may cause environmentally conscious consumers to change their purchasing decisions based on firms' environmental performance (Konar and Cohen, 1997; Jobe, 1999).

Previous literature on the Pollution Release and Transfer Register (PRTR) system has focused on the effects of the U.S. Toxics Release Inventory (TRI), and particularly the relationship between a firm's environmental performance and its financial performance. Two important characteristics of PRTR and TRI systems are (1) that facilities periodically send a mandatory report to the relevant authorities on their releases into the air, water, and soil and the disposal of other wastes, and (2) that the emissions data of specific pollutants from individual facilities are accessible to the public.

The goal of this study is to provide a measurement of change in total factor productivity (TFP) based on environmental (i.e., nonmarket) outputs. It is important to note that we could not judge whether the index increases over time because the regulations requiring more stringent pollution decreases do not necessarily change productivity.[2]

Table 12.1 Pollution abatement cost and expenditures (PACE) in U.S. industry (million U.S. $)

	(1) Value of shipments	(2) PACE	PACE per shipment ratio [(2)/(1)]	Breakdown of abatement cost			
				Treatment	Prevention	Recycling	Disposal
All industries	4,735,384	20,678	0.44%	52%	17%	8%	22%
Food	534,878	1,573	0.29%	55%	11%	7%	28%
Textile	41,149	221	0.54%	63%	7%	9%	21%
Paper	162,848	1,796	1.10%	60%	11%	7%	23%
Petroleum	476,075	3,746	0.79%	51%	35%	7%	8%
Chemical	604,501	5,217	0.86%	53%	16%	8%	24%
Plastics and rubber	200,489	503	0.25%	43%	16%	10%	32%
Nonmetallic mineral	114,321	696	0.61%	57%	18%	7%	18%
Primary metal	201,836	2,291	1.14%	54%	12%	10%	24%
Fabric metal	288,068	763	0.26%	46%	11%	12%	31%
Machinery	302,204	316	0.10%	34%	16%	11%	39%
Electrical equipment	373,932	624	0.17%	54%	9%	10%	27%
Transportation equipment	687,288	1,319	0.19%	45%	13%	12%	30%

Source: Pollution Abatement Cost and Expenditures 2005, U.S. Bureau of the Census

The U.S. Census Bureau published a list of pollution abatement costs and expenditures (PACE) in 2005 according to business type (Table 12.1). We summarized the value of shipments, PACE, and PACE-per-shipment ratio by type of business. The PACE-per-shipment ratio is high in the textiles, paper, petroleum, chemical, nonmetallic mineral, and fabric metal industries. In contrast, the PACE-per-shipment ratio in the machinery, electrical equipment, and transportation industries is lower than in the other sectors. The industries with high PACE-per-shipment ratios mainly incur their abatement costs for pollution treatment, which is essentially an end-of-pipe solution. In contrast, industries with lower PACE-per-shipment ratios tend to incur their abatement costs for recycling and disposal.

12.2 Background

In 1984, a pesticide (methyl isocyanate gas) leak caused an accidental explosion at a Union Carbide India Limited (UCIL) plant in Bhopal, India. The next year, another toxic gas leak accident occurred at a Union Carbide facility in West Virginia and sent more than 100 people to the hospital. These incidents launched an international movement to understand the consequences of the increasing use of chemical substances in industry. Public interest and environmental organizations in the U.S. and Japan accelerated demand for information on toxic chemicals from the facilities that used them (Khanna, 1998). Consequently, the U.S. Emergency Planning and Community Right-to-Know Act (EPCRA) passed in 1986. Toxics Release Inventory (TRI) reporting is required by Section 313 in the EPCRA. The TRI is a publicly available U.S. Environmental Protection Agency (U.S.EPA) database that contains information on toxic chemical releases and waste management activities, which is reported annually by certain industries and federal facilities.[3]

Japan has enforced PRTRs since 2001; its first public release of PRTR data was on March 20, 2003. Under this system, facilities that have more than 21 employees and produce or use chemicals on a list of 354 substances, specified by law, must annually report the quantities they use to the central government.[4] The central government then sorts the reported data by industry type and geographic location and provides the information to the public. Although the central government does not specify facility-level emissions in their aggregated reports, they must disclose facility-level data when a citizen requests them. The PRTR in Japan plays an important role in reducing and managing the development of toxic chemicals.

Table 12.2 shows a historical overview of the laws and regulations on toxic chemical substances in the U.S. and Japan. The U.S. began to enforce pollution restriction laws in the 1940s and 1950s, and Japan began to do so at the end of the 1960s. PRTR laws were established in 1986 as TRI in the U.S. In 1991, the U.S. government began a unique environmental pollution reduction plan known as the 33/50 Program. The 33/50 Program targeted 17 priority chemicals, such as benzene and toluene, and set the goal of a 33% reduction (using a 1988 baseline) in the release and transfer of these chemicals by 1992 and a 50% reduction by 1995. The primary purpose of the EPA's growing series of voluntary programs was to demonstrate the benefits of voluntary partnerships. Previous studies have shown that voluntary approaches bring about targeted reductions more quickly than would regulations alone (Khanna and Damon, 1999; Gamper-Rabindran, 2006). In 2006, Japan also established a volatile organic compound (VOC) reduction plan, which has a target of a 30% reduction in the release of VOC chemical substances and is based on the voluntary efforts of companies and business associations. With these new toxic chemical substances regulations, technologies for toxic chemical substances abatement have advanced and spurred innovations such as plasma chemical degradation (Pascala et al., 2010) and the photocatalytic process method (Doana and Saidi, 2008).

12.3   Literature review and objective

In the analysis of emissions management, it is important to understand whether pollution abatement technologies are utilized efficiently (Kolominskas, 2004) because efficiency at least partially influences the cost of production and pollution abatement technologies (Jaffe et al., 2005). Two opposing incentives result from

Table 12.2 History of law and regulation about toxic chemical substances

Year	United States	Japan
1985	– Clean Water Act (1948)(CWA was revised in 1972, 1977, 1987) – Clean Air Act (1955)(CAA was revised in 1970, 1977, 1990) – Toxic Substances Control Act (1976)	– Basic Law for Environmental Pollution (1967–1993) – Air Pollution Control Law (1968) – Water Pollution Control Law (1970) – Chemical Substances Control Law (1973)
1985–1989	– Emergency Planning and Community Right-to-Know Act (EPCRA) (1986) – Toxics Release Inventory (TRI) started (1986)	– Amendment of Chemical Substances Control Law (Start restriction of Chlorinated Organic Solvent) (1986)
1990–1994	– EPA establishes the 33/50 Program (1991) – Expansion of the chemical list raised the number of chemicals and chemical categories reported to TRI from 336 to over 600 (1994)	– Law Concerning Special Measures for Total Emission Reduction of Nitrogen Oxides and Particulate Matte (1992) – Basic Environment Law (1993) – The Basic Environmental Plan (Defined concept of environmental risk) (1994)
1995–1999	– Facility/industry expansion[1] (1997) – Chemical Use Reporting[2] (1997)	– Pollutant Release and Transfer Registers (PRTR) Law (1999)
2000–2004	– EPA held an online public dialogue on options for reducing the burden on the regulated industry associated with the Toxics Release Inventory (TRI) program (2003)	– Law Concerning Special Measures Against Dioxins (2000) – Amendment of Chemical Substances Control Law (Induced concept of environmental risk impact into ecological system) (2003)
2005–2009	– EPA revised the TRI reporting requirements to reduce burden and promote recycling and treatment as alternatives to disposal and other releases (2006)	– Amendment of Air Pollution Control Law (Started restriction of VOC emission) (2006)

Notes:
1. Seven new industry sectors are added.
2. Expansion of the TRI to gather chemical use information and expansion of the EPA Community Right-to-Know Program to increase the information available to the public on chemical use.

environmental policy on productivity growth, and as a result, two possibilities may emerge (Managi et al., 2005). First, abatement pressures might encourage a growth in productivity that reduces the actual cost of compliance below the originally estimated cost (Bunge, 1996). Second, in contrast, firms might be reluctant to increase productivity if they believe that regulators will respond by ratcheting up standards even further. In addition to changes in environmental regulations and technology, management levels influence productivity. Therefore, the question of whether productivity and technological frontier levels increase over time requires empirical study.

We can divide the previous studies that focused on productivity in the context of toxic chemical substances into two types: one group focused on entire industrial sectors, and the other group analyzed firm-level data. If we use data on entire industrial sectors to estimate productivity, then the industrial characteristics largely determine productivity. However, most of the studies that used firm-level data focused on one industrial sector (Färe et al., 2001; Kwon, 2006; Koehler, 2007). Although the PRTR system was enforced in all industrial sectors in the same year, the technical difficulties associated with reducing toxic chemical emissions differ between industries. It is clear that the necessary capital equipment and labor for reducing toxic chemical substances differs between industries because the chemical products that are used as intermediate materials differ. We therefore compared sector-level TFP by considering the emission of toxic chemical substances (called environmentally sensitive productivity, or ESP).

We selected U.S. and Japanese manufacturing companies for our study for the following reasons. First, they are significant emitters of chemical substances; in 2008, the U.S. and Japanese industrial sectors emitted 3.85 and 0.44 billion pounds of chemical substances, respectively. Their total emission of chemical substances is larger than that of other developed countries. Lanjouw and Mody (1996) noted that the U.S. and Japan have dedicated significant research and development expenditures to environmental technology and that their share of environmental patents worldwide is high. Additionally, their share of pollution abatement costs and expenditures, in terms of GDP, is high. We should also note that the U.S. and Japanese governments freely provide PRTR information on companies on their respective websites. Therefore, information is easily available to the public. This study considered the differences between these industries and compared ESP by focusing on nine manufacturing industries in the U.S. and Japan.

This study aimed to measure the extent to which U.S. and Japanese manufacturing firms have improved their productivities with respect to the toxic chemical substances under consideration. In this paper, we hope to clarify how ESP changes after certain environmental standards are enforced and consider how environmental standards in the domestic market and the international market affect firm performance. Below, we discuss the gap between efficient and inefficient firms.

The TRI system in the U.S. began in 1986 and has operated for over 20 years. In contrast, the PRTR system in Japan is relatively new; it started in 2001. Some of the differences in the two countries' respective levels of ESP might result from the different levels of experience that their manufacturing companies have with this type of policy. We aimed to investigate how experience with this policy affects environmental performance; for example, more experience might increase marginal abatement costs if firms use up their easily reduced emissions. However, if voluntary action requires additional time from the firms, the opposite result might occur. The goal of this paper is to outline policy strategies for firms to reduce toxic chemical substances and maintain their market competitiveness.

In this study, we could not segregate cleaner production costs from pollution abatement costs because there are no data on the former. Recently, several environmentally proactive firms disclosed their pollution abatement costs in their environmental accounting reports, but even these reports did not fully reveal the costs of cleaner production. Separating cleaner production costs from other production costs is difficult because manufacturing firms commonly calculate at least some of their cleaner production costs in the costs of the overall production process.

According to Frondel (2007), regulatory measures and environmental policies are more crucial for end-of-pipe technology. Moreover, cost saving, general management systems, and specific environmental management tools tend to promote cleaner production in OECD countries.

We used Sony's corporate activity report as a case study to interpret the results of above study. Sony has successfully developed a mercury-free alkaline button battery (Sony, 2009). Based on past sales, we estimated that this new battery, in addition to Sony's existing mercury-free silver oxide button batteries, would reduce the firm's mercury use by approximately 470 kg per year.

Using these cases, we tried to identify the effect of a cleaner production approach on the reduction of toxic chemical pollution. The cleaner production approach has advantages for corporate economic performance that outweigh those of the end-of-pipe approach (Frondel et al., 2007). Thus, a general shift in pollution reduction approaches, from an end-of-pipe type to a cleaner production type, can improve productivity. Environmentally sensitive productivity is an appropriate method for this study because it evaluates both environment and economic performance and allows us to identify how manufacturing firms can reduce environmental pollution without hindering economic performance.

12.4   Method and data

This study measured environmentally sensitive productivity changes in U.S. and Japanese manufacturing firms. We applied the directional distance function (DDF) to measure the Luenberger productivity indicator to estimate ESP (Chambers et al., 1998; Fujii et al., 2010). DDF evaluates productive efficiency using a nonparametric production function. Luenberger-type productivity is considered to be a more general measure than the widely used Malmquist Index (Chambers et al., 1998). We can break down a change in the Luenberger productivity indicator into technical change and efficiency change (see Appendix in detail).

We obtained financial data on the U.S. firms from the Mergent online financial database and chemical substances data from the TRI database of the EPA. The

Table 12.3 Firms by industry type

Industry type	Type of business	Code	U.S.	Japan
Basic material industry	Rubber and plastic products	RUBB	14	43
	Chemicals and allied products	CHEM	54	122
	Paper and pulp	PAPER	16	19
	Steel, non-ferrous metal	STEEL	23	63
	Fabricated metal	FABRI	19	28
Processing and assembly industry	Industrial machine	MACHINE	49	68
	Electric product	ELEC	78	30
	Transportation equipment	TRANS	39	69
	Precision instrument	PREC	38	24

Japanese manufacturing firm–level data cover the period of 2001–2008, and the U.S. manufacturing data cover the period of 1999–2007. The financial data on the Japanese firms were provided by the Nikkei NEEDS financial database, and the chemical substances data were from the PRTR database from the Ministry of Economy, Trade and Industry (METI). The sample included 386 U.S. firms and 466 Japanese firms (see Table 12.3). This paper focuses on the nine industries discussed above.

We categorized the nine sectors into two main industries: the basic material industry and the processing and assembly industry. The basic material industry includes rubber and plastic, chemical, paper, steel, and fabricated metal. The processing and assembly industrial sectors include industrial machinery, electronics, transportation, and precision instruments.

We used the total revenue of a firm as the market output variable and capital stock, and the number of employees and the intermediate material input as the market input variables. These variables were deflated from the year 2000 prices according to the type of industry. We obtained the deflators for the U.S. firms from the OECD database and the deflators for the Japanese firms from the Statistics Bureau and Bank of Japan databases. We used the integrated toxic chemical substances risk score (i.e., the toxic risk score), which is estimated with the toxicity weight given by the U.S. EPA, with undesirable output data to estimate productivity (see Tables 12.4 and 12.5).

Our dataset had three limitations. First, it covered different numbers of chemical substances between the U.S. and Japan. There are 426 chemical substances in the TRI database published by the U.S. EPA, and the toxicity weight covers all of the chemical substances in the TRI database. However, there are 354 chemical substances in the PRTR published by the METI in Japan, and the toxicity weight covers only 134 chemical substances. Thus, it was difficult to compare the toxic risk scores directly. Therefore, we focused on the time series of productivity change in each country and industry. The second limitation is that the U.S. firm data provide

Table 12.4 U.S. industrial firms data description

	Total revenue (millions U.S.$)		Capital stock (millions U.S.$)		Cost of sales (millions U.S.$)		Number of employees (person)		Toxic risk score (integrated million pound)	
	Mean	St.dev.	Mean	St.dev.	Mean	St.dev.	Mean	St.dev.	Mean	St.dev.
1999	3,676	12,774	1,102	3,419	2,414	8,714	15,137	36,610	154	635
2000	4,083	13,759	1,187	3,578	2,622	9,797	16,048	36,877	159	627
2001	4,099	13,418	1,227	3,728	2,721	9,819	15,520	35,437	130	497
2002	4,206	14,084	1,275	3,996	2,750	9,980	15,501	34,835	145	589
2003	4,429	14,180	1,335	4,288	2,822	10,169	15,277	34,403	181	827
2004	4,905	15,103	1,359	4,662	3,003	10,536	15,661	34,547	136	647
2005	5,067	14,909	1,335	4,733	3,070	10,649	16,049	35,442	125	577
2006	5,338	15,617	1,389	4,937	3,125	10,258	16,455	34,499	144	674
2007	5,603	14,980	1,442	5,036	3,271	10,361	16,792	34,510	124	623

Table 12.5 Japanese industrial firms data description (1$=100 yen)

	Total revenue (millions U.S.$)		Capital stock (millions U.S.$)		Cost of sales (millions U.S.$)		Number of employees (person)		Toxic risk score (integrated million pound)	
	Mean	St.dev.	Mean	St.dev.	Mean	St.dev.	Mean	St.dev.	Mean	St.dev.
2001	1,934	5,824	2,849	6,731	1,371	3,848	1,333	4,268	389	2,045
2002	1,990	6,032	2,689	6,394	1,370	3,890	1,389	4,486	264	1,487
2003	2,057	6,166	2,584	6,082	1,462	4,225	1,408	4,537	193	1,052
2004	2,821	6,771	2,547	5,986	1,500	4,376	1,494	4,838	151	798
2005	2,523	7,861	2,557	6,021	1,618	4,689	1,628	5,360	140	815
2006	2,842	8,928	2,588	6,112	1,680	4,929	1,782	5,939	176	1,296
2007	3,082	9,755	2,601	6,025	1,758	5,060	1,301	5,218	23	261
2008	2,970	9,235	2,652	6,183	1,677	4,620	1,113	4,382	22	261

different types of information compared with the Japanese firm data. The Mergent online database provides consolidated financial data, and, therefore, the TRI database includes parent company names. We used this information to integrate each plant's toxic chemical substance emission data into company-level data. In contrast, the Japanese PRTR database does not include parent company names; it only includes company names. We thus integrated the Japanese PRTR data into non-consolidated, company-level data. The last limitation is the availability of capital data for the U.S. firms. We used capital stock data for the Japanese firm analysis, but we used net property, plant, and equipment as the capital stock for the U.S. firm analysis because comprehensive capital stock data are not available. In general, net property, plant, and equipment are lower than capital stock because these variables do not include intangible assets, whereas capital stock does.

12.5   Results

The results are shown in Figures 12.1 to 12.4 and Tables 12.6 and 12.7. To investigate productivity changes in the U.S. and Japan, we set the base year at 1999 for U.S. firms and 2001 for Japanese firms. ESP, EFFCH, and TECHCH in the base year equal zero in Figures 12.1 to 12.4. Figure 12.1, Figure 12.2, and Table 12.6 show the U.S. firms' results. Figure 12.3, Figure 12.4, and Table 12.7 show the Japanese firms' results.

12.5.1   Results for U.S. industries

Figure 12.1 shows that the ESP for the five U.S. basic material industries, especially the rubber and steel industries, improved from 2002 to 2007. For the processing and assembly industry, Figure 12.2 shows that the ESP improved rapidly in the machine, electronics and precision instrument industries, and the ESP of these three industries showed similar trends from 1999 to 2007. One interpretation of this rapid ESP improvement in the processing and assembly industry is that the

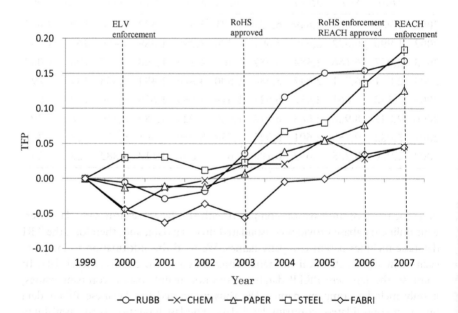

Figure 12.1 Total factor productivity of basic material industry in the U.S.

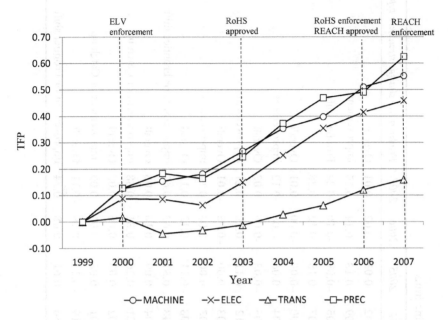

Figure 12.2 Total factor productivity of processing and assembly industry in the U.S.

information technology field achieved substantial technological innovations in this period, including the semiconductor and electronic component sector. In particular, processing and assembly companies invested large amounts of capital and research and development funds to develop new products.

ESP improvements in the processing and assembly industry might also be related to the enforcement of environmental standards in Europe. There are three strict environmental standards for the processing and assembly industry: (1) the Restriction of the Use of Certain Hazardous Substances in Electrical and Electronic Equipment (RoHS); (2) the Registration, Evaluation, Authorization and Restriction of Chemicals (REACH); and (3) the End-of-Life Vehicles Directive (ELV).[5] Under the RoHS and ELV directives, all electric and vehicle products with a level of toxic chemicals above a certain threshold cannot be sold in the European market. These environmental standards have provided an incentive for U.S. firms that export to the European market to begin the management of toxic chemical substances. Therefore, the ESP improvement in the processing and assembly industry was mainly due to rapid technological progress and environmental standards in the European market. The transportation industry had a lower score than the other industries, which may be due to the poor financial performance of the U.S. auto industry and other related industries.

Table 12.6 shows the results of the estimation of TECHCH and EFFCH and suggests that the ESP improvement was mainly caused by the growth in TECHCH from 1999 to 2007 in the U.S. manufacturing industry. The level of EFFCH decreased for several industries; therefore, this structure is the "frontier

Table 12.6 Results of EFFCH and TECHCH indicators in U.S. manufacturing firms

	Indicator	1999	2000	2001	2002	2003	2004	2005	2006	2007	Productivity change structure type
RUBB	EFFCH	0.00	0.02	0.01	-0.00	0.00	0.02	0.03	0.02	0.01	Overall
	TECHCH	0.00	-0.02	-0.04	-0.01	0.03	0.09	0.13	0.14	0.15	improvement
CHEM	EFFCH	0.00	-0.05	-0.08	-0.20	-0.10	-0.05	-0.09	-0.10	-0.24	Frontier shift
	TECHCH	0.00	-0.00	0.06	0.20	0.12	0.07	0.15	0.12	0.28	
PAPER	EFFCH	0.00	-0.01	-0.02	-0.00	-0.01	-0.00	-0.00	-0.00	0.01	Overall
	TECHCH	0.00	0.00	0.00	-0.01	0.01	0.04	0.06	0.08	0.12	improvement
STEEL	EFFCH	0.00	-0.02	0.00	-0.02	-0.01	-0.05	-0.03	-0.06	-0.03	Overall
	TECHCH	0.00	0.05	0.03	0.03	0.03	0.12	0.11	0.20	0.21	improvement
FABRI	EFFCH	0.00	-0.02	-0.06	-0.05	-0.07	-0.03	-0.00	-0.05	-0.01	Overall
	TECHCH	0.00	-0.02	-0.00	0.01	0.02	0.03	0.00	0.08	0.14	improvement
MACHINE	EFFCH	0.00	-0.00	-0.03	-0.04	-0.07	-0.08	-0.11	-0.12	-0.11	Overall
	TECHCH	0.00	0.13	0.18	0.22	0.34	0.43	0.51	0.63	0.67	improvement or Frontier shift
ELEC	EFFCH	0.00	0.03	0.14	0.10	0.05	0.04	0.09	0.10	0.08	Overall
	TECHCH	0.00	0.06	-0.06	-0.04	0.10	0.21	0.26	0.31	0.38	improvement or Catch up
TRANS	EFFCH	0.00	-0.00	-0.00	0.00	-0.00	0.02	0.03	0.06	0.07	Overall
	TECHCH	0.00	0.02	-0.04	-0.04	-0.01	0.01	0.03	0.06	0.09	improvement or Catch up
PREC	EFFCH	0.00	-0.12	-0.09	-0.08	-0.15	-0.19	-0.14	-0.19	-0.11	Overall
	TECHCH	0.00	0.25	0.28	0.24	0.39	0.56	0.61	0.68	0.74	improvement or Frontier shift

Note: EFFCH: Efficiency change, TECHCH: Technical change

shift type". In frontier shift type productivity change, efficient firms on the frontier line achieve technological progress. However, inefficient firms do not keep up with this technological development, and, therefore, the efficiency gap increases. Nevertheless, the main factor in increasing ESP was the improvement of EFFCH in the transportation industry sector. We call this structure the "catch up type". In catch up type productivity change, an inefficient firm's productivity improvement is faster than an efficient firm's technological progress, and the efficiency gap shrinks. Therefore, we noted an "overall improvement type" if TECHCH was positive and EFFCH was approximately zero. In an overall improvement type productivity change, the speed of the efficient firm's technological progress is nearly equal to that of the inefficient firm's productivity improvement.

Table 12.6 shows that, for the chemical manufacturing industry, TECHCH was positive and EFFCH was negative. This finding implies that the efficiency gap between the efficient firms, including frontier and inefficient firms, grew between 1999 and 2007. One interpretation of this result is that environmentally proactive firms produced better systems to manage toxic chemical substances due to new environmental standards. However, firms may also maintain a reactive environmental management system to minimize their environmental protection costs because the TRI system does not regulate the emission of toxic chemicals. That is, firms that focus on the domestic market might have fewer incentives to reduce toxic chemical substance emissions.

Furthermore, EFFCH was negative in the industrial machine and precision instrument industries, which implies a widening efficiency gap. The processing and assembly industry tends to export to the European market, and, thus, these manufacturers have an incentive to manage toxic chemicals proactively to adjust to stringent environmental standards such as the RoHS and ELV. These proactive firms reduced their consumption and emission of toxic chemical substances efficiently. Therefore, firms that do not export to the European market might also be affected through their supply chain management, although this effect is limited. Therefore, firms' perceptions of environmental preferences and environmental standards differ, which might be one reason why some firms manage toxic chemical substances well and others do not.

Our results suggest the importance of consistency between nations and economic unions and the benefit of shared policies to reduce asymmetric shocks in the economy. There have been several cases of a developed country (e.g., Japan) adapting its environmental regulations to reflect the policies in other developed economies, such as the EU. For example, Japan's *marking for the presence of specific chemical substances for electrical and electronic equipment* (J-MOSS) was enforced in July 2006. It is an eco-labeling system that targets six chemical substances (the same as those in the RoHS restriction) and seven electrical and electronic products, and it was enforced in tandem with the RoHS restriction.

One of the main motivations for this development in Japan is the protection of domestic manufacturing companies. In general, production lines are almost the same whether they target the domestic market or global markets (in developed countries). When the EU enforces stringent environmental regulations, firms in Japan need to change their production processes to comply with these standards. However, manufacturing firms in developing countries, which do not export to the EU and do not adopt its restrictions, then increase the competitiveness of their exports to Japan because they do not face the additional pollution abatement costs that are imposed on Japanese manufacturers producing for the EU market. Japan, then, enforced its own new environmental regulations, similar to those of the EU, to protect the competiveness of domestic manufacturing companies. Another relevant example is that of the EU emission trading system, which might harm European industry if countries such as the U.S., Japan, and China do not adopt similar policies.

In contrast, EFFCH was positive in the electronic product and transportation equipment industries, which shows that efficiency gaps in these industries shrank from 1999 to 2007. This result might be explained by the fact that these industries mainly use chemical substances for paints and bonds, and firms can reduce their toxicity by switching from highly toxic chemicals to less-toxic chemical materials. Currently, decreasing the use of toxic chemical substances is costly, but technological innovations can reduce this cost and address several constraints, such as bonding power and color quality. As a result, inefficient firms may be able to use less-toxic chemical materials.

12.5.2   Results for Japanese industries

Figure 12.3 shows that the five Japanese basic material industries improved on average in terms of ESP from 2001 to 2007. In particular, the ESP of these five industries rapidly increased from 2006 to 2007. Then, because of the financial crisis, the ESP

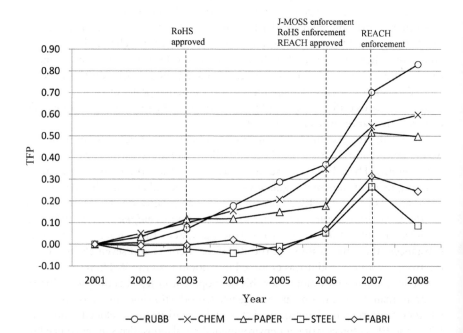

Figure 12.3 Total factor productivity of basic material industry in Japan

of the steel and fabricated metal industries decreased due to a decrease in capital productivity. We might attribute the changes over 2006 and 2007 to the VOC restrictions that were implemented in 2006. This environmental standard encouraged manufacturing companies and business associations to reduce VOC chemical substances through partially mandatory educational seminars and workshops. These activities supported small and medium-scale firms, which tend to have difficulty reducing VOC chemical substances because of a lack of financing and knowledge.

The ESP of the rubber, chemical, and paper industries improved rapidly. In particular, the chemical industry experienced a decrease in its toxic risk score from 2001 to 2008 due to the proactive work of the Japanese Chemical Industry Association (JCIA). The JCIA consists of 180 chemical industrial firms and 75 business associations. In 1997, the JCIA started its own PRTR system to determine how many toxic chemical substances were being emitted. It also holds workshops and seminars to spread knowledge on effective toxic chemical substance reduction among its member firms. This progressive approach helps reactive firms and firms with low levels of environmental technology to reduce their toxic risk score without undermining their financial performance.

Figure 12.4 shows the results for the Japanese processing and assembly industry. This sector improved its ESP from 2001 to 2008, and the electronics industry showed a particularly dramatic increase. In general, toxic chemical materials are used for paints and bonds in the processing and assembly industry. Additionally, toxic chemical materials are used for melting down and solidifying in the basic material industry. Paint and bond materials are relatively easy to replace with other

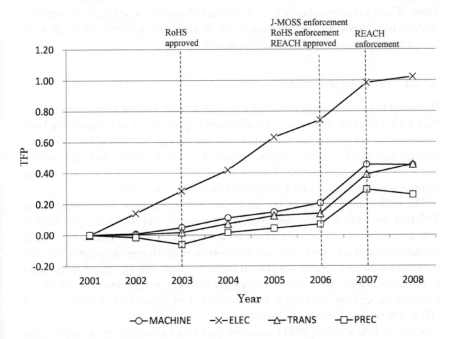

Figure 12.4 Total factor productivity of processing and assembly industry in Japan

low-toxicity chemical materials, but many toxic chemicals used in the basic material industry are difficult to replace. Therefore, the processing and assembly industry has an advantage in reducing its toxic risk score compared to other industries. Table 12.7 shows the results for EFFCH and TECHCH in the Japanese manufacturing firms. Between 2001 and 2008, the ESP of most industries shifted from a frontier shift type to an overall improvement type, which implies that the efficiency gap between the efficient and inefficient firms did not shrink.

The REACH directive was adopted in 2006 in Europe and required firms that export to the European market to be more proactive in controlling toxic chemical substances. In 2018, the REACH directive plans to cover 30,000 chemical substances in firms treating more than 1 ton per year. Progressive firms can play a key role in addressing this stringent environmental standard and maintaining competitiveness in the international market by spreading knowledge and solving problems cooperatively through seminars and workshops in business associations. Additionally, the REACH directive gives firms access to comprehensive environmental management strategies through supply-chain management and makes firms more efficient by requiring them to procure their materials in an environmentally sound manner.

When we compared the U.S. and Japanese results, we identified several industries in the U.S. with an ESP that is shifting to the catch up type, but we did not find this result in Japan. One interpretation of this finding is that the PRTR started in 2001 in Japan, and, thus, both efficient and inefficient firms are still learning about the management of toxic chemical substances (i.e., lower marginal abatement). In contrast, U.S. firms have had sufficient time to promote the management of toxic chemical substances because the TRI was implemented in 1986. Thus, environmentally proactive firms should have applied cost-efficient abatement technologies and management. In this case, it is difficult for firms to have a high and positive TECHCH indicator.

12.5.3 Policy implications

We aimed to identify the structure of productivity changes in each industry. Industries with a frontier shift type of productivity improvement introduced the latest technologies for toxic chemical substances abatement, such as plasma chemical degradation and the photocatalytic process method. However, industries with a catch up type of productivity improvement used traditional but cost effective technology that the advanced companies had already installed.

The policy implications of our study are as follows. First, industries with an ESP that has shifted to the catch up type and overall improvement type have an incentive to innovate new technology because efficient firms might find it difficult to make technological progress in these productivity change structures. Second, industries with an ESP that has shifted to the frontier shift type have an incentive to transfer technology and share knowledge through governmental seminars and business association workshops because inefficient firms do not catch up with efficient firms in a frontier shift structure.

Stern and Aronsson (1984) raise the problem of policies promoted by the spread of information. They show that the information policy regarding energy

Table 12.7 Results of EFFCH and TECHCH indicators in Japanese manufacturing companies

	Indicator	2001	2002	2003	2004	2005	2006	2007	2008	*Productivity change structure type*
RUBB	EFFCH	0.00	0.00	0.03	0.01	0.02	0.03	-0.41	-0.37	Overall improvement or Frontier shift
	TECHCH	0.00	0.01	0.04	0.17	0.27	0.34	1.11	1.20	
CHEM	EFFCH	0.00	-0.02	0.01	0.02	-0.00	0.04	-0.22	-0.20	Overall improvement or Frontier shift
	TECHCH	0.00	0.07	0.09	0.14	0.21	0.31	0.76	0.80	
PAPER	EFFCH	0.00	0.02	0.01	0.01	0.02	0.01	-0.04	-0.05	Overall improvement or Frontier shift
	TECHCH	0.00	0.02	0.11	0.11	0.13	0.17	0.55	0.55	
STEEL	EFFCH	0.00	0.02	0.03	0.01	-0.00	-0.03	-0.24	-0.39	Overall improvement or Frontier shift
	TECHCH	0.00	-0.02	-0.04	0.01	-0.03	0.10	0.55	0.63	
FABRI	EFFCH	0.00	0.01	-0.03	-0.03	-0.03	0.01	-0.16	-0.18	Frontier shift
	TECHCH	0.00	-0.05	0.01	-0.01	0.02	0.05	0.43	0.26	
MACHINE	EFFCH	0.00	-0.00	0.03	0.06	0.05	0.06	-0.14	-0.19	Overall improvement or Frontier shift
	TECHCH	0.00	0.01	0.02	0.05	0.10	0.15	0.59	0.64	
ELEC	EFFCH	0.00	-0.03	0.28	0.26	0.29	0.31	-0.16	0.00	Overall improvement or Frontier shift
	TECHCH	0.00	0.17	0.01	0.16	0.34	0.44	1.15	1.02	
TRANS	EFFCH	0.00	0.05	0.08	0.06	0.06	0.08	-0.04	-0.07	Overall improvement or Frontier shift
	TECHCH	0.00	-0.05	-0.06	0.01	0.06	0.06	0.43	0.53	
PREC	EFFCH	0.00	-0.00	-0.01	0.01	0.00	0.00	-0.18	-0.19	Overall improvement or Frontier shift
	TECHCH	0.00	-0.01	-0.05	0.01	0.04	0.07	0.47	0.45	

Note: EFFCH: Efficiency change, TECHCH: Technical change

conservation policies has proved poor in regard to actually implementing the information received. This is consistent with our results showing that a significant gap exists between frontier firms and others. Instead, Stern and Aronsson (1984) suggested that a more effective policy would be an individual audits system – that is, a system where the companies receive specific information that will become more important and necessary for manufacturing firms. In particular, this argument might be helpful for small and medium firms that do not have sufficient human resources and equipment to manage toxic chemical substances efficiently.

12.6   Conclusion

Productivity improvements play an important role in reducing pollution and improving standards of living. This paper contributes to the literature on productivity changes in several ways. As a policy instrument, the Pollution Release and Transfer Register system has emerged in recent years as a mainstream regulatory tool to manage manufacturing firms' toxic chemical substance emissions. To explore how information provisions provide firms with an incentive to improve environmental performance, we measured and compared environmental performance in terms of productivity.

We found that productivity improved in all industrial sectors in the United State and Japan from 2001 to 2007. In particular, the electronics industry improved rapidly after 2002. These increases might be attributed to the enforcement of the Restriction of the Use of Certain Hazardous Substances in Electrical and Electronic Equipment and Registration, and the Evaluation, Authorization and Restriction of Chemicals directives in Europe. These stringent cross-border restrictions on toxic chemical substances provide strong incentives for U.S. and Japanese firms, which export to the European market, to reduce their use of restricted toxic chemical substances.

This study makes two contributions to productivity literature: the first is our effort to measure productivity by studying toxic chemical emissions by industry base. Previous studies used overall industry data without regard for the heterogeneous characteristics of industries. Understanding sector-level productivity is important because the capital equipment and labor that are needed to reduce toxic chemical substances differ by industry. Furthermore, the chemical products consumed as intermediate materials also differ. Our second contribution is to clarify the structural change of the productivity and efficiency gap between frontier firms and inefficient firms. This information is useful for policy making, which we found should adopt a bottom-up approach or frontier shift approach.

A cleaner production approach is absolutely imperative for manufacturing firms to achieve production improvement because cleaner production allows them to reduce intermediate chemical input and treatment costs for pollution abatement (Frondel, 2007). In other words, industries can improve productivity by applying a cleaner production approach. However, future research is necessary to clarify the technological details involved in this approach.

Appendix: Methodology

A1. Directional distance function (DDF)

Let $x \in \Re_+^L$, $b \in \Re_+^R$, and $y \in \Re_+^M$ be the vectors for inputs, environmental output (or undesirable output), and market outputs (or desirable output), respectively. Define the production technology as

$$P(x) = \{(x, y, b) : x \text{ can produce}(y, b)\}. \tag{1}$$

We assume that good and bad outputs are null-joint; a company cannot produce a desirable output without producing undesirable outputs.[6]

$$(y, b) \in P(x); \; b = 0 \Rightarrow y = 0. \tag{2}$$

We also assume weak disposability, which implies that the pollutant should not be considered freely disposable.

$$(y, b) \in P(x) \text{ and } 0 \leq \beta \leq 1 \Rightarrow (\beta y, \beta b) \in P(x). \tag{3}$$

According to the null-joint hypothesis and weak disposability, the directional distance function for firm k can be computed with the following optimization problem:

$$\vec{D}^{WD}\left(x_k^l, y_k^m, b_k^r, g_{x^l}, g_{y^m}, g_{b^r}\right) = \text{Maximize}_k, \tag{4}$$

$$\text{s.t.} \sum_{i=1}^{N} \lambda_i x_i^l \leq x_k^l + \beta_k g_{x^l} \qquad l = 1, \ldots, L, \tag{5}$$

$$\sum_{i=1}^{N} \lambda_i y_i^m \geq y_k^m + \beta_k g_{y^m} \qquad m = 1, \ldots, M, \tag{6}$$

$$\sum_{i=1}^{N} \lambda_i b_i^r = b_k^r + \beta_k g_{b^r} \qquad r = 1, \ldots, R, \tag{7}$$

$$\lambda_i \geq 0 \qquad (i = 1, \ldots, N), \tag{8}$$

where l, m, and r are the input, the desirable output, and the undesirable output, respectively; x is the input factor in the L × N input factor matrix; y is the desirable output in the M × N desirable output factor matrix; and b is the undesirable output factor in the R × N undesirable output matrix. In addition, g_x is the directional vector of the input factor; g_y is the directional vector of the desirable output factors; and g_b is the directional vector of the undesirable output factors. β_k is the inefficiency score of the kth firm, and λ_i is the weight variable. To estimate the inefficiency score of all firms, we must apply the model independently N times for each firm. Therefore, to apply the output-oriented Luenberger indicator, we set the directional vector as $g = (0, y^m, b^r)$.

A2. Luenberger productivity indicator

The ESP is computed with the results of the DDF model and is derived as follows (Chambers et al., 1998):

$$\text{ESP}_t^{t+1} = \text{TECHCH}_t^{t+1} + \text{EFFCH}_t^{t+1}, \tag{9}$$

$$\text{TECHCH}_t^{t+1} = \frac{1}{2}\left\{\vec{D}^{t+1}(x_t,y_t,b_t) + \vec{D}^{t+1}(x_{t+1},y_{t+1},b_{t+1}) \right.$$
$$\left. - \vec{D}^t(x_t,y_t,b_t) - \vec{D}^t(x_{t+1},y_{t+1},b_{t+1})\right\}, \tag{10}$$

$$\text{EFFCH}_t^{t+1} = \vec{D}^t(x_t,y_t,b_t) - \vec{D}^{t+1}(x_{t+1},y_{t+1},b_{t+1}), \tag{11}$$

where x_t represents the input for year t; x_{t+1} is the input for year t + 1; y_t is the desirable output for year t; and y_{t+1} is the desirable output for year t + 1. b_t is the undesirable output for year t, and b_{t+1} is the undesirable output for year t + 1. $\vec{D}^t(x_t,y_t,b_t)$ is the inefficiency score of year t based on the frontier curve in year t. Similarly, $\vec{D}^{t+1}(x_t,y_t,b_t)$ is the inefficiency of year t + 1 based on the frontier curve in year t + 1.

The ESP score indicates the productivity change compared to the benchmark year. The ESP includes all categories of productivity change, which can be broken down into Technical Change (TECHCH) and Efficiency Change (EFFCH). TECHCH shows shifts in the production frontier, and EFFCH measures changes in a production unit's position relative to the frontier (i.e., catching up).

Studies that employ the DDF model usually assume either constant returns to scale (CRS) or variable returns to scale (VRS). In this study, we assumed CRS to avoid infeasible calculations in the time-series analysis. For example, Färe et al. (1994, 1996) pointed out that it is not possible to compute productivity change in the VRS model. Likewise, in our study, the calculation of productivity change under VRS was infeasible. Therefore, we only used the CRS model.

Notes

1 Productivity can be defined as efficiency of production (called total factor productivity [TFP]), which includes all categories of productivity, such as labor productivity and capital productivity (see Managi et al., 2004).
2 The linear expansion of pollution abatement costs and pollution reduction does not necessarily change pollution reduction per abatement cost (Pethig, 2006; Khanna and Plassmann, 2007).
3 Under TRI, the reports must be filed by the owners and operators of facilities that meet all of the following three criteria. (1) TRI reporting requirements are limited to the manufacturing facilities within the major SIC code groups 20 through 39. In 1997, the U.S. EPA added seven additional industry sectors to the TRI requirements. These sectors started to report submissions in the reporting year 1998. (2) The number of full-time employees must be 10 (or the equivalent of 20,000 hours of work per year) or more. (3) Any facility that manufactured or processed more than 25,000 pounds or otherwise used more than 10,000 pounds of a listed toxic chemical during the course of the calendar year is required to submit a report.

4 These data include, for example, the annual amount handled. More specifically, this requirement applies to facilities with an annual amount of 1 ton or more (5 tons or more for the initial 2 years) – 0.5 tons or more for specific Class 1–designated chemical substances – or to business operators with facilities that meet the following criteria: (1) they fall under the Mine Safety Law, (2) are sewage disposal facilities, (3) are domestic waste disposal facilities/industrial waste disposal facilities, or (4) fall under the Act on Special Measures against Dioxins.

5 RoHS, REACH, and ELV passed in 2003, 2006, and 1997, respectively, and were enforced in 2006, 2007, and 2000, respectively.

6 Some production plants achieve zero emission-levels, in which the producer can produce desirable outputs without undesirable output emission. However, for example, a zero emission-level for one emission is associated with an increase in another emission, such as a recycling system of solid waste. In this case, the environmental burden will be zero for one emission, but solid waste is generated at a higher level. By aggregating these emissions, we apply a null-jointness assumption. This assumption implies that industrial firms always produce undesirable outputs. With the production of more undesirable outputs, desirable production can be increased, given the same available technology (i.e., not considering future technological progress) each year.

Bibliography

Akao, K., Managi, S. (2007) The Feasibility and Optimality of Sustainable Growth Under Materials Balance. *Journal of Economic Dynamics and Control.* 31(11), 3778–3790.

Arora, S., Cason, T. (1996) Why Do Firms Volunteer to Exceed Environmental Regulations? Understanding Participation in the EPA's 33/50 Program. *Land Economics.* 72(4), 413–432.

Bunge J., Cohen-Rosenthal E., Ruiz-Quintanilla A. (1996) Employee Participation in Pollution Reduction: Preliminary Analysis of the Toxics Release Inventory. *Journal of Cleaner Production.* 4, 9–16.

Chambers R.G., Chung Y.H., Färe R. (1998) Profit, Directional Distance Functions, and Nerlovian Efficiency. *Journal of Optimization Theory and Applications.* 98(2), 351–364.

Doana, H.D., Saidi, M. (2008) Simultaneous Removal of Metal Ions and Linear Alkylbenzene Sulfonate by Combined Electrochemical and Photocatalytic Process. *Journal of Hazardous Materials.* 158(2–3), 557–567.

Färe, R., Grosskopf S. (1996) *Intertemporal Production Frontiers: With Dynamic DEA.* Kluwer Academic Publishers, Boston.

Färe, R., Grosskopf S., Norris M., Zhang Z. (1994) Productivity Growth, Technical Progress and Efficiency Change in Industrialized Countries. *American Economic Review.* 84(1), 66–83.

Färe R., Grosskopf S., Pasurka C.A., Jr. (2001) Accounting for Air Pollution Emission in Measures of State Manufacturing Productivity Growth. *Journal of Regional Science.* 41(3), 381–409.

Frondel, M., Horbach, J., Rennings, K. (2007) End-of-Pipe or Cleaner Production? An Empirical Comparison of Environmental Innovation Decisions Across OECD Countries. *Business Strategy and the Environment.* 16(8), 571–584.

Fujii H., Kaneko S., Managi S. (2010) Changes in Environmentally Sensitive Productivity and Technological Modernization in China's Iron and Steel Industry in the 1990s. *Environment and Development Economics.* 15, 485–504.

Gamper-Rabindran S. (2006) Did the EPA's Voluntary Industrial Toxics Program Reduce Emissions? A GIS Analysis of Distributional Impacts and By-Media Analysis of Substitution. *Journal of Environmental Economics and Management.* 52, 391–410.

Jaffe A.B., Newell R.G., Stavins R.N. (2005) A Tale of Two Market Failures: Technology and Environmental Policy. *Ecological Economics.* 54(2–3), 164–174.

Jobe M.M. (1999) The Power of Information: The Example of the US Toxics Release Inventory. *Journal of Government Information.* 26, 287–295.

Khanna M., Damon, L.A. (1999) EPA's Voluntary 33/50 Program: Impact on Toxic Releases and Economic Performance of Firms. *Journal of Environmental Economics and Management.* 37, 1–25.

Khanna M., Quimio W.R.H., Bojilova D. (1998) Toxics Release Information: A Policy Tool for Environmental Protection. *Journal of Environmental Economics and Management.* 36, 243–266.

Khanna N, Plassmann F. (2007) Total Factor productivity and the Environmental Kuznets Curve: A Comment and Some Intuition. *Ecological Economics.* 63(1), 54–58.

Koehler D.A., Spengler J.D. (2007) The toxic release inventory: Fact or fiction? A case study of the primary aluminum industry. *Journal of Environmental Management.* 85, 296–307.

Kolominskas C., Sullivan R. (2004) Improving Cleaner Production Through Pollutant Release and Transfer Register Reporting Processes. *Journal of Cleaner Production.* 12, 713–724.

Konar S., Cohen M.A. (1997) Information As Regulation: The Effect of Community Right to Know Laws on Toxic Emissions. *Journal of Environmental Economics and Management.* 32, 109–124.

Kwon H.M. (2006) The Effectiveness of Process Safety Management (PSM) Regulation for Chemical Industry in Korea. *Journal of Loss Prevention in the Process Industries.* 19, 13–16.

Lanjouw, J.O., Mody A. (1996) Innovation and the International Diffusion of Environmentally Responsive Technology. *Research Policy.* 25(4), 549–571.

Lyon T.P., Maxwell J.W. (2004) *Corporate Environmentalism and Public Policy.* Cambridge University Press, Cambridge.

Managi, S., Opaluch, J.J., Jin, D., Grigalunas, T.A. (2004) Technological change and depletion in offshore oil and gas. *Journal of Environmental Economics and Management.* 47, 388–409.

Managi, S., Opaluch, J.J., Jin, D., Grigalunas, T.A. (2005) Environmental Regulations and Technological Change in the Offshore Oil and Gas Industry. *Land Economics.* 81(2), 303–319.

Pascala, S., Moussaa, D., Hnatiucb E., Brisset, J.L. (2010) Plasma Chemical Degradation of Phosphorous-Containing Warfare Agents Stimulants. *Journal of Hazardous Materials.* 175(1–3), 1037–1041.

Pethig R. (2006) Non-Linear Production, Abatement, Pollution and Materials Balance Reconsidered. *Journal of Environmental Economics and Management.* 51(2), 185–204.

Sony (2009) *CSR Report Executive Summary.* http://www.sony.net/SonyInfo/csr_report/issues/report/2009/pdf/CSR2009E_all.pdf

Stern, P.C. Aronson, E. (eds.) (1984) *Energy Use: The Human Dimension.* Freeman, New York, pp. 237.

Tietenberg T., Wheeler D. (2001) Empowering the Community: Information Strategies for Pollution Control, in Henk Folmer (ed.), *Frontiers of Environmental Economics.* Edward Elgar, Cheltenham, UK, and Lyme, USA.

13 Contributions of the private sector to global biodiversity protection

Tania Ray Bhattacharya and Shunsuke Managi

13.1 Introduction

Since the inception of the UN Convention on Biological Diversity (CBD) in 1993, little progress has been achieved in terms of involving the business community in protecting biological diversity worldwide. According to the CBD, biodiversity refers to "the variability among living organisms from all sources including, inter alia, terrestrial, marine and other aquatic ecosystems and the ecological complexes of which they are part; this includes diversity within species, between species and of ecosystems" (Article 2, Convention On Biological Diversity). Even for guiding investment, the biodiversity convention is perhaps the least specifically prescriptive global environmental convention (Moran et al. 1996). A wide gap still exists between the actions inducing climate change and the conservation of ecosystem and biological diversity (Heller and Zavaleta 2009). Thus far, efforts have been made mainly by the non-commercial sector, including non-governmental organizations (NGOs). Most international funding for biodiversity conservation is received from high-income countries' Overseas Development Assistance (ODA). All market-based mechanisms, including ecotourism, environmentally friendly products marketing, and payments for ecosystem services (PES), provide approximately 1 to 2 billion USD per annum (Gutman and Davidson 2007), which is profoundly insufficient to meet the current need . Most funds are used for biodiversity and ecosystem service–related academic work and for a few demonstration projects that have limited impact on the ground (Gutman and Davidson 2007).

It has been estimated that the global biodiversity resource has been declining continuously over the last several decades mainly due to increasing anthropogenic interferences (FAO 2010)[1]. The CBD targets for 2010 are yet to be achieved fully in any aspect, including policy intervention, international finance, technology transfer, and patent issues (Butchart et al. 2010). In the recent statement of the Executive Secretary of the CBD in the Rio+20 Summit (June 2012), it is clearly mentioned that CBD has so far failed in all its given assignments. In the process of investigating the reasons for such failure, it is also identified that the lack of mainstreaming ecosystems and biodiversity in the economic planning and economic sector as one of the major reasons (CBD 2012). As a matter of fact, the business sector has a major role to play in terms of mainstreaming ecology and biodiversity conservation, not only to have a sustainable business but also to mitigate the impacts of biodiversity loss caused by the economic and business activities across the world. In the 2010 Report for Business in The Economics of Ecosystems and Biodiversity (TEEB 2010), which is so far one of the most comprehensive reports on the general issues of business and biodiversity linkage, the importance of business sectors' involvement in the whole process of conservation and protection of ecology, biodiversity, and environment was repeatedly emphasized. The business sector, with its financial and technological resources, can indeed play a key role in the whole process. Conversely, in many cases, businesses are also responsible for the loss of biodiversity. For example, most multinational companies now operate their manufacturing units outside of their countries of origin to enjoy multiple benefits, such as low production costs, less stringent laws and regulations (including environmental laws), and relatively easier utilization of natural resources, all of which can accelerate the loss of local biological diversity (Mahidhar et al. 2009). Compared with climate change issues, biodiversity has generated low levels of international response (Heller and Zavaleta 2008).

Biodiversity is a public good whose open and free use by one person doesn't bar others to use it freely at the same time, and its true value is thus not realized by the market. As a result, the economy is unable to quantify the cost of externalities of biodiversity loss (Metcalfe et al. 2010). Sustained investment in global biodiversity monitoring and development of measurable indicators are essential to track and improve the effectiveness of biodiversity protection initiatives (Walpole et al. 2009). The public and private sectors are equally important in this process. A growing amount of evidence indicates that private-sector companies engaged in the mitigation of biodiversity loss are now reporting corresponding positive commercial and reputational impacts on their business activities (Metcalfe et al. 2010). If policies such as labeling for environmentally friendly goods are produced in a less costly operational method and sell well in the market, this provides opportunities for win-win situations. On the one hand there is growing amount of scientific evidence on rapid loss of biodiversity, which predicts severe impacts on sustainable development, and on the other hand there is lack of mitigation tools that can halt the loss of biodiversity. There is no single silver bullet for these problems – multifaceted actions are required, which include the mainstreaming of ecosystem and biodiversity conservation in economic and business planning and activities.

Since biodiversity and ecosystems act as business inputs, the negative impact that they suffer from eventually poses risks to companies. For water-intensive business processes such as agribusiness, power generation, and pulp and paper processing, negative impacts on water availability and water quality might create severe business risks in terms of raw material supply constraints, higher procurement costs, and quality of production. Similarly, for companies that are heavily dependent on land resources, biodiversity loss in land and soil may result in additional business risks resulting from yield reduction, soil contamination, pesticide overflows, and other related consequences[2]. Biodiversity loss or degradation can affect not only business outputs but also company reputation and goodwill due to a degraded local environment and adverse health impacts on the local communities.

Understanding the importance of biodiversity and ecosystems in the context of sustainable business and development, a growing number of studies are now being published in this area. A majority of the current literature discusses the relationships between biodiversity and business in terms of the corporate social responsibilities (CSRs) of the private sector to protect biological diversity (TEEB for Business 2010). Rondinelli and Berry (2000) conducted a content analysis of the environmental performance reports of 38 companies; their findings showed that multinational companies (MNCs) of different sizes and from different industries are adopting similar types of sustainable development programs (including biodiversity protection) because proactive environmental management provides immediate and direct business benefits, i.e., lower costs, fewer risks and liabilities, and more efficient operations. However, they concluded that externally oriented programs such as corporate citizenship activities reflect a small portion of the environmental management activities and frequently do not provide the most potential for achieving sustainable development. The review of multinational companies' environmental performance reports indicates that regardless of the type of green activities, most of the companies operate proactively when they see business benefits derived from a responsible environmental image (Rondinelli and Berry 2000). Dyke et al. (2005) argued that publicity for environmental action is an important issue for the timber industry. Most of the publicity issues are related to the corporate forest management, but forestry certification, wildlife management, and land exchanges were also ranked as popular topics.

The TEEB Report for Business (2010) also argued that the business sector is motivated to invest more in the protection of biodiversity and ecosystems provided they observe that the serious damage to the ecosystem caused by business activities can jeopardize the company's reputation or disrupt the supply chain of raw materials, and that protection activities can bring a good payback in the near future.

Vickerman (1999) further argued that private players must have an important role in the protection of biological diversity. In this context, the importance of public-private partnerships, in addition to individual company efforts, was emphasized. Private lands must be included in biodiversity protection strategies to bring more ownership to the entire process than there would be with public lands. Therefore, incentive schemes like stewardship incentive programs and tax incentives could be used to entice individuals to work to conserve biodiversity. The Millennium Ecosystem Assessment (MEA) presents a concrete account of biodiversity loss and ecosystem degradation (MEA 2005). The TEEB (2010) also analyzed business leaders' growing concerns about the risk of biodiversity loss and the requirements for preserving ecological limits.

Martens et al. (2003) identified declining biodiversity to be not only an environmental problem but also a socio-economic problem. Hence, the preservation of biodiversity requires that industries' and consumers' production patterns change. The TEEB for Business (Chapter 2, 2010) discussed the interconnections between business and biodiversity that are highly influenced by consumer preferences. A recent survey of over 13,000 individuals further supports that idea. The survey found that 82 percent of Latin American consumers were more concerned, followed by 56 percent in Asia, 49 percent in the United States and 48 percent in Europe. The demand for products that are ecologically certified by the Forest Stewardship Council (FSC) and the Marine Stewardship Council (MSC), as well as the demand for Rainforest Alliance–certified coffee, supports these findings.

For branded fast-moving consumer goods, eco-labeling is moving from niche to mainstream markets. Examples include Domtar (FSC-certified product), Mars (Rainforest Alliance cocoa), Cadbury (Fair-Trade cocoa), and Unilever (Rainforest Alliance PG Tips). Walmart now scores its suppliers based on their concern for the protection of biodiversity and natural resources and uses eco-labels for all of its brands. Cosmetics companies such as Natura and L'Oreal have adopted the sustainable use of biodiversity as the main driver of innovation and aim to use plant-based ingredients in the manufacturing of their products. Essentially, the TEEB for Business (Chapter 2, 2010) showed the general impact and dependence on biodiversity and ecosystem services across several business sectors.

Doremus (2003) suggested a policy portfolio approach to protecting biodiversity on private lands. In the United States, more than 90 percent of the listed endangered and threatened species maintain their habitats on private lands, and approximately two-thirds of these species depend on these lands for the majority of their habitat (U.S. General Accounting Office 1995; Groves et al. 2000). However, biodiversity protection for privately owned lands has always been problematic. No particular policy measure is perfect; rather, a broad spectrum of conservation options is more likely to be effective, and the optimal portfolio of policies may combine state and private actions.

The participation of private actors is only possible under specific conditions. According to Olson's theory (Olson 1965), rational self-interested individuals will not act in the interest of the group because individual costs exceed individual benefits. Without selective incentives to motivate participation, collective action is unlikely, even by large groups of people with common interests. Because biodiversity protection may not provide an immediate economic gain, an external regulatory force is necessary (e.g., a civil society such as Global Action Network) to solve the collective action problem. Thus, civil society's role in conservation and biodiversity policies is important (Glasbergen 2010). A range of public policy measures like green development finance (GDF) and payment for ecosystem services (PES) can increase the scale of biodiversity and ecosystem conservation services to generate more business opportunities. Such measures can be defined as a voluntary transaction, where a well-defined ecosystem service or a land use policy is likely to be secured while the service is purchased by at least one buyer from at least one provider (Wunder 2005), creating access and benefit sharing, tax incentives, and performance standards, among other benefits. (TEEB for Business Chapter 5, 2010). Generally, neither the government nor the private sector includes the protection of biodiversity and ecosystem services in its financial accounting and reporting. The World Business Council for Sustainable Development (WBCSD) is currently working on this limitation.

The previous discussion is based on the existing literature and provides important information on the private sectors' role and potential importance in terms of conserving biodiversity and ecosystems on the earth. The importance of private sectors' role in terms of financial support, which is the key for the success of these conservation activities, has also been discussed. This is an important issue because biodiversity protection requires significant financial support that is contingent on active private-sector participation. Although the existing literature focuses on the private sector's concern for biodiversity protection and makes policy recommendations for the same, there is a gap of business sectoral analysis in the context of biodiversity and ecosystem conservation. It is so far understood that business and biodiversity has a causal relationship, but its functioning and complicacy has yet to be revealed. This study attempts to bridge the gap between the general understanding of the relationship of business and biodiversity and the business sector–specific relationship, which is assumed to be different for every sector. Within this context, this chapter first assesses the involvement of Fortune 500 companies in biodiversity protection with respect to the clarity of their policies regarding biodiversity and their contributions towards achieving the targets set by the CBD. Section 13.2 discusses existing works on business and biodiversity that distinguish this study. Section 13.3 explains the data and methodological issues. Section 13.4 presents this study's findings and Section 13.5 analyzes related policy issues, where we show how several policy recommendations regarding biodiversity protection may be incorporated effectively into long-term business strategies.

We believe that this study will benefit policy makers and the private sector. Although the private sector is increasingly funding a number of ecosystem services, particularly carbon sequestration, little is known about the potential willingness of this sector to fund other ecosystem services, such as biodiversity conservation (Waage et al. 2007). Our research aims to address this knowledge gap. By indicating the leading Fortune 500 companies' concerns about the protection of biodiversity and ecosystem services, this study can help policymakers and the private sector with their future environmental protection activities.

13.2 Data and methodology

This study primarily collected data and information on companies' biodiversity policies from the major 500 U.S. companies mentioned in the 2007 Forbes Fortune 500 list (CNN 2007). The selection of companies is made following the Fortune 500 list published by *Fortune* magazine. All 500 companies are selected for this study at the first stage. Then classification has been done based on their respective business categories. We thoroughly analyzed the contents of these companies' CSR reports, sustainability reports, and/or annual reports (depending on the availability from each company's website) to determine whether the companies have specific biodiversity policies.

13.2.1 Data structure and definitions

In this study, whether or not a firm has a specific biodiversity policy depends on the clarity of the biodiversity protection reporting in the CSR report, sustainability report, and annual report. Firms that lack such specific reporting but still conduct several similar activities funded by NGOs/NPOs are not considered to have specific biodiversity policies. Many companies with specific policies related to various ecosystem services, such as water resource protection, but without a description of specific biodiversity policies also were not considered to have specific biodiversity policies.

During the first step of the assessment, we analyze the top 500 companies listed in the April 30, 2007, issue of *Fortune* magazine published online by CNN, which is a Time Warner Company (web source: http://money.cnn.com/magazines/fortune/).[3] We analyze the various biodiversity protection initiatives reported in the publications of these companies, including annual reports, corporate social responsibility reports, environmental assessment reports, and environmental impact assessment reports; our main purpose is to identify the companies' ongoing and overall activities related to biodiversity. Finally, whether a company has a specific biodiversity policy based on its direct reporting on biodiversity protection and related activities under any of its action plan (not indirect action) has been considered in our analysis. For example, several companies have specific policies related to various ecosystem services such as water resource protection; when a company issues no work or policies on issues directly related to biodiversity, we do not consider this company to have a biodiversity policy. To avoid double counting and overlapping with other policies, we consider only the directly mentioned policies.

The top 500 companies are selected based on their annual revenue generation (in dollars) in the 2007 fiscal year. First, we obtain all 500 companies' biodiversity-related policy actions on a binary response (i.e., "yes"/"no") basis. This initial screening reveals two sets of companies: those with and those without biodiversity-related policies. Next, we categorize all companies into 74 sectors consistent with the *Fortune* magazine classification. Finally, for each sector, we calculate the percentage of companies with direct biodiversity policies. This percentage indicates how many companies of a particular sector are concerned with biodiversity issues. We call this a measure of a company's biodiversity policy responsiveness. Sectors are ranked from 1 to 74 based on these percentage figures and on the annual revenue generation of the companies provided by the Fortune 500 list.

13.2.2   *Classification of the companies*

The Fortune 500 is a list compiled by *Fortune* magazine ranking the top 500 public corporations of the U.S. as measured by their gross revenue adjusted to their excise duty payment. Based on the North American Industry Classification System (NAICS), the Fortune 500 list inherently became categorized likewise into manufacturing, utilities, finance and banking, retail, etc. It has been estimated that manufacturing, finance, retail, and utilities comprise around 70 percent of the total 500 companies in the list. Further, World Economic Forum (WEF) (for the convenience of analysis of the business sector and its impact on the environment) categorized the remaining 30 percent of the companies into 4 additional categories: consumer goods, consumer services, health care, and technology and business services. Therefore, Fortune 500 companies fall into 8 major categories. However, in this study we created further sub-categories of the 500 businesses, following a combination of the sector definitions from the NAICS and WEF for the purpose of detailed assessment. We therefore created 74 sub-categories of companies spread over 8 major sectors. Each sub-category is thus unique in business nature and mutually exclusive to other sub-categories. Such exclusivity was necessary to provide independence to the result obtained in the process of our analysis.

13.3 Results

In this section we will first describe the classification of the 500-odd companies under the broad categories of business activities, along with their corresponding activities related to the biodiversity and ecosystem conservation and protection and certain important percentage indicators. Second, we will discuss the relationship between various indicators of biodiversity policy adoption, and finally we will discuss the causal relationship between business risks, business revenue, and biodiversity policy adoption under different business categories among the Fortune 500 companies.

13.3.1 Sectoral classification and characteristics of the Fortune 500 companies in terms of biodiversity policies

We aggregated the 74 sectors into 8 major sectoral business categories based on the World Economic Forum report on business and biodiversity. Table 13.1 shows the behavior of the primary and utility sectors in terms of percentage of companies that report their biodiversity policies under each sector category and percentage among the total 500 companies. The last column describes the reasons for adoption/no adoption of a biodiversity protection policy. Table 13.1 further demonstrates that almost all the companies under the primary and utility sectors have certain biodiversity policies in place.

Table 13.2 shows the behavior of the consumer sectors in terms of the percentage of companies that report their biodiversity policies under each sector category and the percentage among the total 500 companies in the context of biodiversity policy adoption. There are two major categories of businesses: consumer goods and consumer services. Almost all the companies in the consumer goods sector have their own biodiversity protection policy. However, a very few companies in the consumer service sector have biodiversity policies. Reason behind such dismal levels of performance could be attributed to their businesses having no or very limited interaction with the nature and environment directly.

Table 13.3 shows the behavior of the industrial sector in terms of percentage of companies that report their biodiversity policies under each sector category and the percentage among the total 500 companies in the context of biodiversity policy adoption. Unlike the consumer services sector, the industrial sector has many more biodiversity protection policies, as the majority of the companies listed under this category have direct interaction with the environment. A few special cases have been noted in this category, like real estate companies. They are non-starters in terms of adopting any biodiversity protection policy, even though they have a direct impact on land and land use change and a corresponding effect on the environment and local ecology.

Table 13.4 shows the behavior of the service sector in terms of the percentage of companies that report their biodiversity policies under each sector category

Table 13.1 Assessment of the primary and utility sector's biodiversity policies

Sectors	Subsectors	No. of companies per sector	% of companies among F500	% of companies with biodiversity policies	Impact on biodiversity levels and objectives to adopt specific policies on biodiversity
Primary Industries	Mining, Crude-Oil Production (MCP)	9	1.8%	90%	The extraction of oil is responsible for the deforestation, degradation, and destruction of lands across the globe. The oil extraction process also releases toxic drilling by-products into local rivers, while broken pipelines and leakages result in persistent oil spillage. The construction of roads for accessing remote oil sites opens wild lands to colonists and land developers. Due to these serious impacts created during their production processes, 90% of MCP companies adopt direct policies on biodiversity protection.
	Petroleum Refining (PR)	10	2.0%	70%	Gas flaring during oil refining produces highly poisonous chemicals, which create severe negative impacts to biodiversity. To mitigate these impacts, 70% of petroleum refining companies adopt direct policies to protect biodiversity and ecosystems.
	Chemicals	17	3.4%	52%	52% of chemical companies adopt biodiversity protection activities and policies to mitigate impacts on protected species and to reestablish complex ecosystems, as their production process/operation occur in mines located in the sensitive native ecosystems.

Energy	13	2.6%	38.5 %	While constructing new power plants (green field projects), biodiversity levels are hampered, and sometimes restoration of the forest in a different place is required, with necessary relocation of the species living in the forest. Thus, 38.5% of energy companies adopts biodiversity policies
Metals	8	1.6%	50%	Indigenous forests and their flora and fauna are affected during mining activities. Rehabilitation of indigenous people from the mining area is also important for the metal industry. After the mining, site restoration plays a major role, in terms of conservation and protection of the biodiversity. Thus 50% of metal companies have biodiversity policies.
Tobacco	2	0.4%	0%	Neither of the two tobacco companies have any specific biodiversity policies. But they mention some activities related to wetland protection, as the tobacco industry's long-term success relies on sustainable natural resources, although they don't create significant impacts on biodiversity levels.
Utilities: Gas and Electric	26	5.2%	70%	During the construction of new power plants for electricity production, biodiversity protection of the local areas is important. Sometimes, restoration of the forest is required with necessary relocation of species living in that forest. Route selection for gas reserves and distribution is also important, as the routes may go through sensitive areas (e.g., homelands of indigenous peoples, rich biodiversity, old-growth forest, a conservation unit, etc.). Thus, 70% of utility companies adopt biodiversity protection policies.

Utilities

Table 13.2 Assessment of the consumer sector's biodiversity policies

Sectors	Subsectors	No. of companies per sector	% of companies among F500	% of companies with biodiversity policies	Impact on biodiversity levels and objectives to adopt specific policies on biodiversity
Consumer Goods	Food Production (FP)	5	1.0%	40%	Around 40% of companies in the food production (FP) sector report clearly about their biodiversity policies. Their main objective is to create a sustainable food supply chain.
	Motor Vehicles and Parts (MVP)	15	3.0%	18%	Only 18% of motor vehicle and parts (MVP) manufacturing companies have specific biodiversity policies, as they don't create much impact on biodiversity levels through their operation processes.
	Food Consumer Products (FCP)	14	2.8%	50%	Among the food consumer products (FCP) companies, around 50% have policies on biodiversity. Their objective is mainly to maintain environmentally friendly agricultural supply chains.
	Household and Personal Products (HPP)	6	1.2%	80%	For the household and personal products (HPP) companies, around 80% have specific policies related to biodiversity, as they consider biodiversity as important environmental indicator for their business operations.
	Beverages	6	1.2%	16%	Only 16% of beverage companies have policies on biodiversity protection. Though this sector doesn't create many impacts directly on the biodiversity levels, the only company in this subsector, i.e., Pepsi Bottling, has a biodiversity policy in the form of sustainable agriculture principles.

	Forest and Paper Products (FPP)	3	0.6%	100%	All three companies in the forest and paper products (FPP) sector have specific biodiversity policies, which refer to different certifications (e.g., FSC), as the major Fortune 500 companies in the U.S. look for biodiversity-certified companies in the supply chain for their paper procurement policy
	Miscellaneous	3	0.6%	33%	Only one company, 3M, mentions a biodiversity policy, whose objective is to preserve and enhance biodiversity as an important part of their environmental sustainability strategy.
	Apparel	4	0.8%	0%	No company has a biodiversity policy, as their business processes don't create any direct impacts on biodiversity levels.
	Home Equipment, Furnishings (HEF)	3	0.6%	0%	Biodiversity policies not adopted.
	Building Materials, Glass (BMG)	2	0.4%	50%	Only one of two companies, Owens Corning, has a biodiversity policy. Their objective is to take care of environmental damage, including biodiversity loss and stressed vegetation, while evaluating potential properties and operations for acquisition purposes.
	Toys, Sporting Goods (TSG)	1	0.2%	100%	Here, only Mattel has a biodiversity policy regarding their paper procurement process in the supply chain.
	Furniture	1	0.2%	0%	Biodiversity policy not adopted.
Consumer Services	General Merchandisers (GM)	10	2.0%	0%	Biodiversity policies not adopted.

(Continued)

Table 13.2 (Continued)

Sectors	Subsectors	No. of companies per sector	% of companies among F500	% of companies with biodiversity policies	Impact on biodiversity levels and objectives to adopt specific policies on biodiversity
	Specialty Retailers (SR)	24	4.8%	8.3%	Only 8.3% of companies have biodiversity policies, mainly related to forestry policies and paper and wood procurement policies.
	Food and Drug Stores (FD)	10	2.0%	20%	Here, 20% of companies have biodiversity protection policies related to food standards through research and engagement with the relevant stakeholders.
	Entertainment	6	1.2%	33.3%	33.3% of entertainment companies report on biodiversity protection policies, as tourism can generate revenue to protect and preserve biodiversity and the environment, especially in developing countries. Besides preserving the environment, profits have a greater potential to reach local and rural communities when compared to profits in other sectors.
	Airlines	7	1.4%	0%	No biodiversity policies are adopted.
	Mail, Package, Freight Delivery (MPF)	2	0.4%	50%	One of two companies, FedEx, has a biodiversity policy, mainly for reforestation.
	Automotive Retailing, Services (ARS)	8	1.6%	0%	Biodiversity policies not adopted.
	Wholesalers: Diversified (WD)	9	1.8%	0%	Biodiversity policies not adopted.

Wholesalers: Food and Grocery (WFG)	4	0.8%	Biodiversity policies not adopted.
Packaging, Containers (PC)	7	1.4%	Biodiversity policies not adopted.
Food Services (FS)	4	0.8%	Biodiversity policies not adopted.
Hotels, Casinos, Resorts (HCR)	5	1.0%	Biodiversity policies not adopted.
Publishing, Printing (PP)	4	0.8%	Biodiversity policies not adopted.
Temporary Help (TH)	2	0.4%	Biodiversity policies not adopted.
Waste Management (WM)	2	0.4%	Biodiversity policies not adopted.
Transportation and Logistics (TL)	2	0.4%	Biodiversity policies not adopted.
Trucking, Truck Leasing (TTL)	2	0.4%	Biodiversity policies not adopted.

Table 13.3 Assessment of the industrial sector's biodiversity policies

Sectors	Subsectors	No. of companies per sector	% of companies among F500	% of companies with biodiversity policies	Impact on biodiversity levels and objectives to adopt specific policies on biodiversity
Industrials	Aerospace and Defense (AD)	10	2.0%	10%	One out of ten companies has a biodiversity policy in its CSR reports, which considers only renewable fuel sources that minimize biodiversity impacts.
	Computers, Office Equipment (COE)	8	1.6%	37.5 %	37.5 % of companies have biodiversity policies, with the main emphasis on forest stewardship for their paper procurement.
	Industrial and Farm Equipment (IFE)	13	2.6%	7%	7% of companies have biodiversity policies, considering biodiversity as an important environmental indicator.
	Homebuilders	11	2.2%	27.3 %	27% of companies adopt biodiversity policies to show that ecology and biodiversity are considered at the design and planning stages, and to describe how ecology is managed on site.
	Network and other Communications Equipment (NCE)	6	1.2%	33.3%	In the coming years NCE will be the key technology enabler to monitor, manage, and reduce environmental impacts and to deliver solutions for energy and resource management, and will apply these solutions for their own operations. Thus 33.3% of companies adopt biodiversity policies.
	Wholesalers: Electronics and Office Equipment (WOE)	7	1.4%	0%	Different organic compounds and metals used by the WOE manufacturers have carcinogenic effect and also act as neurotoxicants which can severely affect biodiversity levels and the ecosystem. To mitigate these impacts 42.9% of companies adopt policies related to biodiversity protection.

Semiconductors and other Electronic Components (SEC)	7	1.4%	42.9%	To mitigate these impacts, 42.9% of SEC companies adopt policies related to biodiversity protection.
Pipelines	6	1.2%	33.3%	Pipeline impacts on biodiversity could be measured in many ways. If a hydrocarbon reserve is located inside a "sensitive area" (e.g., homelands of indigenous peoples, rich biodiversity, old-growth forests, etc.), directional drilling can avoid damage to the sensitive area by drilling laterally as far as possible. To mitigate these impacts, 33.3% of companies adopt biodiversity policies.
Oil and Gas Equipment, Services (OGE)	5	1.0%	80%	80% of companies mention their biodiversity policies and action plans in relation to sustainable technologies and environment protection. Route selection for the oil and gas reserve and distribution is very important in this regard, as the routes may be through the sensitive areas (e.g., homelands of indigenous peoples, rich biodiversity, old-growth forests, a conservation unit, etc.).
Railroads	4	0.8%	0%	Biodiversity policies not adopted.
Electronics, Electrical Equipment (EEE)	4	0.8%	0%	Biodiversity policies not adopted.

(Continued)

Table 13.3 (Continued)

Sectors	Subsectors	No. of companies per sector	% of companies among F500	% of companies with biodiversity policies	Impact on biodiversity levels and objectives to adopt specific policies on biodiversity
	Medical Products and Equipment (MPE)	5	1.0%	40%	Two out of five companies (40%) reported their biodiversity activities and policies in their CSR reports. The connections between human health and a healthy environment are inseparable. That's the objective behind the MPE companies' policies on biodiversity.
	Engineering, Construction (EC)	5	1.0%	60%	60 % of EC companies report on their biodiversity policies, mainly for the protection of wildlife habitats and the biodiversity protection as environmental stewardship.
	Scientific Photo Control equipment (SPC)	3	0.6%	33.3%	One out of three SPC companies (33.3%), i.e., Eastman Kodak, reports on its biodiversity and natural habitat policy for maintaining its environmental stewardship.
	Computer Peripherals (CP)	3	0.6%	66.7%	66.7% of CP companies have biodiversity policies. They claim that they have indirect impact on biodiversity, but they also claim to use system approach for environmental sustainability, including biodiversity, to influence their business.
	Transportation Equipment (TE)	2	0.4%	0%	Biodiversity policies not adopted.
	Real Estate (RE)	2	0.4%	0%	Biodiversity policies not adopted.

Table 13.4 Assessment of the service sector's biodiversity policies

Sectors	Subsectors	No. of companies per sector	% of companies among F500	% of companies with biodiversity policies	Impact on biodiversity levels and objectives to adopt specific policies on biodiversity
Health Care	Wholesalers: Health Care (WHC)	5	1.0%	0%	Biodiversity policies not adopted.
	Pharmaceuticals	9	1.8%	67%	67% of major pharmaceutical companies, including Pfizer and Wyeth (now Pfizer), mention biodiversity protection under their water policies. These corporations are undergoing research in the rainforests for a variety of reasons. There is a great deal of pharmaceutical research going on in the labs of these particular companies – only 1% of all known plant and animal life have been examined for their medicinal potential. Thus the main objectives behind adopting biodiversity policies is to discover new drugs to treat human diseases worldwide.
	Health Care: Insurance and Managed Care (HIM)	7	1.4%	0%	Biodiversity policies not adopted.
	Health Care: Pharmacy and other Services (HPO)	5	1.0%	0%	Biodiversity policies not adopted.
	Health Care: Medical Facilities (HMF)	6	1.2%	0%	Biodiversity policies not adopted.

(Continued)

Table 13.4 (Continued)

Sectors	Subsectors	No. of companies per sector	% of companies among F500	% of companies with biodiversity policies	Impact on biodiversity levels and objectives to adopt specific policies on biodiversity
Finance	Diversified Financials (DF)	9	1.8%	33.3%	33.3% of DF companies have biodiversity policies as their environmental liability, although they don't create any impact on biodiversity directly.
	Commercial Banks (CB)	21	4.2%	23.8%	The commercial banks may not have direct biodiversity or ecosystem protection policies, but for their paper procurement policy in the supply chain, they mention biodiversity and forest conservation.
	Insurance: P & C (stock) (IPC)	18	3.6%	5.6%	5.6% of IPC companies have policies on biodiversity, mainly as their part of environmental stewardship, as their business processes don't create any direct impacts on biodiversity level.
	Securities	7	1.4%	83 %	Five out of seven securities companies' report on their biodiversity consciousness and policies in their CSR or sustainability reports, mainly for their service related to the market-based solutions for environmental issues.
	Insurance: Life, Health (stock) (ILHS)	10	2.0%	20%	Only 20% of ILHS companies have policies on biodiversity as a part of environmental stewardship, but their business processes don't create any direct impact on biodiversity level.
	Insurance: Life, Health (mutual) (ILHM)	8	1.6%	0%	Biodiversity policies not adopted.

				Description
	Insurance: P & C (mutual) (IPCM)	2	0.4%	50%	50% of companies mention biodiversity and ecosystem protection concerns in their environmental responsibility sections of CSR, although their business processes don't have any direct impact on biodiversity levels.
	Savings Institutions (SI)	2	0.4%	0%	Biodiversity policies not adopted.
	Financial Data Services (FDS)	4	0.8%	0%	Biodiversity policies not adopted.
Technology and business	Advertising, Marketing (AM)	2	0.4%	0%	Biodiversity policies not adopted.
	Telecommunications	13	2.6%	0%	Biodiversity policies not adopted.
	Computer Software (CS)	2	0.4%	0%	Biodiversity policies not adopted.
	Information Technology Services (ITS)	5	1.0%	20%	20% of ITS companies mention biodiversity policies, mainly in their forest policies. Their business processes don't create any direct impact on biodiversity levels.
	Internet Services and Retailing (ISR)	6	1.2%	16.7%	Only one out of six companies, i.e., Google, mentions their biodiversity concerns and policies as a part of their overall environment concerns, but other companies don't have any policies, as this business doesn't create any direct impacts on biodiversity levels.
	Diversified Outsourcing (DO)	1	0.2%	0%	Biodiversity policy not adopted.
	Payroll Services (PS)	1	0.2%	0%	Biodiversity policy not adopted.

and the percentage among the total 500 companies in the context of biodiversity policy adoption. The service sector includes health care, finance, and technology. As a matter of fact, the financial sector has much wider environmental policies, including biodiversity protection, when compared with the other two sectors. The technology and business sector and the health care sector are not that progressive in adopting biodiversity protection policies, which could be attributed to the nature of their businesses, which are not directly involved with the environment and ecology.

13.3.2   Assessment of the Fortune 500 companies' biodiversity policy responsiveness

We discussed earlier that most of the Fortune 500 companies do not systematically record their activities regarding biodiversity conservation and mitigation; therefore, collecting information on biodiversity-related investments was difficult. These data limitations therefore prompted the use of revenue as a normative indicator of the companies' expected behavior. We assumed that if the company has higher revenue, then it is expected that it would be well organized in all of its planning and policies, including the policies related to biodiversity. Ciocirlan and Pettersson (2012) and Ahmed et.al. (2003) also argued that there is some positive correlation between revenue and companies' decision-making processes towards environmental protection. The assumption informing this logic is that higher revenue corresponds to a greater likelihood of working seriously on issues related to biodiversity and ecosystem services. Hence, revenue has been considered as one of the indicators in the study.

The Fortune 500 companies' annual and corporate social responsibility reports rarely mentioned monetary investments that were specifically for biodiversity protection. We mainly get the overall investment amount for the purpose of overall environmental protection purposes, including usage of renewable energy, water resource reservation, climate change, ecosystem services, etc. In some cases, separate investment components are mentioned for climate change protection but not for biodiversity protection. In addition, we used the companies' revenue data mainly to determine a company's economic position and to rank the companies financially. We studied the companies' policies and activities regarding biodiversity protection separately. In this respect, the companies' revenues and contributions towards biodiversity protection are unrelated.

Figure 13.1 indicates the link between the companies' revenues and their activities in relation to biodiversity protection. Our initial assessment shows that companywide acceptance of biodiversity policies is heterogeneous, although nearly all Fortune 500 companies maintain a global presence that is as broad as their geographical operational presence. The company's revenue is critical in determining the relative ranking on the Fortune 500 list. We hypothesize that such a revenue ranking method would influence the companies' responsible behavior towards society and the environment. The incorporation of a proper biodiversity protection policy in the overall corporate policy is one indicator for such behavior. Our result shows that the correlation between revenue ranking and biodiversity policy adoption is 0.42, which indicates that high-revenue-earning companies on the Fortune 500 list are not necessarily concerned about their biodiversity impacts and corresponding measures. Figure 13.1 illustrates the relative ranking of different subsectors based on their revenue, their acceptance of biodiversity policies, and the percentage of companies within a sector with specific biodiversity policies.

13.3.3   Comparison of risk, revenue, and mitigation policy measures of Fortune 500 companies and their biodiversity conservation policies

In this section, we first analyze the activities and reporting schemes of the major companies within each sector from Table 13.1, mainly to identify the current status of their biodiversity risk exposure.

We also analyze the companies by sector according to their revenue and specific adoption of biodiversity-related policies. Therefore, we consider mainly those companies that have the highest revenues in their sector and specific biodiversity-related policies. We discuss a few well-known companies that may not have a specific biodiversity policy but that are involved in unique biodiversity conservation activities, e.g., McDonald's (consumer service sector) marketing strategy.

The sectors discussed here were sequentially selected according to their sector biodiversity policy adaptation ranking.

a)   Utilities

In the utility sector (electricity/gas/water), the business risks from biodiversity loss rank 2 (out of 6), and approximately 70 percent of the companies have specific biodiversity policies. This sector is ranked first in biodiversity policy acceptance, eighth in revenue and second in biodiversity risk. These rankings indicate that the utility sector, although low in revenue, is highly active in adopting protective measures because of its high risk of exposure to biodiversity loss. In this sector, the highest ranked company Dominion Resources has a clear biodiversity policy, with specific measures for aquatic life protection, avian protection, rare plant protection, and wildlife protection. Another high earning company, Southern, promotes the biodiversity conservation of its own land and partners with others in programs including Power of Flight, Longleaf Legacy, and Five Star Restoration. Edison International specifies a clear biodiversity policy for vegetation and an integrated pest management plan. Pepco Holding's biodiversity policy includes wetlands delineation, threatened and endangered species identification, forest stand delineation, oyster bed and essential fish habitat assessments, and an aquatic survey.

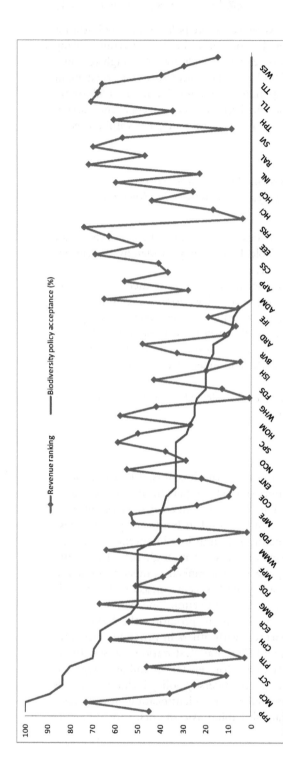

Figure 13.1 Comparative ranking of revenue and percentage of biodiversity policy acceptance of Fortune 500 companies

Note: Sector abbreviation detail: Forest & Paper Products = FPP; Toys, Sporting Goods = TSG; Mining, Crude-Oil Production = MCP Household and Personal Products = HPP; Securities = SCT; Oil and Gas Equipment, Services = OGS; Petroleum Refining = PTR; Utilities: Gas & Electric = UGE; Computer Peripherals = CPH; Pharmaceuticals = PHR; Engineering, Construction = ECR; Chemicals = CHM; Building Materials, glass = BMG; Food Consumer Products = FCP; Food Services = FDS; Insurance: P & C (mutual) = ISM; Mail, Package, Freight Delivery = MPF; Metals = MTL; Waste Management = WMM; Semiconductors and Other Electronic Components = SCE; Food Production = FDP; Hotels, Casinos, Resorts = HCR; Medical Products & Equipment = MPE; Energy = ENG; Computers, Office Equipment = COE; Diversified Financials = DFS; Entertainment = ENT; Miscellaneous = MSC; Network and Other Communications Equipment = NCO; Pipelines = PIP; Scientific, Photo, Control Equipment = SPC; Packaging, Containers = PKG; Homebuilders = HOM; Publishing, Printing = PPT; Wholesalers: Food and Grocery = WHG; Commercial Banks = CBK; Food & Drug Stores = FDS; Information Technology Services = ICT; Insurance: Life, Health (stock) = ISH; Motor Vehicles & Parts = MVP; Beverages = BVR; Internet Services and Retailing = ISR; Aerospace and Defense = ARD; Specialty Retailers = RET; Industrial & Farm Equipment = IFE; Insurance: P & C (stock) = ISS; Advertising, Marketing = ADM; Airlines = ARL; Apparel = APP; Automotive Retailing, Services = AUT; Computer Software = CSS; Diversified Outsourcing = BPO; Electronics, Electrical Equipment = EEE; Financial Data Services = FDS; Furniture = FRS; General Merchandisers = GMD; Health Care: Insurance & Managed Care = HCI; Health Care: Medical Facilities = HCM; Health Care: Pharmacy and Other Services = HCP; Home Equipment, Furnishings = HEF; Insurance: Life, Health (mutual) = INI; Payroll Services = PRS; Railroads = RAL; Real Estate = RES; Savings Institutions = SVI; Telecommunications = TEL; Temporary Help = TPH; Tobacco = TBC; Transportation and Logistics = TLL; Transportation Equipment = TRE; Trucking,

b)   Primary industries

Approximately 90 percent of companies in the mining and crude oil production (MCP) sector report their biodiversity protection activities and policies in their CSR report. For example, Occidental Petroleum clearly mentions their biodiversity and habitat preservation policy and goals; Apache notes its conservation policy for wetland and wildlife.

Seventy percent of petroleum refining (PR) companies reported biodiversity policies. ExxonMobil, which is a highly ranked company in terms of revenue, claims that their sites incorporate biodiversity protection to limit the impacts on sensitive areas. Their mitigation actions include participating in initiatives to enhance the wildlife and habitat attributes of their properties as well as modifying engineering design, construction, and operating practices to protect particular species and sensitive habitats. Marathon Oil is certified by the Wildlife Habitat Council.

Fifty-two percent of chemical companies and 50 percent of metal companies report their biodiversity protection activities and policies in their CSR report. For example, Alcoa's biodiversity policy states that the successful operation of their mines, even in sensitive native ecosystems, must avoid any impact on protected species and should follow targeted values to reestablish complex ecosystems. Although the top chemical company, Dow Chemicals, invests in various biodiversity protection activities, it offers no declarations of biodiversity policies in its CSR report. PPG Industries has a biodiversity policy for wildlife protection activities, whereas Ashland mentions a biodiversity policy for water bodies.

Among all the energy companies, 38.5 percent report biodiversity policies. For example, Constellation Energy and the Baltimore Gas and Electric Company (BGE) are collaborating to apply an Integrative Vegetation Management approach to their sites that involves the targeted use of environmentally benign herbicides to remove tall-growing, woody vegetation; in addition to complying with reliability requirements, this biodiversity policy reduces competition from invasive and undesirable plants that crowd out native and more beneficial plants.

c)   Consumer goods

Approximately 40 percent of companies in the food production (FP) sector clearly report their biodiversity policies, especially in CSR reports. In this sector, the company that generates the highest revenue, Archer Daniels Midland, is working to create a sustainable supply chain for palm oil in which one criterion is species conservation; however, this company only has general biodiversity policies for palm oil and soy production. Tyson Foods, which lacks business activities in or adjacent to legally protected biodiversity hot spots, does not describe its policy and activities related to biodiversity.

Among food consumer product (FCP) companies, approximately 50 percent have biodiversity policies. Major companies in this sector, such as PepsiCo, Sara

Lee, General Mills, and Kellogg, include biodiversity policies for their agricultural supply chain initiatives. Sara Lee implements a biodiversity policy mainly in its coffee production, and enhances the global multi-stakeholder initiative that functions to increase the sustainability in the mainstream coffee sector. General Mills commits to responsibly sourcing palm oil by ensuring that its purchases are not associated with rainforest deforestation. In contrast, a few companies, such as Hershey, have no formal program or strategy for managing their biodiversity impacts and claim that they presently do not significantly impact biodiversity levels.

Approximately 80 percent of household and personal products (HPP) companies have specific biodiversity policies. Major companies, including P&G, Kimberly-Clark, Colgate-Palmolive, and Avon Products, consider biodiversity to be an important environmental indicator of their business operations. Avon Products and Kimberley-Clark clearly report on biodiversity indicators in their global reporting initiative (GRI). In its CSR report, Avon Products declares its full support for forest management practices that protect biodiversity and ecosystem integrity, whereas Kimberly-Clark mentions its activities on habitat protection and restoration in the GRI.

Only 16 percent of beverage companies have biodiversity protection policies. Pepsi Bottling is the only company that mentions a biodiversity policy in its sustainable agriculture principles. Only 18 percent of motor vehicle and parts (MVP) manufacturing companies have specific biodiversity policies. Among them, only General Motors indicates its volunteer-based efforts to preserve its community's biodiversity.

Companies in the forest and paper products (FPP) sector have specific biodiversity policies. For example, International Paper, Weyerhaeuser, and Boise Cascade Holdings hold certifications for forest management, fiber procurement, and chain of custody certification, such as the FSC, the sustainable forestry initiative (SFI), the Brazilian forest certification standard (Cerflor), and the American Tree Farming System (ATFS) certification. In their paper procurement policy, most of these companies seek biodiversity-certified companies throughout the supply chain and are engaged in various biodiversity-related activities, such as the conservation of biodiversity hotspots, major tropical wilderness areas, and threatened and endangered species.

The miscellaneous sector contains three Fortune 500 companies, and only one company, 3M, mentions its biodiversity policy; it claims that preserving and enhancing biodiversity constitutes an important aspect of its environmental sustainability strategy. In addition to activities such as maintaining and protecting sustainable forestland and preserving water quality in critical areas, 3M's main concern is to create and fund "new ways to keep wild areas wild".

In subsectors such as furniture, apparel, and home equipment and furnishings (HEF) industries, no companies have policies related to biodiversity and ecosystems, probably because they create less impacts on biodiversity and are affected less by changes in biodiversity.

In the building materials and glass (BMG) sector, only one company, Owens Corning, has a specific policy related to biodiversity. When Owens Corning evaluates potential properties and operations for acquisition purposes, environmental consultants review the potential property and surrounding areas to assess existing environmental damage, including biodiversity loss and stressed vegetation; when selecting operational sites, they consider world heritage and biosphere sites, including forests, mountains, lakes, deserts, monuments, buildings, and cities considered by the United Nations Educational Scientific and Cultural Organization (UNESCO) to be of special cultural or physical significance.

In the toys and sporting goods (TSG) sector, only Mattel clearly mentions a biodiversity policy, primarily for paper procurement.

d) Industrial

The industrial sector (construction, aerospace components) ranks fourth in terms of the risk from biodiversity loss; 27.8 percent of the companies report on their biodiversity policies and activities. This sector ranks fifth in revenue generation. In this sector, subsectors such as wholesalers of electronics and office equipment (WOE), railroads, electronics and electrical equipment (EEE), transportation equipment (TE), and real estate (RE) have 0% biodiversity policy acceptance. In the homebuilders' category, 27.3 percent of companies report biodiversity concern and policies; for example, Lennar mentions the preservation and enhancement of wetlands and wildlife habitat in its CSR report.

In the oil and gas equipment and services (OGE) subsector, 80 percent of the companies have environmental policies related to biodiversity. Baker Hughes mentions its biodiversity policy and action plan in relation to its GRI report on sustainable technology and environment protection.

In the computer peripherals (CP) subsector, 66.7 percent of companies report on their biodiversity protection policy. Although companies such as EMC claim that their impact on biodiversity is largely indirect, they also claim to use a systems approach to environmental sustainability (including biodiversity) to drive their businesses.

Sixty percent of companies in the engineering and construction (EC) subsector report on their biodiversity policies. In adopting sustainability as a goal, Fluor, the top EC company, uses the "Triple Bottom Line" model, which considers the protection of wildlife habitats and biodiversity as environmental stewardship.

In the scientific photo control equipment (SPC) subsector, one of the three companies (33.3 percent), Eastman Kodak, reports a biodiversity and natural habitat policy. In the medical products & equipment (MPE) subsector, two out of five companies (40 percent) reported a biodiversity activity and policy in their CSR reports. In addition, 33.3 percent of pipeline-manufacturing companies and 42.9 percent of semiconductor and other electronic component manufacturing (SEC) companies reported biodiversity policies.

In the aerospace and defense (AD) subsector, only one of the ten topmost companies, Boeing, has a biodiversity policy in its CSR report, which pledges to consider only renewable fuel sources that have a minimal biodiversity impact.

In the computers and office equipment (COE) category and in the network and other communications equipment (NCE) category, 37.5 percent and 33.3 percent of the companies, respectively, report biodiversity consciousness and policies. In the industrial & farm equipment (IFE) category, only 7 percent of the companies, i.e., Deere, mention a concern for biodiversity protection.

e)   *Financial institution*

Approximately 83 percent of the securities companies (five of six) report biodiversity consciousness and policies in their CSR or sustainability reports. Goldman Sachs uses biodiversity policies for a major service related to market-based solutions for environmental issues. Morgan Stanley expresses concern about diversity, probably because its environmental policy statement is developed by its major business units in consultation with external stakeholders.

Although companies in the insurance for life and health (mutual) (ILHM) category did not report policies related to biodiversity protection, one of the two insurance P & C (mutual) (IPCM) companies, State Farm Insurance, mentions biodiversity and ecosystem protection concerns in the environmental responsibility section of its CSR; State Farm states that its environmental responsibility covers conservation issues beyond land and wildlife, and that it considers the preservation of biodiversity and fragile ecosystems to be integral to this responsibility.

Savings institutions (SI) and financial data services (FDS) companies do not report on these issues but may be considering their indirect impacts. One of 18 (i.e., 5.6 percent) insurance of P & C (stock) (IPCS) companies and 20 percent (2 out of 10) of insurance of life and health (stock) (ILHS) companies report biodiversity-related concerns and policies. For example, the ILHS company MetLife reports on its biodiversity policy and its biodiversity protection activities for the New York Botanical Garden.

Among diversified financial (DF) companies and commercial banks (CB), 33.3 percent and 23.8 percent, respectively, report biodiversity policies. The commercial bank JPMorgan Chase reports its plantation and natural habitat protection policies and activities. Many commercial banks may not have specific biodiversity or ecosystem protection policies but mention biodiversity and forest conservation in their paper procurement policies.

f)   *Consumer services*

In the consumer services sector, biodiversity risk ranks fifth, aggregated biodiversity policy acceptance ranks sixth, and aggregated revenue generation ranks third. Companies in the general merchandiser (GM), airline, automotive retailing and services (ARS), wholesalers: diversified (WD), temporary help (TH), transportation and logistics (TL), and trucking and truck leasing (TTL) subsectors do not report biodiversity consciousness or policies because they have no direct impact on biodiversity levels. In the specialty retailers (SR) subsector, only 8.3 percent of companies have biodiversity policies, which primarily relate to their forestry policies and paper and wood procurement policies.

In the food and drug stores (FD) subsector, 20 percent of companies report biodiversity policies. For example, through research and engagement with the relevant stakeholders in the food industry, Safeway adopts a biodiversity protection policy for food standards. In addition, 33.3 percent of entertainment companies report biodiversity protection policies. Time Warner relates its biodiversity policy mainly to forest management policy by supporting suppliers with proper forest certifications. One out of two (50 percent) mail, package, and freight delivery (MPF) companies, FedEx, reports biodiversity concern and policies, particularly in relation to reforestation.

Among the packaging and container (PC) companies, 28.6 percent report biodiversity policies. The topmost company, Smurfit-Stone Container, reports biodiversity policies in relation to sustainable forestry; 25 percent of wholesalers: food and grocery (WFG) companies and 50 percent of food services (FS) companies report biodiversity policies. The well-known food services company McDonald's may not have direct biodiversity or forestry policies, but its "Endangered Animals Happy Meal" effectively relates marketing to biodiversity. The food services company Starbucks has a biodiversity policy for coffee production, with organic and traditional shade-growing agricultural methods that protect the forest's birds and biodiversity.[4]

In the hotels, casinos and resorts (HCR) subsector, 40 percent of the companies report biodiversity policies. Hotel Marriott International has clear policies on biodiversity protection primarily in terms of forest management, as it considers rain forest preservation to be an important policy. Twenty-five percent of publishing and printing (PP) companies and 50 percent of waste management (WM) companies report biodiversity policies. For the publishing and printing company R.R. Donnelley & Sons, biodiversity conservation and forest ecosystem protection constitute one of their sustainability principles. The waste management company Allied Waste Industries' biodiversity-related policies and activities concern wildlife habitat and wetland habitat conservation.

g) Health care

In the health-care sector (pharmaceuticals, biotechnology, health-care providers), the risk of biodiversity loss and revenue generation rank third and sixth, respectively. Only 13.3 percent of the sector, however, expresses a clear biodiversity policy, and only pharmaceutical companies report clearly about their biodiversity policies and activities. Companies from the wholesalers: health care (WHC), health care: insurance and managed care (HIM), health care: pharmacy and other services (HPO), and health care: medical facilities (HMF) subsectors do not have specific policies regarding biodiversity. The topmost pharmaceutical companies, such as Johnson & Johnson, are considerably active in biodiversity protection; Johnson & Johnson specifies that it has more than 55 conservation projects underway around the world, and 66 percent of these aim to enhance or conserve off-site biodiversity. Some major pharmaceutical companies, such as Pfizer and Wyeth (now Pfizer), include biodiversity protection in their water policies.

h)   Technology and business services

In the technology and business services sector, business risks due to biodiversity loss is the lowest (rank 6) among the sectors discussed, whereas revenue generation rank is 7 and only 5.2 percent of the companies in these sector have clear biodiversity policies.

The advertising and marketing (AM), telecommunications, computer software (CS), diversified outsourcing (DO), and payroll services (PS) sectors have no biodiversity policies or protection activities. In the information technology services (IT) subsector, only one of five (20 percent) of the companies, Affiliated Computer Services (a Xerox company), mentions a biodiversity policy, which is mainly incorporated into its forest policy. In the Internet services and retailing (ISR) subsector, only one of six (16.7 percent) of the companies, Google, mentions biodiversity concerns and policies.

13.3.4   Comparison of revenue, risk, and action among Fortune 500 companies

To analyze the companies' biodiversity-related policies within each sector, we first identified the companies' risk perception in terms of business activities and then converted them into risk profiles based on risk characteristics. This analysis provides 12 different types of risk that a company can face when their operations negatively impact biodiversity and ecosystems. During the content analysis of the individual companies' policies, we determined that companies mainly attempt to conceal these risks. In most cases, the policies appear to focus narrowly on immediate targets. Based on the 12-category risk spectrum, we have identified the level of risk exposure for each sector (TEEB Report for Business 2010 [Chapter 4], Economic Evaluation of Environmental Impacts of Asian Development Bank) and compared risk profiles to respective revenue and biodiversity policy adoption rankings.

Figure 13.2 shows the correlations between the three indicators used in this study, i.e., the biodiversity risk ranking, revenue ranking, and biodiversity policy acceptance ranking. We have eight sectors (mining, electricity, and financial, among others) and three indicators: company revenue, biodiversity loss related risk, and biodiversity policy adoption. For the revenue, a higher rank number indicates higher earnings by a company. In context of risk, a higher rank number indicates that the sector is highly exposed to the risk related to loss of biodiversity. Similarly, for the indicator of policy adoption, a higher rank number means that the sector is highly aware of the importance of biodiversity and taking necessary actions to protect biodiversity by taking company level policies and vice versa. Since there is no single indicator or index to measure the

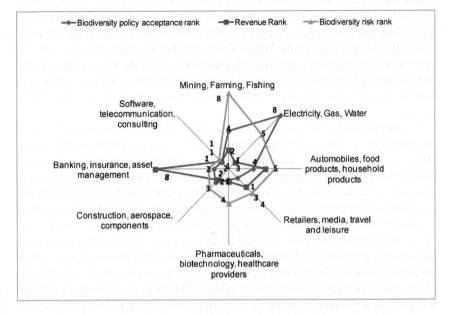

Figure 13.2 Comparison between business risk due to biodiversity loss, policy acceptance, and Fortune 500 revenue rank

companies in the context of impacts on biodiversity, we had to create certain parameters which are most likely indicating the targeted performance of the companies.

The financial sector, which includes banks and insurance companies, has the highest revenue levels. Although this sector demonstrates considerably low levels of biodiversity-related policy adoption, it also has lower levels of risk related to biodiversity loss. Furthermore, the utility sector, which includes electricity, water, and gas companies, has the lowest revenue levels but is ranked high in the areas of risk related to biodiversity loss and the adoption of specific biodiversity mitigation policies. Thus, these indicators exhibit little or no correlation. Using these rank and risk characteristics for the eight different sectors, we analyzed each sector in terms of its biodiversity loss risk, economic performance, and level of biodiversity protection policy acceptance.

13.4 Discussion and conclusion

This study illustrates that in most cases, biodiversity loss and its related risks to businesses are not fully addressed by company policies. Therefore, despite bearing high levels of biodiversity risk exposure and related business risks, companies have yet to adopt specific biodiversity policies for day-to-day activities. A clear gap is found in the lack of a proper assessment tool for estimating the impact of biodiversity losses in terms of financial, social, and environmental measures.

Unless companies are aware of their economic impact on the loss of biodiversity and understand the benefits of risk-mitigating measures in terms of finance or reputation, the companies are highly unlikely to seriously address biodiversity. It has been reported by the World Economic Forum that globally only 27 percent of the companies are somewhat concern about the loss of biodiversity and its related impact on business. The major reason for such poor response is found to be the very slow impact of biodiversity loss on business activities (WEF 2010).

In contrast to the responses related to climate change, those related to bio-diversity loss are not significant relative to the scale of business operations. However, the increased concerns from the companies for wildlife protection activities and related ecosystem conservation issues indicate an improved general awareness of these issues. In most cases, the companies' biodiversity policies are concealed within general environmental protection measures and CSR activities; as a result, these actions lack the systematic organization that can benefit com-panies and their consumers. The results of our study indicate that companies that directly generate biodiversity loss are more likely to formally specify their concern for biodiversity through reporting. This effect is probably a consequence of the public perception of company liability. Our analysis of company reports and published documents reveals a clear lack of direction and commitment to addressing the problem of biodiversity loss. In fact, the reporting of biodiversity-related activities is rare even in the GRI guidelines, which exacerbate the impact of biodiversity loss globally. In the Economics of Ecosystems and Biodiversity report for 2010, it has been further mentioned that companies that have direct interaction with ecosystems, like tobacco, food, and beverage companies, are more proactive in biodiversity conservation and protection measures (TEEB 2010).

In summary, the major findings are as follows:

1. Companies' revenue profiles do not significantly affect their acceptance of specific biodiversity-related policies. Large companies thus have yet to act responsibly with respect to biodiversity protection.
2. Companies' business activity profiles significantly influence their decisions to adopt biodiversity protection policy and measures. Therefore, unless com-panies consider the impact of biodiversity loss on their business activities, it may be difficult to encourage them to adopt mitigation actions.
3. Companies' business risk profiles might influence their acceptance of biodi-versity-related policies, although minimal initiative has been taken.

This study shows that companies in the utility sector, which bears a high operational impact on ecosystems, rank high in the adoption of specific biodi-versity mitigation policies despite generating low revenues, whereas the financial sector ranks lower on biodiversity protection policy adoption and the risk of biodiversity loss, even though it generates high revenues. In primary industries, the revenue generation is lower, but the risk of biodiversity loss, and thus the rate of the adoption of biodiversity mitigation policies, is comparatively higher.

However, most Fortune 500 companies with direct biodiversity-related policies prefer mitigation hierarchy measures that are cost-effective, less tedious, and easy to understand and implement. Practices designed to reduce the impact of business development on biodiversity are known as compensatory mitigation (Madsen et al. 2010). Few countries are in the early stages of the adoption or investigation of compensatory mitigation, but in most geographical regions, compensatory mitigation is developed or developing around different economic, political, institutional, and cultural circumstances that give rise to a variety of programs (Madsen et al. 2010). However, no corresponding frameworks are available to guide business sectors in setting up such a mitigation hierarchy. Consequently, we recommend a three-step approach for preparing a sector-specific mitigation hierarchy framework to assess and mitigate the damage caused by ecosystem and biodiversity losses. Initially, such a framework at the level of the sector rather than the company will be important because more detailed information and data are required for a company-specific framework. Such a sector-specific framework can be developed by companies within a particular sector by collecting the relevant preparatory information.

Step 1: Prepare a revenue risk profile for all member companies within the sector to reflect the current and future positions based on various external factors such as market risk and regulatory risk.

Step 2: Prepare the sector's business process risk profile based on a life cycle assessment, which will identify potential sources or causes of biodiversity and ecosystem losses. This step can also factor in future technological changes, which might alter companies' business processes and activity profiles and their corresponding impact.

Step 3: Prepare a detailed sector-wide business risk mapping based on market research, which should be linked to each step of the business process. For example, if pesticides are a significant source or cause of biodiversity loss for a particular sector, then all sources of pesticides in all business activities should be consolidated and mapped against the nature of their risk impact, e.g., reduced productivity.

A limitation of this chapter is our lack of attention to the details concerning the companies' actual implementation of work related to ecosystem services and biodiversity protection; we are thus unable to surmise much beyond popular reporting. In addition, we primarily used publicly available information and data to evaluate companies' policies for combating biodiversity-related losses; our results are thus indicative rather than definitive in nature. Future research could examine each company's activities in greater detail.

Notes

1 Food and Agriculture Organization (FAO) reported that since 1900 more than 75% of the total global plant genetic diversity has been lost. (The Second Report on the State of the World's Plant Genetic Resources for Food and Agriculture 2010).

2   Previous studies identified the potential burdens and stressors to water and land created by the different sectors in various stages of their life cycles (Asian Development Bank 1997) Businesses create emissions during various stages of their life cycle that potentially impact the biodiversity. However, to prepare the life cycle analysis of these industries, more significant efforts could be made to apply sustainability accounting using fieldwork and case-oriented research methods (Lamberton 2005).

3   The revenue ranking is based on 2007 because only figures for that year were available online (accessed October 2010) during the course of this research. However, these rankings have not changed much between 2007 and 2010 (the ranking correlation for the two years is 0.987), so our data are sufficiently up to date. The company websites were accessed in October 2010.

4   Studies show that species richness of all ants and birds and of forest ant and bird species is lower in most coffee agro ecosystems (where intensified coffee management process is followed) than in natural forests. But rustic coffee, which is grown under native forest canopies/natural shade trees have equal or greater ant and bird richness than nearby forests. Thus rustic coffee production is better for maintaining biodiversity levels (Philpott et al., 2008). Starbucks is also adopting biodiversity policies to follow traditional rustic coffee production system, which utilizes native forest canopies, and as a way to decrease the biodiversity loss.

Bibliography

Ahmad J, O'Regan N, Ghobadian A. (2003) Managing for Performance: Corporate Responsibility and Internal Stakeholders. *International Journal of Business Performance Management.* 5 (2/3): 141–153.

Asian Development Bank. (1997) Economic Valuation of Environmental Impacts in *Guidelines for the Economic Analysis of Projects.* Manila (Philippines): Asian Development Bank.

Bishop J, Bertrand N. (2010) *Report for Business: The Economics of Ecosystems and Biodiversity.* Malta: United Nations Environment Programme.

Butchart S, Walpole M, Collen B, Stien A. (2010) Global biodiversity: indcators of recent declines. *Science.* 328 (5982): 1164–1168.

CNN. (2007) *List of Fortune 500 Companies in the United States.* [cited in October 2010].

Ciocirlan C, Pettersson C. (2012) Does Workforce Diversity Matter in the Fight Against Climate Change ? An Analysis of Fortune 500 Companies. *Corporate Social Responsibility and Environmental Management.* 19:47–62.

Convention on Biological Diversity (1992) Article 2. United Nations Environment Program.

Convention on Biological Diversity. (2012) *The Statement of the Executive Secretary of the CBD on the Occasion of the UNCTAD and BIOTRADE Congress.* Rio De Janeiro (Brazil).

Doremus H. (2003) A Policy Portfolio Approach to Biodiversity Protection on Private Lands. *Environmental Science and Policy.* 6: 217–232.

Dyke J, Cash S, Brody S, Thornton S. (2005) Examining the Role of the Forest Industry in Collaborative Ecosystem Management: Implications for Corporate Strategy. *Corporate Social Responsibility and Environmental Management.* 12 (1): 10–18.

Economics of Ecosystems and Biodiversity, The (2010) *The Economics of Ecosystems and Biodiversity: Mainstreaming the Economics of Nature: A Synthesis of the Approach,*

Conclusions and Recommendations of TEEB. Geneva (Switzerland): United Nations Environment Program (UNEP).

Food and Agriculture Organization. (2010) *The Second Report on The State of the World's Plant Genetic Resources for Food and Agriculture.* Rome (Italy): Food and Agriculture Organization.

Glasbergen P. (2010) Global Action Networks: Agents for Collective Action. *Global Environmental Change.* 20: 130–141.

Gutman P, Davidson S. (2007) *A Review of Innovative International Financial Mechanisms for Biodiversity Conservation With a Special Focus on the International Financing of Developing Countries' Protected Areas.* Washington, D.C. (USA): World Wildlife Fund's Macroeconomics Program Office .

Groves CR, Kutner, LS, Storms DM, Murray MP, Scott Schafale JM, Weakley M, Pressey AS. (2000) Owning Up to our Responsibilities: Who Owns Lands Important for Biodiversity in Stein BA, Kutner LS, Adams JS, *Precious Heritage: The Status of Biodiversity in the United States.* New York: Oxford University Press, pp. 275–300.

Heller EN, Zavaleta E. (2009) Biodiversity Management in the Face of Climate Change: A review of 22 Years of Recommendations. *Biological Conservation.* 142 (1): 14–32.

Lamberton G. (2005) Sustainability Accounting – A Brief History and Conceptual Framework. *Accounting Forum.* 29 (1): 7–26.

Levrel H, Fontaine B. (2010) Balancing State and Volunteer Investment in Biodiversity Monitoring for the Implementation of CBD Indicators: A French Example. *Ecological Economics.* 69 :1580–1586.

Madsen B, Carroll N, Moore BK. (2010) *State of Biodiversity Markets Report: Offset and Compensation Programs Worldwide.* Washington, D.C. (USA): Ecosystem Marketplace.

Mahidhar V, Giffi C, Kambil A, Alvanos R. (2009) Rethinking Emerging Market Strategies: From Off Shoring to Strategic Expansion. *A Deloitte Review (Issue-4).* Washington, D.C.: Deloitte Development LLC.

Martens P, Rotmans J, Groot D. (2003) Biodiversity: Luxury or Necessity? *Global Environmental Change.* 13 :75–81.

Merriam W. (1997) Life Cycle Assessment. *A Report of West Virginia University Extension Program.* Morgantown (USA): West Virginia University.

Metcalfe J, Vorhies F. (2010) Exploring the Case for a Green Development Mechanism. *Article presented in the International Workshop on Innovative Financial Mechanisms.* Bonn (Germany). Convention on Biological Diversity.

Millennium Ecosystem Assessment. (2005) *Ecosystems and human well-being: biodiversity synthesis.* Washington (DC): World Resource Institutes.

Moran D, Pearce D, Wendelaar A. (1996) Global Biodiversity Priorities: A Cost-Effectiveness Index for Investments. *Global Environmental Change.* 6 (2): 103–119.

Olson M. (1965) *The Logic of Collective Action: Public Goods and the Theory of Groups.* Boston (USA). Harvard University Press.

Philpott SM, Arendt WJ, Armbrecht I, Bichier P, Diestch TV, Gordon C, Greenberg R, Reynoso-Santos R, Soto-Pinto L, Tejeda-Cruz C, et al. (2008) 'Biodiversity loss in Latin American coffee landscapes: review of the evidence on ants, birds, and trees.' *Conserv Biol.* 22(5): 1093–1105.

Rondinelli DA, Berry MA. (2000) Environmental Citizenship in Multinational Corporations: Social Responsibility and Sustainable Development. *European Management Journal.* 18 (1): 70–84.

U.S. General Accounting Office. (1995) *Endangered Species Act: Information on Species Protection on Nonfederal Lands,* edited by U.S.G.A. Office. Washington D.C. General Accounting Office.

Vickerman S. (1999) A State Model for Implementing Stewardship Incentives to Conserve Biodiversity and Endangered Species. *The Science of the Total Environment.* 240 :41–50.

Wagge S. (2007) Investing in the Future: An Assessment of Private Sector Demand for Engaging in Markets & Payments for Ecosystem Services. *PESAL Papers Series No. 2.* Rome (Italy): UN Food and Agriculture Organization.

Walpole M, Almond A, Besancon C, Butchart S. (2009) Tracking Progress Toward the 2010 Biodiversity Target and Beyond. *Science.* 325: 1503–1504.

Walter R. (2005) *Millennium Ecosystem Assessment: Ecosystems and Human Well-Being.* Washington, D.C. (USA): Island Press.

World Economic Forum (2010) Biodiversity and Business Risk. *A briefing paper for participants engaged in biodiversity related discussions at the World Economic Forum Davos-Klosters Annual Meeting. Geneva.* World Economic Forum.

Wunder S. (2005) Payments for Environmental Services: Some Nuts and Bolts. *Occasional paper No. 42.* Jakarta (Indonesia): CIFOR.

14 Ecologically friendly transportation
Cost analysis of subsidy and tax reduction scheme

Kenta Tanaka and Shunsuke Managi

14.1 Introduction

The amount of CO_2 emissions from the transportation sector accounts for a large proportion of total emissions. However, reducing CO_2 emissions in this sector is relatively difficult because of a growing population, a higher share of automobile owners, and an improvement in infrastructure, which all contribute to emissions. Although the total aggregated greenhouse gas (GHG) emissions of Annex 1 parties decreased overall from 1990 to 2004 in the majority of energy-consuming sectors, the transport and energy industry sectors were exceptions (Meyer et al., 2007). Thus, the reduction of emissions in the transportation sector is an important problem facing both developed and developing countries.

To encourage a reduction in emissions, several developed countries have introduced incentives for buyers who purchase hybrid cars and ecologically friendly cars (i.e., eco-cars). These incentives include subsidies and tax reductions for individuals who purchase an energy-efficient car. Several researchers have examined the cost effectiveness of policies that promote hybrid cars and eco-cars (see, e.g., Chandra et al., 2010; Beresteanu and Li, 2011). However, the effects of tax reductions and subsidies are difficult to understand, particularly because of the complex car and energy tax systems in different countries. In Japan, for example, car owners must pay several taxes, including a car tax, a car volume tax, and a car acquisition tax. Beresteanu and Li (2011) examined how the cost effectiveness of car taxes depends on which method of tax reduction is used. An additional factor for consideration is how a change in fuel costs may affect a buyer's inclination to purchase a new car. Thus, to determine the cost effectiveness of each approach, we must further analyze how significantly the different methods of tax reduction affect the overall outcome.

In this chapter, we analyze the cost effectiveness of tax reductions and subsidies with regard to the reduction of CO_2 emissions in Japan. We classify the effect of each subsidy and tax reduction (i.e., car tax, car volume tax, car acquisition tax) and then discuss the cost effectiveness of each tax reduction and subsidy approach.

14.2   Background

14.2.1   Previous studies

Although numerous studies have examined automobile demand (e.g., Berry et al., 1995), recent studies have focused on countries' diffusion policies concerning eco-cars. The diffusion of energy-efficient goods is a key issue for developed countries, several of which have implemented tax reductions and subsidies for the purchase of eco-cars. However, an effective diffusion policy is challenging to implement, primarily because the purchase behavior concerning durable goods, such as cars, is difficult to understand. In reality, as previous studies have found, people do not purchase durable goods in a rational way (see, e.g., Allcott and Wozny, 2013). To implement an effective diffusion policy, we must consider the cost effectiveness of each diffusion policy that has been implemented in the past, including an examination of previous studies that have evaluated the diffusion policies regarding eco-cars.

Chandra et al. (2010) estimated the cost of CO_2 emissions by examining a Canadian rebate program for purchasers of hybrid cars, using province-level panel data to control for unobservable attribution. These researchers estimated the abatement cost of the tax rebate as 195.20 Canadian dollars per CO_2 ton on average. In a separate study, Beresteanu and Li (2011) analyzed the income tax incentive for the purchase of a hybrid car in the United States, estimating the abatement cost of the program as \$177 per CO_2 ton. The study also showed that the cost effectiveness of a federal tax program could be improved by a flat rebate program. Additionally, Gallangher and Muehlegger (2011) assessed the relative effect of tax incentives, gasoline prices, social preference, and other non-monetary incentives. Their study found that sales tax incentives have a much greater effect than income tax incentives on the demand for hybrid cars.

14.2.2   Tax reductions and subsidies for eco-cars

Because the diffusion of eco-cars is an important policy in Japan, the country has implemented several preferential treatments for purchasers of eco-friendly vehicles. Beginning in 2004, the government began to reform the tax system for cars. In April 2009, Japan implemented a large-scale financial plan to encourage hybrid and eco-car purchases through tax reductions (eco-car tax reductions) and subsidies (eco-car subsidies) for automobile purchases. Although the tax reductions for hybrid cars and eco-cars were changed in 2012, the eco-car tax reductions have continued, as shown in the summary of eco-car tax reductions in Table 14.1. People who purchase a new car that meets the gas mileage and emission standards of 2005 are permitted to pay lower taxes (car weight taxes and car acquisition taxes).

One eco-car subsidy, implemented from April to September 2009, was applied to the purchases of new cars that met gas mileage and emission standards in 2010. A summary of the eco-car subsidy is shown in Table 14.2. People who purchased new cars that met the gas mileage and emission standards in 2010 were eligible to receive the subsidy. Although it depends on the situation of

Table 14.1 Summary of eco-car tax rebates

	Car volume tax	Car acquisition tax
Hybrid car	Free tax	Free tax
☆☆☆☆ and gas mileage standard + 25%	75% reduction	75% reduction
☆☆☆☆ and gas mileage standard + 20%	50% reduction	50% reduction
☆☆☆☆ and gas mileage standard + 15%		

Note: ☆☆☆☆ mean emissions of air pollution are 75% less than the rate for meeting the standard in 2005.

Table 14.2 Summary of eco-car subsidy

	Standard Car	Light car
Subsidy for purchasing new car (Replacement of 13-year-old car with new eco-car)	250,000 JP yen	125,000 JP yen
Subsidy for purchasing a new car (☆☆☆☆ and gas mileage standard +15%)	100,000 JP yen	50,000 JP yen

Note: In this table, we define a new (eco)car as the rate for meeting standards in 2010.

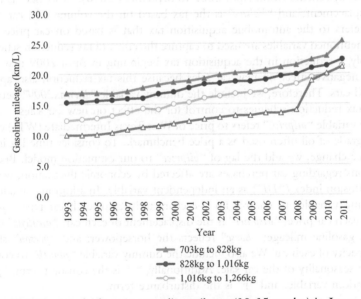

Figure 14.1 The trend of average gasoline mileage (10–15 modes) in Japan

Note: Each line shows the average gasoline mileage based on each volume class

purchasing a new car, buyers could receive a subsidy of as much as 250,000 Japanese yen. An additional eco-car subsidy was implemented in 2012.

Overall, eco-car tax reductions and eco-car subsidies have been shown to effectively promote the diffusion of eco-cars. Figure 14.1 shows the trend of average gasoline mileage (10–15 modes) in Japan, reflecting a gradual improvement over time. Notably, the gasoline mileage of high-volume cars (1266 kg to 1518 kg)[1] dramatically improved in 2009.

14.3   Model

14.3.1   *Estimation of new eco-car sales by subsidy and tax reduction*

First, we estimate the effect of subsidies and tax reductions on the diffusion of hybrid cars and eco-cars. In this estimation, we use a random effect model and panel data. We estimate the following equation:

$$
\begin{aligned}
Car_{i,t} = {}& \beta_1 Car_{i,t-1} + \beta_2 Car_{i,t-2} + \beta_3 Car_{i,t-3} + \beta_4 Subsidy_{i,t} + \beta_5 Cartax_{i,t} \\
& + \beta_6 Voltax_{i,t} + \beta_7 Buytax_{i,t} + \beta_8 Buytax2009_{i,t} + \beta_9 oilprice_{i,t} + \beta_{10} oilprice_{i,t-1} \\
& + \beta_{11} oilprice_{i,t-2} + \beta_{12} DI_t + \beta_{13} price_i + \beta_{14} displace_i + \beta_{15} gmilege_i + \beta_{16} horce_i \\
& + \beta_{17} person_i + month_t + c + \mu + v
\end{aligned}
\tag{1}
$$

where i represents each type of car, t is the month and "*Car*" is the number of new car registrations. "*Subsidy*" is the variable representing what portion of a subsidy was paid for each type of car within the implementation periods of the subsidy scheme (from April 2009 to September 2010). "*Car tax*" is based on displacement, and "*Voltax*" is the tax based on the volume of a car. "*Buy tax*" refers to the automobile acquisition tax that is based on car price. The aforementioned variables are used to capture the effect of tax reduction schemes. Notably, a reduction in the acquisition tax beginning in April 2009 may have had a negative effect on new car sales because this tax reduction also applied to used cars. Therefore, we include the dummy variable "*Buytax2009*" between these tax reduction schemes to control for the effect on new car sales.

The variable "*oilprice*" refers to price of West Texas Intermediate (WTI) crude oil, a grade of oil often used as a price benchmark. To consider time lag in the oil price change, we add the lag of "*oilprice*" to our estimation model. Because decisions regarding car purchases are affected by economic fluctuation, we add the diffusion index ("*DI*") as an independent variable. In addition, we add the following variables to control for the characteristics of each car type: "*price*" shows each car price; "*displace*" is the displacement of each car; "*gmilege*" refers to the gasoline mileage; "*horse*" reflects the horsepower; and "*person*" shows the capacity of each car. We also include the dummy variable "*month*" to control for the seasonality of the car sale. Additionally, "*c*" is the constant term, "μ" is the random variable, and "*v*" is the disturbance term.

14.3.2   *Estimation of CO_2 reduction by subsidy and tax reduction scheme*

First, we estimate the amount of eco-car diffusion associated with each subsidy and tax reduction approach. Based on the number of eco-cars that are diffused by subsidy and tax reductions, we simulate the amount of CO_2 reduction that occurs. We establish an assumption to simulate the amount of CO_2 reduction, based initially on the total distance traveled by cars over a typical lifetime. Because this amount differs in each country and region, it is difficult to estimate the actual distance. However, used cars whose odometers reach 100,000 km generally have a value of zero in the Japanese used car market; therefore, we establish the anticipated running distance of new cars as 100,000 km.

The second assumption relates to the tenure of a new car, which is also difficult to ascertain. Based on statistics from the Automobile Inspection and Registration Information Association (2013), the average age of cars in Japan is 8.07 years, whereas the average duration of car use is 12.58 years. Overall, people tend to own their cars longer than they did in the past. To reflect these statistics, we establish 10 years as the amount of time spent using a car.

The third relevant assumption relates to the concept of switching. For example, people do not always exclusively use new cars; instead, they might simultaneously use an old car and a new car. Other people might sell their old car to a used car market. Although we can suppose several situations, in this study we hypothesize that people who purchase new hybrids or eco-cars trade in or sell their previous cars. The framework for this simulation is depicted in Figure 14.2.

We estimate the amount of eco-car diffusion according to β_4 and the amount of subsidy for each car type. In addition, we simulate how much gasoline is consumed by new cars. From the gasoline consumption of new cars and the CO_2 emission coefficient (0.0023t per ℓ), we can simulate how much CO_2 is produced. Conversely, CO_2 emissions from the purchaser's previous automobile disappear. By comparing the emissions of the older cars[2] to the emissions of the new cars, we can estimate the amount of emissions reduction that is achieved by each subsidy scheme. Dividing the abatement amount of the CO_2 emissions by the cost of each scheme, we can understand the abatement cost of each scheme per CO_2 ton. In this analysis, we also simulate each tax reduction scheme based on the same method.

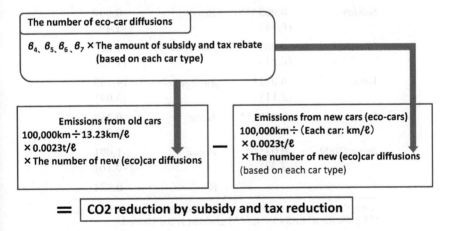

Figure 14.2 Simulation of CO_2 reduction

14.3.3   Data

Our statistics include the number of new car registrations and car information for each car type in January 2005 and December 2010. The registration data were obtained from the Japanese Automobile Dealers Association's annual report on new car registrations. The price data for each car type were obtained from The Car Information Ltd.'s (2010) reference chart on domestically produced car prices. Information about each car type was obtained from the Society of Automobile Engineers of Japan's (2010)[3] specification sheet on automobiles. Our analysis included data on 234 car types. The diffusion index was obtained from the Japanese government's public database (Cabinet Office, Government of Japan, 2014), and WTI prices came from the public database of the International Monetary Fund (2014).

14.4   Results

14.4.1   Estimation results

Table 14.3 shows the estimation results of Equation (1). The lags of the dependent variables show positive coefficients, suggesting that car demand is affected by the time trend of car sales. Each variable that captures the scheme effects

Table 14.3 Estimation results of random effect model

Car_{t-1}	0.575*** (70.11)	$oilprice_t$	−0.005 (−0.01)
Car_{t-2}	0.089*** (9.25)	$oilprice_{t-1}$	0.951 (0.49)
Car_{t-3}	0.253*** (31.39)	$oilprice_{t-2}$	0.820 (0.58)
Subsidy	0.002*** (6.84)	Price	−0.000 (−1.49)
Cartax	0.001 (0.31)	displacement	29.027 (1.23)
Voltax	0.011** (2.11)	gmilege	14.152*** (5.04)
Buytax	0.018*** (3.03)	Horse	0.268 (0.81)
Buytax2009	−0.02*** (−3.32)	Person	−1.091 (−0.16)
		R^2	0.874

Note: Values in parentheses are t-values. *Significant at the 10% level, **Significant at the 5% level, ***Significant at the 1% level.

shows a positive coefficient. Comparing the coefficients of policy variables, "*Buytax*" shows the largest coefficient. However, "*Cartax*" does not show a significant correlation with the dependent variable in this estimation. Thus, a car tax has limited effectiveness regarding new car demand. Additionally, "*Buytax2009*" shows a negative relationship with the dependent variable. The detailed impact of each policy will be analyzed in a later section.

Conversely, variables related to oil prices do not have a significant relationship with the dependent variable. These results are consistent with previous studies (see, e.g., Allcott and Wozny, 2013). In reality, many people do not consider their future gasoline consumption when purchasing vehicles (Allcott, 2011). Instead, our results identify gasoline mileage as an important factor in the selection of cars. As noted by researchers, people often misunderstand the performance of durable goods, for example, with regard to miles per gallon (MPG) in car use (see, e.g., Larrick and Soll, 2008). Our results also may have captured similar effects.

14.4.2   Simulation results: cost of each scheme

Based on the results of random effect estimation we simulate the cost of each scheme, as shown in Table 14.4. Comparatively, subsidies are the most effective approach regarding emissions reduction. At the other end of the spectrum, car acquisition taxes demonstrate the highest costs of all schemes. This result implies that car acquisition taxes decrease cost efficiency. In recent years, consumers have tended to buy compact and fuel-efficient cars that are less expensive than hybrid cars. However, because car acquisition taxes are based on car prices, this type of tax does not contribute enough to diffuse a hybrid car. These results help to explain how different types of tax rebates affect overall cost effectiveness.

Conversely, the car weight tax reduction may provide incentives for purchasing hybrid cars because hybrids are heavier than other cars. Hybrid cars demonstrate good performance with regard to emissions reduction; thus, the implementation of this tax increases cost effectiveness. In addition to covering a wide range of car types, the subsidy provides benefits that people can easily understand.

Table 14.4 Evaluation of each policy for the diffusion of eco-cars

	Car weight tax	Car acquisition tax	Subsidy
Emissions reduction by each policy (CO_2-kt)	739.590	1173.557	1903.720
Reduction of fuel consumption by each policy (10,000 kl)	31.879	50.584	82.057
Cost of emissions reduction (Japanese yen/ton)	21755.697	47373.700	20653.390

14.5   Discussion and conclusion

This study examines the cost effectiveness of tax reductions and subsidies with regard to the purchases of hybrids and eco-cars. Our results provide several important policy implications. First, we find differences in the cost effectiveness of each tax reduction scheme. For example, a reduction in the car weight tax is better than a reduction in the car acquisition tax for purposes of emissions reduction. Because the diffusion of energy-efficient goods is an important policy goal of many countries, these findings can help governments to implement cost-effective policies for the reduction of CO_2 emissions. Second, our results show that the cost effectiveness of diffusion schemes for eco-cars in Japan is lower than that of other developed countries. Thus, the government of Japan has the opportunity to improve the cost effectiveness of each scheme by considering alternative policies, including tax reductions for eco-cars and hybrid car purchases.

Notes

1 This volume class of car includes several major hybrid cars, e.g., the Toyota Prius.
2 We use the averages of the gasoline mileages of cars (13.23 km per 1) that are not included in subsidy and tax reduction schemes as the gasoline mileage of the old cars.
3 Our sample is based on monthly data. However, the information and price data of each car type is not based on monthly change. We use the information and price data of each car type in 2010 as variables.

Bibliography

Allcott, H. (2011) "Consumer' Perceptions and Misperceptions of Energy Costs", *American Economic Review*, 101(3), 98–104.

Allcott, H., and Wozny, N. (2013) "Gasoline Prices, Fuel Economy, and the Energy Paradox", *Review of Economics and Statistics*, 96(5), 779–795.

Automobile Inspection and Registration Information Association. (2013) "Trend of the Car Ownership in Japan", Automobile Inspection and Registration Information Association [in Japanese].

Beresteanu, A., and Li, S. (2011) "Gasoline Prices, Government Support, and the Demand for Hybrid Vehicles in the United States", *International Economic Review*, 52(1), 161–182.

Berry, S., Leviosohn, J, and Pakes, A. (1995) "Automobile Prices in Market Equilibrium", *Econometrica*, 63, 841–890.

Cabinet Office, Government of Japan. (2014) "Result of Diffusion Index", http://www.esri.cao.go.jp/jp/stat/di/di.html [in Japanese]

Car Information Ltd. (2010) "Reference Chart of Domestically-Produced Car Price", Car Information Ltd [in Japanese].

Chandra A., Gulati, S, and Kandlikar, M. (2010) "Green Drivers or Free Riders? An Analysis of Tax Rebates for Hybrid Vehicles", *Journal of Environmental Economics and Management*, 60, 78–93.

Gallangher, S. K., and Muehlegger, E. (2011) "Giving Green to Get Green? Incentive and Consumer Adaptation of Hybrid Vehicle Technology", *Journal of Environmental Economics and Management*, 61, 1–15.

IMF (2014) "IMF Primary Commodity Prices." http://www.imf.org/external/np/res/commod/index.aspx

Japan Automobile Dealers Association (each year) "The Annual Report of the Number New Car Registration", *Japan* Automobile Dealers Association.

Larrick, R.P., and Soll, B. (2008) "The MPG Illusion", *Science*, 320(5883), 1593–94.

Meyer, I., Leimbach, M., and Jaeger, C.C. (2007) "International Passenger Transport and Climate Change: A Sector Analysis in Car Demand and Associated CO_2 Emissions from 2000 to 2050", *Energy Policy*, 35, 6332–6345.

Society of Automobile Engineers of Japan (2010) "Specification Sheet of Automobiles", *Society* of Automobile Engineers of Japan [in Japanese].

Conclusion

Kei Kabaya and Shunsuke Managi

We have discussed a wide range of issues in *The Economics of Green Growth: New indicators for sustainable societies*. This concluding chapter will summarize and highlight the essence of this book.

Sustainable development cannot be fully measured by the conventional GDP, which intensively highlights the needs of current generations. For securing the needs of future generations, the sources of GDP, namely the stocks of capitals, have to be maintained for the future. Since our economic activities do not solely depend on man-made capitals but utilize broader capitals such as human capacity, natural resources, social relations, and knowledge and techniques, the indicators for sustainable development should include and measure all these capitals ideally as attempted by the Genuine Savings and the Inclusive Wealth Index. The data availability and methodological accuracy are always challenges in doing so, but more and more open data have become available and accessible recently, and the ways to improve the estimation methodology have been proposed as discussed in this book.

Sustainability is not only an issue for one country but also an issue for the entire globe in such a highly interconnected world. Several indicators have been proposed to assess the impacts of our economic activities on global natural environments (e.g. planetary boundary) in order to provoke a discussion about the unsustainability of current consumption and production patterns. According to these indicators we may have already exceeded the supporting capacity of the Earth in a sense, while there still exist people who suffer from absolute poverty with limited material use. To combat these two polarized issues simultaneously, more debate on fairer allocation of consumption opportunities among current generations needs to be instigated.

Measuring the natural resource use of each country will be the first step to unveil the impacts of respective domestic consumptions on their natural environments. What is worth considering is to measure resource use and emissions embodied in trade (i.e. resources used for and pollutants emitted from the production of import and export goods, e.g. virtual water and embodied carbon emissions). The indicators adding to or deducting from these factors will provide a more holistic picture of global environmental impacts caused by the consumption in one country, and may encourage the actions based on the principle of Common But Differentiated Responsibilities agreed at the Rio Summit.

Green economy (or green growth) raised as the central issue at the Rio+20 will require fundamental changes of the current economic systems to enable sustainable consumption and production. Its progress will be measured by a wide variety of indicators, ranging from low-carbon to resource efficiency, eco-system services, economic growth, employment, social inclusiveness, and poverty reduction. The policy measures for promoting green economy also vary widely, from tax and allowance to subsidy reform, environmental regulations and infor-mation, technological innovation, investment in green infrastructure and green procurement. Several chapters of this book touched upon this issue, showing the importance of environmental regulations to encourage technological devel-opment and private voluntary actions to mitigate environmental damages. The necessity to consider the cost effectiveness of tax and subsidy schemes was also pointed out. Meanwhile, it was also revealed that temporal measures do not necessarily improve the environmental quality, but rather may cause the exac-erbation of the problems.

The overarching goal of sustainable development and green economy is the improvement of people's well-being. Since material wealth does not necessarily coincide with well-being, the measurement scope needs to be widened to include the subjective happiness of individuals and influential factors to evaluate the progress towards this goal. The Better Life Index proposes multiple indicators that are considered to be relevant to human well-being (note that the focus is on OECD countries), and we suggested one methodology to aggregate these indicators into one and to customize those taking into account the national context, enabling cross-border comparison and more precise estimations of well-being.

We have introduced various types of indicators and showed several approaches to improve their accuracy and usefulness. As noted in the Introduction, however, there still exists room for enhancing even these upgraded indicators in terms of scopes and methodologies. The current capital approach of indicators for sustainable development does not capture the mental and spiritual factors of humans, while the scope of well-being indicators lacks sustainability elements. Neither of them may properly mention the biological capacity of the Earth and the quality of current generations. Further studies on how to tackle these issues, for instance unifying all the indicators into one or using several indicators in parallel, will be required.

Index